Beyond Steel

Beyond Steel

Pittsburgh and the Economics of Transformation

Christopher P. Briem

The Kent State University Press Kent, Ohio

ISBN 978-1-60635-502-2 (paperback)
ISBN 978-1-63101-582-3 (epub)
Published in the United States of America

Unless otherwise noted, illustrations are by Christopher P. Briem.

Cataloging information for this title is available at the Library of Congress.

Contents

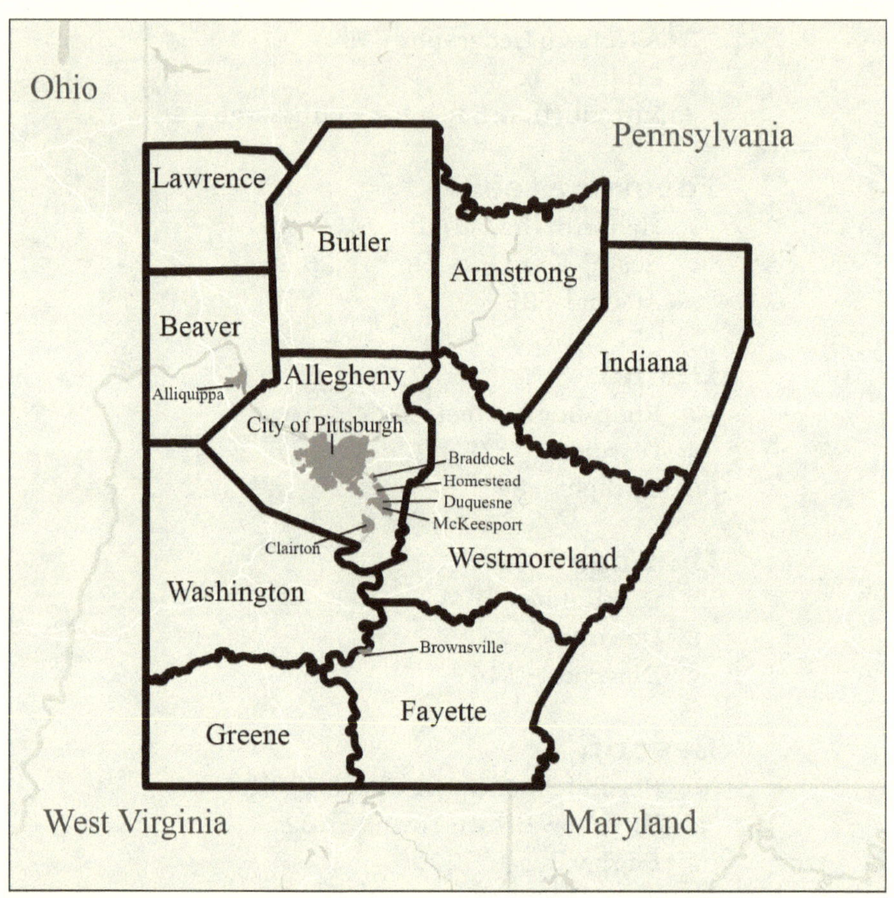

Southwestern Pennsylvania

A Note on Geography

The *City of Pittsburgh* is just one of 128 municipalities entirely within Allegheny County, Pennsylvania. The *Pittsburgh* metropolitan statistical area is a formal geography deliniated by the US Office of Management and Budget, which has been variously defined over different decades. In the 1950s, the Pittsburgh metropolitan area was typically considered to be comprised of four counties in southwestern Pennsylvania: Allegheny, Beaver, Washington, and Westmoreland Counties. By 2024, the definition of the Pittsburgh metropolitan statistical area had expanded to eight counties, also including four additional Pennsylvania counties: Armstrong, Butler, Fayette, and Lawrence Counties. Where *southwestern Pennsylvania* is discussed, it generally refers to a ten-county region that also includes Greene and Indiana Counties, a region that rests atop the Appalachian Low Plateau of Northern Appalachia.

The spirit of adventure in Pittsburgh has thus far been economic.

Robert A. Woods, "Pittsburgh: An Interpretation of Its Growth," *Pittsburgh Survey* (1914)

Preface

In early 2014, colleagues in the media relations department at the University of Pittsburgh forwarded to me a voicemail they said was from an independent journalist looking for information on the communities of Pittsburgh's Mon Valley, once one of the primary centers of steel production in southwestern Pennsylvania. The query was common; the unending plight of the former industrial region defined by the lower Monongahela River remained a recurring topic for writers after it became the nexus of US deindustrialization in the 1980s. Once the most concentrated steelmaking region in the United States—where serial entrepreneur Andrew Carnegie began his last and most successful business commodifying steel production—the Mon Valley saw the bulk of its heavy industry shut down over just a few years in the early 1980s. Recurring stories of the area's collective plight have evolved into a distinct literary genre: ruin porn, or maybe a more apropos description for greater Pittsburgh and its environs: rust porn. Writers looking for background information on the history and current conditions in Pittsburgh's most struggling communities were often redirected my way.

Listening to the message, I quickly realized the request was from someone who definitely did not need any basic primer on either the decline of the steel industry or the history of the Mon Valley. From the 1950s through the 1980s, John Hoerr was one of the nation's preeminent labor reporters—a beat that has become virtually extinct in the modern era. His professional career covered the critical decades that transformed the US steel industry from the dominant global leader to a chronic patient struggling to revive. His 1988 book *And the Wolf Finally Came: The*

Decline of the American Steel Industry remains for many of us the authoritative history of the breakdown in labor-industry relations and its destructive impact on the competitiveness of the US steel industry.[1] John was also a native of McKeesport, the Mon Valley's largest city and the second-largest municipality in southwestern Pennsylvania for the bulk of the twentieth century. The trauma of McKeesport and its neighboring mill towns was embedded within his broader narrative tracing the contraction of the steel industry, which Hoerr had chronicled as it was taking place.

Hoerr was cycling back, intending to write again on the ongoing plight of the region where he grew up. He was seeking an answer to why revitalization and redevelopment had failed to come to his hometown a generation past the steel industry's regional nadir. I was fortunate enough to begin a conversation with him in the year before he passed in 2015, unfortunately too soon for him to complete his project. Our conversations broadened to a far more universal topic: Why do some communities, or even whole regions, sustain growth while others do not? In recent years, Pittsburgh has garnered ever more headlines proclaiming that it has successfully transitioned from industrial anachronism to a paragon of technology-based economic development, a hagiography that simplifies a far more conflicted path. What John knew better than most was that headlines fail to tell a complete story.

And the Wolf Finally Came suggests to some a counterfactual—that if relations between labor and management in the steel industry had not devolved so completely in the decades leading up to the 1980s, the US steel industry could have maintained its competitiveness. Even if true, the corollary many assume—that Pittsburgh and the Mon Valley could have simultaneously retained the corpus of their legacy steel production—begs a harsher economic reality. Pittsburgh's competitiveness as a location to produce steel had been in decline long before the 1980s. Southwestern Pennsylvania has long since been passed over as the region best positioned for new investment in steel production. Today, future prospects for greater Pittsburgh are decoupled from the prospects of the steel industry, a reality that remains difficult to accept for a region identified for so long with the once-monolithic industry.

Growing up in Pittsburgh, I saw the collapse of the region's heavy industry reach its apogee when I was a young teenager in the early 1980s. Before that decline arrived, I spent some of my earlier childhood on Pittsburgh's South Side, an entire neighborhood that existed literally in the shadow of the massive South Side Works of the Jones & Laughlin Company. For over a century, a vast steel complex had spanned both sides of the Monongahela River within line of sight of Downtown Pittsburgh. As I was growing up, no living resident could have had any memory of the neighborhood's existence independent of the plant. For me, an almost daily trip involved crossing the river as a passenger on the Port Authority's 54C bus, traversing the Brady Street Bridge, and crossing the Monongahela River into the center of the city. The bridge's midpoint provided the optimal vantage point to view the still-extant orange glow emanating from blast furnaces hugging the riverbanks. If only J&L's South Side had shut down, it would have been a devastating blow to the economy of both the city and region of Pittsburgh. When it closed in the mid-1980s, the shutdown of steel production at J&L, by then fully absorbed into the LTV Corporation, was only one small part of a far vaster contraction of the regional steel industry.

On the ground, the rapid collapse of so much of Pittsburgh's industrial core early in the 1980s was a shock so unexpected it was disorienting. Only decades later, in graduate school, I learned of research completed in the 1960s predicting the future decline of heavy industry in Pittsburgh with fatalistic accuracy. What seemed a complete surprise was predicted in the *Economic Study of the Pittsburgh Region,* a four-year project taken up by University of Pittsburgh economists Edgar M. Hoover and Ben Chinitz between 1960 and 1964. That Pittsburgh had the opportunity to alter its seemingly predestined trajectory long before it arrived remains a muted point in Pittsburgh's history, as if the region wants to forget that it failed to heed the dire warnings. Trying to understand why repeated prognostications of steel's future decline in the region were so consistently ignored was the genesis of this project.

It takes a fair amount of hubris to attempt to retell the Pittsburgh story, given the detailed narratives that have already been authored. The story of Pittsburgh's postwar renaissance and the unprecedented partnership between business and political leaders has been retold ad nauseum, which is not to diminish its impact reshaping the region's urban core. Then, after decline set in, the plight of former steel communities has been told not just by John Hoerr but in narratives such as William Serrin's detailed history *Homestead: The Glory and Tragedy of an American Steel Town* (1992) or Judith Modell's *A Town Without Steel: Envisioning Homestead* (1998) and many others too numerous to list here. More recently, in *Nuclear Suburbs: Cold War Technoscience and the Pittsburgh*

Renaissance, geographer Patrick Vitale has thoroughly documented the research milieu that coalesced in Cold War–era Pittsburgh. In *Beyond Rust: Metropolitan Pittsburgh and the Fate of Industrial America,* historian Allen Dieterich-Ward has covered the story of Pittsburgh's postindustrial transformation, emphasizing the very real fact that Pittsburgh's story is not just a metropolitan history but extends even beyond Pennsylvania's borders to Weirton, West Virginia, and Steubenville, Ohio, just as it does to Johnstown, Pennsylvania, and Youngstown, Ohio, and beyond. Most recently, work by historian Gabriel Winant in *Next Shift* has looked at what the shift from a manufacturing-centric to healthcare workforce has meant in Pittsburgh. Each of these versions of Pittsburgh's transformation is predicated on an underlying economic narrative driven by the growth and decline of steel across southwestern Pennsylvania.[2]

Today, regions nationwide focus considerable resources on attracting new industries and retaining existing ones. How best to shape those efforts is unclear as regions everywhere are forced to react to ever more rapid shifts in industrial competitiveness. Pittsburgh may be an extreme case of how much and how fast economic circumstances can change. Still, its story provides guidance for regions everywhere that will inevitably face economic challenges imposed by factors far outside their control.

Pittsburgh's transformation is incomplete, uneven, and ongoing. Every story of technology-based resurgence is matched by an underreported story of the failure of many of the region's former mill towns, unable to rebuild past prosperity. Despite oft-repeated stories of how Pittsburgh worked collectively to shed the occluded air that gave it a multicentury description as the "Smoky City," the region regularly registers some of the most polluted air in the nation. Pittsburgh has likewise failed to find any solution to deep and exceptional levels of racial disparities, a blight that has persisted through both periods of economic growth and decline, suggesting causal forces that go far deeper than the story of steel's rise and fall.

The region's economic implosion of the 1980s was a moment of reckoning that forced Pittsburgh and its environs to address compound dysfunctions simultaneously. Loss of industry begat a loss of population and workers that would reshape regional demographics for decades into the future. At the same time, the region was left with a surfeit of heavily polluted industrial land needing reclamation and repurposing on an unprecedented scale. New jobs would eventually be generated across a range of industries, but they would not appear quickly. Resilience came slowly but steadily across a range of industries, most notably in regional educational and health industries. Then, early in the twenty-first century, new technology was applied to ancient shale deposits in Pennsylvania, jump-starting an energy revolution and re-creating for Pittsburgh yet another boom generated from extractive mining industries.

These vectors of change have converged to define modern Pittsburgh. Any transformation that has come to Pittsburgh first required moving on from a steel-dependent economy, a shift far more difficult than is commonly believed today. Today, the battle between visions of old and new Pittsburgh has reemerged with vengeance, as debates rage over where the region will find prosperity in the future. Many of Pittsburgh's old battles are new again.

Readers will be disappointed if they expect this to be a concise cookbook describing the policies regions should follow to promote regional growth or avert decline. Caution should be applied to any purported answer meant to apply to all regions and all eras. The uniqueness and complexity of most regional economies make broad generalizations problematic at best. If there is a core message here, it is that regions need to be prepared for change and can set the conditions that facilitate economic resilience. Pittsburgh provides an extreme example of the pitfalls of deferring change for so long. It also stands out as a region that believed a singular industrial trajectory could continue indefinitely and eventually faced the consequences when those beliefs were proven false. If there is an exceptionalism to Pittsburgh's story, it is in how much change the region had to face up to and the repeated efforts it has taken to rebuild economic stability. Pittsburgh's lesson is that there has been no silver bullet that catalyzed change. Repeated efforts to generate a renaissance, many of which failed along the way, are as much the story for the city and Pittsburgh's greater region. More than anything else, change in Pittsburgh necessitated moving past its long reliance on heavy industry, but that shift did not come easily.

Pittsburghers know that the times are out of joint. Somehow they're expecting the prosperity to blow up in their faces.

Fortune Magazine, 1941

INTRODUCTION

Say It Ain't Pittsburgh

May 28, 2009

White House Press Secretary Robert Gibbs began a routine Thursday afternoon briefing by passing on scheduling ephemera to the assembled journalists: "The United States will host the next G20 summit, September 24th through the 25th."[1] A decade after being formed, the G20 rapidly emerged as the nexus of international financial diplomacy. Short for "Group of Twenty Finance Ministers and Central Bank Governors," the organization had spent much of its first decade in the semi-obscurity typical of most international bureaucracies. A group of nineteen nations and the European Union, G20 sponsored meetings typically attended by the finance ministers, or sometimes just their deputies or other surrogates, of member nations.

Circumstances were vastly different in the spring of 2009. Nations worldwide focused on turning back a global economic crisis that had metastasized over the previous two years. The US economy lost over seven hundred thousand jobs in 2008, the largest annual decline since the Great Depression. Interconnected financial markets spread a growing economic contagion around the globe. Financial markets worldwide came to a virtual halt following the September 2008 bankruptcy of the investment bank Lehman Brothers. The ensuing economic contraction was so deep that journalists labeled it the Great Recession, and in the spring of 2009, nobody knew when the plunge would stop. The previous fall, the G20 not only began bringing together senior finance officials but also convened national leaders in Washington in the hope that they could bring stability back to the global economy. In April 2009, world leaders came together again in London. With the worldwide recession continuing unabated, plans immediately began for a follow-on summit that fall.

Still, Gibbs's announcement on the timing of the upcoming meeting did not make headlines as much as its planned location. Continuing his prepared statement, the press secretary matter-of-factly explained that the forthcoming summit would be hosted "in Pittsburgh, Pennsylvania." The press corps in attendance responded to the announcement with murmurs and more than a few audible laughs in appreciation of what they presumed was press secretary's deadpan humor before jumping into the substance of the day's briefing.[2] Following summits in Washington, DC, and London, only the highest profile venues could expect to host so many visiting foreign potentates. There was no reason to seriously consider the possibility that Pittsburgh could have even made a short list of potential locations.

Journalists beyond the White House press contingent were equally incredulous. In *The Atlantic* a few days after the announcement, senior writer Derek Thompson summarized the common consensus by asking, "Why in the World is the G20 Meeting in Pittsburgh?" He and others found it odd that the organization would choose to meet in a region that was still the "mascot for steel subsidies."[3]

Gibbs was almost forced to explain that he was not joking. Pittsburgh "has seen its share of economic woes in the past," but the city's ongoing economic transformation was the core of a new narrative: "Because of foresight and investment [it] is now renewed, giving birth to renewed industries that are creating the jobs of the future."[4] In an instant, Pittsburgh was no longer the apocryphal Rust Belt city continuing to struggle in the face of inexorable economic decline.

Pundits quickly discovered that their dour perceptions were based on memories of a Pittsburgh past. The undeniable reality was that the steel industry had long faded as the economic engine for both Pittsburgh and southwestern Pennsylvania. Thompson unequivocally retracted his initial judgment on the choice of Pittsburgh and replaced his commentary, writing that Pittsburgh had not only "manifestly emerged from its rusty reputation as a tech leader" but had become a model for "how subsidy-reliant cities and regions can transform themselves to compete in a 21st-century environment."[5]

The media's cognitive dissonance was not unreasonable. Indeed, for decades, Pittsburgh had been indelibly branded by the collapse of a US

G20 Pittsburgh Summit, 2009 (Wikipedia / Presidencia de la Nación Argentina)

steel industry long concentrated there. At the beginning of the 1980s, the economic trajectory of both the city and greater region of Pittsburgh was abruptly altered by a tempest of economic shocks. Mass obsolescence of industrial capital, expanding domestic and global competition, a deep and extended national recession, and disruptive technological change within the steel industry seemed to instantaneously come together to eviscerate the Steel City's competitive advantage in producing steel. The result was a localized economic miasma rarely seen in the peacetime history of the United States. If Pittsburgh had still been defined by its Rust Belt legacy, it would have been the most incongruous location for a summit focused entirely on generating new economic growth.

Throughout the 1980s, half of the manufacturing jobs across southwestern Pennsylvania disappeared permanently. The nation's unemployment rate peaked at 12 percent during the recession that stretched from July 1981 until November 1983, at the time the longest and most severe recession since the Great Depression. The unemployment rate for the Pittsburgh metropolitan area—a conservative measure of the region's economic distress—peaked at over 18 percent in early 1982. The ten counties of southwestern Pennsylvania employed more than three hundred thousand manufacturing workers at the beginning of the 1980s. Just over

160,000 manufacturing jobs remained in the region by the end of the decade, a number that would be cut in half again by early in the twenty-first century. Industrial contraction also took with it the jobs directly or indirectly supported by the mills and the considerable earnings of their workers, affecting nearly every worker, firm, family, and institution across southwestern Pennsylvania.

The magnitude of Pittsburgh's decline was in direct proportion to how long southwestern Pennsylvania had depended on heavy industries for its collective prosperity. Sheer geography had guaranteed that a metals industry emerged in nineteenth-century Pittsburgh. Southwestern Pennsylvania fortuitously rested atop a thick seam of bituminous coal. The nearby Connellsville coal field, just one part of the immense Pittsburgh Seam, remains the source of some of the best metallurgic coal in the world, ideal for making the industrial coke essential for smelting iron. The Monongahela River and its tributaries directly connected Pittsburgh with the seemingly inexhaustible supply of energy-rich bituminous coal. At Pittsburgh, the Monongahela and Allegheny Rivers form the Ohio, which connects the city with a continent of customers for its industrial output. A certain geographic fate resulted in metal foundries clogging the riverbanks of Pittsburgh before the onset of the Civil War.

The city of Pittsburgh has remained relatively small in both size and population, making up only a fraction of the larger Allegheny County, itself just one part of a more expansive southwestern Pennsylvania region that would all be shaped by the expansion of steelmaking. Before the end of the nineteenth century the economic corpus of Pittsburgh had pushed far beyond the city's urban center. Defying the common monocentric city model of regional growth—which theorized that a region's highest value production was concentrated in a centralized business district—much of Pittsburgh's heavy industry had built up along the floodplains of the river valleys that sinewed out far from Downtown Pittsburgh.

Despite its industrial cohesion, no local government has ever represented the full extent of economic Pittsburgh, far from it. In the twenty-first century, the city of Pittsburgh proper covers just 55 square miles, today not even encompassing all of the urban core of a far larger Greater Pittsburgh region that has maintained no single definition. Since 2023, the federal government has defined the Pittsburgh metropolitan statistical area as eight counties of southwestern Pennsylvania—home to over 2.4 million people across 5,706 square miles and governed by no fewer than seven hundred individual local governments. Pittsburgh is the core of an alternative definition of the region, the Pittsburgh–Weirton–Steubenville combined statistical area that in 2024 encompasses thirteen counties and extends into both West Virginia and Ohio. Steel would drive the history of that wider geography and beyond.

What was a fortuitous location for producing iron had an even greater competitive advantage in the production of commodity steel once Bessemer technology, imported from Europe, enabled the industry to shift from artisan to industrial-scale output. Through the latter half of the nineteenth-century, "coal and metallurgy came together" in Pittsburgh "like twin supernovae, impelling into rapid expansion all elements of the economy which were aligned with them" but also "expelling into oblivion those which were not."[6] Many industries had proven they could be successful in nineteenth-century Pittsburgh: iron, glass, shipbuilding, and even cotton works—but no industry benefited as much as steel did from the natural resources uniquely colocated in southwestern Pennsylvania. The production of raw steel in unprecedented quantities eventually displaced much of the industrial diversity that wanted to spring forth in the region. An excessive comparative advantage shaped Pittsburgh's trajectory for more than a century.

The steel industry's sustained output and extraordinary concentration in Pittsburgh produced an existential side effect: an almost intentional blindness to the inevitability that someday the industry would fade as the region's economic engine. Before 1980, at best insufficient plans were made for a future Pittsburgh unreliant on steel production. The steel industry's long history in the region made the development of almost any other industry difficult or possibly even unwanted. When change was forced upon it, greater Pittsburgh was unprepared for a postindustrial future and collectively dazed by how rapidly that future had arrived.

Even as job losses peaked in the early 1980s, a stubborn denial remained for industry, workers and communities across southwestern Pennsylvania. The cyclical pattern of economic booms and recessions had long been a defining part of the nation's manufacturing economy, especially for industries like steel that are dependent on highly variable flows of new capital investment. Periodic spikes of double-digit unemployment rates were common enough to be considered routine. Since the end of the Great Depression, the Pittsburgh metropolitan area experienced double-digit unemployment rates of 11.6 percent in 1954, 14 percent in 1958, 13.8 percent in 1961, and 11.1 percent in 1963, each peak reaching above comparable national rates.[7] Pittsburgh's downturns were seen as part of a recurring cycle from which the region always rebounded. Knowledge of that pattern inured not just residents and workers but also experts to the structural shifts that were bearing down on southwestern Pennsylvania. At the very worst of Pittsburgh's downturn, in the spring of 1983, a top regional economist opined, "Once the recovery gets underway, that will go a long way toward curing the problems that now appear to be incurable and permanent ones in the Pittsburgh area."[8] In reality, the problems were just beginning.

As the 1980s progressed, mill towns that had been built around steel plants sank into an unprecedented economic abyss. Layoffs that had been temporary in previous business cycles became permanent for virtually all of the region's unemployed steelworkers. During the national recession officially dated to extend between December 2007 and June 2009, the nation's unemployment rate peaked at exactly 10 percent; a rate sustained for just a month in October 2009 before dropping. A decade later, the pandemic-induced recession of 2020 briefly resulted in four months of double-digit unemployment, but it again quickly dropped. In the first half of the 1980s, Pittsburgh's unemployment rate remained above 10 percent for three straight years, and a full decade passed before that rate again reached prerecession employment levels. The depth of the region's economic collapse became impossible to deny as firms began announcing they were shutting down plants permanently, not preserving them for future production. The permanence of job losses hit home as firms that had been in existence for generations went bankrupt or abandoned their steelmaking operations. By the time the blast furnaces were dismantled—or violently demolished, in most cases—denial had evolved into an indisputable economic depression for all of southwestern Pennsylvania.

Concentrated job destruction begat an even more traumatic population loss. The uniqueness of Pittsburgh's economic decline was not just the scale of job loss but how quickly jobs disappeared. An innumerable number of laid-off workers were forced to leave in search of better economic opportunities. As a result, the region recorded the single largest population drop among literally all metropolitan areas in the United States between the 1980 and 1990 decennial censuses. What was arguably one of the largest regional exoduses in the nation's peacetime history left an enduring mark on all who remained. Few US regions refer collectively to their former residents as a diaspora in the way Pittsburgh remembers its lost residents.

Pittsburgh's demographic decline defied common economic theories of how major metropolitan regions grow and change. Smaller and even midsized regions inevitably face traumatic contractions when their core industries decline. Larger regions were believed to nurture an economic diversity that inoculated them against outright contraction. In the 1960s, economist Wilbur Thompson postulated that large metropolitan areas exhibit an urban size rachet. Regions that have grown beyond a critical threshold, perhaps as low as a population of a quarter million, will perpetually be able to generate future growth, or at the very least avert decline.[9] Regions such as Pittsburgh—once one of the nation's five largest metropolitan areas—should never shrink. Pittsburgh's sharp contraction in the 1980s defied Thompson's hypothesis with a vengeance.

Pittsburgh was far from the only US region to ever experience deindustrialization and decline. US mass production dates to the construction of the nation's first integrated textile factory at Waltham, Massachusetts, in 1813. New England textile production continued through the nineteenth century but began a structural decline dating back at least to the 1920s. Houston and the greater Texas oil patch declined during the extended oil bust of the 1980s, and southern California's cluster of aerospace and electronics industries experienced a severe post–Cold War contraction in the early 1990s. In each of those cases, declines were either followed by quick rebounds or were much slower than what most steel communities experienced. The decline of New England's textile industry was extended over several decades, with a core of the region's textile-producing firms surviving into the 1950s. The extended waning accommodated growth in new industries and time for both workers and firms to shift into entirely new sectors. Houston's energy-induced recession barely slowed the region's continued demographic growth and was mitigated by an industry and a workforce that had long been tempered by consistent volatility. Southern California's severe but localized recession was relatively brief, and growth across a panoply of other industries continued through the worst of its downturn.

Before Pittsburgh in the 1980s, Seattle's Boeing Bust of the late 1960s was considered the worst regional downturn in the United States since the Great Depression. After World War II, Seattle shared with Pittsburgh a magnified concentration in a specialized industry. William Boeing founded the Pacific Aero Products Company in the city on July 15, 1916, the beginning of a century-long dominance in aircraft production.

Like steel in Pittsburgh, the aircraft industry in Seattle was spurred by the concentration of natural resources available nearby. Northwest Washington provided a ready supply of the spruce wood then essential to aircraft construction. Seattle's aerospace industry expanded as air transportation increased, with demand spiking during two world wars and the Cold War that followed.

In the late 1960s, Boeing's cancellation of a planned supersonic commercial airplane and the waning of Vietnam War defense contracts forced the company to lay off sixty-four thousand workers.[10] The contraction pushed metropolitan Seattle's unemployment rate to a peak of 13.8 percent. Also, like Pittsburgh a decade later, Seattle experienced a spike in outmigration caused by the rapid loss of jobs. So bad were conditions perceived to be in Seattle that in 1971 two local real estate brokers paid $160 of their own money on would become an iconic billboard asking: "Will the last person leaving SEATTLE—Turn out the lights?" Yet, the billboard has been perpetually misunderstood. The real estate agents who paid for it intended it to be more parody than criticism. Their counterintuitive goal was to highlight how attractive Seattle remained, despite a barrage of negative economic news coming from the region. Their optimism was prescient.[11]

Even at its nadir, Seattle's historic downturn paled in comparison to what Pittsburgh faced a decade later. Seattle's overall job losses soon abated, and even the region's manufacturing employment increased from 1972 onward. By 1975, the region's total employment had returned to 1969 levels. By the end of the 1970s, Seattle employed more manufacturing workers than ever before. Southwestern Pennsylvania, in contrast, never recouped any of the steel jobs lost during the 1980s. New economic growth, or even just stability, would have to come from entirely different vectors.

It is a remarkable story that steel had not only survived but thrived in Pittsburgh for so long, bestowing tremendous profit to the region over an unprecedented epoch. Yet, by the penultimate decade of the twentieth century, steel had become the region's greatest obstacle to growth in the twenty-first century. So deep was its economic and demographic decline, many questioned whether Pittsburgh could continue as a major metropolitan area. Maybe the region that had birthed one of mankind's greatest concentrations of industrial output had become an unneeded anachronism once efficient steel production became far more distributed across the nation and globally. What was the future for a region based on steel once the production of steel moved elsewhere? For much of the world, Pittsburgh at the beginning of 2009 was frozen in time, still struggling to find an answer to those questions.

Yet, even at the region's economic nadir, there were signs of the path that would reshape Pittsburgh's future. A discordant surprise came in 1985, when the Rand McNally Corporation published its first *Places Rated Almanac.*[12] Many were piqued by the anomaly that Pittsburgh of all places was named the "Most Livable" region, compared to all 329 other metropolitan regions across the United States. Rand-McNally was the corporate sponsor for those metropolitan rankings, but it was the second edition of statistics compiled by researcher David Savageau. Both academic and media analysts were taking a greater interest in the measurement and of quality of life, an amorphous metric but one that was being taken ever more seriously as an important source of regional competitiveness.

Described as "marvels of data collection, manipulation, and synthesis," Savageau's work expanded the scope of the evolving field of regional benchmarking.[13] Pittsburgh's top ranking opened up his methodology to increased scrutiny.[14] The Associated Press expressed skepticism by asking: "What next? A city known to outsiders for recession-silenced steel mills, 9.1 percent unemployment, and labor violence has been named the most livable city in the United States."[15]

Pittsburghers found the region's top ranking incongruous with the economic pall continuing to unfold around them. Savageau and his coauthor, Richard Boyer, visited Pittsburgh soon after the release of the *Places Rated Almanac* and were offered a key to the city from Mayor Richard Caliguiri. Inconceivable to many was that the region's industrial contraction might be part of the reason its livability rankings were improving. During his visit, Savageau commented, "The city's decline as a major steel producer is as much responsible for its rating as are any other criteria."[16] Few Pittsburgh denizens at the time could understand such a positive spin while enduring the seemingly cataclysmic loss of jobs.

One expert in survey techniques, University of Washington psychology professor Geoff Loftus, was particularly incredulous. He decompiled Savageau's methodology and concluded that Pittsburgh's top ranking was mostly an artifact of debatable techniques used in aggregating the final results from many data subcategories. Loftus applied his own weighting to Savageau's data and created an alternative ranking that gave San Francisco, not Pittsburgh, the highest overall quality of life. His results were published in the journal *Psychology Today* in an article titled "Say It Ain't Pittsburgh."[17]

Academic skepticism notwithstanding, Savageau's analysis presaged an emerging competitiveness that sustained Pittsburgh through the worst of its economic downturn. Pittsburgh in 1985 compared favorably to other regions in its cost of living, low crime rates, and access to medical care and education. The factors Pittsburgh excelled at were not ones that necessarily made it an attractive place for industrial site selection, but they were ever more important to workers and their families. Loftus's reworked analysis concluded that Pittsburgh ranked twelfth among the nation's metropolitan regions. Given the extraordinary economic handicaps the region was enduring, it remained an enviable result.

As the G20 summit began a quarter-century later, the core of the Pittsburgh region's economy bore little resemblance to its former self. Long one of the most specialized manufacturing regions, a new Pittsburgh was sustained by jobs across a far broader range of industries, giving it an economic diversification it had lacked at least since early in the nineteenth century. Change had come neither easily nor quickly. Efforts to preserve a regional steel industry persisted long after any realistic chance of regional reindustrialization had faded. Eventually, economic development policies were forced to shift away from historic priorities in attracting the largest of factories and toward efforts to grow technology-based and smaller businesses. Entirely new economic development tools had to be created to even begin planning new uses for the surfeit of industrial brownfields left by economic contraction. And while Pittsburgh had created an enviable model of civic leadership over the course of the twentieth century—most notably the Allegheny Conference, a public–private partnership that has been credited with the city's post–World War II Renaissance—the scale of problems the region faced in the 1980s required repeated evolutions of its civic infrastructure.

To understand Pittsburgh's transformation in the decades following the rapid contraction of the steel industry begs an underlying question: Why did change not begin sooner or progress further? Pittsburgh faced such a stark transformation because it had deferred change for so long. In retrospect, it is clear that the competitiveness of the steel industry there began draining away early in the twentieth century. While the historic plant closures and layoffs of the early 1980s were a shock for most who experienced them, past warning signs were neither rare nor hidden. That those signs were repeatedly misinterpreted or dismissed only magnified the trauma of Pittsburgh's historic contraction. The region eventually moved beyond steel because it was forced to, but it never chose this path willingly.

Few roadmaps foreshadowing Pittsburgh's economic trajectory over the last half century were as prescient as one presented in the *Economic Study of the Pittsburgh Region* (*ESPR*)—a four-year project sponsored by the Ford Foundation and the Pittsburgh Regional Planning Agency. Between 1960 and 1964, University of Pittsburgh professors Edgar M. Hoover and Benjamin Chinitz and a team of researchers produced four volumes analyzing the state of the economy in southwestern Pennsylvania and projecting how it would evolve over the coming decades. In addition to ominously predicting steep employment declines for Pittsburgh's steel industry, the *ESPR* had lessons applicable for all regions. One of its core conclusions was that in the future "factors of strategic transport advantage or availability of materials, fuels, and energy, exert far less of a constraint" on any region's economic growth. The report foreshadowed a greater role for talent attraction and workforce development that would only become central to economic development policy decades in the future. It proposed "a whole field of action involving improvement of the Region's attractiveness as a place to live and work."[18]

Competition between regions has only expanded since the 1960s, producing ever-starker disparities between winners and losers. Regions worldwide continue to struggle to devise policies effective at attracting new investment and incubating new industries. As planner Richard Florida has described the growing economic divergence between regions, some attain the status of "superstar cities," while others do not.[19] Competition is not just among the largest regions but now extends across the continuum of its small and medium-sized regions globally. Some are sustaining enviable growth rates, while others fall farther behind their peers.

There is no consensus among economic development practitioners over what metric defines success, though a nearly universal metric is employment. "Jobs über alles" is almost always a central goal of economic policy. Yet, even that clarity of objective is becoming less insightful in crafting policies to achieve it. Where population and labor force growth was once seen as an inevitable result of job creation, that fundamental causality is being questioned more and more. "Do people follow jobs, or do jobs follow people?" has become an ever more central question in regional economic development. It may seem new, but in 1964 the *ESPR* concluded, "People rather than geography will play the largest role in shaping our future."[20] Hoover and his team had reached a conclusion would be far more mainstream only decades later. In virtual apostasy, given their location, they surmised that policies to promote prosperity and regional growth ought not to focus on *smokestack chasing*—a term that would only be coined decades in the future—and instead should work to "provide a far higher level of convenience, sightliness, public services, recreation and cultural and educational opportunity than was ever before the case."[21] How closely Pittsburgh followed that advice is the story both of the region's early 1980s economic collapse and its later rebound.

The now-common strategy that building and sustaining a competitive workforce is critical to future prosperity was foretold long before Pittsburgh was ready to abandon its industrial heritage. For decades, persistent industry-centric policies led to an almost inevitable economic paroxysm. A 1961 prognostication wondered what historians would conclude twenty-five years in the future: "Did it grow, prosper and find the right road toward the 'good life' in the intervening 25 years? Or are the pressures and problems of today—1961—merely to be multiplied by 15? Will the city as Lewis Mumford says urban civilizations tend to do, advance its own destruction?"[22]

A strong case can be made that the problems Pittsburgh faced in 1961 were indeed multiplied severalfold by the time the quarter century passed. Troubling economic trends identified repeatedly through the first half of the twentieth century continued mostly unchecked for decades. When 1986 finally arrived, there was no similar public prognostication of what Pittsburgh would look like a further twenty-five years into the future. The most rational projections would likely have been too dour to publish.

Forever Steel

1

To know Pittsburg thoroughly is a liberal education in "the kind of culture demanded by modern times."

James Parton, "Pittsburg,"
Atlantic Monthly, January 1868

Hell with the Lid Off

December 12, 1900

At a private University Club dinner in New York City, a banquet was held in honor of Carnegie Steel's president, Charles Schwab.[1] Three years earlier, the then-thirty-five-year-old Schwab had been appointed president and put in charge of the formidable steel leviathan assembled by Andrew Carnegie. Schwab's speech focused on how Carnegie Steel benefited from vertical integration and economies of scale, allowing it to control all facets of steel production. Schwab opined that steel could be produced at an ever-greater efficiency if its manufacture could be further consolidated across the industry. Schwab's speech and a half-hour conversation with J. P. Morgan following dinner changed US corporate history.

Through Schwab, the financier solicited from Carnegie the cost of buying him out whole. Carnegie returned a note with a single price, which Morgan immediately accepted. The final details were worked out at a speed unheard of by modern standards, given the scale of the transaction. By February, rumors of a massive new consolidation within the steel industry were already being repeated. In March, U.S. Steel acknowledged it was in discussions to sell the company. The final deal was announced less than eighty days after the lunch when Schwab first met Morgan. The "unexpected consequences" of the deal have "vibrated through every decade" since.[2] Nowhere have those consequences reverberated deeper and longer than in Pittsburgh.

For $480 million, Carnegie parted with the company he built, with his personal payout valued at over $225 million. In later life, Carnegie said he gave Morgan a bargain, and Morgan obliquely acknowledged he would have accepted a figure $100 million higher.[3] Carnegie spent the rest of his life working to give the inconceivable fortune away. Equity other than Carnegie's was distributed among executives and partners at Carnegie Steel. Andrew Carnegie deserves inordinate credit for creating the vast wealth J. P. Morgan instantly monetized for him, but steel did not come to Pittsburgh because of any single entrepreneur. Carnegie was just the most successful at taking advantage of the geography fortuitously bestowed on southwestern Pennsylvania.

Before Steel

Long before Pittsburgh was conceived, early European visitors found the inland Appalachian plateau ideal for agriculture, but difficult transportation over the Allegheny Mountains limited access to the major markets still clustered along the coast. Farmers distilled crops of rye into alcohol, which proved to be the only product they could profitably transport to cash markets. So valuable was the flow of grain alcohol coming from northern Appalachia that the cash-starved federal government exploited it as an early source of revenue. Congress passed a federal duty on all distilled alcohols in 1791, a tax that bore down hard on the northern Appalachian farmers near Pittsburgh. Opposition to the new tax spurred one of the young nation's first major crises when the Whiskey Rebellion erupted just south of Pittsburgh. Outright insurrection and violence targeted at federal excise collectors spurred President Washington and his treasury secretary, Alexander Hamilton, to lead federal forces into the region south of Pittsburgh in 1794. The uprising quickly faded in the face of the overwhelming federal response.

As the young nation expanded, westward population migration conferred economic benefits on Pittsburgh. The Ohio River was an early superhighway for ever-increasing flows of settlers moving inward on the North American continent. Early national commerce depended on riverborne transportation, and Pittsburgh was a natural incubator for the industries supplying the United States' westward expansion. As far back as 1770, envisioning Pittsburgh as a transportation node for the westward flow of goods, Benjamin Franklin accurately predicted that Fort Pitt would become a shipbuilding center for an inland empire he foresaw.

From its earliest settlement, Pittsburgh and its environs benefited from an economic engine just below the surface. The first known map of the northern Appalachian coal was prepared in 1749 by Joshua Fry, who would briefly be George Washington's commanding officer in the Virginia militia four years in the future, and Peter Jefferson, father of the future president.[4] Their map documented that the region yet to be named Pittsburgh fortuitously rested atop a thick seam of bituminous coal created from organic remains first deposited there 300 million years earlier, when western Pennsylvania sat atop a vast coastal plain. Epochal time and immense pressure had first transformed the carbon-rich sediment first into peat and then into lignite, also known as brown coal. Eventually, the process created its own ocean of bituminous or black coal, which was not just vast but so accessible that outcrops often could be extracted directly from the surface.

By 1760, a mine on Coal Hill—later named Mount Washington and directly across the Monongahela River from Fort Pitt—was providing fuel to heat the garrison stationed there. Little effort was needed to mine the coal from outcrops of the sedimentary rock exposed on the hillside. Extracted coal only needed to be rolled down the hill and ported over the river. Not limited to local uses, Pittsburgh seam coal was soon exported from the region and became the primary fuel of the Industrial Revolution in North America.

The Pittsburgh Coal Seam stretches over eleven thousand square miles across three states. The de facto limitless fuel catalyzed an alternate vector of economic growth for the region. Abundant and accessible fuel made Pittsburgh a very different type of frontier town, with industry growing alongside commerce. Economist and early US Treasury official Tench Coxe reported that the "plenty of pit-coal in Pennsylvania will very soon give it an immense advantage over all the interior country north and east of it." In 1796, the French engineer Victor Collor, surreptitiously surveying the Ohio and Mississippi Rivers for the French government, went further, noting that Pittsburgh "will certainly become one of the first inland cities of the United States" because a "rich vein of coal is found on the summit of one of the mountains which bounds the Ohio on the left.[5]

Coal sourced from western Pennsylvania became ever more important once steamboats became the modal form of transportation on the western rivers, creating demand for Appalachian coal all along the Ohio and Mississippi Rivers. With unparalleled advantages in coal supplies and transportation, energy-intensive iron and glass production all but spontaneously erupted in the valleys of western Pennsylvania. By 1797, James O'Hara—whom President Washington had appointed quartermaster general of the US Army—and Isaac Craig had established a glassworks along the Ohio River within eyesight of Fort Pitt. The first Pittsburgh iron forge dates at least as far back as Joseph McClurg's 1804 foundry along the Monongahela River. Iron production quickly spurred secondary industries, and the region's first rolling mill—which transformed raw metal into more usable forms—was built by Englishman Christopher Cowan in 1811.[6] Pittsburgh's industrial fate was sealed before the first decades of the nineteenth century had elapsed.[7]

Pittsburgh's early economic growth was far from limited to metalworking industries. Fulfilling Benjamin Franklin's prediction, Pittsburgh became a center of steamboat production. Its shipyards constructed at least 196 steam-powered vessels between 1811 and 1835.[8] Other industries followed. In 1804, Peter Eltonhead of Manchester, England, came to Pittsburgh to open the city's first cotton mill.[9] Seven cotton mills operated there by 1850, making it one of the region's largest industries. Pittsburgh's energy-intensive glass industry grew through most of the nineteenth century, much of its output was used to ship other locally produced goods westward. In 1880, Allegheny County produced nearly 27 percent of the nation's output of glass, a staggering concentration that put it far ahead of Philadelphia, the nation's second-largest supplier, which produced 7.7 percent of the national total.[10]

Pittsburgh's enduring competitive advantage showed itself in the growth of ironworks and foundries that increased in number through the first half of the nineteenth century. By the 1850s, more than 113 different owners of rolling mills were operating in Pittsburgh.[11] Not dominated by any single firm, the iron industry across southwestern Pennsylvania was made up of a myriad of small and medium-sized producers. At midcentury, much of the region's iron production was concentrated along the riverbanks. The Jones & Lauth Company established its ironworks along the Monongahela River in 1853—less than three miles from Fort Pitt. In 1861, the firm expanded to include a blast furnace and foundry, making it the city's first integrated ironworks.

The concentration of metal works was a unique sight for visitors to the city. Travel writer James Parton arrived in Pittsburgh in 1866. His travelogue about the city, published in *The Atlantic* in 1868, includes one of the most repeated, if misconstrued, descriptions of industrial Pittsburgh. Looking down from a nearby hill, he described the expansive industry clustered in the river valley below as akin to "Hell with the lid off." Parton's description has long been interpreted as a pejorative, though the author did not intend it as such. His article was an elaborate hagiography extolling Pittsburgh as a destination. The opening paragraph did not impugn the growing city but rather implored: "Here all is curious and wonderful; site, environs, history, geology, business, aspect, atmosphere, customs, everything. . . . To know Pittsburg thoroughly is a 'liberal education in the kind of culture demanded by modern times.'"

The partial sentence most often quoted from Parton's longform work is almost always clipped from its original context. Parton had ascended Cliff Street, part of what would far later be known as the city of Pittsburgh's Hill District. Looking down from the heights were not the massive iron- or steelworks that would be built in subsequent decades but innumerable smaller manufacturers clinging to the riverbanks. In full context, Parton's words were far from critique:

> There is one evening scene in Pittsburg which no visitor should miss. Owing to the abruptness of the hill behind the town, there is a street along the edge of the bluff, from which you can look directly down upon the part of the city which lies low, near the level of the rivers. On the evening of this dark day, we were conducted to the edge of the abyss, and looked over the iron railing upon the most striking spectacle we ever beheld. It is an unprofitable business, view-hunting; but if anyone would enjoy a spectacle as striking as Niagara, he may do so by simply walking up a long hill to Cliff Street in Pittsburg, and looking over into—hell with the lid taken off.[12]

As awed as Parton was in 1866, Pittsburgh's mid-nineteenth-century agglomeration of manufacturing would be magnified many times over in the steel revolution just beginning. Catalyzed by access to river and rail networks and, more than anything else, the nearby concentration of metallurgic coal, ever-greater steel production from the valleys of southwestern Pennsylvania was an inevitable geographic destiny.

Heated to as high as 2,000 degrees Fahrenheit but prevented from combusting in a low-oxygen environment, coal becomes industrial coke. The transformation required forcing volatile gases and moisture out of the organic rock. The desiccated and purified coal burns cleaner and at the higher temperatures essential to industrial-scale iron and steel production. The first use of coke in small iron furnaces dates back at least to Isaac Meason's Plumsock puddling furnace in Fayette County, built southwest of Pittsburgh in 1817.

A decisive point in Pittsburgh's economic history came in 1859 when the Clinton Furnace at the base of Coal Hill—today Mount Washington—proved that coal from Connellsville could be used in blast furnaces to smelt iron ore. The engineered fuel became central to iron and steel production for a century. The low sulfur content of Connellsville-sourced coke made it the ideal metallurgical coal. Even coal from other veins of the Pittsburgh Seam proved less effective as a feedstock for producing blast furnace coke. By 1880, over 82 percent of all coking coal in the United States came from western Pennsylvania. More than anything else, the unique advantages of Connellsville coal made southwestern Pennsylvania the dominant center of iron and steel production in North America.

Both iron and steel were limited to small-batch production well into the nineteenth century. From antiquity, iron was smelted from iron ore in charcoal-fueled bloomeries. The heavy use of wood-charcoal is blamed for the deforestation across much of northern Europe in the sixteenth century. Early metal furnaces were forced to remain small in both Europe and the United States as they often moved once they had denuded local supplies of wood. Bloomeries produced a sponge-iron, or directly reduced iron, a concoction of iron and slag that could be further refined into wrought iron, but only in limited batches.

Steel was not a new product, had been a niche product since mankind's Iron Age, which began in parts of the world more than three millennia earlier. Iron with precise amounts of carbon forms the harder, stronger, and lighter steel. Too little carbon and iron remained soft and malleable, ideal for blacksmiths, who could form the iron after heating in their own furnaces, but not strong enough for more demanding uses. Too much carbon and molten pig iron could be cast into shapes, but was too hard and brittle for most uses. Carbon steel, with 0.1 percent to 2 percent carbon, was stronger and lighter than either wrought or cast iron. Despite the clear advantages of steel for most uses, the difficult task of precisely adding carbon to iron inhibited production at scale and limited steel to only niche uses.

For more than a millennium, extending into the beginning of the nineteenth century, the most common methods of steel production were forms of cementation or crucible processes. In cementation, small batches of low-carbon wrought iron were packed alongside layers of charcoal and then heated for periods stretching from days to weeks. Once the iron had absorbed sufficient carbon, the output was reheated by similar means and then worked under a forge to distribute the carbon. It was a fuel-, time-, and manpower-intensive process that did not produce a homogeneous product and could not be scaled up to industrial-scale levels of output. Crucible steel was manufactured by melting pig iron or cementation steel in smaller vats with various forms of flux, including glass and sand, but could not produce higher quality or homogenous steel at scale.

At the onset of the Industrial Revolution, a process was developed to refine pig iron in much larger batches and without reliance on scarce charcoal. Large vats of molten pig iron, or puddle, were exposed to air, forcing oxidation of impurities including carbon within the industrial cauldron. The molten metal begins forming into spongy balls of wrought iron weighing as much to ninety pounds. Only the strongest men could manually stir the alchemic mixture using iron rods weighing up to seventy pounds—rods that were typically consumed in the process—and then extract the puddle balls that formed. To complete their task, puddlers needed not only rare strength and endurance but difficult to acquire manual skills. Their tacit knowledge was only acquired from those who had mastered the alchemic art of manually distilling steel from liquid iron.[13] Ironworks relied on these specialized workers, giving puddlers rare power compared to other nineteenth-century industrial workers. As a result, puddlers were among the best-paid of mid-nineteenth-century industrial workers and were among the first to successfully organize for collective bargaining. In 1858, puddlers came together in Pittsburgh to form the Sons of Vulcan, which immediately became one of the earliest and most powerful US labor unions. Puddlers' advantages proved to be fleeting as technology would soon arrive to eviscerate their indispensable role in iron production.

Bessemer

Andrew Carnegie exploited Pittsburgh's economic advantages as only a serial entrepreneur could. Steel was far from his first business, and he had learned how to build and manage ever larger enterprises. Having made respectable fortunes first in the railroad industry and then in the oil and gas discoveries of northwest Pennsylvania, Carnegie entered the ironmaking business. In 1863, he fronted the investment, making his brother Thomas a partner at a small Pittsburgh ironworks. Carnegie and business partners then founded an independent Cyclops Iron Mills in 1864 which was merged the following year with Thomas's earlier ironworks to form the Union Iron Mills, just one of many successful iron producers already operating in Pittsburgh.

Carnegie then became a builder of bridges, as the industry shifted from wood to iron construction. He cofounded the Keystone Bridge Company in 1865—reorganized from the Piper-Shiffler Bridge Building Company operating at Twenty-Ninth Street in Lawrenceville, Pennsylvania.

Keystone Bridge supplied the material for the base of the Brooklyn Bridge, and later constructed thirteen spans along the lower Ohio River. In 1871, to supply the business with iron, Carnegie invested in a new Lucy Furnace set up alongside the Keystone Bridge Company in Lawrenceville—an area just recently merged into the city of Pittsburgh. It was Carnegie's experience as a subcontractor for the great bridge in St. Louis that motivated him to enter the steel industry directly. The bridge's designer and later namesake, James Eads, insisted on using steel for parts of its superstructure. The Keystone Bridge Company was the principal subcontractor for the superstructure, but the company was not capable of producing the steel trusses called for in Eads's design, forcing Carnegie to subcontract steel fabrication to the Butcher Steel Company in Philadelphia.[14]

Carnegie and his partners set out to build a new steel plant near Pittsburgh. They acquired land alongside the Monongahela River near where General Edward Braddock met his demise during the French and Indian Wars over a century earlier. The site not only offered direct river access but was also located alongside two separate rail lines: the Pennsylvania Railroad and the Baltimore & Ohio. The Pittsburgh region provided an optimal location to source the vast quantities of coal and coke needed by the new plant and to deliver final products. Carnegie and Coleman became partners in a new firm: Carnegie, McCandless, & Company which began construction of a new dedicated steelworks on 107 acres of land in 1873. Carnegie hired Andrew Holley—arguably the leading steel engineer of the period—to design the new plant, which he fatefully built around a new Bessemer furnace.

Bessemer technology was revolutionizing steel production in the late nineteenth century, transforming it from small-scale, virtually artisan production to industrial-scale mass production. The new process forced air through large vats of molten pig iron to catalyze the removal of carbon. Within the Bessemer vessel, impurities that do not burn off form solid slag, which is removed after smelting. The elimination of highly skilled and highly paid puddlers, and the larger-scale output of Bessemer furnaces, dramatically lowered the cost and consistency of steel production.

Carnegie had observed Bessemer furnaces himself on a visit to a plant in Sheffield, England. In each of his previous industries, Carnegie's obsession, and the key to his commercial success, had been lowering the cost of production. The Bessemer process was the ideal tool to apply the same business model to steel production. The new plant in Braddock dwarfed the smaller size of the typical iron and steel producers previously clustered in Pittsburgh and proved to be an immediate commercial success.

Initially, the relationship between Carnegie's new plant and Pittsburgh's existing mills was symbiotic. As the plant began production, the market demand for steel was insufficient to meet the oversized output of the Edgar Thomson Works. Excess steel ingots were sold to other local crucible steel producers that used Carnegie's Bessemer-made steel as an input to produce a wider range of steel products.

Within a few years, increasing demand for steel rail more than absorbed the excess supply of steel ingots Carnegie had been selling to other Pittsburgh-based mills. To compete, many of Pittsburgh's older steel producers banded together to construct a Bessemer-based steel plant on par with Carnegie's. In 1881, the Pittsburgh Bessemer Steel Company came online at Homestead, barely three miles downriver from Carnegie's Braddock plant. The consortium quickly faced repeated financial and labor difficulties. When Pittsburgh Bessemer was forced to liquidate, Carnegie acquired the Homestead Steelworks in 1879 for $350,000. A reformed group of Pittsburgh iron producers incorporated the Duquesne Steel Company to build a Bessemer-based plant just three miles upriver from Braddock. Reorganized as the Allegheny Bessemer Company, the plant was completed and began production in 1889. Within a year, Carnegie acquired the new plant in Duquesne as well, cementing his dominance in the steel industry just as the demand for the commodity was rapidly expanding. Operation of all three plants was consolidated under a reorganized Carnegie Steel Company in 1891.

Pittsburgh's Jones & Laughlin Company converted to Bessemer-steel production by 1886. While some crucible steel production continued, and Pittsburgh's very last puddling furnace only shut down in 1961, Bessemer-based production dominated the steel industry by the end of the nineteenth century. Carnegie and his competitors used Bessemer production to make southwestern Pennsylvania the greatest concentration of steel production in the nation. In 1874, just under 10 percent of the nation's steel ingot production came from within Allegheny County. By 1894, a remarkable 43 percent of the nation's steel ingots were sourced from the one county.[15]

Carnegie quickly set a new standard for integrating all stages of steel production. In 1881, he joined forces with coal magnate Henry Clay Frick

Carnegie Steel Furnaces at Braddock, 1905 (Library of Congress / Detroit Publishing Company)

to ensure supplies of the industrial coke his steelworks depended on. When the steel industry's demand for iron ore outstripped nearby supplies, Carnegie took advantage of new iron ore discoveries in the Mesabi Range of Minnesota after 1892. Carnegie partnered with John D. Rockefeller—considered the richest individual in US history, due to profit from the Standard Oil Company—to not just acquire a single ore mine but to contract to buy the output of the entire region. Even though the new source of iron ore was geographically distant from his southwestern Pennsylvania steel plants, Carnegie minimized costs by shipping ore via lake steamers operated by Carnegie subsidiaries to a Carnegie-owned port at Conneaut, Ohio, and then transported by rail to his Mon Valley–based operations.

Alongside Carnegie through the last three decades of the century, George Westinghouse created an equally impressive string of successful businesses, all based in Pittsburgh. Building on his invention of an effective air brake for railroads, Westinghouse had gone on to build a natural gas business and then founded Westinghouse Electric, in 1885. Pittsburgh was also central to the creation of the modern aluminum industry when the Pittsburgh Reduction Company, later Alcoa, was formed there in 1888. By 1886, Pittsburgh's original oil exchange evolved into first the Pittsburgh Coal Exchange, which later became the Pittsburgh Stock Exchange. Few regions anywhere could claim such a concentration of industrial output, entrepreneurism, and financing at the peak of the Second Industrial Revolution. In the penultimate decade of the nineteenth century, *The New York Times* could with little exaggeration claim that "no part of America holds out more golden promises to the enterprising manufacturer than Pittsburgh."[16]

By the turn of the century, Pittsburgh's rich entrepreneurial milieu was being displaced by the ever-larger industrial enterprises coalescing there. Carnegie Steel in 1900 only trailed Standard Oil as the single most valuable industrial firm in the world. If Carnegie's operations had been the only manufacturers located in proximity to Pittsburgh, it would have been enough to define the city as an industrial center without rival within the United States. Carnegie's competitors only added to the region's industrial dominance. At the time, the Pittsburgh Works of the Jones & Laughlin Company was itself one of the nation's largest factories, with more than eight thousand employees, comparable in size to Carnegie's operations at Homestead. By 1900, steel producers across southwestern Pennsylvania were interconnected in a mature network including coal and coking operations stretching out from Pittsburgh in all directions.[17]

When Andrew Carnegie sold his entire steel portfolio to J. P. Morgan for a then-inconceivable $480 million in 1901, the Duquesne Works, along with Homestead Works and the Edgar Thomson plant at Braddock, became the core of the even more behemoth U.S. Steel trust. Morgan acquired not only Carnegie's profitable steel operations but the industrial assets of thirty other companies, in an unprecedented amalgam of production. What emerged was not merely a company proficient at producing steel but one that entirely dominated the market for steel in North America, a market that explicitly defined Pittsburgh as its geographic and economic center.

There can be perfect competition and, at the same time, perfect cooperation.

Elbert Gary, U.S. Steel president (1901–11), 1927

Basing Point Pittsburgh

July 21, 1924

On July 21, 1924, the Federal Trade Commission (FTC) issued a cease-and-desist order to the U.S. Steel Corporation and seven of its subsidiaries, enjoining them to immediately discontinue using the "Pittsburgh Plus" pricing system.[1] For decades, the basing point pricing system had been integrated into US steel markets, despite opposition from federal regulators. Still, the content of the ruling was not as surprising as how long it took to be issued. Federal antitrust litigation against U.S. Steel had been ongoing since 1911, when the Justice Department first filed suit seeking to break up the massive new trust. By 1924, the federal government's era of active trustbusting was over three decades old. Since U.S. Steel came into existence in 1901, Presidents Roosevelt, Taft, and Wilson each had substantial successes in legal battles against many of the largest firms in the nation, but U.S. Steel was different. Not only had the corporation evaded persistent antitrust efforts through its first two decades of existence, few large US corporations had been impeded less by federal regulators.

Basing point pricing was nothing less than a codified form of price fixing. The system required steel producers nationwide to artificially charge consumers based on the market price set in Pittsburgh. In addition, distant purchasers of steel had to pay the entirely fictional freight cost of shipping product from Pittsburgh, regardless of where the actual production took place. The mandatory freight charge was commonly called "phantom freight," though it was a real cost to the buyers and a competitive disadvantage for producers distant from Pittsburgh. The FTC's sharply worded ruling quantified the economic harm caused by the use of Pittsburgh Plus pricing. Upward of $30 million annually was added to the cost of steel products purchased in eleven western states, the equivalent of nearly a half billion dollars at the beginning of the twenty-first century.

The primary target of the FTC's order was U.S. Steel, which had been virtually synonymous with the US steel industry since the conglomerate was created in 1901. The corporate merger engineered by J. Pierpont Morgan of Carnegie Steel, and its major competitors was the largest in US history. With an initial capitalization of $1.4 billion, U.S. Steel instantly became the nation's first billion-dollar corporation. Not only did the new corporate entity dwarf its competitors, it was also able to force most of the nation's steel consumers to adhere to a pricing scheme that worked almost entirely to their disadvantage. The ruling was not merely a warning. The directive was intended to conclusively end the use of basing point pricing, the core of U.S. Steel's business model, across the nation.

Not the result of any government-mandated statute or regulation, Pittsburgh Plus pricing was enforced solely by U.S. Steel's domineering role in the steel industry and was unapologetically intended to limit new competition that otherwise might capture profit from long-established producers. Not only did the imposition of phantom freight charges put new producers at a disadvantage, but the system also impeded innovation almost by design. Even if firms elsewhere produced steel more efficiently, they were precluded from undercutting the prices charged by producers near Pittsburgh. The system reinforced the status quo across the steel industry, not just benefiting established producers, but protecting the regions where they those producers were concentrated. As long as the artificial basing point system remained in effect, Pittsburgh benefited more than any other region could.[2]

Elbert Gary

Basing point pricing was an almost inevitable result of the immense concentration of production controlled by U.S. Steel early in the twentieth century. At its inception in 1901, U.S. Steel was a new form of business enterprise. Not limited to steel, the holding company encompassed twelve subsidiaries spanning the iron, coal, cement, railroad, steel, wire, and mining industries, but at its core the new conglomerate was built around the cluster of steel production Carnegie amassed in Pittsburgh. Employing over 168,000 employees at its inception, the new U.S. Steel rivaled in scope the vast industrial trusts that came into existence at the end of the nineteenth century. U.S. Steel initially produced just under two-thirds of the nation's pig iron, half of its finished steel, and three quarters of the nation's tin production.

The new conglomerate was not just far larger than Carnegie Steel—which Andrew Carnegie sold outright to J. P. Morgan—but it lacked almost any of the entrepreneurial ethos that defined each of the enterprises Andrew Carnegie founded. Chicago attorney Ebert Gary was named the first U.S. Steel chairman after serving as president of Federal Steel in Chicago, which was also part of the grand merger that created U.S. Steel. Gary's rise within the industry could not have diverged more from Andrew Carnegie's hyper-entrepreneurial life story. As an attorney, Gary served two terms as a judge in DuPage County, Illinois. He had practiced law for more than twenty-seven years before becoming the general counsel of Illinois Steel. When Illinois Steel acquired Lorraine Steel and other firms in 1898 to form Federal Steel—the nation's second largest steel producer—Gary was named the firm's president. Throughout Carnegie's business career, he was obsessed with lowering production costs. Gary had little experience on the front lines of any business operation. His strategic vision was focused on maintaining stable prices for the firm's products. In his view, market disruptions and the pricing volatility caused by unfettered competition only interfered with the efficient management of the oversized firm.

Within the conglomerate's first decade, a national economic crisis allowed the firm to solidify its near monopoly power within the steel industry. April 18, 1906, the Great San Francisco Earthquake riled financial markets in both the United States and Europe. The natural disaster produced an immense need for reconstruction funding, which pulled cash from highly leveraged banks in New York. A bear market descended on US financial markets. British insurance companies backed many of the claims that resulted from the disaster. Unprecedented capital outflows from the United Kingdom forced the Bank of England to increase interest rates to maintain a stable exchange rate between the pound sterling and the dollar. Persistent financial turmoil precipitated one of the most severe recessions in US history in the spring of 1907.

The national recession of 1907 spurred desperate price competition that threatened to eviscerate the conglomerate's profits. U.S. Steel did not prioritize minimizing costs but instead worked to limit production and maintain prices across the industry. Limiting production would disadvantage U.S. Steel if competitors replaced production. To manage steel output nationwide, Gary convened quarterly meetings of the nation's steel executives. At the Gary Dinners—as the meetings were widely known—representatives of the largest steel producers announced the prices they were offering. Though no formal agreements were made, virtually all steel producers followed the lead of the major firms and the prices they disclosed. By almost any definition, the Gary Dinners were a deliberate exercise in price collusion intended to limit competition within the industry, yet the meetings faced little opposition from federal regulators.

The dinners, held at the Waldorf Hotel in New York City, persisted long after the financial crisis that begat them subsided. No attempt was made to shield the dinners from public view—the media regularly reported on them—and Gary himself was anything but apologetic about their anti-competitive goals. The dinners continued until 1911, when they were institutionalized by the formation of the American Iron and Steel Institute which continued representing the collective interests of the steel industry over the next century. Gary never wavered from his core beliefs, declaring in 1912: "I do not believe in destructive competition, which is calculated to drive out the weak so that only the strong may survive."[3]

The new U.S. Steel did not envision its future constrained to Pittsburgh. Soon after the conglomerate was formed, Pittsburgh collectively fretted over its future as the center of US steel production. Those concerns only accelerated as U.S. Steel began construction of a massive new steelworks in Indiana. So big was the new plant that a town needed to be created alongside the new plant—a town later named for Judge Gary himself.

In 1911, the newly appointed president of U.S. Steel, James A. Farrell, visited Pittsburgh to reassure the city that its "position in the iron and steel trade as the center and leader of the world is so solidly assured that claims of rivals passing her in importance are not to be considered seriously." Farrell argued that Pittsburgh "can afford to be indifferent to the natural rivalry of other places."[4]

Growing economic angst motivated Pittsburgh's business community to begin actively looking for new investments. In 1911, the Pittsburgh Industrial Commission was created to market the city to potential investors. Over $136,000—the equivalent of $3.5 million in 2018—was spent on

Editorial cartoon, 1911 (*Pittsburgh Sun-Gazette*)

a three-year project aimed at the "securing of more industries and building up the Pittsburgh district and its immense commercial possibilities."[5]

Farrell came to Pittsburgh soon after William Howard Taft began his single term as president. In October 1911, the Taft administration broke sharply with President Roosevelt's more lenient policy toward the corporation and filed suit against the U.S. Steel for violating the Sherman Antitrust Act of 1890. The lawsuit initiated under President Taft continued into the Wilson administration. A four-judge circuit court ruled against the government in June 1915 with a subsequent appeal before the US Supreme Court scheduled in March 1917. With the United States' entry into World War I in April 1917, the hearing was postponed until October 1919. On March 1, 1920, the Supreme Court, by a four to three vote, issued a ruling against the federal government and, again, in favor of U.S. Steel.[6] Despite the adverse ruling, executive branch efforts to rein in U.S. Steel barely paused. Undaunted, the FTC initiated a new investigation of U.S. Steel in May 1920. In July, the FTC rejected these new charges in a 3–2 vote.[7]

The case was reconsidered yet again the following year. In April, the FTC issued a formal complaint charging U.S. Steel with violations of both Article 2 of the Clayton Act and Section 5 of the Federal Trade

Commission Act. Article 2 proscribed price discrimination, or the offering of different prices to different consumers, for commodity products. Section 5 focused on unfair or deceptive acts or practices.

The federal charges centered around the corporation's continued use of the Pittsburgh Plus pricing system, which was generating increasing complaints from both steel producers and consumers in markets distant from Pittsburgh. Midwestern resentment against the practice was reflected by the nearly daily appearance of demands to "abolish Pittsburgh Plus," on the *Chicago Daily Tribune* editorial pages.[8] The FTC's 1920 action was initiated by the a consortium of Midwestern firms, including the Western Association of Rolled Steel Consumers of Chicago, Illinois; the Superior Commercial Club of Superior, Wisconsin; the State of Minnesota; the Civic Associations of Duluth, Minnesota; the Southern Association of Steel Fabricators based in Atlanta, Georgia; and the Birmingham (Alabama) Civic Association and the Birmingham Base Steel Bureau. No plaintiff anywhere near Pittsburgh argued against the status quo. It would have been irrational for any stakeholder in Pittsburgh to take a position against the basing point system in use. The FTC's ruling banning Pittsburgh Plus pricing only arrived in 1924.[9]

U.S. Steel sought no appeal of the commission's order, instead only filing a formal statement of intended compliance. For the most part, U.S. Steel simply ignored the directive. A technical reading of the ruling only required the firm to cease using a single basing point. Pittsburgh had been the geographic nexus of the pricing system for decades. Nominal compliance came from modification of the system to use a limited number of alternative basing points. First, Chicago was added as an alternative location for geographic reference, with Birmingham, Alabama; Middleton, Ohio; and Sparrows Point, Maryland, added later.[10] Multiple locations for the basing point system barely attenuated the economic advantage the system provided southwestern Pennsylvania. Pittsburgh's reckoning with its own future was likewise deferred.

Protected by its own dominance across the industry, U.S. Steel in its first decades was "more concerned with centralization and consolidation than with innovations leading to improved productivity."[11] The corporation was notably deficient in new innovations and investment in research and only established a formal research laboratory in 1927. For decades, U.S. Steel's early research operation remained marginal when compared to the corporation's enormous size. By the 1920s, U.S. Steel was the largest firm in the nation other than General Motors. Yet, the

66 employees U.S. Steel employed at its primary research lab ranked as only the twenty-sixth largest corporate laboratory in the country. In comparison, Bell Labs employed 2,000 employees dedicated to research activities; the chemical company Du Pont employed 943; and General Electric: 672. In 1927, the industry trade journal *Iron Age* critically opined, "The Steel Corporation as a whole has had no conspicuous place in fundamental research in iron and steel."[12]

Steel Codes and the Great Depression

Just five years after the FTC's largely ignored ruling against Pittsburgh Plus pricing, the stock market's Black Tuesday on October 29, 1929, precipitated a national depression that would freeze in place the nation's industrial geography. The Great Depression was made that much more difficult by the prosperity that had preceded it, especially for steel regions. Through the roaring 1920s, continuing economic growth and the rapid adoption of the automobile fueled an ever-increasing demand for steel. In March 1929, the nation's steel producers operated at nearly 99 percent capacity. That year the nation's raw steel production exceeded 50 million tons for the first time ever.[13]

During the Great Depression, Pittsburgh suffered more than other steel centers because the region even lacked diversity within the metals industry. Pittsburgh was "known as a tonnage city," producing the bulk of the nation's raw steel ingots, but had never built a similar advantage in steel fabrication or the production of finished goods. By the early twentieth century, the region was no longer competitive in the production of lighter metal castings.[14] The large integrated producers concentrated in Pittsburgh fared worst of all during the Depression because they were the source of steel rails and structural shapes that recorded some of the largest drops in demand during the Depression. Consumer goods—to include steel beer cans, which experienced new growth once Prohibition's ending, in 1933—used commodity strip steel, which had dispersed production across the nation.

New Deal economic policies intentionally prioritized price stability over competition, reinforcing the steel industry's preexisting geography. Congress passed the National Industrial Recovery Act in June 1933. The law suspended most existing antitrust laws and permitted collusion among firms. Directed by the National Recovery Administration (NRA), industries adopted trade practices that both limited competition and inflated prices. The steel industry became one of the first covered by the new NRA codes. A new federal agency, the Steel Code Authority, was directed by the board of directors of the American Iron and Steel Association; the formal organization begat of the Gary Dinners a quarter century earlier.[15]

The new Steel Code Authority explicitly limited investment in new steel capacity, all but preventing the emergence of new competition for existing producers. Firms were required to seek permission before opening any new plants or expanding any productive capacity at existing plants. The anticompetitive regulations were intended to counter overcapacity that was seen to be crippling prices across many industries. The codes inhibited the industry's geographic dispersion and favored large existing producers that were able to shift production between plants. Newer and smaller manufacturers complained of the impact such restrictions had on their businesses.[16] With reinvesment curtailed by federal reglators, many smaller producers were unable to make essential capital improvements, leaving them less able to compete in the future.

In 1935, the US Supreme Court deemed the NRA and the steel codes unconstitutional, but the ongoing Depression continued to suppress the emergence of new competitors in the capital-intensive steel industry. Where there was new steel capacity constructed during the Depression, much was concentrated in traditional steelmaking regions and mostly at existing plants. A $10 million expansion in Homestead, Pennsylvania, including a new hundred-inch semicontinuous plate mill with a capacity of 729,000 tons per year, opened in 1937. The same year, U.S. Steel announced a $60 million investment to improve Pittsburgh-area plants. A total of $45 million was invested at U.S Steel's Clairton Works to build a new hot strip mill and an expanded coking plant. Another $15 million was invested in a new slabbing mill at Carnegie Steel's original steel plant at Braddock. U.S. Steel was not alone in expanding its Pittsburgh-based steel operations. Jones & Laughlin invested just under $24 million in a new ninety-six-inch continuous strip mill in Pittsburgh in 1937.

One of the last entirely new steel plants to be constructed in Pittsburgh came in December 1938, when U.S. Steel opened its new Irvin Works in West Mifflin, nearly adjacent to the firm's Duquesne Works. Fitting yet another industrial steel works in the region was a gargantuan task, as industry had long put to use most usable parcels of land along the rivers. Over $60 million dollars was needed to displace 4.4 million cubic yards of earth—said to be second only to what was required in the construction of the Panama Canal—to make a suitable site within the hilly topography of the heavily industrialized Monongahela Valley. When the new plant opened, headlines seemed to go out of their way to report that it was "the best possible evidence of faith in Pittsburgh as the steel capital of the country."[17]

Reinvestment in traditional steel regions during the Great Depression reversed for a brief period an inexorable westward shift of the US steel industry. The industry's geographic center had moved westward an average six miles a year since first calculated in 1874, when it was first estimated to reside in Juniata County, Pennsylvania—a hundred miles east of Pittsburgh. By 1933, the center had moved past Pittsburgh and into western Ohio. If not for the onset of the Depression, the westward drift would likely have continued, but between 1933 and 1936 the industry's trajectory reversed course and retreated thirteen miles, determined to rest near an apple tree outside of Mansfield, Ohio.[18]

The brief retrograde only masked a growing realization among experts that Pittsburgh's competitiveness as a manufacturing center was declining. By 1935, the Bureau of Business Research at the University of Pittsburgh concluded that the city had already "passed through its period of mushroom growth in the eighties and nineties of the last century and the first decade of the present one." More significantly it explained, the development of byproduct coke ovens freed the steel industry from its dependence on nearby Connellsville coal, giving distant steel producers new advantages. Coupled with the Depression's devastating impact, Pittsburgh's steel industries were expected to soon stagnate.[19] The economic prognosis was only delayed by historic events emerging far beyond Pittsburgh.

Every time I approach Pittsburgh, especially by plane, I get a sense of tremendous power, a sense of accomplishment. Pittsburgh thrills you, and frightens you a little, too.

Frank Knox, secretary of the Navy, circa 1943

Arsenal

April 14, 1945

In the final months of World War II, the USS *LST-1059* slipped down the Neville Island ways of the Dravo Corporation shipyard, just three miles downriver from the head of the Ohio River and Downtown Pittsburgh. The navy's newest warship was a Landing Ship, Tank (LST), designed to do what most ships avoid at all costs: beach itself directly onto the shore. The purpose-built vessel was capable of discharging cargo without accessible port facilities, making it invaluable to military operations around the world. Far from the only warship to be built in Pittsburgh during the war, *LST-1059* was the last of 146 nearly identical ships the Dravo Corporation alone had mass-produced at its Neville Island facility.

The frenetic pace of ship construction during the war dwarfed the smaller rivercraft the company had specialized in before the war. Dravo's Neville Island facility first began construction of steel barges during World War I. Dravo-designed barges became the standard for transporting coal and other bulky products by river.[1] Other than the unpowered barges, the shipyard had produced only a limited number of small towboats and river dredges, rarely more than two hundred tons displacement. Weighing over sixteen hundred tons, each of the LSTs was far larger than all the ships Dravo had built to date with one exception: the two-thousand-ton sidewheel railcar ferry George H. Walker completed in 1923.[2]

Once a center of steamboat construction, Pittsburgh's previous shipbuilding era had mostly ended over a century earlier. World War II necessitated the industry's unforeseen reemergence. The German invasion of France prompted passage of the Two-Ocean Navy Act in July 1940. Federal orders for new warships overwhelmed the nation's traditional shipyards. The Navy turned to smaller inland shipyards, including some with little or no shipbuilding experience, to rapidly expand ship construction. Dravo received orders for small submarine chasers by the end of 1940. Workers laid the keel for *LST-1* in July 1942—an entirely new ship design—just seven months after Pearl Harbor.

A similar conversion occurred at the nearby American Bridge Company, a subsidiary of the U.S. Steel Corporation that traced its roots to the Keystone Bridge Company, which Andrew Carnegie and partners founded in 1865. American Bridge facilities in Coraopolis, adjacent to Neville Island on the Ohio River, produced an additional 126 LSTs during the war. Together, Dravo and American Bridge produced over 40 percent of the of the 650 LSTs commissioned between 1942 and 1945. In addition, the two Pittsburgh shipyards built destroyer escorts and minesweepers as well as hundreds of smaller watercraft for the army and navy. By 1945, the two exigent shipyards made Pittsburgh into one of the most prolific shipbuilding centers still functioning anywhere in the world.

Other Pittsburgh companies quickly transformed their production lines for the duration of the war. The H. J. Heinz Company took just three months to convert several canned-goods manufacturing lines to the production of combat gliders needed by the Army Air Corps. Wartime orders made a Pittsburgh plant the world's largest grease producer, eventually producing over 5 million pounds of "Eisenhower Grease," an essential water repellent needed for virtually all amphibious equipment. No part of Pittsburgh's industrial ecosystem was untouched by the war effort. Even the Shenango Pottery Company of New Castle, forty miles north of Pittsburgh, shifted entirely to defense production for the duration. Early in the war, the firm delivered a million-dollar order of dinnerware for the army and navy before converting its expertise in ceramics to produce landmines.[3]

Southwestern Pennsylvania's already prodigious industrial capacity began expanding even before the nation formally declared war on the Axis powers. Across the region, entirely new manufacturing facilities were built to meet the industrial needs generated by a nation mobilizing for a global conflict. On a farm twenty miles northwest of Pittsburgh, the Curtiss-Wright Corporation constructed a plant to mass-produce aircraft propellers in 1940—essential to meeting President Roosevelt's goal

Launching of LST 1038, Neville Island, January 1945 (National Archives)

of producing fifty thousand warfighting aircraft annually. The revolutionary plant along the Ohio River in Vanport, Beaver County, was designed to be "the largest individual aircraft propeller manufacturing plant in the United States."[4] The new plant produced alloy steel propellers until the very end of the war. So vital was the plant's output that its location was expected to be one of the prime targets should German strategic bombers ever reach the continental United States.[5] In 1942, within sight of the new propeller plant, the Koppers Company of Pittsburgh began construction of a new plant to produce butadiene and styrene, essential ingredients in the production of synthetic rubber. Synthetic rubber became crucial to the war effort after the fall of both Singapore and the Philippines cut off the nation's natural rubber supplies. The Blaw-Knox Corporation—a Pittsburgh-based builder of construction equipment—was awarded the contract to handle all engineering and design work for the War Department's BunaS synthetic rubber program across the nation.[6]

More than anything else, Pittsburgh contributed steel to the global war effort. Steel was formed into armor for ships, tanks, aircraft, and innumerable types of armaments. National economic mobilization filled the orderbooks for virtually all of the steelworks of Pittsburgh, instantly shifting the region from the doldrums of the Great Depression to near-capacity production. Between 1940 and 1945, the blast furnaces of the greater Pittsburgh Ordnance District produced 95 million tons of steel, virtually all allocated for wartime products.

Steel was more important in World War II than in any conflict before or since. A vast expansion of navy and merchant fleets made ship construction the nation's single largest consumer of steel. In 1940, US shipbuilding in used just 998,858 tons of steel. By 1943, steel needed for ship construction alone increased to over 13 million tons. Each of the 1,167 US combat vessels built during the war required armor plate and structural steel far in excess of what was needed to fabricate a typical merchant ship.[7] In addition, the steel needed for tanks, trucks, and vehicles of all types offset many times over the loss in demand from civilian automobile production curtailed by wartime regulation.

Virtually all of Pittsburgh industry was quickly reoriented to meet surging demand for wartime products. The steel fabrication infrastructure of the Pittsburgh region was crucial to the production of aerial bombs. Over 11 million such devices were produced in the Pittsburgh Ordnance District during the war, as were an estimated 28 million large artillery shells. The district's total wartime output was valued at over $19 billion in price-controlled dollars, the rough equivalent to over $520 billion in 2024. As the nation mobilized, not only was steel needed in unprecedented quantities, it was needed faster than was imaginable at the time. Vast amounts were even needed to rapidly construct new steel production facilities, but the new facilities could not come online rapidly enough. The only realistic way to meet the expanding demand was to run existing facilities as close to capacity as possible, if not beyond.

The impact of the global war on Pittsburgh stood in stark contrast to the fate of major industrial centers elsewhere. Safely ensconced the nation's strategic rear, plants in Pittsburgh were able to produce uninterrupted through the end of the war. Rival industrial regions around the world faced very different fates. Most manufacturing centers in both Europe and Japan were strategic targets through much of the conflict. Many industrial regions outside the United States, peers to Pittsburgh in the production of steel prior to the war, saw their industrial infrastructure decimated during the conflict or deliberately deconstructed soon afterward. Immediately after the war, Allied powers imposed extensive reparation policies that began with the systematic démontage of their surviving industrial capital.[8] Entire plants were dismantled and reconstructed in lands controlled by the victors. At the end of the war, no single region in the world equaled Pittsburgh's raw industrial output.

Mobilization

It was a full ten years after Wall Street's Black Tuesday, October 29, 1929, before the Great Depression definitively came to an end for Pittsburgh. Escalating conflict in Europe had not immediately generated new economic activity for US manufacturing firms, or for the city of Pittsburgh. Through 1938, US sales to belligerents in Europe were curtailed by domestic politics and an aversion to being pulled into the war. Even the German invasion of Czechoslovakia in January 1939 did not have a major impact on US industrial output. Still adhering to an isolationist foreign policy, the country responded by extending the 1937 Neutrality Act—due to expire that year—for an additional two years. The act explicitly limited the ability of US firms to accept industrial orders from any of the European powers at war.

Existing plants could not meet the surging demand for steel, but industry executives resisted new investment to increase capacity. The industry's experience following World War I and through the subsequent Depression gave steel executives pause before initiating major new investment on their own. In a dramatic failure of prescience, the October 1939 edition of the Department of Commerce's *Survey of Current Business* detailed the multiple reasons industrial leaders opposed new capital investment. Businesses argued, "The war may not prove to be a long one, in which case no significant demand for our exports may arise" but also prognosticated that the war "is on a much smaller scale than in 1914."[9] Few companies were willing to accept the risk of investing in new capital-intensive steel production.

By early 1940, little surplus capacity was available at any of the nation's already saturated steel mills, but no Federal policies were in place to incentivize investments to expand production. Limited mobilization planning only began with the creation of the short-lived War Resources Board in August 1939, which disbanded before the end of the year due to political factions trying to keep the US out of the war. Roosevelt formed a new National Defense Advisory Commission (NDAC)—tasked with coordinating economic mobilization efforts—in May 1940. The commission's advisor on industrial matters was U.S. Steel Chairman Edward Stettinius. NDAC staff immediately realized the nation was facing dire supply constraints across all strategic commodities, but especially in steel. In September, the NDAC received a report from its Division of Research and Statistics that the nation's steel production capacity was grossly insufficient for the anticipated defense buildup. The National Research Council had reached a similar conclusion earlier that year.[10] National mobilization was expected to require over 90 million tons of steel per year. At the time, the notional capacity of all US steel producers combined amounted to 70 million tons of ingot production annually.

Virtually all mobilization plans were being slowed by the nation's limited steel production. Yet, steel executives continued to resist making the new investments necessary to increase industrial capacity, arguing that the projected shortages could be addressed by lowering production of civilian consumer goods, which would free up capacity for defense needs. Demand jumped even further in mid-1940, when the federal budget authorized an additional $9 billion for new army appropriations, along with $4 billion for a complementary Two-Ocean Navy expansion. The $13 billion surge in defense appropriations was a fortyfold increase over an average $340 million in annual appropriations for the army and navy over the prior two decades.[11]

Increasing the nation's capacity to produce steel was a major challenge, but allocation of the vital commodity across so many competing requirements posed compound problems. Early in the war, steel was considered the "No. 1 Bottleneck" holding up production across a range of vital war products.[12] Efficient allocation of steel production was inhibited by both "small-order" and "commercial-customer" problems.[13] The small-order problem resulted from steel producers' difficulty in responding to the growing number of small-batch orders for specialized military equipment. Many of these orders were vital to the production of other wartime products, but in normal circumstances, such small orders were not a priority for profit-maximizing steelmakers. The "commercial-customer" problem resulted from steel producers' desire to give priorities to their commercial customers ahead of new wartime orders. Wartime orders were expected to end as soon as the conflict drew to a close. Producers looking toward the future preferred to continue supplying their commercial customers, which were expected to return once peace returned. Each of these problems was exacerbated by widespread hoarding of critical material in anticipation of even greater shortages to come. Resolving these concurrent problems required coordinated economic planning very much anathema to the normal operation of the free market, economic planning on a scale that the United States had little experience implementing.

Even if all existing steel supply was efficiently distributed, the nation needed additional production to come online quickly. In late 1940, the navy declared that the problem of expediting steel deliveries to its shipyard contractors had assumed "gargantuan" proportions. Despite protests from the mobilization bureaucracy, the steel industry remained reluctant to invest its own capital in new capacity. If there was going to be a rapid expansion in steel production, the government was being forced to become the investor of last resort.

In 1940—even after a decade of New Deal federal programs—policy tools did not exist for the government to take on comprehensive economic coordination within any industry. A solution was found in dormant legislation and a quiescent Depression-era agency. Set up by the Hoover administration, the Reconstruction Finance Corporation (RFC) had been authorized in January 1932 to address growing economic problems during the Great Depression, disbursing $1.5 billion in 1932 and $1.8 billion in both 1933 and 1934. Wartime necessities forced the RFC to take on a very different and much more expansive role.

With the passage of the Lend-Lease Act in March 1941, most neutrality restrictions limiting exports were lifted. New orders from belligerent nations poured in, further swamping US industries. Allied nations were also no longer constrained by a lack of cash to pay for new orders. The new legislation permitted the US government to front the cost for most new foreign orders. A total of $7.27 billion of material goods was pledged to the United Kingdom and the Soviet Union in 1941 alone.[14]

By May 1941, all grades of iron and steel were added to a list of precious commodities by the Army and Navy Munitions Board, effectively placing their trade under direct federal control. Mobilization plans anticipated that the national steel industry had to immediately jump to producing

92 million tons a year and rapidly increase to 110 or 120 million tons annually, nearly 50 percent more than the 83 million tons the industry was capable of producing at the time. "These figures appear fantastic and their realization at this moment seems highly problematical," declared an industry magazine.[15]

Bureaucracy

The private sector would not be left to its own devices to meet the escalating demand for steel. Coordination of steel production fell to the RFC. In 1940, the repurposed federal agency established eight new subsidiary corporations to implement wartime mobilization efforts: the Metals Reserve Company, the Rubber Reserve Company, the Defense Plant Corporation, the Defense Supplies Corporation, the War Damage Corporation, the US Commercial Company, the Rubber Development Corporation, and the Petroleum Reserve Corporation. Each of these had a major impact on Pittsburgh during the war, but none greater than the investments of the Defense Plant Corporation (DPC). The DPC "was established to supply the almost unlimited capital needed to expand the nation's industrial base."[16] The new agency not only financed new industrial capacity but also became the owner of a large part of the nation's industrial base, even if existing firms were contracted to manage and operate the new plants for the duration.

With the declaration of war against the Axis powers, vastly increasing industrial output immediately became central to the nation's military strategy. A reworked national mobilization plan developed by the US joint chiefs of staff envisioned a 9 million–man army along with a future Army Air Force and a navy, each larger than ever supported in the history of the United States. Those plans faced immediate economic constraints. The scale of matériel and munitions needed to build such a force could not be produced quickly enough for use in the war plans for which they were designated.

In July 1942, economist Donald Nelson, the War Production Board chairman, came to Pittsburgh to urge labor and management to work together to increase steel production at local plants.[17] During his tour of Pittsburgh's "Victory Valley," he called for a "renewed production effort going beyond anything we have yet achieved."[18] So crucial was the production of raw and fabricated products from Pittsburgh that the eventual timing of the D-Day invasion was largely determined by how long it would take US industry to construct the combined air, land, and sea forces that crossed the English Channel in June 1944.

The rapid expansion of industrial output required government intervention in the US economy on a scale unprecedented before or since. Not only were comprehensive wage and price controls implemented across the economy, but a mandatory diversion to military production subsumed virtually all of the nation's industrial output. A comprehensive Controlled Materials Plan was imposed on strategic commodities, effectively controlling all steel, copper, and aluminum trade.[19] Steel, aluminum, and copper production was placed under the tightest controls because by "controlling the use of these key metals you in fact control practically all production."[20] In June 1942, a mandatory Production Requirements Plan was imposed on any plant that used or produced or anticipated needing just $5,000 or more of any critical metal.[21] All new investments were financed directly by the federal government or determined entirely by new government orders. The normal functioning of a free market was held virtually in abeyance as the national economy focused on maximizing war-related production.

The DPC alone was responsible for $9.6 billion in new investment between 1941 and 1945, most of which was channeled to build new industrial capacity across the nation. Federal investment expanded the industrial capacity of Pittsburgh faster than any single investor or firm ever had previously, including Andrew Carnegie himself. During the war, the Pittsburgh Industrial District received over $511 million in direct investment, much of which had been dispersed early on for the expansion of existing plant capacity.

New or expanded facilities financed by the DPC were federal government property, even if leased back to private companies. Workers often did not realize they were de facto government workers, but the corporations were isolated from most commercial risks normally part of private sector investment. Investments made by the DPC fueled expansions the private sector was unwilling to make, even with guaranteed wartime orders. Other than a Curtiss-Wright plant built to manufacture aircraft propellers in Beaver County, most of the DPC's investments in Pittsburgh focused on expanding existing capacity at the region's metal works. The Aluminum Company of America expanded its Canonsburg and New Castle plants with DPC investment. U.S. Steel expanded its Duquesne Works with three new electric furnaces and its Homestead Steel with seven open-hearth furnaces, all financed by the DPC.

The DPC operationalized two types of leases for the new capital it financed. Companies engaged in the production of goods directly for the military paid just $1 per year for the use of federally owned equipment, while the rent for firms that produced semifinished products for further processing at other war-production plants was based on the volume of its sales.[22] No matter how leases were structured, detailed production schedules were firmly controlled by federal bureaucrats executing broad mobilization plans.

So intertwined were business and government during the war that the distinction between the public and private sector often confounded other levels of government. In 1940, the Mesta Machine Company of Homestead was awarded one of the largest ordinance contracts in Pittsburgh history for the production of 355 large-caliber 155-millimeter guns. In January 1942, based on the new investment, the Allegheny County property assessor increased the valuation on the property and equipment located at the firm's Homestead plant. The updated valuation increased the firm's annual property taxes by $5,137.[23] Mesta claimed the incremental increase in value derived from equipment owned by the federal government and was therefore exempt from local property taxes. The company appealed against the tax increase by filing a lawsuit in Allegheny County's Court of Common Pleas. When the county court upheld the higher assessment value, the company appealed to the Pennsylvania Supreme Court. Further appeals eventually reached the US Supreme Court. Only in January 1944 did the Supreme Court conclusively side with the company's argument that the equipment on the site was indeed federally owned and, therefore, tax-exempt.[24]

Wartime demand generated an enormous expansion of industrial capacity across the Pittsburgh region. In addition to DPC funding, Mesta reinvested $4 billion at its existing Pittsburgh plants in 1940 and 1941, an amount greater than the firm's cumulative capital investment between 1929 and 1939. Much of the additional manufacturing capacity was dedicated to products with limited peacetime uses. Mesta's World War II specialty in large caliber artillery extended to the construction of "Little David," an experimental thirty-six-inch mortar system, the largest artillery piece in the world. Designed for bunker busting in a planned invasion of mainland Japan, the gun was effectively obsolete before hostilities ended.

Little stood in the way of the myriad plant expansions necessitated by the war. Navy Secretary Frank Knox designated U.S. Steel's Homestead Works as the primary facility to supply the Navy's Speed Up Program, essential to ramping up shipbuilding production. Extension of the Homestead Works became the largest wartime expansion of a steel plant anywhere in the nation. With an $86.2 million contract from the DPC and $75 million provided by Carnegie-Illinois Steel, then a subsidiary of U.S. Steel, the firm opened eleven new open-hearth furnaces in 1943. Expansion of the plant required the displacement of nearly eight thousand residents from their homes.[25] A total of 1,566 families were uprooted as 121 acres of residential Homestead were taken over for the plant's expansion. Demolished were 1,363 buildings, twelve churches, five schools, and two convents.[26] In August 1941, the federal government raised an additional $117 million for investment concentrated in the Mon Valley, already the industrial heart of the region's steelmaking capacity.[27] Collectively, the wartime expansion of Carnegie's original plants at Braddock, Duquesne, and Homestead was equivalent to the rapid construction of a new fully integrated steelworks.[28]

When Secretary of the Navy Frank Knox visited Pittsburgh during the war, he likely flew into what is now the Allegheny County Municipal Airport, in just south of the city of Pittsburgh. Planes approaching the airport flew through the nonstop plumes being generated by the hyper-industrialized Monongahela River Valley. The blast furnaces below were generating a twenty-four-hour glow that lit the sky unlike any artificial illumination in history. The view was an unbelievably magnified version of what had awed nineteenth-century writer James Parton when he described the much smaller industries of 1866 Pittsburgh.

Knox observed Pittsburgh after a full century of virtually unabated industrial expansion and from a much greater height than Parton could have achieved. He looked down on concentrated industrial production several orders of magnitude greater than anyone would have thought possible in the mid-nineteenth century. As the war came to an end, US producers accounted for over half of global steel production, and 40 percent of US production came from plants in southwestern Pennsylvania. With civilian production of almost all durable goods suspended for the duration of the war, for a full half decade Pittsburgh had been entirely subsumed by a war economy directed by federal planners.

The End of Basing Point Pricing

The beginning of the end for basing point pricing in the steel industry only came in 1938, when Congress passed the Wheeler-Lea Act, which primarily addressed the FTC's power to regulate against false advertising. The act included a minor clause making all unchallenged past orders of the FTC automatically effective unless respondents filed an appeal before May of that year. The FTC's order ending Pittsburgh Plus pricing, though much ignored since 1924, had never been challenged in court. The corporation hastened to file an appeal against what was by then a fourteen-year-old cease-and-desist order.

Just as happened during World War I, most pending regulatory cases against industrial concerns were held in abeyance during World War II. Only after the conflict concluded was U.S. Steel's challenge to the 1924 ruling reactivated and merged with eleven other appeals filed by plaintiffs against similar FTC rulings. The lead case was an appeal by the Cement Institute against a similar ruling by the FTC against the use of basing point pricing in the cement industry. In 1948, the consolidated case made it to the US Supreme Court. The court's final ruling in *FTC vs. Cement Institute* voided the remaining appeal in the case on August 28.[29] Basing point pricing was deemed illegal.

Even in the face of the Supreme Court's definitive ruling, the steel industry did not immediately abandon support for basing point pricing. Instead, it lobbied for new legislation that would give it a statutory exemption from the ruling. Pennsylvania Senator Francis Myers was successful in getting the Senate to pass a bill placing a moratorium on implementation of the ruling.[30] Because the House of Representatives declined to schedule required hearings on the amendment, the legislation was not passed during the session. Repeated efforts the following congressional session were less successful. Only at the end of 1950 did legislative efforts to preserve basing point pricing in the steel industry come to a conclusive end.

By 1950, U.S. Steel was almost a half century old, and Pittsburgh's dominance of the US metals industry had endured for nearly a century. The city's economy had completely conformed to its dominant industry, growing into one of the most specialized industrial centers in the world. Protected by an institutionalized pricing system entirely to its advantage, the Pittsburgh region had less incentive to innovate and change than almost anywhere else in the nation. If steel had followed the path typical of other industries, maturity should have brought deconcentrating as firms moved away from the locations of early agglomeration. Yet, steel remained the dominant industries of the Monongahela and Ohio River valleys stretching out from Pittsburgh. New production had emerged around Birmingham, Alabama, and U.S. Steel built from scratch the Gary Works in Illinois, but those expansions did not induce any new industrial diversity in Pittsburgh.

Pittsburgh's hyperspecialized production had been protected by the effectiveness of basing point pricing and the nation's nearly continuous growth in the demand for steel. Plants operating at capacity obscured the reality that Pittsburgh's competitiveness as a location for making steel was draining away by early in the twentieth century. U.S. Steel's new stamping plant built in West Mifflin in 1938 was more exception than rule and relied on steel produced by other blast furnaces in the Monongahela River Valley. The last fully integrated steelworks to be constructed near Pittsburgh was the Midland Works of Crucible Steel, built thirty-six miles down the Ohio River in 1911.[31]

The Great Depression and the wartime exigencies that immediately followed not only deferred any decline in steel but reinforced Pittsburgh's reliance on heavy industry. U.S. Steel had almost singlehandedly checked the normal evolution of an entire industry and by sheer corporate fiat artificially inflated Pittsburgh's role as a manufacturing center. Only as World War II came to an end would Pittsburgh begin to face the competitive pressures that it had been insulated from for so long.

Denial

4

But what many Americans do not know is that their own steel industry is bigger than those of all other nations on earth put together!

No other nation in the world could have matched that record. It is a record that stands as a glorious tribute to the men who make steel and the men who built steel in America.

U.S. Steel advertisement, January 2, 1951

Rhapsody of Steel

October 18, 1944

The Reconstruction Finance Corporation—the federal agency that had become the de jure owner of a large swath of industrial United States it had financed during World War II—was planning for the future. In mid-October 1944, the federal agency publicly announced a detailed list of industrial plants soon to be designated as war surplus. War on all fronts continued unabated at the beginning of the month. In Europe, the Battle of the Bulge was still two months in the future. In the Pacific, the battle to retake the Philippines was ongoing. However, even with the outcome of the global conflict uncertain, the home front bureaucracy was preparing for a future peace.

The initial list included twenty-two industrial plants to be disposed of near Pittsburgh and a total of seventy facilities across Pennsylvania.[1] Western Pennsylvania plants to be privatized read like a blue-ribbon directory of Pittsburgh's industrial heritage: a hundred acres at the Homestead Works of Carnegie-Illinois Steel, a subsidiary of U.S. Steel—where seven new open-hearth furnaces had been built in 1941; three new electric furnaces at the neighboring Duquesne Works; a synthetic rubber plant built by the Koppers Company in Beaver County; and nineteen other industrial facilities spread across the region. Demobilization was the next stage of the economic transformation wrought by the massive industrial expansion necessitated by the wartime exigencies. "America today is going through an industrial expansion that may tend to reshape the entire industrial picture," declared a federal official in 1942.[2]

Pittsburgh leaders were distinctly worried about how demobilization would affect the region's future. In June 1944, *The Wall Street Journal* noted that the war years had seen significant population gains across most western states but that Pennsylvania's population had declined by over 6 percent between 1940 and 1943, a greater loss than could be explained by the military draft still underway. The newspaper gave Pittsburgh a *D* rating for its future growth potential, categorizing it in a group of metropolitan areas that "cannot be expected to grow rapidly or even recoup their losses in the postwar period."[3] Pittsburgh's economic future was threatened not only by expected plant closures locally but by new plants built far from western Pennsylvania during the war. Federal policies during the war explicitly tried to disperse as much new industrial capacity as possible away from the nation's "industrial triangle," thought to have Pittsburgh; Boston; and Wilmington, Delaware, as its three vertices.[4]

Any shift of industrial activity away from traditional manufacturing regions explicitly threatened Pittsburgh. The fear of new publicly subsidized competition hit home in Pittsburgh even before construction of most of the new plants began. As early as August 1940, the Pittsburgh Industrial Commission formed an emergency committee to lobby against federal policies attempting to shift manufacturing activity toward less industrialized areas. Citing more than two thousand plants already available for defense work in the region, the commission argued that government-induced shifts were inefficient and politically motivated. Instead, regions should contribute to the war effort based on their existing specializations. Business leaders in Pittsburgh cited the parable of Pliny the Elder: "Let the shoemaker stick to his last."[5]

At the beginning of 1941, the federal Office of Production Management took executive control of the nation's ever-expanding mobilization bureaucracy. Federal agencies began allocating orders among existing industrial plants and controlled where new industrial capacity could be located. In May, the office established a Plant Site Board with broad authority to regulate the location of industrial investment across the nation.[6] Approval was required before any new industrial facility could be constructed, even for any major expansion at existing plants.

Portending future challenges for Pittsburgh, the new bureaucracy issued formal guidance to locate new plants away from highly industrialized areas.[7] Early in the war, the prime consideration for the location of new industrial sites was their ability to be defended from enemy attack. Areas considered vulnerable included those with excessive concentrations of industrial activity, and few regions were as concentrated as Pittsburgh. While Pittsburgh saw many of its historic factories expand during the war, most of the nation's entirely new industrial plants built between 1941 and 1945 were in distant regions with little history in heavy manufacturing.

As early as July 1944, the navy—which had generated an inordinate proportion of the wartime demand for steel—set up a dedicated bureaucracy focusing on terminating wartime contracts and beginning reconversion to peacetime activity.[8] On December 1, 1944, more than five hundred prime defense contracts valued at over $250 million—equivalent to more than $4.5 billion at in 2025—were canceled in the Pittsburgh Ordnance District. As 1944 drew to a close, Pittsburgh's manufacturing plants employed a record 365,000 workers—at least 60 percent above 1929 levels—but payrolls dipped in December for the first time since the war began.[9] Few expected war-induced employment levels to be sustained long into the coming peace. The same month, a committee appointed by the governor of Pennsylvania dourly reported that a congressional plan for peacetime reconversion could result in the loss of 35 percent of all jobs in Pennsylvania.[10]

Plant slowdowns and more than a few outright closures expanded by mid-1945 as the war drew to a close. After nearly five years of full employment, 45,000 Carnegie Steel workers in the Pittsburgh region were on layoff at the end of August. Whether their unemployment was temporary or permanent remained an unknown for most. Postwar labor conflict compounded the slowdown as workers sought wage gains suppressed by statutory wage freezes in force through much of the war. In January 1946, nearly 750,000 steelworkers nationwide went on strike. Regional steelworks were "sprawled lifeless" as workers began picketing.[11] The following April, nearly 350,000 coal workers joined them, with over 200,000 railroad workers striking by May. Curtailment of coal supplies hindered electricity supplies, compounding the economic slowdown as utilities required regional dimouts, and limited freight transport via rail.

The westward march of the US steel industry—briefly reversed during the Great Depression—not only restarted but accelerated during the war.[12] Induced by federal policy and financing, the war had generated investment in new steel plants in western states that never before had significant concentrations of heavy industry. Production began in 1944 at an integrated steel plant built by U.S. Steel, in partnership with Columbia Steel in Geneva, Utah, while shipbuilding magnate Henry

Kaiser financed the 1942 construction of a similar plant in California's San Bernardino Valley. In August 1945, Pittsburgh-based steel executives predicted the "war-born Western Steel industry" was a threat that could "topple this district from its steel throne."[13] In October 1946, a *Time* magazine journalist quipped, "A postcard mailed in Washington to 'New Ghost Town, Pa.' last week, did not make the postmen think twice. It was promptly delivered in Pittsburgh."[14] In May 1946, the steel industry's trade magazine *Iron Age* declared, "Pittsburgh is yielding its crown as the leading steel producer to Chicago," and that "no new industry has come into the city in 30 years."[15] A more optimistic August 1946 op-ed in *The New York Times* counterintuitively belied the economic angst growing in Pittsburgh: "There is too much steel and sinew in the Pittsburgh region to fit the description of 'Ghost Town' painted by local and provincial pessimists who looked at the wartime westward trend of steel through jaundiced eyes."[16] A local editorial the same month acknowledged Pittsburghers' deep concerns about their future: "The postwar period also produced a war of nerves for anxious Pittsburghers through the renewal of rumors that United States Steel might build a new major plant on the Atlantic seaboard. These rumors added to the doubts of Pittsburghers as a future of the steel city."[17]

Econometric Institute

In 1943, a new Allegheny Conference on Postwar Community Planning for the Metropolitan Area of Allegheny County was formed specifically to address the economic problems Pittsburgh was expected to face once wartime production inevitably slowed. In June of 1944, one of the first studies initiated by the new organization was exhaustively titled "Economic Problems: A Study of What Industries Are Needed Here; Why New Industries Have not Located Here; Local Tax Problem; Problems of Small Business Enterprises and Research to Develop Basic Information Relating to the Region."[18]

In September 1944, the new organization—renamed upon incorporation the Allegheny Conference on Community Development (ACCD)—warned that Pittsburgh's postwar planning efforts were falling behind. Local governments in southwestern Pennsylvania were advised to accelerate planning for major public works projects, expected to be a significant source of employment for returning service members. The committee urged: "Every borough and township, no matter how small, should have at this time some appropriation and plan to create jobs for service-men who are unable to find work in industry."[19] Like the New Deal economic programs that came earlier, peacetime reconversion was universally expected to be centrally planned, financed, and largely managed by the public sector.

The Conference, as the ACCD has been commonly referred to since it was formed, was a hybrid public–private partnership that immediately took a leading role in addressing Pittsburgh's most pressing problems. Air pollution, transportation, urban redevelopment, and even public parking were all targets of early ACCD initiatives, which quickly began transforming the landscape of the city of Pittsburgh. Much the result of ACCD initiatives, Downtown Pittsburgh was transformed in the decade following World War II. In October 1945, Governor Ed Martin approved a comprehensive redevelopment proposal for Downtown Pittsburgh submitted jointly by the Pittsburgh Regional Planning Association and the ACCD.[20] Based on a 1939 proposal authored by Robert Moses, famed New York Parks commissioner, work began to construct a new thirty-six-acre Point Park at the head of the Ohio River. A complementary twenty-three-acre office and retail development was constructed adjacent to the future park. Once a rundown warehouse and industrial district, Pittsburgh's central business district became a showcase of urban redevelopment.

ACCD lobbying was also central to the less-heralded but arguably the most crucial outcome of the revitalization efforts that collectively became known as the Pittsburgh Renaissance: comprehensive flood control efforts that alleviated much of the chronic flooding that recurred in the city. Federal construction of dams along the Allegheny River resulted in projects like the Kinzua Dam, completed by the US Army Corps of Engineers in 1965. While the dam successfully mitigated flooding and supported economic redevelopment in Pittsburgh, it had severe consequences for the Seneca Indians who lived in proximity to it. The construction submerged over ten thousand acres of their land in McKean County, Pennsylvania, and Cattaraugus County, New York. It displaced hundreds of households and abrogated the 1794 Treaty of Canandaigua, which had guaranteed the Seneca permanent ownership of their territory.

The extent of what was accomplished in Downtown Pittsburgh made the ACCD a model of public and private collaboration that other regions attempted to emulate for decades into the future. As the initial projects were still under construction, Downtown Pittsburgh was popularly hailed as the region's "Golden Triangle." For all the successes the Conference had in urban redevelopment, inducing more fundamental economic shifts would prove far more difficult.

In the spring of 1945, the ACCD requested the Greater Pittsburgh Chamber of Commerce to undertake a comprehensive economic assessment of the Pittsburgh region.[21] The Econometric Institute, a New York consulting firm, was contracted to complete a focused study of the economy of the Pittsburgh region. The private think tank was led by Charles F. Roos, an accomplished mathematician and economist. In 1930, Roos cofounded the academic Econometric Society, along with Joseph Schumpeter and Ragnar Frisch, the very first economist to be awarded the Nobel Prize in Economic Sciences when the Swedish Central Bank created the award in 1968.[22] A decade later, Schumpeter published the book he would be best known for, titled *Capitalism, Socialism, and Democracy*, which introduced the concept of "creative destruction" as the disruptive force defining modern capitalism. John Maynard Keynes—possibly the best-known economist of the twentieth century—was an early member and served two terms as president of the Econometric Society between 1944 and 1945.[23] Roos himself served as president in 1948. From its inception, the Econometric Society became one of the preeminent economic research organizations in the nation.

In 1938, Roos had formed the auxiliary Econometric Institute Inc. to facilitate economic consulting for privately sponsored research. Before World War II, the firm produced a report for General Motors that used groundbreaking econometric models to predict industry trends. The project in Pittsburgh was one of the organization's first contracted efforts following World War II. The Econometric Institute delivered to the Chamber of Commerce an extensive and scathing report concluding that Pittsburgh faced myriad economic challenges. It argued that Pittsburgh, severely lacking industrial and labor force diversity, "will, however, slowly decline unless new industries employing women and those engaged in the production of consumer goods are attracted to the area."[24]

The report and its prognosis for the Pittsburgh economy were not well received. The Pittsburgh Chamber of Commerce accepted an initial version on February 1, 1946, and a copy reached the Allegheny Conference on February 25. The next day, the Chamber of Commerce recalled the report and directed the Econometric Institute to revise the entire analysis. On May 14, the Econometric Institute submitted a rewritten report—not shared with the public—retaining the core of its critical conclusions on the weaknesses in the Pittsburgh economy. So alarmed by the content of the report, the ACCD immediately formed a series of committees to review the results before they could be released to the public. The reviews were still ongoing when part of the report was inadvertently made public in late October, prompting stories in Pittsburgh's three major daily papers. Park Martin, ACCD executive director, admonished the Chamber of Commerce for the leak, saying that "releasing a report of the character of the Econometric Report to reporters without explanatory materials and interpretations is seriously open to question."[25]

The Allegheny Conference's review committees unequivocally rejected nearly all of the Econometric Institute's dour conclusions, describing the entire report as "unsatisfactory in many respects." Furthermore they said it "lacks the authenticity that may be described to it," and "if quoted indiscriminately, there is a very real danger that the Report may mislead potential investors and other business interests and may perhaps influence present property owners to make inadvisable moves."[26] One subcommittee even attempted to redefine the very nature of what "natural resources" meant in the region: "There are facilities in Western Pennsylvania, so permanently a part of the area and so important that they would be considered as 'Natural resources' by most business men. Among these are the electrical power facilities, the iron and steel industry, the glass industry, and the existing labor force."[27]

So embedded was heavy industry in Pittsburgh, so *permanent*, as the subcommittee wanted to believe, that business leaders considered industrial infrastructure akin to the seemingly inexhaustible supply of coal in the ground. Denying economic trends already long underway, reviewers found inconceivable the notion that Pittsburgh's defining industries could someday find other regions more competitive locations for future investment. Another subcommittee found just one point of agreement with the report: Pittsburgh needed better marketing and advertising to attract new investment, which implied that the major economic problem facing Pittsburgh was misperception about the region's economy elsewhere in the nation.

Presaging later efforts to improve the region's quality of life, the report included a detailed survey asking business leaders who had relocated why they left the city. "We want to get away from the dirt," summarized most of the responses. "We've made a mess here, and now we are beginning to feel that the best solution for it is just to move away from it," one respondent explained. Poor environmental issues contributed to an inferior, and distinctly uncompetitive, quality of life: "Now the fact is that Pittsburgh has no fishing, no water sports, not enough parks, few good night clubs, not enough taxis, and an insufficient water supply."[28]

Less noticed, but equally prescient, findings within Roos's report portended trends that became apparent only in subsequent decades. The report noted that residential housing values near the city's urban core were declining and that only real estate prices in sections of the city near universities were holding their own.[29] When completed, the full report would be suppressed and only limited summaries released to the public. Even that minimal disclosure seemed the result of the unanticipated public disclosure of an early draft in 1946.[30] Public release of the full report did not occur until 1954, eight years after the original was submitted.[31]

U.S. Steel Chairman Benjamin Fairless made no mention of the Econometric Institute report when he addressed the ACCD's fourth annual dinner in September 1948, even though many attendees were certainly members of the committees that had reviewed the report. Instead, Fairless focused almost solely on what the impending demise of the Pittsburgh Plus pricing system meant for the steel industry and more specifically on what the ruling portended for Pittsburgh: "Surely this region is not anxious to move toward or occupy a less impressive position than its present one in the production of steel in the United States." Fairless added: "Pittsburgh is long on the production of steel and short on consuming capacity."[32] Even without referencing Charles Roos's conclusions, Fairless reinforced the core message that Pittsburgh's lack of industrial diversity was a glaring economic weakness that threatened its future.

Even three years after the end of the war, Fairless decried the continuing impact of publicly financed investments on the steel industry. He encouraged the rapid liquidation of the remaining federally owned industrial plants as soon as practical. He described the plants' continuing public ownership as "in the direction of state socialism." Yet, he implicitly acknowledged that private capital had not sustained investment necessary to keep older plants viable: "A number of these government-owned plants are probably more modern and more efficient than similar facilities owned by private industry."[33] A disproportionate share of those older industrial plants were the Pittsburgh plants of U.S. Steel.

Also missing from Fairless's remarks was any acknowledgement of the environmental harm industry had brought to Pittsburgh and the cumulative damage done to the region's quality of life. The dystopian industrial apparition many inferred from James Parton's 1866 observations on industrial Pittsburgh became prophecy just a month after Fairless's address. On the morning of Tuesday, October 26, 1948, an industrial smog settled in over the Monongahela Valley town of Donora—twenty-five miles southeast of Downtown Pittsburgh. A concoction of industrial gases and coal smoke became trapped over the town as a cold front arriving from the southwest displaced a lingering high-pressure system. A rare anticyclone pushed a band of warm air counterclockwise over southwestern Pennsylvania. The resulting temperature inversion kept the cold valley air close to the surface. The deep Monongahela River valley and its tributary valleys formed blind alley tunnels from which the toxic smog could not escape.[34]

Diffused within the smog were byproducts of zinc production that included sulfur and hydrofluoric acid, which normally diffused into the air from atop the forty-foot stacks of the Donora Zinc Works. As long as the warm industrial effluent lofted upward, the result was little noticed by residents, who were long inured to the emissions, but the lingering temperature inversion kept the toxic smog near the surface where it persisted. The following days provided no relief, and by Thursday the smog had "stiffened adhesively into a motionless clot of smoke," as described later by medical journalist Berton Roueché in *The New Yorker.*[35] So routine were corrosive atmospheric conditions, residents maintained their regular routines and the valley's industrial plants continued normal operation, continuously adding to the atmospheric soup. By Friday, local firefighters were unable to drive through the town, making it difficult to get vital oxygen to residents calling for assistance. The first death attributed to the smog occurred before the end of the day, the very first recorded US death attributed to air pollution. The following day, seventeen more Donora residents died as a result of inhaling the toxic gas, and two more fatalities were recorded on Sunday. An abnormal spike of fifty more deaths occurred over the following month, though the death count from the event was recorded as just the twenty who perished by the end of the weekend.[36] No toxicological cause was ever officially ascribed to the health disaster that unfolded, but an independent analysis conducted before the end of the year concluded that hydrofluoric acid mixed in with the smog caused acute fluoride poisoning in an uncounted number of residents.[37]

Environmental concerns had never inhibited the growth of steel production across southwestern Pennsylvania, but as the nation emerged from World War II, the industry itself clearly did not have an optimistic view on the inevitability of Pittsburgh's future as a production center. In

1950, Allegheny County issued a property reassessment that increased the value of Carnegie-Illinois Steel facilities under its purview by 40 percent, resulting in a proportional increase in taxes. Appealing the new valuations, Carnegie-Illinois's president, Clifford F. Hood, argued: "Because of the shift in population and gradual decline of its natural resources advantages, Pittsburgh is losing its crown as steel king of the world."[38] The legal arguments accidentally disclosed an enduring legacy of heavy industry on the communities where the corporation's facilities were located. U.S. Steel claimed its plants were located "on property not desirable for [other] business or residential uses." Most major steel plants in western Pennsylvania were located on what would otherwise be prime riverfront parcels that should have had a range of alternative uses. It was the long history of steel production that made the expansive riverfront real estate unfit for almost any alternative use.

Even as Fairless addressed the ACCD in 1948, he was overseeing a vast expansion of new steel capacity at locations far from Pittsburgh. In April 1951, Fairless keynoted the groundbreaking at a four thousand-acre site U.S. Steel was investing in along the Delaware River—just outside of Philadelphia—which provided direct access to ocean trade routes. Named the Fairless Works, newly constructed integrated steel plant began output on December 11, 1952.

Ben Moreell

Despite the warnings of the Econometric Institute and from the University of Pittsburgh's Bureau of Business Research more than a decade earlier, and even despite the demise of a Pittsburgh-based point pricing system, Pittsburgh's government and business leaders worked collectively to expand the region's steel production. The Urban Redevelopment Authority of Pittsburgh (URA) partnered with business leaders to facilitate the expansion of the Jones & Laughlin (J&L) Corporation's South Side Works. Following closely the strategy that had been used to redevelop much of Downtown Pittsburgh, the URA exercised its power of eminent domain in conjunction with private-sector investment to complete the project.

For nearly a century, J&L's steelworks spanned both sides the Monongahela River, coexisting alongside the densest Pittsburgh neighborhoods. On the southern riverbank, the plant crowded next to the flats of the city's South Side, part of an independent Borough of East Birmingham until it merged with the city of Pittsburgh in 1872. The plant pushed up directly against the neighborhood's busy Carson Street retail thoroughfare. Further plant expansion was not possible without a mass repurposing of urban real estate. Following the core strategy of the Pittsburgh Renaissance, the city declared a large swath of property in the neighborhood as blighted, thus enabling the URA to exercise its power of eminent domain to acquire eighty acres of densely used real estate, land which was then made available to J&L.

Across the Monongahela River, J&L's expansion continued when the firm added space to its coking operation in 1952, again displacing much of an existing neighborhood. The thirty-acre expansion displaced more than five hundred families from what was known as the Scotch Bottom section of Pittsburgh's Hazelwood neighborhood. Again, the homes could only be acquired via the legal authority vested in the URA, and again only after the needed real estate was legally designated as blighted.[39]

Chairman and Chief Executive Ben Moreell introduced J&L's expansion project to the Pittsburgh City Council in October 1952. The company's expansion plans included the construction of no fewer than eleven new open-hearth furnaces on the newly acquired property within the city. Moreell explained the decision to expand in Pittsburgh: "It is no secret that in steel and other industries, there was talk that the steel industry in Pittsburgh was on the down grade. We don't believe in that. We put our cash on the line and let it ride." In gambling parlance, Moreell and J&L were doubling down on Pittsburgh. The investment in Hazelwood, Moreell said, made "Pittsburgh the permanent base" for the company's future production.[40]

Moreell began efforts to expand J&L's production soon after he took charge of the firm in 1948. An expert in concrete, the retired admiral had spent thirty-one years on active duty in the navy's Civil Engineering Corps. In 1937, he was selected as rear admiral and put in charge of the navy's Bureau of Yards and Docks. With the onset of World War II, Moreell was singularly responsible for the creation of the navy's Construction Battalion (Seabee) force, which built the bases across the Pacific. He retired in September 1946 as a four-star admiral, the first staff corps officer in the history of the navy to ever achieve that rank. Afterward, he immediately began a business career, as president of the Turner Construction Company. In 1947, he left Turner when he was named president, chief executive officer, and chairman of the board of J&L.

Moreell immediately focused the corporation on expansion. By the first half of 1948, J&L reported investing more than twice its net income on improvements at its existing plants concentrated in Pittsburgh.[41] Moreell was undeterred by the demise of basing point pricing and publicly argued it would actually improve Pittsburgh's industrial future. Counterintuitively, he predicted an "inevitable movement" of steel fabricators into the Pittsburgh district as a result of the Supreme Court ruling ending basing point pricing in the industry.[42]

Expansion by J&L and other regional steel producers appeared to pay off in the short run. Countering expectations, the end of the war did not precipitate the protracted prolonged depression many feared. National strikes in 1946 were resolved with workers receiving significant raises, a boon to industrial workers concentrated in Pittsburgh. With major consumer purchases deferred during the war, civilian demand ramped up quickly while rebuilding efforts in Europe created additional new orders for US industry. Raw steel production in the United States reached 80.4 million tons in 1948, just below the 81.3 million tons produced during the peak of wartime production in 1944.[43] By 1950, U.S. Steel confidently claimed to be the dominant leader of a US steel industry unmatched worldwide. A national advertising campaign sponsored by the corporation immodestly pointed out that the US "steel industry is bigger than those of all other nations on earth put together."[44]

Less acknowledged was that a large part of the reason for US industrial dominance was the economic restrictions Allied powers placed on their former adversaries. Soon after the war, many German plants were ordered to be destroyed, and others were systematically deconstructed to be rebuilt as war reparations elsewhere. Germany's heavy industries were initially limited to just 50 percent of their 1938 production by the Level of Industry plan the Allied powers imposed in March 1946. Greater restrictions were placed on German steel production, which was limited to just under 6 million tons per year, equivalent to just 25 percent of prewar production levels.[45] Similar deconstruction was planned for Japanese industries, but more effective strategic bombing had left the nation with less industry to raze at the end of the war. The onset of the Cold War soon pushed the western powers to moderate reparation policies and shift decisively to encouraging industrial expansion in both countries. Aided by US financing, reconstruction of the steel industry in both West Germany and Japan went forward based on the latest technologies.[46]

The onset of the Korean War in June 1950 again spiked demand for US steel. Unlike production during World War II, the new military orders came on top of robust civilian consumption and business investment that did not slow during the conflict. Even before the additional military orders, the US steel industry was again operating near capacity, challenged to meet ever-growing domestic and international demand. The United States produced literally half of all worldwide steel production, and Pittsburgh remained the center of nation's production. The combined Pittsburgh–Youngstown industrial district produced just under 40 percent of all steel ingots in the nation.[47]

So strained were steel producers that capacity utilization of US steel plants reached an unsustainable 100.9 percent in 1951. At the time, more than ample demand existed to absorb expanded steel production in Pittsburgh and elsewhere. Other Pittsburgh producers likewise reinvested in their existing plants to increase capacity. In 1954, the Pittsburgh Steel Corporation completed a four-year, $65 million expansion of its plants in the Pittsburgh district, including the construction of the half-million tons of open-hearth capacity at its plant in Allenport, thirty miles south of Pittsburgh along the Monongahela River. In addition, new rolling mills installed at the time were hailed as the "most modern in the industry."[48] The same year, Allegheny Ludlum, a company with roots in Pittsburgh dating back to the Revolutionary War, invested over $12 million in a new cold rolling mill in Brackenridge.

Despite the Econometric Institute's predictions, regional economic trends through most of the 1950s countered the dismal prognostications for the future of heavy industry in Pittsburgh. Early in the decade, manufacturing output across the region surged even higher than the artificial wartime peaks of a decade earlier. Manufacturing employment in the four-county Pittsburgh metropolitan region reached over 379,000 jobs in 1952—surpassing even an estimate of the region's wartime peak employment of 365,000 industrial workers in 1944.[49] At the time, a remarkable 44 percent of all regional workers were directly employed by manufacturing industries. An even greater number of local workers were employed in industries dependent on the steel industry's vast supply chain or on the spending of steelworkers and their families. Still, industry in Pittsburgh remained concentrated not only in steel but in very basic steel forges, as it had been since Carnegie's revolution that began in Braddock seven decades earlier. Also contrary to Ben Moreell's forecast, the end of basing point pricing did not induce a wave of steel fabricators, nor any other industry, to expand in Pittsburgh.

Maintaining the region's competitive advantage was not a concern, as long as virtually all steel producers filled their order books. Through the 1950s, producers were able to repeatedly increase prices, generating record profits and deferring further any incentives to diversify away from steel production. The only hiccup came in April 1952, when President Truman attempted to nationalize the steel industry hours before a national strike called by the United Steelworkers of America. The threatened work stoppage put at risk steel supplies needed for armaments production in the middle of the Korean War. The US Supreme Court declared the federal action illegal by the beginning of July, returning control of the businesses to the private sector but prompting a national strike, which lasted seven weeks. The two sides only came to an agreement on July 23 after Truman pressured both U.S. Steel's President Benjamin Fairless and the United Steelworkers of America's President Philip Murray to end the work stoppage. Despite the strike and mirroring the robust corporate earnings of most major steel producers, new capacity at J&L contributed to a string of record profits for the company during the 1950s.

Despite the facile business climate, Pittsburgh business leaders still vigorously defended against any potential economic threat, near or far, by any means. Nearby Youngstown, Ohio, was also a steel region, but had long been poorly served by rail lines and did not have the water access Pittsburgh producers had collectively taken advantage of since the nineteenth century, so Youngstown leaders advocated for construction of a canal connecting the Ohio River with Lake Erie. The project would have equalized freight transportation costs between Pittsburgh and Youngstown producers and was envisioned to include a new Grand Lake reservoir that would have provided both flood control and recreation benefits for Northeast Ohio. Proponents argued that the seaway would significantly lower shipping costs for raw materials like iron ore, coal, and limestone—critical inputs for steel production—but these were advantages that would mostly accrue to Youngstown producers. As a result, Pittsburgh leaders were less than supportive of the project. In 1956, the Greater Pittsburgh Chamber of Commerce issued a 105-page report arguing that the benefits of the Lake Erie to Ohio River Seaway project was not worth pursuing. The report was honest enough to admit that the effects on the Pittsburgh economy "would be potentially hazardous at this time."[50] The scale of the project required federal funding and likely additional funding from both Ohio and Pennsylvania state governments. Lacking support from Pennsylvania politicians, the project failed to move forward, and no canal has yet to be constructed.

At the beginning of the 1960s, the US steel industry had sustained enviable and unabated growth for over two decades, growth that many expected to continue. Nonetheless, the steel industry was more than aware of emerging threats. In the late 1950s, it began to take notice of increasing competition from alternative materials, including plastics and aluminum for a range of consumer products.[51] Steel's first industrywide marketing effort highlighted a range of new uses for steel, in particular the potential of stainless steel. In 1958, the American Iron and Steel Institute crafted a new steelmark logo—comprising three stylized hypocycloids—as part of the new marketing effort.

Marketing efforts were extended in 1959 when the American Iron and Steel Association sponsored a commercial movie—*Rhapsody of Steel*—telling the story of steel from primitive to modern times. It ascribed

Rhapsody of Steel banner, Horne's department store–1962 (Copyright Brady Stewart Studio, used with permission)

virtually all technological progress to the widespread use of steel. With corporate funding, the movie's score was composed by Dimitri Tiomkin, one of the giants of Hollywood music at the time, and recorded by the Pittsburgh Symphony Orchestra; it was the first movie score ever recorded by the organization. Immodest in scope, the film's goal was to "renew confidence in the economic system which has made such progress and provided the sinews of the free world's new strength."[52] The film and its coordinated public relations campaign could only reinforce a belief that the steel industry had little to worry about in the future, a message Pittsburgh was more than willing to hear.

In 1962, U.S. Steel and the American Iron and Steel Institute launched a national marketing campaign designed to show steel's contributions to modern life. A weeklong marketing event in Pittsburgh took place in October to introduce the new campaign. Any doubts about Pittsburgh's economic future—a future still entirely dependent on the success of local steel producers—were still mostly ascribed to misperceptions. Keynoting the event, a top U.S. Steel executive advised Pittsburghers "to rely on 'confidence in self' to assure the continuing success of the city, its industries, and its people."[53] More fundamental change, and in particular any significant diversion from legacy industries, was not on the agenda.

So concentrated was steel production in Pittsburgh late into the 1950s that the entire region, and in particular the hyper-concentration of steel production that remained in the Monongahela River Valley, was considered a strategic vulnerability in the new atomic age. A 1957 study concluded that nuclear attacks on Chicago and Pittsburgh could cripple 57 percent of the nation's steelmaking facilities.[54] The concerns were not new. To minimize the vulnerability of industrial output in southwestern Pennsylvania, a 1948 federal plan had proposed that Pittsburgh-area industries be spread along the newly constructed Pennsylvania Turnpike as far as Bedford, 120 miles to the east of Downtown Pittsburgh.[55]

In April 1952, operating military forces were deployed into the Pittsburgh region for the first time since the Civil War. That month, two army battalions, the first elements of what would be named the Pittsburgh Air Defense Command, rumbled through the streets of McKeesport to set up a ring of 90-mm antiaircraft guns to protect against aerial attacks.[56] The conventional artillery was supplemented, and then replaced, by a battery of state-of-the-art Nike guided missiles at twelve locations surrounding Pittsburgh in 1954, and further upgraded to Nike-Hercules missiles in 1959. Pittsburgh was among the very first regions to receive the counter-bomber deployments precisely because the area held such an extraordinary concentration of heavy industry.

The Economic Study of the Pittsburgh Region

The prolonged concentration of heavy industry in Pittsburgh had produced a regional economy that functioned differently from other major US regions. In 1963, Benjamin Chinitz of the University of Pittsburgh authored a paper, "Contrasts in Agglomeration: New York and Pittsburgh," published in the *American Economic Review.*[57] Mirroring the conclusions Charles Roos and the Econometric Institute had published fifteen years earlier, Chinitz noted Pittsburgh remained severely challenged by its lack of industrial diversity and severely oligopolistic corporate structure. Pittsburgh was dominated by a small number of larger firms vastly different from the industrial diversity and ownership patterns in New York. Pittsburgh's monolithic industrial structure, Chinitz theorized, could be the root cause of the low rate of entrepreneurial activity that had long been observed in the region. Large industrial firms concentrated there just did not incubate the growth of small businesses, new innovations, and new industries at rates common elsewhere.

Chinitz's article was an extension of economic research ongoing in Pittsburgh at the beginning of the 1960s. In 1958, economist Edgar M. Hoover was recruited to University of Pittsburgh and appointed director of a regional economic study sponsored by the Pittsburgh Regional Planning Association. The $400,000 allocated to the *Economic Study of the Pittsburgh Region* (*ESPR*)—equivalent to over $4.4 million in 2024—made it one of the largest studies of a regional economy ever conducted. Funding came from the Ford Foundation, matched with support from local organizations including Pittsburgh's Regional Industrial Development Corporation, a quasi-public agency that had recently been formed to promote economic development efforts. The project mirrored analysis on the New York City region, where Hoover and Economist Raymond Vernon were completing the "first full-scale scholarly effort to reveal to the public the need for areawide planning."[58] Hoover's work in regional economics was central to the "stages" theory of regional development, explaining how regional transformations inevitably followed the introduction of improved technology. For Pittsburgh, the rapid development of Bessemer technology had indeed once catalyzed growth of the region's steel industry. Hoover's task was to explain why that evolution had not continued.

Hoover and Chinitz, associate director of the project, along with a staff of fifty, began a monumental three-year study of industrial Pittsburgh. Their "immersion in regional economics," as Chinitz later called the project, documented Pittsburgh's economic history and produced detailed forecasts of how the region was expected to change over the coming quarter century. When completed, the report warned without equivocation that the economic advantages Pittsburgh had long relied on were in decline and had been for decades. In the face of automation and increasing labor force productivity across manufacturing sectors, even maintaining employment levels in the region was expected to be a challenge. On the future of Pittsburgh's industrial base, the report concluded that "unless the Pittsburgh Region were to increase its share of steel output of the nation and raise its output by at least 95 percent by 1985, the industry's employment in the Region will continue to fall." The report virtually dismissed any possibility that Pittsburgh's loss of competitive advantage in heavy industries could be reversed, dourly raising an existential question for Pittsburgh's economic future: "Such a radical deflection of trend could only come from some very strong and rapid bolstering of the Region's competitive position through technological or market shifts. Are any such shifts in sight?"[59]

Not just looking backward, the study produced detailed projections of how Pittsburgh's economy would evolve over the coming quarter-century. Employment in its primary metals industry alone was projected to decrease from 108,000 in 1960 to 63,000 in 1985. The prediction must have been as unbelievable to the public at the time as overly optimistic it proved to be in retrospect.

The observation that the steel industry in Pittsburgh had long been in decline flew in the face of the industry's continuing dominance within the region's economy. Superficial observation confirmed that the region's historic steel plants, some now more than a century old, were still in operation. The scale of past investments profoundly masked declines long underway. Industrial facilities common across western Pennsylvania were "massive, immobile, indivisible and long-lived." Investments that had made sense long in the past played a role "in protecting old and large steel centers like Pittsburgh," at least for a while, but not forever. The *ESPR* could not find "any inkling of possibilities for location of major new integrated steelworks in the Pittsburgh area."[60] A group of private-sector leaders was brought together by the Allegheny Conference to address the *ESPR*'s findings acknowledged that Pittsburgh was "little better off economically than it was 20 years ago when, at the end of World War II, the outlook for Pittsburgh was at best uncertain."[61]

Chinitz, Hoover, and their colleagues observed a difficult truth: Industry in Pittsburgh lacked the dynamism of business enterprises in other regions. Steel producers there had long been protected from the scale of competition common in other industries. Pittsburgh and its core industries had been molded around those artificial advantages. In 1960, U.S. Steel's sixtieth year of existence, the national magazine *Businessweek* observed that the corporation was only then getting around to transforming itself into a commercial enterprise but "still had a ways to go."[62] Emerging economic threats went unnoticed because steel production continued to expand. In 1960, U.S. Steel announced a major new investment at its Duquesne Works. The Dorothy Six blast furnace—the world's largest at the time—began production in 1963, just as the final *ESPR* reports were being published. The opening of the largest and most modern blast furnace in the world easily overshadowed whatever pessimism was predicted in an academic report focused on the seemingly distant future.

New plants and strong economic growth through the 1960s suppressed any public debate about the region's future competitiveness. An expanding national economy generated increased levels of capital spending, inevitably boosting steel and industries still concentrated in Pittsburgh. Soon after the final *ESPR* reports were released, Chinitz addressed the Economic Club of Pittsburgh. Despite the improving economic conditions at the time, he foretold more than accurately an ominous potential future: "Should something go wrong in steel . . . the rate of unemployment could rise precipitously in a very short time."[63]

What Pittsburgh continued to lack through much of the twentieth century was any of Schumpeter's "creative destruction," which he described as essential to modern capitalism. Without the normal churn of new businesses being created year in and year out, the region was less able to adapt and change than others were. Chinitz's speech concluded with a warning for the region's future if it continued on its inertial path dependent on steel: "If we permit the current recovery to blind us to our long term needs we will be repeating precisely the mistakes of the past. Then we didn't know better. Now we do."[64]

Like warnings earlier, Chinitz's came long before there was an audience willing to listen, let alone take meaningful action to shift Pittsburgh's inertial economic trajectory.

The process of Creative Destruction is the essential fact about capitalism. It is what capitalism consists in and what every capitalist concern has got to live in.

Joseph A. Schumpeter, *Capitalism, Socialism, and Democracy*, 2013

Disruption

October 12, 1969

At a new factory in Darlington, South Carolina, a mostly rural community a hundred miles southeast of Charlotte, a company with no history of making steel opened the nation's newest steel furnace. The Nuclear Corporation of America, as the company was then known, really had no right to still be in business, let alone investing in an entirely new business operation.

The small company traced a long and circuitous corporate ancestry dating back to 1905, when it was founded by Ransom E. Olds, whose brand and car company was acquired by General Motors in 1904. Lending his initials to a new independent company, the REO Motor Company eventually failed as an independent auto producer and filed for bankruptcy in 1938. Reorganized, the company survived as a truck producer during World War II but generated only minimal profits after the war. After a new surge of orders during the Korean War came to an end, the company's directors considered winding down the business and dissolving it. A dissident group of shareholders objected and in 1955 forced the company to acquire a small firm engaged in producing a few products related to the nascent nuclear industry. Renamed the Nuclear Corporation of America, over the following decade the company diversified further by acquiring a range of disparate firms, few of which turned a profit.[1]

In 1965, the firm went bankrupt yet again but somehow reorganized and remained in business, a testament to the redemptive power of US bankruptcy law. Going forward, the Nuclear Corporation of America concentrated on its one profitable subsidiary, a small steel fabrication company in South Carolina it had acquired only in 1962. Prior to the construction of the Darlington plant, the company primarily relied on foreign steel, which it reworked into steel joists—a staple of the construction industry.

Darlington was a community about as far removed from Pittsburgh as it could be. Near no ready supply of coal, nor any major river, the location, indeed the entire plant, bore little resemblance to the massive integrated steel plants that defined Pittsburgh. By the beginning of the twentieth century, the expansion of Bessemer steel production at larger integrated steelworks had long since displaced all that had remained of South Carolina's earlier artisan metals industry. But at the end of the 1960s, there was a resurgence of steelmaking in the unlikely state. In 1969, West Germany's Korf Company had begun a steel minimill in coastal Georgetown, South Carolina.[2] The Darlington steel plant would become South Carolina's second of the modern era.

The Nuclear Corporation was almost forced into the steelmaking business. Lacking sufficient domestic supplies of raw steel, and with escalating tariffs limiting its ability to source inputs from overseas, the company built its own steel plant. It was a decision of expediency, far from a strategic decision to compete against existing steel firms. Lacking sufficient capital for any larger project, the company had decided to build a smaller, more limited steel minimill.

So little experience did the Nuclear Corporation have in making steel that the very first pour of molten steel broke out of its containment vessel and hot metal poured onto the caster, melting it.[3] It was an inauspicious start for a firm that within two decades would become one of the largest steel producers in the world. When opened, the new plant was likely little noticed at the headquarters of U.S. Steel in Pittsburgh, four hundred miles north. It was unimaginable that the barely functioning plant posed any commercial threat to existing steelmakers in Pittsburgh or elsewhere. Yet, the company was more successful in its new venture than any of its innumerable previous incarnations. By the early 1970s, the company had morphed yet again, fully dedicating itself to steel production. It was renamed Nucor, which by early in the twenty-first century would become the largest US steelmaker. By the time executives in Pittsburgh paid attention to the success of the new venture, it was in many ways too late. It was also not the only threat to Pittsburgh's position in steel production.

Global Competition

Global steel production entered a rapid growth phase in the decades after World War II. Major steel producers around the globe regrouped following the traumatic contractions wrought by the war and began unprecedented expansion. Sustained Japanese growth—later named the Japanese economic miracle—was fueled by savings and investment rates far above what was typical in the United States or other advanced industrialized countries at the time. Japanese investment levels first caught up with, and then exceeded, those in the United States over the course of the 1960s. In 1965, capital expenditures in the US steel industry exceeded $1.82 billion, far above an estimated $510 million investment in Japanese steel industries. By 1970, capital expenditures in the Japanese steel industry had jumped to $1.89 billion, exceeding for the first time the level of investment in the US steel industry, which had declined to $1.7 billion.[4] What made Japanese steel production a threat was not the just the scale of new capacity coming online but the advanced technologies Japanese steelmakers were implementing as they expanded. While most new US steel investments during the 1950s—including the major expansions at Pittsburgh's J&L works—used older open-hearth production technologies, the Japanese steel industry was putting in place newer basic-oxygen process plants.

A half century earlier, open-hearth steel production had displaced most of the nation's Bessemer-based steel production. Though slower than Bessemer technologies, open-hearth furnaces were capable of producing higher quality steel. Like Bessemer technology, open-hearth steel furnaces used air to catalyze oxidation of impurities, including carbon within a mixture of iron ore and scrap metal. Henry Bessemer himself knew pure oxygen was a far better catalyst than air, but until the middle of the twentieth century, technical limitations and the high cost of producing pure oxygen limited its use in metal production. During World War II, Germany's V2 rocket program spurred technical advances that dramatically lowered the cost of producing pure oxygen at industrial scales. After the war, those technologies would be applied to new commercial uses. In 1952, a prototype of an oxygen-based steel furnace was built in Austria.

Pure oxygen reacts far more violently than air, self-generating heat, which both accelerated the steelmaking process and offset fuel costs. Basic-oxygen process furnaces shortened the average time for a typical heat by from as long as twelve hours to under an hour. Also, these furnaces needed less industrial coke, further eviscerating much of the geographic advantage of steel production in proximity to the Connellsville coal seam. Pollution controls could also be implemented on basic-oxygen process furnaces at far lower costs—an advantage that would take on even greater importance in later decades. Economists looking back at the steel capacity added by US firms in the 1950s—to include much of the investment in Pittsburgh—concluded unequivocally that "no *new* OH [open-hearth] furnaces should have been built."[5]

Beginning with the first Japanese basic-oxygen process plant in 1957, Japanese steelmakers "became the fastest to adopt BOP [basic-oxygen] furnaces, a superior technology that both economized on scrap and offered productive efficiencies."[6] Between 1960 and 1974, Japanese steel production expanded by over 437 percent, while the US steel industry expanded production by just 41.7 percent.[7] Expanding production required ever more customers. National reconstruction initially generated ample demand for new Japanese steel production, but eventually Japanese producers needed to look for new markets overseas. Japanese steel producers were in search of new markets just as US markets provided an opening to foreign producers.

On July 15, 1959, over a half million steelworkers nationwide, including over 125,000 in the Pittsburgh region, did not report to work as the United Steelworkers of America initiated a strike against all major steel producers.[8] The bulk of US steel production was shut down for an unprecedented 116 days. Foreign producers, especially rapidly growing Japanese production, filled much of the resulting gap in US steel. In 1959, US steel imports exceeded exports for the first time in nearly three quarters of a century. In 1960 and 1961, immediately following the strike, US steel imports initially decreased, but from 1962 onward, steel imports increased every year through the end of the decade.[9] By 1968, over 18 million tons of imported steel accounted for 16.7 percent of domestic steel consumption, more than enough to get the attention of an industry looking to prevent any further erosion of market share.[10]

US steel executives began pressing for the imposition of new tariffs and explicit trade restraints to limit foreign steel coming into the United States. However, formal trade barriers ran counter to the global free-trade regimes that had been championed by US foreign policy since the end of World War II. The US State Department advocated for less stringent voluntary measures to limit steel imports. Voluntary Export

Restraints had emerged as a tool of US trade policy in the 1950s, to limit, first, Japanese tuna sold into US markets and later, textile imports. In January 1969, Japan and the European Coal and Steel Community—a predecessor of the European Union—accepted new voluntary restraints agreements limiting exports of steel into US markets until 1972. Far from protecting existing steel producers from competition, depressed imports incubated new competition, which eventually displaced much of the steel sourced from Pittsburgh. Multiple threats to the US steel industry, and in particular to the legacy integrated steel production of Pittsburgh, were coming together at the same time.

Minimills

There lurked an even greater domestic threat to the steel industry in Pittsburgh. In 1963, The *Economic Study of the Pittsburgh Region* (*ESPR*) noted almost in passing that "technologic developments are in sight which are likely to have the effect of reducing the cost disadvantages of smaller scale steelmaking operations"—a development the report concluded would unavoidably be detrimental to Pittsburgh and its historic concentration of the largest integrated steel complexes.[11] The report did not identify the new technology enabling the success of smaller steel plants, but it was deeply prescient describing the future impact of steel minimills across the global steel industry.

Minimills operate on a very different business model than the large integrated steelworks pioneered by Andrew Carnegie and his early competitors. The behemoth integrated steel mills clustered in Pittsburgh brought together all aspects of making steel, from the smelting of iron ore to final milling, often with colocated coke works. This business model took full advantage of Pittsburgh's geography and its proximity of metallurgic coal. Minimills, in sharp contrast, were designed as far more modest operations that concentrated on reprocessing scrap steel, making them virtually independent from supplies of coal and industrial coke and access to navigable rivers.

Throughout the 1960s, minimills were a barely noticed niche of global steel markets. Early minimills were only capable of limited types of steel production, such as rebar, structural beams, and wire rod. The smaller plants struggled with flat-rolled products such as hot-rolled coil and automotive-grade sheet steel. The reliance on scrap led to high residual elements, like copper and tin, making it difficult to achieve the purity required for advanced applications. Additionally, early minimills lacked refining technical capabilities such as vacuum degassing, limiting their ability to produce ultraclean, high-strength steel.

Prior to 1970, steel production at existing minimills was not even included in official statistics of national steel production. When the output of minimills was aggregated with the production of traditional mills for the first time in 1970, the smaller mills collectively constituted barely 2 percent of all US steel production. The percentage of minimill-produced steel, in the United States and globally, would not remain low for long.[12]

Decades later, Harvard economist Claton Christensen would identify the rise of steel minimills as a prototypical disruptive technology that fundamentally changed the business model of the global steel industry.[13] Most consequential for Pittsburgh was that steel minimills dramatically shifted the geography of regional competitiveness within the steel industry. With basing point pricing a distant history, new minimills faced few obstacles to where production facilities could be located. In the latter half of the twentieth century, optimal sites for new minimills were closer to fast-growing regional markets, areas typically far from traditional steel centers. In addition, supplies of scrap steel were dispersed across the country or imported from overseas, again to Pittsburgh's disadvantage. Relying on electric arc furnaces, there was no advantage for locations with nearby sources of coal, an advantage that had once predestined western Pennsylvania as the optimal location for blast furnaces.

Nucor's first minimill in South Carolina was so successful that the firm constructed a second plant in Norfolk, Nebraska, in 1972, and then a third plant in Jewett, Texas—halfway between Dallas and Houston—in 1974. The geographic pattern of the new mills, had it been noticed in Pittsburgh, should have given pause to any optimistic projections for the steel industry there.

Real Estate

As the competition from minimills emerged, U.S. Steel attempted an entirely different transformation. Not focused on improving its existing steel production, the company diverted resources into areas disconnected from its historic production lines. Internally at least, U.S. Steel acknowledged the declining growth prospects in its legacy business units. Through the 1960s, the company attempted to diversify its manufacturing portfolio with greater investment in its chemical divisions, including the 1968 acquisition of Armour Chemicals.[14] In early 1969, the corporation made an even more discordant shift when it formed a subsidiary, U.S. Steel Realty Development, ironically as the new minimills in South Carolina were completing construction.[15]

Through its new real estate subsidiary, U.S. Steel began investments not just far from Pittsburgh, but in ventures mostly unrelated to raw steel production. The company was the general contractor for two hotels that opened in 1971 at the Disney World in Florida. U.S. Steel diversified its manufacturing output to include steel-framed prefabricated hotel rooms at a plant in Marion, Ohio, three hours west of Pittsburgh.[16] Few of U.S. Steel's new real estate ventures benefited Pittsburgh, with one major exception. In 1969 construction began on U.S. Steel's new headquarters, in Downtown Pittsburgh. The massive new building was completed early in the next decade. More real estate projects followed. Later in the 1970s, U.S. Steel began plans to construct another major skyscraper in Downtown Pittsburgh, adjacent to its new headquarters. The building was originally to be leased to the Dravo Corporation, one of Pittsburgh's historic manufacturing firms, but would be named the Mellon Bank Center, after Dravo canceled plans to occupy the building, which opened in 1983. Most of U.S. Steel's real estate ventures were gradually sold off. The Mellon Bank Center was sold in 1983, and U.S. Steel eventually sold its own headquarters building 2011, though it maintained its headquarters there.

Pittsburgh's Jones & Laughlin (J&L) Corporation would not pursue similar diversification efforts, but it would become the diversification target of other firms. In 1968, the Texas-based conglomerate Ling-Temco-Vought, Inc. purchased a controlling stake in the company. J&L operated independently for the next six years, before Ling-Temco-Vought, renamed LTV in 1971, took full control, leading the company to shift its headquarters to Cleveland by the end of the decade.

Skybus

Regional leaders were beginning to recognize the need for new industries in Pittsburgh. Early efforts to diversify Pittsburgh's economy came via an unlikely source. In December 1961, the executive director of the newly formed Southwestern Pennsylvania Regional Planning Commission (SPRPC), Patrick Cusick, sent a letter to Pittsburgh's major corporate leaders introducing a recent transit study. The letter requested Pittsburgh's business leaders come up with relevant transit ideas that could be implemented locally. In response, the Westinghouse Electric Company made a strategic decision to enter the market for transit systems.[17] Though the company did not produce transit systems, Westinghouse was a leader in automation and control systems—expertise it wanted to apply in new markets. Possibly anticipating Westinghouse's new transit system, the association adopted a Golden Triangle Master Plan in June 1962, which advocated for "an automated rapid transit system serving areas to the east and south of the Triangle." Building the new system was actually part of a multipronged economic development strategy intended to "promote the city as a center of the rapid transportation industry." The overarching goal was to incubate an entirely new transportation vehicle industry cluster based in Pittsburgh. The effort was essentially a top-down industrial targeting strategy aimed at diversifying Pittsburgh's economy away from its reliance on the metals industry.[18]

In June 1963, Allegheny County's public transit system, the Port Authority of Allegheny County (PAT), partnered with state, county, and federal governments and a collection of companies in a $5 million demonstration project testing the Westinghouse Transit Expressway System, an entirely new type of driverless rubber-wheeled vehicle designed to operate on elevated concrete treadways.[19] The goal was not just to build a new transit system but to develop one that could be marketed to a wide range of midsized regions across the country. Westinghouse pitched the new concept as optimal for medium-sized regions with transit flows along routes with between five and twenty thousand riders an hour.[20] For lower density transit flows, travel demand could best be met by bus service. Traditional rail lines, that is, steel wheel on steel rail, were more efficient for higher density transit flows.

Skybus was arguably the first deliberate attempt to push Pittsburgh's economy away from metals industries. Early in 1964, the head of the Regional Industrial Development Corporation argued that a transportation equipment industry held "great potentialities for the area in terms of increased employment and economic growth." The following year, the Chamber of Commerce sponsored the creation of an Urban Transportation Development Council, which was charged with making Pittsburgh "a center of mass transit production and design."[21] Richard

King Mellon, along with the Allegheny Conference for Community Development (ACCD), backed the plan. Three philanthropic foundations affiliated with Mellon—the Richard King Mellon Foundation, the Sarah Scaife Foundation, and the A. W. Mellon Educational and Charitable Trust—quietly accumulated property adjacent to the U.S. Steel Building, anticipating future resale to PAT to be used for a new downtown transit depot.[22] At the same time, new federal funding encouraged the development of new transit systems. The 1964 Urban Mass Transportation Act created the Urban Mass Transit Administration and allocated $375 million for largescale urban public or private rail projects.[23]

Opposition to Skybus emerged from political and business constituencies. In 1969, an alternative plan—to build a more conventional and less costly system based on steel rail lines was presented to the PAT board of directors by WABCO, the century-old company George Westinghouse founded to produce an air brake system for railroads.[24] The fight over Skybus became a battle not just within Pittsburgh's business community but between two of George Westinghouse's legacy companies. WABCO might have generated its proposal because it believed Westinghouse had violated a noncompete agreement between the two firms.[25] The existence of the alternative proposal, albeit one with far less potential to spur a new transportation vehicle industry in Pittsburgh, coalesced opposition to the novel Skybus system. As the fight over Skybus deepened, longstanding political alignments at the core of Pittsburgh's postwar Renaissance frayed. Pittsburgh Mayor Pete Flaherty formed a de facto alliance with the minority Republican County Commissioner William Hunt to oppose Skybus. At the time, Allegheny County's executive leadership comprised a three-commissioner executive board. Hunt's opposition did not align with nearly a decade of support for the new transit system from the more Republican aligned R. K. Mellon and the ACCD.[26]

Skybus may have been doomed by the threat Pittsburgh's dominant steel industry perceived. Though there was never public opposition from the industry, it was believed steel interests were more sympathetic to the WABCO proposal and its use of traditional steel rail.[27] Flaherty slowed planning efforts by refusing to permit a crucial parcel of land downtown, the real estate that foundations associated with R. K. Mellon had quietly acquired for use as a transit depot.[28] Flaherty and a coalition of suburban mayors filed suit against PAT's entire Early Action Program, a strategic plan for the region's public transit that had been pursued for over a decade. A 1972 injunction issued by an Allegheny

County judge temporarily halted Skybus progress. Still, as late as May 1973, not only did people believe that "U.S. funding was assured" for the construction of Skybus, but plans were approved that month for an extension of the system between Downtown Pittsburgh and Oakland.[29] By the time the injunction was overturned that year, the collapse of unified support doomed the potential for additional federal funding. By the end of the year, PAT effectively abandoned efforts to implement the innovative Skybus program. Westinghouse's Transit Expressway Revenue Line eventually found some limited success elsewhere, with Skybus-inspired "people-mover" systems eventually constructed in Miami, Tampa, and Orlando, but no significant cluster of transportation equipment industries would emerge in Pittsburgh.

Through the latter half of the 1960s, public concerns over Pittsburgh's economic future diminished. Economic optimism in Pittsburgh was buttressed by the nation's 106-month economic expansion beginning in February 1961—the longest period of such expansion until the 1990s. In the second half of the decade, the Vietnam War added to demand for Pittsburgh's industrial output. In December 1966, the unemployment rate for the Pittsburgh metropolitan area dropped to 2.2 percent, the lowest since 1946, when metropolitan labor force statistics were first consistently compiled, and remained under 3 percent for thirty of the thirty-six remaining months in the decade.[30] Again, predictions of steel's decline in Pittsburgh had been proven wrong, reinforcing further beliefs in the region's economic resilience.

Some realized that much of Pittsburgh's sanguine economy of the late 1960s was at least partially the result of the Vietnam War. In 1968, Congressman Elmer J. Holland, who represented the South Side of the city of Pittsburgh—still home to J&L's behemoth steelworks, which spanned both sides of the Monongahela River—requested that the US Department of Labor study the future economic prospects of the Pittsburgh region.

The congressman was looking ahead. He wanted to know what the region could expect when the war ended. The answer he received was remarkably pessimistic. The final report, *Pittsburgh: A Study of a Static Economic-Area Situation* came to a now-repeated conclusion: "The position of the basic industry is not the problem. The problem is that the area simply does not have the proper industrial mix to give it the

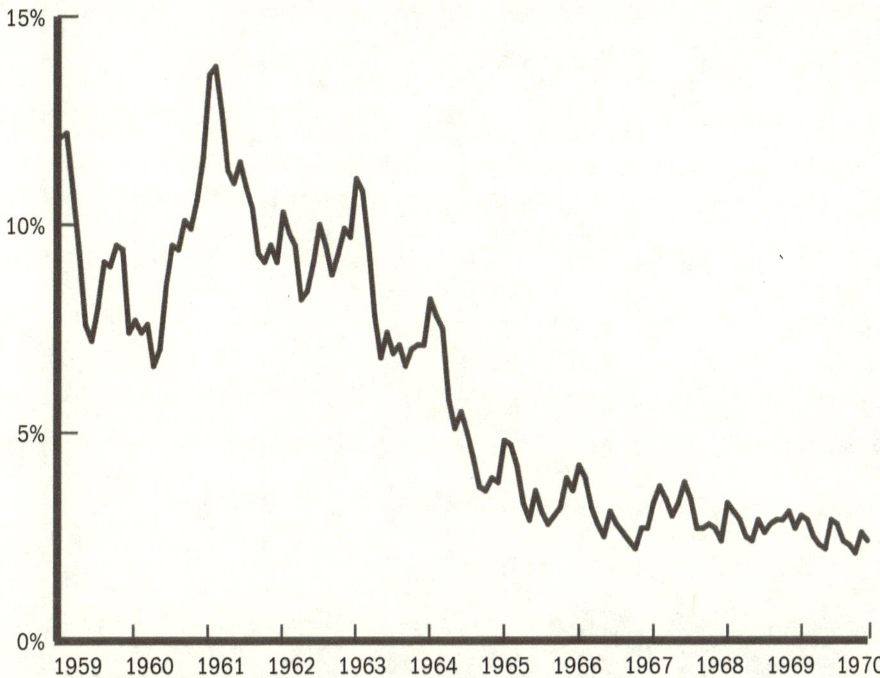

Pittsburgh region unemployment rate, 1959–70

viability of other metropolitan areas." The region suffered from not just from a narrow mix of industries but narrow skills within its labor force. The Department of Labor predicted that future economic adjustment in Pittsburgh would be difficult because laid-off steelworkers would not be able to readily find jobs in alternative occupations or industries and that previous efforts to diversify the region's economy had mostly failed. It also highlighted a chronic underemployment for women in the region's workforce. The report gives some of the clearest evidence that the *ESPR* was not well received by Pittsburgh's broader business community. *ESPR* proponents were described in the report as part of a "New Coalition" at odds with existing business leadership. It cited University of Pittsburgh professor Robert Weidenhammer, who said the Pittsburgh business community was made up of a heavy industry "establishment" and that the "establishment has literally had its feet encased in steel thereby shutting out what the city needs most—a mixed industrial base."[31] His was a heretical opinion in Pittsburgh at the end of the 1960s.

Did we make a mistake locating our headquarters in Pittsburgh?

U.S. Steel advertisement,
Pittsburgh Press, May 18, 1976

Twilight

January 18, 1970

At the very beginning of the 1970s, the business editor of the *Pittsburgh Press* accurately, if colorfully, reported that "Steel—Pittsburgh's bread and butter industry—spent most of 1969 in the gravy."[1] It was gratuitous to observe that steel remained at the center of Pittsburgh's economy. Rarely idled since a national steel strike a decade earlier had ended, blast furnaces remained clustered along the riverbanks of southwestern Pennsylvania, much as they had for over a century. Pittsburgh and its environs remained among the most concentrated agglomerations of steel production anywhere in the world.

Output from Pittsburgh's mills had never been higher, but advancing labor force productivity meant employment at regional manufacturing plants had slowly been declining since reaching a peak of over 379,000 jobs at the height of the Korean War in 1952.[2] Still, in 1969 more than 320,000 workers were employed directly by manufacturing industries across the ten counties of southwestern Pennsylvania, roughly a third of the region's 1 million workers. More local workers were part of the vast network of suppliers providing goods and services to regional steel plants or were dependent on their output. Even a recent surge of commercial construction in the city was a secondary impact of the region's steel industry. Nearing completion was construction of the largest skyscraper ever to be located in Downtown Pittsburgh—the tallest building ever built between New York and Chicago—destined to become the new headquarters of the U.S. Steel Corporation, by far the single largest employer across western Pennsylvania.

Manufacturing remained good for the region's economy, particularly for its workers. Unemployment across the Pittsburgh metropolitan area was extremely low, dropping to a low of 2.1 percent in October 1969—a rate well below what many economists, before or since, have defined as full employment.[3] Pittsburgh's economic prognosis appeared sanguine because the national economic expansion that began in February 1961 continued unbroken through the end of the decade. As the decade turned, US steel plants had just finished producing 141 million tons of raw steel in 1969, more than had ever been produced in any prior year.[4]

Less obvious in January was that 1970 marked a transition year for the US economy. Later calculation determined that a mild national recession had begun in December 1969.[5] Lasting until November 1970, the eleven-month recession ended the longest continuous economic expansion to date for the US economy. Nonetheless, the economic slowdown barely registered as a recession at all. The nation's gross national product declined just 0.2 percent from peak to trough, making the single mildest US recession to date.

A 1970 *Pittsburgh Press* article hinted at some of the broader changes underway within the steel industry, changes that unavoidably impacted Pittsburgh. Almost in passing, the article noted that a year had passed since both the European Coal and Steel Community and Japan had volunteered to limit exports to the United States in January 1969. Two years remained on the three-year agreement, a compromise in a decadelong fight US steel producers had been waging against escalating steel imports. International trade machinations were just the leading edge of the decades' macroeconomic tumult that was bearing down on the industrial regions in the United States.

Gold

On August 5, 1971, the French government formally requested $191 million of its dollar reserves be exchanged for gold. The postwar Bretton Woods monetary system made the US dollar fully convertible to gold bullion, a system that relied on a US promise to exchange gold on demand. On August 15, to avoid further depletion of the nation's gold reserves, President Nixon effectively terminated the gold convertibility of the dollar, an act that led to an immediate depreciation in the value of the dollar in world currency markets. The unavoidable consequence was a spike in the cost of all goods imported into the United States. Higher prices quickly began spreading through the entire economy.

Industrial regions such as Pittsburgh initially benefited from the rapid depreciation of the US dollar. The less expensive dollar improved the competitive position of US producers in world markets. US manufacturing expanded, and US gross national product grew by more than 6 percent between 1971 and 1972. Coupled with a decline in imports, the trade deficit the United States maintained with the world declined in 1972. Between 1972 and 1973. US employment grew by over 2.6 million jobs—the largest annual increase since the beginning of World War II.

Later in 1973, international politics injected a new round of monetary turmoil into the US economy. That October, the Organization of Arab Petroleum Countries declared an oil embargo against the United States in response to support it gave Israel in the Yom Kippur War then raging. The new embargo caused the market price for oil to jump over 70 percent at the end of 1973, as compared to what it had been just a year earlier. Increasing energy prices compounded price increases cascading through the national economy. The spike in inflation precipitated the second national recession of the 1970s, which began in November 1973 and lasted until March 1975.

The mid-decade recession was the longest since the Great Depression four decades earlier. Surprising economists, economic decline did not significantly slow rampant inflation. The contradictory juxtaposition of both rising prices and lack of growth gave rise to the ominous new term *stagflation.* Persistent inflation, coupled with unprecedented price controls imposed by the Nixon administration in August 1971, eventually caused escalating disruptions across the steel industry. Steel prices were constrained by the mandated price freeze, but the industry could not escape the escalating costs of essential inputs, much of which were purchased from unconstrained international markets. A depreciating dollar pushed up the price of virtually all imported commodities, including many basic inputs needed for raw steel production. Between 1973 and 1974, the price of scrap steel rose by 153 percent; zinc by 250 percent, and fuel prices by 244 percent.[6]

Driven by macroeconomic fluctuations, the economy of southwestern Pennsylvania was a near constant roller coaster through the first half of the decade. In February 1970, the Pittsburgh region's 3.1 percent unemployment rate was markedly below the low national rate of 4.2 percent. The region's unemployment rate more than doubled to 7.3 percent by

August 1971, peaking above the nation's 6.1 percent that month. By 1974, Pittsburgh's unemployment rate had dropped back down to 4.0 percent, only to peak again at 8.3 percent in August 1975. Overall employment levels in the region experienced less volatility. Despite the year-over-year volatility, outward signs suggested that the regional economy remained strong. Other than dipping slightly during the 1973–75 recession, total employment in the Pittsburgh metropolitan region rose every year between 1971 and 1979, gaining 118,000 jobs.

Rising inflation threatened to bring new strikes to the steel industry as workers sought higher wages to maintain their purchasing power. Once common, few major labor stoppages had affected the industry since the national steel strikes of 1959. Preventing future work stoppages was the primary goal for the industry as it prepared for contract negotiations. In 1973, both workers and management had strong incentives to prevent major work stoppages as a coordinating committee of ten major steel producers began negotiations with the United Steelworkers of America. The parties agreed to the first Experimental Negotiating Agreement (ENA) crafted primarily "to avoid industrywide strikes or lockouts or government intervention."[7]

The ENA set up a strict schedule for anticipated 1974 industrywide contract negotiations. The agreement's key innovation was that workers surrendered the right to strike if negotiations failed. If an agreement was not reached between labor and management, the union agreed to accept binding arbitration—effectively precluding the potential of any major strike. In return for the historic concession, firms agreed to a guaranteed cost of living adjustment to wages on top of three percent wage increases each year of the contract.[8] These adjustments protected workers from losing purchasing power even in the face of escalating price inflation. Workers and industry renewed the ENA again in 1977, to govern labor-management relations in the steel and mining industries through the end of the decade.

The guaranteed wage increases of the ENA were only feasible because the steel industry was planning for continued growth and greater profits. In March 1973, U.S. Steel's president, Edgar Speer, was pressured to assure the public not that the industry was in decline but that it had sufficient capacity to keep up with ever-increasing demand.[9] Expanding global demand was straining the industry, pushing the US steel industry to produce at a nearly unsustainable 97 percent capacity in 1973—the highest level since the Korean War. Total US steel production jumped by over 14 percent between 1972 and 1973, reaching a record 151 million tons of raw steel. Though it was not realized at the time, the US steel industry would never again produce as much in a single year.

Following its peak output, US steel production declined only slightly in 1974 as a national recession set in. So mild was the decline that in May 1975, Speer described the mid-decade recession as the U.S. Steel's "best recession ever." The company added a significant amount of new production capacity in 1974 and had just finished two years of producing over 25 million tons of steel annually, a new company record.[10] "I can't recall another time when the future has been more favorable." Yet the corporation's output was plunging as he made those comments. U.S. Steel's 1975 output dropped precipitously to a fourteen-year low.[11]

If the mid-decade recessions were mild for U.S. Steel, so, too, were they for Pittsburgh. Before decline returned, Pittsburgh believed it had escaped a recurring paradigm of magnified regional declines during national recessions. Early in the 1970s, the region's manufacturing employment dipped only slightly, a dip easily attributed to US involvement in

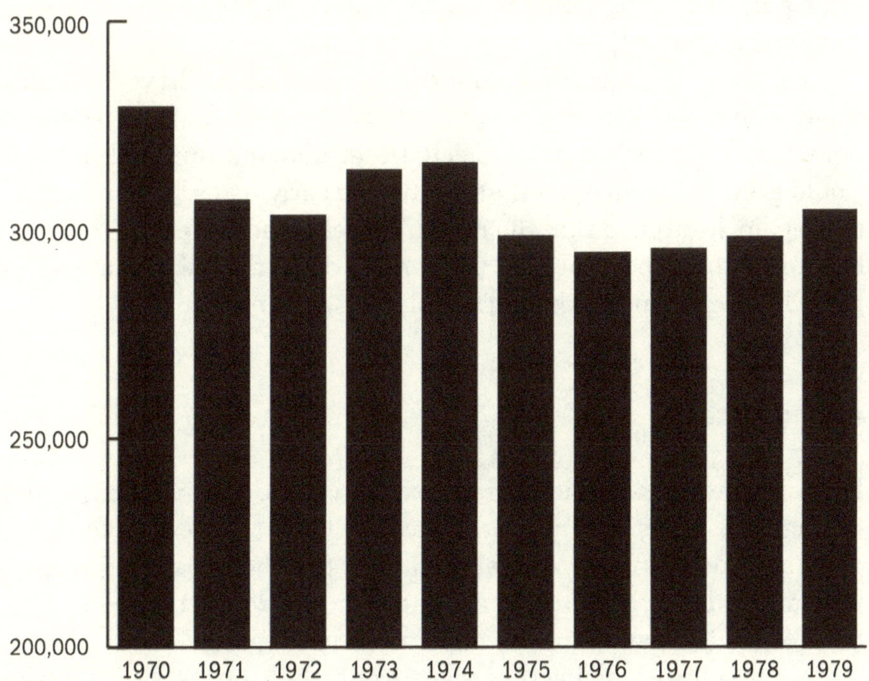

Southwestern Pennsylvania manufacturing employment, 1970–79

the Vietnam War coming to an end. Through the remainder of the 1970s, regional manufacturing employment did not sustain gains but remained remarkably stable given the turbulent macroeconomic headlines. Even during the worst of the 1973–75 recession, continued strong demand for steel protected Pittsburgh from much of the nation's cyclical decline. A 1975 headline went so far to declare: "Steel Is Pittsburgh's Hedge on Recession." The article quoted the senior economist of the region's largest bank: "It used to be said that when the economy caught a cold, Pittsburgh caught pneumonia. Now it seems the other way around."[12]

Despite the recessions, and national concerns over inflation, there were other reasons Pittsburgh's economy seemed to be faring well. The mandatory wage increases of the ENA and expansion across the steel industry fueled higher wages in Pittsburgh. Between 1970 and 1980, steelworkers' inflation-adjusted wages increased 37 percent.[13] Increasing wages within the steel industry translated directly into disproportionate gains for southwestern Pennsylvania. A 1978 study concluded that per capita personal income in the Pittsburgh region had increased over the preceding decade at a faster rate than in all other major metropolitan regions in the United States, except for Houston—which was inordinately benefiting from the global surge in oil and gas exploration—and Washington, DC.[14]

Long forgotten was Ben Chinitz's warning about how Pittsburgh would fare in any future steel industry contraction. In his first annual report as chairman, Speer projected that demand for steel products would grow by 3 percent annually into the early 1980s.[15] For producers to keep up, he argued that the nation's steel capacity needed to expand by more than 30 percent over the coming decade, growth that was expected to require more than $17.5 billion in new investment.[16]

Air and Water

Publicly, the threat regional steel executives worried about the most through the 1970s was not foreign competition, nor even the rapidly growing production from steel minimills, but the expanding scope of local and federal environmental regulations. Through the 1960s, Pittsburgh's lauded paradigm of cooperation between civic and business leaders steadily eroded across many fronts, but the most dire conflict emerged over environmental policymaking and enforcement. An updated Allegheny County pollution code took effect on January 1, 1970, which mandated far stricter enforcement of environmental regulations. Unlike past efforts, which had relied far more on informal suasion, local government was taking the steel industry to court. Over the first eleven months of 1970, Allegheny County issued 533 notices of violation, filed 82 criminal complaints, and investigated 4,607 pollution complaints received from the general public.[17]

Local activism was buttressed by increasingly active federal environmental regulation. The Federal Clean Air Act of 1970 expanded the enforcement authority of the federal government. The new rules coincided with the creation of the Environmental Protection Agency (EPA) on December 2, 1970. Steel manufacturing was an early target of the new EPA bureaucracy, an enmity that was, unsurprisingly, reciprocated. When William Ruckelshaus, the EPA's first director, paid an early courtesy call on U.S. Steel Chairman Edwin Gott, he later recalled being told, "You know we don't like you very much" and "we certainly don't like your agency."[18]

Pittsburgh's historic advantages in producing steel derived almost entirely from the quality of metallurgic coal readily available in southwestern Pennsylvania. The integrated steel plants concentrated in Pittsburgh more than anywhere else in the United States relied on industrial coke to fuel their blast furnaces. But the transformation of coal into industrial coke was unavoidably one of the dirtiest industrial operations. Compliance with new regulations was hardest for older coke works built long before limiting pollution was a priority. U.S. Steel's Clairton Coke Works—thirty miles southeast of Pittsburgh—began operation in 1918 and remained the largest coke plant in the nation. In 1970, the giant plant included twenty batteries made up of more than thirteen hundred individual ovens. U.S. Steel's largest competitor, Jones & Laughlin (J&L), operated a comparably large coke works within the urban core of the city of Pittsburgh adjacent to the city's Hazelwood neighborhood, where beehive coke ovens first began production in the 1850s while another coke works had operated on Neville Island on the Ohio River just outside the city of Pittsburgh since the 1930s.

Coal becomes coke after impurities—including tar, benzene, naphtha, and other byproducts—are forced out of the organic rock. Controlling the byproduct-infused emissions posed a nearly intractable engineering challenge unto itself, but the final step in the process required quickly removing the coke from the ovens and quenching it with large volumes of water to prevent oxidation. The water used to cool the coke becomes contaminated with toxic phenols, ammonia, hydrogen sulfide, and cyanide. Coking operations at Clairton were in immediate violation of the new limits on phenols imposed by Allegheny County's 1970 Pollution Code, forcing U.S. Steel to seek a variance to continue operating.

U.S. Steel's petition focused less on health issues, but on a tangential economic argument. The corporation emphasized that the coke works could not remain open if forced to comply with the strict environmental regulations recently approved. With a network of regional steel production dependent on coke produced at Clairton, shutting down coking operations meant jobs across the greater Pittsburgh region would be put at risk. To highlight the point, U.S. Steel quantified the economic role the Clairton Works played in the larger economy of southwestern Pennsylvania. It counted 29,500 regional jobs directly dependent on output from the Clairton Works and argued that another 75,000 regional jobs were dependent on the wages of workers and their families. Some considered the company's argument "economic blackmail," but the logic could not be ignored in heavily industrialized Pittsburgh. Deliberations over the variance extended over an unusual length of time, and in November 1971, fifteen months later, the county's regulatory Variance Board eventually disapproved U.S. Steel's request.

The corporation immediately appealed the ruling, placing the fate of the Clairton Works before Allegheny County courts. Preempting any significant regulatory clamp down, the presiding judge ordered the parties to quickly come to an agreement that would keep the Clairton Works operating. In September 1972, U.S. Steel and Allegheny County agreed to a consent decree that effectively exempted the coking operations at Clairton from state and local pollution limits for a full decade. U.S. Steel nominally agreed to make capital improvements to the plant that would eventually make it economically feasible for the plant to operate in compliance with the latest pollution standards.

The consent decree provided only a brief hiatus in the ongoing legal battle between the corporation and regulators. In 1973, state official rejected the plans submitted by the corporation. In 1975, the Commonwealth of Pennsylvania and Allegheny County jointly filed charges against U.S. Steel alleging 241 violations of the 1972 consent decree. U.S. Steel's response would not be limited to the courts. The corporation took its economic argument directly to the public at large. In May 1976, U.S. Steel placed full-page advertisements in both of Pittsburgh's major daily newspapers: the *Pittsburgh Press* and *Pittsburgh Post-Gazette.* The ads were not intended to sell any product, nor even to promote U.S. Steel's corporate image. Instead, they conveyed a less than subtle threat: "Did we make a mistake by locating our new headquarters building in Pittsburgh?" Lest there be any confusion over the message, the advertisement made clear: "There were considerable discussions for over a year about whether these efficient steelmaking furnaces should be installed here or in some other part of the country."[19]

Support for stricter environmental regulation was far from universal even, or especially, in communities in close proximity to the largest emitters. "If the antipollution people want to feed us and pay our bills, then I'm for it," a resident of Clairton commented at the time. For Clairton, like so many other mill towns, far more than "smoke makes money," the fight was one of "smoke vs. survival."[20] The *Pittsburgh Post-Gazette* offered an editorial more than sympathetic with the corporation, opining that U.S. Steel "is to Pittsburgh what peanuts and Jimmy Carter are to Plains, Georgia. Like the fountain at the Point, the Pirates and Steelers, U.S. Steel is an integral part of this community."[21]

Closed-door negotiations between the parties resulted in a reworked legal agreement that ensured the Clairton Coke Works remained in operation. In October 1976, U.S. Steel agreed to make a $600 million investment in the plant by 1983, $155 million of which would be for equipment to bring the site into compliance with local and federal air pollution regulations.[22] Effectively, U.S. Steel was granted the variance it initially sought six years earlier, allowing it to operate out of compliance with the county's pollution codes for at least the next seven years.

In the fight over local environmental regulations, preserving jobs became a singular policy goal. Where once local regulators played an adversarial role, by the late 1970s, "county commissioners and the health department both became far more inclined to protect industry from advanced control requirements than to foster them."[23] Coupled with an omnibus retrenchment of federal environmental policy during the 1980s, the heightened environmental activism of the 1960s and 1970s was overcome by events as the region struggled with existential economic change.

An undeniable economic challenge facing Pittsburgh was the high cost of bringing older industrial capital up to modern environmental standards. The costs to improve many older factories—some in Pittsburgh still using older open-hearth furnaces at the beginning of the 1970s—far exceeded the costs to construct new plants. The cheapest location for a

"Did we make a mistake by locating our new headquarters building in Pittsburgh?"

Edgar Speer, Chairman, United States Steel.

When we built our innovative and efficient headquarters building at 600 Grant Street, we knew we were building a landmark for the whole area.

We also knew we were sticking our necks out.

This building represents a very sizable and visible commitment by United States Steel to remain a vital part of the economy of this area. U.S. Steel provides over 40,000 jobs in Southwestern Pennsylvania—but that doesn't begin to indicate our total involvement in the economic picture.

In 1974, for instance, we bought products, supplies, and services from local companies—about $600,000,000 worth. We paid about $30,000,000 in property and other taxes. And our employees added $20,000,000 in state and local wage taxes.

Adding up all payrolls, purchases, taxes, dividends, and employee benefits—U.S. Steel and its people contribute over *a billion and a half dollars a year* to the economy of Southwestern Pennsylvania, including Pittsburgh.

All this involvement results from a series of carefully considered decisions to spend huge sums of money—to keep our Pittsburgh area operations competitive.

Take the two Basic Oxygen furnaces at our Edgar Thomson plant.

There were considerable discussions for over a year about whether these efficient steelmaking furnaces should be installed here—or in some other part of the country.

We not only decided to build them here—we also planned for a third BOP vessel, so we could modernize an old plant and expand if needed.

We've had to make hundreds of decisions like that, involving hundreds of millions of dollars, and I'll be telling you about some of them in future messages.

But can we continue to make these favorable decisions that benefit this area? I'd like to think so—but our decisions to save jobs or add jobs through modernization or expansion involve more than just spending money. We must consider, too, whether our neighbors want to help us continue to be successful.

For example, as increasing future steel demand requires additional decisions on facility location, will the governmental and environmental climate favor selection of the Pittsburgh area?

We hope it does!

U.S. Steel advertisement, May 1976 (*Pittsburgh Press*)

new plant was almost always on previously undeveloped, or *greenfield* sites unhindered by demolition or environmental remediation costs always required to rebuild existing plants. Yet, there were few such sites available across southwestern Pennsylvania, let alone near Pittsburgh. More than a century of intense industrial development across the topographically challenged region had made use of virtually every site suitable for large industrial plants.

Through the end of his tenure at the head of U.S. Steel in 1978, Speer argued construction of new greenfield sites was far less expensive than the cost to improve the firm's many Pittsburgh-based facilities.[24] That logic was central to the corporation's plans to build a new multibillion-dollar plant on undeveloped land on Lake Erie at the Pennsylvania–Ohio border. In 1976, U.S. Steel began planning for the new \$3 billion—the equivalent of nearly \$17 billion in 2025—Conneaut plant. In 1978, the company applied for a permit to build the plant to the US Army Corps of Engineers.[25]

With so much capital already invested in Pittsburgh-based facilities, any shift of production toward new regions would take time. As a result, the corporation was forced to accept stringent consent orders from both local and national regulators in order to keep its Pittsburgh-based plants operating. Complying with new environmental regulations briefly spurred a new round of investment intended to modernize Pittsburgh's plants. In addition to the new investment required to rebuild coke works at Clairton, in 1979 U.S. Steel negotiated a reprieve from its earlier consent decree by agreeing to build a new blast furnace at its Duquesne Works.

U.S. Steel was not alone in making these new investments. At the beginning of the 1970s, J&L—by then a subsidiary of the LTV Corporation—was still producing steel at its South Side Works spanning both sides of the Monongahela River within eyesight of Downtown Pittsburgh, as it had for 120 years. Dominating the site was a 270-foot blast furnace named Ann—built in 1899, it was one of the oldest operating blast furnaces in the world. Ann had not been upgraded since 1966. By the early 1970s, both local and federal regulators were pressuring the firm to close the older furnaces on the Hazelwood side of the plant. To keep the plant open, the company entered into its own consent decree with the EPA. A \$200 million investment put in place modern electric furnaces at the South Side Works, for a short period the largest and most modern electric furnaces in the nation.[26]

Two national recessions over the course of the 1970s had failed to turn Pittsburgh toward envisioning, or even conceiving, a future without steel. Prior to 1979, the only major steelworks in the region to completely shut down over the previous half century were U.S. Steel operations in Etna along the Allegheny River (closed 1953) and facilities in Donora, where a zinc works was closed in 1957 and remaining operations at the site ended by 1967.[27] Though many promised upgrades would never happen, expanding environmental regulations counterintuitively generated plans for crucial reinvestments that were expected to keep Pittsburgh plants operating ever longer.

The upgrade of its South Side Works was the very last investment the Jones & Laughlin Corporation made in the Pittsburgh region. The company had already begun a systematic retreat from the city. By 1974, the venerable Pittsburgh company was effectively no longer based in Pittsburgh. The Texas holding company Ling-Temco-Vought (LTV) purchased a majority of J&L's stock in 1968. The conglomerate took full control of the company in 1974. LTV's J&L division absorbed the assets of the Youngstown Sheet & Tube Company when it acquired the Lykes Company in 1978. The firm's subsequent consolidation of executive leadership in Cleveland moved more than four hundred executive positions out of Pittsburgh, though many of the relocated workers did not change their permanent places of residence, choosing instead an extended commute.[28] Despite Ben Moreell's Pittsburgh-centered expansion two decades earlier, corporate restructuring pushed LTV to lead the steel industry's broader abandonment of Pittsburgh.

The global expansion of steel production had not slowed, and an emerging surplus in steel capacity was becoming difficult to deny in the latter half of the 1970s. The voluntary export restraints that Europe and Japan had agreed to in 1969 were not renewed when they expired in 1974. The restraints had initially dampened steel imports, and instability in the value of the dollar aided US producers early in the decade. Imports resumed increasing by mid-decade, and in 1977, imports into the United States jumped by a million tons a year, surging over previous record highs. US producers argued that foreign steelmakers were engaged in unfair pricing—effectively dumping steel products into US markets at prices below their cost of production. Federal legislation imposed a new trigger price mechanism that set new limits on steel imports when prices dropped below regulated levels.[29]

For steel production in Pittsburgh, the greater, if still unacknowledged, threat was not international production but steel production elsewhere within the United States. Steel production from minimills increased continuously through the 1970s, further threatening traditional steel producers. At the end of the decade, 15 percent of US steel production came from sixty steel minimills dispersed across the nation. Ominously, no steel minimill had been built in Pittsburgh, nor were any such plants on the horizon.[30] Pittsburgh was being left behind by the early 1980s, by which time minimills had taken entire markets for certain steel products away from integrated steel plants.[31]

Volkswagen

The 1970s saw what was arguably the one of the most successful efforts to diversify Pittsburgh's economy, albeit it was more a diversification within manufacturing industries than a shift into entirely new sectors. A little more than a month before the nation celebrated its independence from Europe two centuries earlier, regional business and economic news was dominated by new investment coming into Pennsylvania from the continent. On the last day of May 1976, Volkswagen announced it had selected New Stanton, Pennsylvania, for a new US automobile assembly plant in. The site in Westmoreland County—forty miles west of Downtown Pittsburgh—was the location of a never-completed factory originally intended to produce automobiles for the Chrysler Corporation. Six years earlier, the onset of a national recession in 1970 had prompted Chrysler to abandon construction there.

Pennsylvania's Volkswagen plant would be the first production facility of a foreign automaker within the United States since Rolls Royce operated a factory in Massachusetts between 1921 and 1929. Governor Milton Shapp euphorically announced the state had "pulled a big rabbit out of the hat," alluding to the subcompact car slated to be produced at the new plant. Even less restrained descriptions hailed the new plant as the "biggest economic prize of the decade," and the Shapp administration was lauded for its "inventiveness in expanding the state's industrial base."[32] The public was told that the plant would immediately create upward of five thousand jobs and spur the creation of an additional twenty-three to twenty-five thousand jobs in a new automobile manufacturing cluster coming to the Commonwealth.[33] "We could have a mini Detroit," predicted one state official.[34]

The fight to attract the new Volkswagen plant represented a paradigm shift in the competition between states. The announcement that the plant would be in Pennsylvania was the culmination of a multiyear battle that pitted states against each other in unprecedented competition to attract the new investment. *The Wall Street Journal* described the frenzy of activity among states to land the new plant as "the greatest industrial courtship of all time."[35] Pennsylvania's success came at a steep price. Volkswagen was provided upward of $78 million in public subsidies to sway its decision. Public incentives on a similar scale only became common in later decades. The package offered to the automobile manufacturer was so large critics called it a "symbol of fiscal lunacy on as grandiose a scale."[36]

What made efforts to attract Volkswagen so different from previous economic development practices was the scale of public subsidies involved and the vastly expanded roles of both state and local governments. In April 1976, *The Wall Street Journal* noted that "virtually every state east of the Mississippi is interested, and nearly every one of their governors has been to Germany to woo VW."[37] When it appeared to have been dropped from a short list of potential sites, the city of Baltimore ran a full-page ad in *The Wall Street Journal* addressing Volkswagen directly: "Baltimore Wants You So Much, We'll Let You Write Your Own Terms. We're Confident That We Can Work Something Out."[38] Pennsylvania later claimed it won the competition despite forty-seven other proposals. Even Puerto Rico threw in its hat, and three states—Tennessee, Arkansas, and Mississippi—collaborated on a joint proposal.

The nascent automobile industry in western Pennsylvania was another counterintuitive benefit of macroeconomic turmoil. In September 1973, Volkswagen had begun exploring the possibility of assembling automobiles in the United States, to escape the impacts of magnifying currency fluctuations early in the decade. Its initial plan to build a completely new plant was abandoned after the corporation's financial condition deteriorated, due to a synchronized global recession affecting both the United States and Western Europe between 1973 and 1975. The company refocused on rehabilitating an existing plant at lower costs. The competition narrowed down to the location in New Stanton and two sites in Ohio: a former Westinghouse appliance factory in Columbus, and a former federal tank plant in the Cleveland suburb of Brook Park. In early 1975, lacking only a formal announcement, Ohio's Brook Park location appeared to have won the competition. Its key advantage was the lower costs required to restart production at the plant, which had produced tanks until 1965, compared to the additional investment needed to complete the unfinished Pennsylvania plant. So clear was the choice that in April, the German weekly *Der Spiegel* printed a photograph of "Volkswagen's future facility in Ohio."[39]

Competition for new investment had evolved and was no longer left entirely to the vagaries of the free market. If Brook Park offered the lower cost alternative, Pennsylvania proved willing to compensate Volkswagen by offering an even more generous publicly funded financial package. Pennsylvania, like several other states, had already offered substantial incentives. State promises to fund necessary road and rail links were already on the table, as were tax breaks and state assistance in recruiting new workers. What pushed Pennsylvania past Ohio was an additional $40 million low-interest loan, which Volkswagen would not be required to make principal payments on until 1998. "When Pennsylvania came up with that low-interest loan . . . we scrambled to see what we could put together. . . . We couldn't come close," said Ohio officials looking back on the deal.[40]

Pennsylvania's incentive package was seminal not only because of the value of the incentives it offered but the leading role state government played in the effort. State and local government played only limited roles when Chrysler had expressed interest in building a new western Pennsylvania automobile plant in 1968. A local utility company acted as the prime agent, pitching a western Pennsylvania location to the corporation.[41] Then, the utility's real estate subsidiary had assembled the parcel of land required for the new plant, with virtually no major incentives provided by the state.[42] Public investment was mostly limited to a commitment for pay for the construction of new water and sewer infrastructure required to support the expansion of industrial activity in the predominantly rural area.

The crucial loan came from the Pennsylvania Industrial Development Authority, then Pennsylvania's primary economic development program. At a time when commercial interest rates ranged between 8 and 10 percent, repayment terms were set at just 1.75 percent for the first twenty years and 8 percent per annum only for the last ten. The below-market interest rate was effectively a direct financial payment to the corporation, no less beneficial than writing Volkswagen a check. The size of the loan exhausted loans available from the development program for the subsequent two years. Other incentives included a $20 million general obligation bond floated by the Commonwealth of Pennsylvania to finance completion of a highway link between the new plant and major highways. A new railroad spur linking the plant and major rail lines would be paid for from federal funds the state was slated to receive due to the federal Railroad Revitalization and Regulatory Reform Act of 1976. Pennsylvania provided additional in-kind subsidies, including training for new workers, and agreed to take on the preliminary screening of an anticipated forty-five thousand job applications. Pennsylvania was concentrating most of its economic development resources to land the one project.

Local governments provided additional incentives, including a five-year property tax abatement by both Westmoreland County government and the local school district. At the new plant site, 147 acres were designated a subzone of the Pittsburgh Foreign Trade Zone. The trade zone reduced customs duties on parts and supplies imported by the plant, producing an unaccounted-for opportunity cost in foregone revenues to the state government. As a result, Volkswagen needed to pay only a duty of about 3 percent on finished automobiles rather than duties as high as 20 percent on certain components.[43] Collectively, Pennsylvania's incentive package was called "the most complex economic development agreement in US history."[44] The value of the entire package was initially appraised at $51.7 million, or 19.6 percent of the full cost of the plant. Later accounting put the value of public incentives at $90 million (equivalent to over $522 million in 2025).[45] The comprehensive set of incentives had omnibus political support within the state. Critics made note of the unprecedented scale of public incentives offered to a private corporation, but naysayers held little sway once Pennsylvania landed the project.[46] Nonetheless, without massive public subsidies, it is unlikely the new plant would ever have been located in western Pennsylvania.

At the time, Pennsylvania's winning bid was critiqued as an example of overpayment by state governments to corporations making major site selection decisions.[47] Volkswagen was ahead of the pack, but soon a bevy of foreign automakers built manufacturing plants in the United States, and all expected and received sizable state incentives for similar investments. In 1994, Alabama offered Mercedes-Benz a package valued at more than $300 million to locate an automobile plant outside of Birmingham. South Carolina provided similar financial incentives to bring a BMW plant to the state in 1992 and also agreed to bear the cost of initial training for the plant's entire workforce.[48] Enabled by what Pennsylvania had willingly put on the table, corporations were quickly trained to pit state governments against one another and expect ever-larger subsidies for major investments.

Criticisms of the incentive package within Pennsylvania evaporated once employment at the New Stanton site ramped up. The plant employed close to four thousand workers within a year of its April 1978 opening. It added a second shift in January 1979, further expanding capacity and jobs. By 1980, employment peaked at more than six thousand workers on site, exceeding early predictions for job creation. The new jobs were expected to last long into the future, and few remembered criticisms of the public subsidies required to bring the plant to Pennsylvania.

While the size of the incentives offered to Volkswagen initially provoked controversy, through the end of the 1970s there was little dispute that economic development policies should be focused on attracting factories like the one Volkswagen brought to Pennsylvania. "Smokestack chasing" remained the preeminent goal for state and local economic development policies. Little effort and even less public funding went into growing smaller firms, promoting entrepreneurial activity or programs aimed at expanding employment in nonmanufacturing industries. Pennsylvania was doubling down on past practices, and as the 1970s ended, the gamble appeared to be paying off.

Inflation

The nation's top economic concern through most of the 1970s was the persistent and historic inflation that defined the decade. President Nixon's August 8, 1974, resignation only passed to his successor the task of fighting the nation's unrelenting inflation. On October 8, President Ford's "Whip Inflation Now" speech—his first before a joint session of Congress—declared inflation "public enemy number one."[49] As late as 1976, inflation remained above 9 percent, but it moderated to below 6 percent in 1977. The worst briefly appeared to be over, but inflation again began to climb in 1978, becoming the top economic problem facing the Carter administration. On October 24, 1978, President Carter addressed the nation in a televised speech focused exclusively on reignited inflation fears.[50] Its opening was blunt: "Good evening. I want to have a frank talk with you tonight about our most serious domestic problem. That problem is inflation. Inflation can threaten all the economic gains we've made, and it can stand in the way of what we want to achieve in the future."

Fears of inflation soon escalated. Through the year, domestic turmoil and widespread oilfield strikes depressed supplies coming from Iran, the world's fourth-largest oil producer. On December 26, the Iranian oil industry virtually shut down amid the turmoil. US energy prices spiked and created rapid price increases throughout the economy. The ongoing energy crisis pushed inflation to unprecedented levels. Inflation in the United States went above 10 percent in March 1979 and remained in double digits for the subsequent thirty-two months. The fears induced were not merely economic but led to greater concerns about the nation's political stature in the world. National political columnist Hobart Rowen argued that "a plunging dollar . . . would force OPEC to raise prices—or worse, price oil in some currency other than dollars."[51] The battle over inflation was becoming a proxy for defending US financial leadership globally. As the 1970s came to a close, the full might of US monetary policy was about to be trained on the nation's unvanquished inflation. Virtually all other economic imperatives—to include the stability of American manufacturing industries, and the stability of US manufacturing regions—became distant and secondary goals.

Damage

7

We have been shocked out of our complacency and smugness. We now realize that American industry has no manifest destiny to be always first, always right, always best.

David Roderick, U.S. Steel chairman, May 1982

Démontage

October 6, 1979

Convening for a rare Saturday meeting, the members of the Federal Open Markets Committee (FOMC) met in Washington on October 6, 1979. The FOMC, made up of the board of governors of the Federal Reserve and the presidents of five regional Federal Reserve banks, sets key interest rates to shape the nation's monetary policy. The unscheduled meeting had been called on short notice and in secret by Paul Volcker.[1] Appointed chairman of the Board of Governors of the Federal Reserve System less than two months earlier, Volcker also automatically became chairman of the FOMC.

Following a series of financial crises, most notably the Financial Panic of 1907, the Federal Reserve was created in 1913 to be the nation's central bank. The Federal Reserve's statutory task is to execute monetary policy and maintain the stability of the US money supply. The Federal Reserve's primary tools include the *discount rate,* the interest rate the Federal Reserve charges for loans it makes directly to member banks and setting a target range for the *federal funds rate,* the interest rate member banks charge for lending excess bank reserves they have on deposit with the Federal Reserve. The discount rate and the federal funds rate influence the *prime rate*—the interest rate banks use to lend to their best customers and a benchmark for setting almost all interest rates used in corporate lending. Even marginal shifts made by the FOMC have immediate and consequential impacts on the level of investment flowing through the US economy.

Under Volcker's leadership, the Federal Reserve unequivocally declared war on inflation. The unprecedented October 6 meeting raised the discount rate by a full percentage point, only the second time in history the FOMC had made such a large move at a single meeting. At 12 percent, the new discount rate was the highest ever set. Simultaneously, the FOMC dramatically widened the target range for the federal funds rate. Prior to the October 6 meeting, the target for the federal funds rate was a narrow half-percentage point range between 11¼ and 11¾ percent. The FOMC opened the target range to an unprecedented four hundred basis points, a four-percentage point range between 11½ percent and 15½ percent.

The historic interest rate hikes and other monetary policies announced that day were a sharp break with the Fed's standing practice of moderation. Over the preceding decades, the Federal Reserve had adopted a de facto policy of gradualism in monetary policy, deliberately avoiding rapid shifts that could potentially unsettle markets. Discarding even the pretense of gradual change, the FOMC was deliberately applying shock treatment to financial markets. During the meeting, Chairman Volcker argued that the Fed's tradition of only making incremental changes had "run out of psychological gas."[2] The moves were immediately labeled the Fed's "Saturday Night Massacre" in anticipation of their unavoidable economic consequences on the nation's economy.

Persistent inflation notwithstanding, the Pittsburgh region's economy appeared to be strengthening as the end of the 1970s drew closer. Regional wage levels were rising in both nominal and real terms, and the regional workforce had recently reached new peak employment levels. "Job rate sets record in district," declared a February 1979 headline as the Pittsburgh metropolitan region recorded total employment of over 1.1 million for the first time in January 1979.[3]

More than most other regions, Pittsburgh workers were protected from the impact of rampant inflation so much in the news. Guaranteed cost-of-living adjustments were codified for steelworkers by the experimental negotiating agreement agreed to between the United Steel Workers of America and major steelmakers earlier in the decade. High levels of unionization in the public and private sectors meant cost-of-living adjustments were replicated by most collective bargaining agreements in the region, ensuring that wages more than kept pace with rising prices. In 1970, the average earnings per job in the Pittsburgh metropolitan statistical area was moderately higher (+5 percent) than national levels. By 1979, the average earnings per job for the region had improved to 14 percent above national levels. Public sentiment reflected the economic conditions across the region. A 1979 *Pittsburgh Post-Gazette* survey found that just 3 percent of the public considered unemployment a major problem in the Pittsburgh area, far less than the 65 percent who considered "road and street conditions" the region's most pressing problem.[4]

Still, the Federal Reserve decided inflation must be brought lower, and the only way to force that to happen was to dramatically slow the nation's economy. As the FOMC began its October 6 meeting, economic indicators had yet to signal the United States had entered into a new recession. Following the meeting, few expected that a recession could be avoided. Higher interest rates quickly choked off access to financial capital, collapsing rates of new investment and creating even greater declines in steel demand. The federal funds rate reached 14 percent by the end of 1979 and peaked at 17.6 percent the following April.[5] Interest rates for most corporate and consumer borrowing reached even higher. Higher interest rates also increased the international demand for the US dollar, pushing up its value against other major currencies, making US exports less competitive in foreign markets, dooming efforts to increase the steel industry's competitiveness overseas. The resulting drop in both domestic and international orders compounded to create an immediate economic crisis for US industries.

Layoffs

The investment climate across the United States was turned on its head. Within weeks, U.S. Steel announced the closing of sixteen plants nationwide, resulting in more than thirteen thousand layoffs. The facilities to be closed were spread across the nation, but the only Pittsburgh-area facilities directly affected were the Ambridge and Shiffler plants of the corporation's American Bridge division, which traced its roots to Andrew Carnegie's Keystone Bridge Company, founded in Pittsburgh in 1865. Located in Pittsburgh's Lawrenceville neighborhood, the Shiffler plant employed fewer than three hundred workers at the time. Both plants concentrated in bridge fabrication, a business that had been slowing for years following elevated rates of infrastructure investment during the 1960s. The corporation declared a $808 million loss based on the book value of the plants being shut down. Even if the losses were mostly in the form of capital write-offs, the company's $561.7 million loss in the fourth quarter of 1979 was, at the time, the single worst quarterly loss ever recorded by a US corporation. U.S. Steel reported a $293 million loss for the year, its worst performance ever.

Just a few years earlier, US steel producers were struggling to expand production fast enough to meet growing domestic and international demand. In 1976, U.S. Steel announced plans to invest more than $2 billion to construct an entirely new steel plant at Conneaut, Ohio, on Lake Erie at the Pennsylvania–Ohio border. The lakeside location reflected U.S. Steel's intention to expand sales in global markets. The Great Lakes provided ready access to the iron ore supplies being shipped across the Great Lakes, but it was also an ideal port for exporting steel via the Saint Lawrence Seaway, which connected the Great Lakes and the North Atlantic. Persistent inflation had depreciated the value of the dollar, making US products more competitive in foreign markets and buttressing US manufacturers' hope they could reverse trade losses that had been growing since the 1960s. Just months after U.S. Steel finally received the necessary permit to begin construction of the Conneaut Plant in May 1979, the Fed's dramatic actions eviscerated the project's economic justification.

Virtually on schedule, the nation entered a new recession at the beginning of 1980. The economic downturn sparked by the Federal Reserve's anti-inflation measures was historically severe but remarkably short. Officially lasting only between January and July of that year, the contraction was the sharpest in half a century. US gross national product (GNP) declined in the second quarter by 7.8 percent, the economy's worst quarterly performance since the end of the Great Depression.[6]

Despite the severity of the brief recession, initial signs reinforced hopes for a rapid economic rebound. The nation's GNP decline abated to a modest 0.7 percent drop for the third quarter of 1980 and then recorded an extremely robust 7.6 percent growth in the first quarter of 1981. The rebound was strong enough that even those plants on the short list of Pittsburgh facilities slated for closure by U.S. Steel in 1979 were spared. Following a vote on wage concessions by workers at the two plants, U.S. Steel announced on December 30 that American Bridge plants at Ambridge and Pittsburgh would remain open and retain all workers. Pittsburgh began the 1980s with the core of its historic industrial heritage unscathed.

The steel industry—and thus Pittsburgh—benefitted from the ongoing energy crisis at the root of the nation's persistent inflation. Higher energy prices generated sustained new investments in energy exploration and development, spiking the demand for tubular steel products needed by both the oil and gas industries. Even through the worst of the 1980 recession, Pittsburgh-based steel facilities producing tubular products operated at near capacity.

Strong demand for tubular products was also the primary force behind a new wave of investments planned across the steel industry. Two companies based in Houston, Hunt Energy and the Quanex Corporation, planned to reopen the former Jones & Laughlin (J&L) Brier Hill plant in nearby Youngstown, Ohio, to produce tubular products.[7] In McKeesport, U.S. Steel's National Tube Division was operating nearly continuously, straining to even keep up with its current order book. Ignoring the national recession, the plant had even brought on fifteen hundred additional workers between 1980 and 1981. Late in 1981, a record 4,350 oil rigs were operating in the southeastern United States, each the front end of a long supply chain needing new steel pipe at every step. Steel industry executives believed the industry could not fully meet the demand for tubular products "for at least a decade."[8] It would prove to be a very unwarranted extrapolation.

Unmet demand for steel pipe justified U.S. Steel's decision to build a new tubular mill at its Fairfield Works, near Birmingham, Alabama. The decision not to expand U.S. Steel's tubular operations at McKeesport would have been more foreboding in Pittsburgh if the mill were not operating at capacity. The lack of space to expand near McKeesport—an enduring liability for southwestern Pennsylvania's industrial facilities—was one of the reasons the new investment was forced to go elsewhere. Also, the Alabama location was closer to the sources of pipe demand along the Gulf Coast. Geography, once the guarantor of southwestern Pennsylvania's economic competitiveness, had become a distinct disadvantage.

Hoarding cash, U.S. Steel entered into a unique "taker-pay" agreement with customers to finance the planned expansion of tubular capacity. A total of fourteen customers fronted $1 billion for the construction of the corporation's new Alabama plant. So tight were tubular markets that producers like U.S. Steel could extract such extraordinary concessions from customers. In return, the deal guaranteed the customer-investors continuous supplies of steel pipe. With the new capacity not expected to come online until later in the decade and existing U.S. Steel facilities unable to meet existing demand for tubular products, the company entered a five-year agreement with the Italian firm Dalmine to import steel pipe into the United States.[9]

Tubular operations powered U.S. Steel's quick return to profitability in 1980. In January 1981, the corporation announced that it had earned $504 million over the previous year. The corporation's historic losses the previous year had mostly been paper losses generated from capital write-downs, but profits earned in 1980 brought in significant new cash. The corporation ended 1980 with $1.3 billion in cash on hand, but little of that ever went into capital improvements at any of its legacy steel operations.[10]

Reversing monetary policies of the previous fall, the Federal Reserve soon hastened a return to growth. By May 1980, with inflation showing signs of moderating, the Federal Reserve began cutting the discount and worked to loosen money supply via other measures. The moves facilitated the quick economic rebound from the recession monetary policy had clearly induced. By the end of the year, idled workers had been recalled at virtually all of the steel plants of southwestern Pennsylvania. By February 1981, the Edgar Thomson Works, which had seen half its workforce idled six months earlier, recalled all of its workers.[11] In June 1981, the American Iron and Steel Institute (AISI) issued a report, "Steel at the Crossroads: One Year Later," which optimistically concluded that the rate of steel plant modernization was improving and that any decline in the nation's steel industry was turning around rapidly.[12]

Any brief resurgence in the regional economy quickly evaporated as the Federal Reserve renewed its battle against inflation. When inflation failed to decline late in 1980, the Federal Reserve saw it as a threat to the economy and its credibility as the nation's monetary authority.[13] Starting in July 1980, the Fed restarted aggressively raising the discount rate. The prime rate reached an all-time peak of 21.5 percent in December 1980, while the national average for residential mortgages reached over 18 percent in September 1981. Like the 1980 recession, the follow-on recession of 1981 was easily predicted.

Officially, the second recession of the 1980s began in July 1981, exactly a year after the previous one had ended. The nation's economy continued to contract for the next sixteen months. Officially ending only in November 1982, the period tied with the recession that stretched between November 1973 and March 1975 as the longest since the Great Depression. For the steel industry and Pittsburgh, it would be a much longer period before economic growth returned. Employment levels in the Pittsburgh region took not sixteen months but sixteen years to return to their pre-1981 peaks.

The new recession soon produced another precipitous drop in industrial orders. Over the weekend of November 6–7, 1981, most of the Homestead Works went idle, the plant's first complete shutdown since the national steel strike of 1959. Many of the plant's workers were laid off for the first time in their careers.[14] On December 30, U.S. Steel announced the Edgar Thomson Works in Braddock was shutting down. A total of 650 plant workers were already on layoff, and the new announcement meant 1,000 of their coworkers would join them. Yet, both plant closures were expected to be temporary; hundreds of workers remained on the job at each facility for maintenance and winterization. Executives expected the plants to restart in the near future, and workers expected to be recalled. It was becoming clear that the 1981 slump was at least "as steep, or steeper than the industry's plunge in the summer of 1980."[15] New layoffs were the beginning of an economic contraction unlike cyclical downturns of the recent past. Unlike past practices, few workers were given a definite recall dates as they were laid off.

The manufacturing-centered downturn only reinforced U.S. Steel's plan to transform itself into something other than a steel company. The corporation had already begun to limit new investments and was building cash reserves in anticipation of a major corporate acquisition. The corporation accumulated cash by selling legacy assets in coal reserves and earning another $975 million in the first nine months of 1981. By September, the corporation held $2.5 billion in cash and an additional $3 billion in bank lines of credit, for a total $5.5 billion working capital—the equivalent of $19 billion in 2025.[16]

Why the corporation was hoarding cash soon became apparent. On November 19, 1981, U.S. Steel announced plans to purchase Marathon Oil, the nation's seventeenth largest oil company. The $6.2 billion deal drew down most of the corporation's cash and forced it to take on $3 billion in new debt. Mobil Oil, the nation's second-largest oil producer, had offered $5 billion in a hostile attempt to acquire Marathon three weeks earlier. U.S. Steel's cash reserve allowed it to outbid Mobil and purchase outright 51 percent of Marathon's stock; the remaining 49 percent was exchanged for shares of U.S. Steel. Just after midnight on January 7, 1982, $3.7 billion worth of checks to seventeen thousand Marathon shareholders were mailed out to consummate the deal.[17] So intent was Mobil to acquire Marathon that the larger corporation briefly considered making a bid to acquire all of U.S. Steel just to take ownership of Mobil's assets.[18] Buying Marathon was not a marginal diversification for U.S. Steel but a deliberate decision to morph the corporation into an entirely different industry. A U.S. Steel executive described the transaction as the firm "electing to swallow a whale."[19] U.S. Steel was not abandoning Pittsburgh as much as it was abandoning the steel industry.

In January 1982, total employment across the US steel industry dropped to 254,000 hourly workers, 45 percent fewer than the 453,000 on the job just three years earlier, and the lowest total since the AISI began monthly tracking of industry employment totals in 1933. The national recession affected all sectors of the economy but had dire consequences for heavy manufacturing industries. There was no escape for Pittsburgh, which remained one of the nation's most concentrated steel regions. In February 1982, unemployment in the Pittsburgh metropolitan area topped 18 percent as the official count of unemployed workers in the region peaked at over 210,000, three times the region's average of 70,000 unemployed through the 1970s.

Closures

As poorly as the economy was faring across western Pennsylvania in early 1982, conditions could have been much worse and soon would be. Demand for the tubular steel products needed by the oil industry remained strong through the very end of 1981. Despite layoffs at other plants, over 90 percent of the workers at U.S. Steel's National Tube Works in McKeesport remained on the job in December 1981. The Fed's growth-inhibiting policies had a secondary impact, effectively ending the energy boom that had continued to generate orders for the steel industry. Energy prices at first stabilized and then retreated from the lofty levels they had sustained through the successive energy crises of the previous decade. The oil shortages that had begat two national recessions in the 1970s turned to an oil glut by 1982. The price of oil dropped from its historic peak in 1979—$39.50 per barrel, equivalent to over $170 per barrel in 2025. Soon, the price fell below its inflation-adjusted rate of a decade earlier. Energy prices were beginning what eventually became a twenty-year slide. Lower oil prices translated directly to lower investment across the energy sector and a collapse in the demand for tubular steel products that had continued to sustain Pittsburgh plants.

In March 1982, major operations at U.S. Steel's National Tube Works in McKeesport shut down, laying off twenty-four hundred of the plant's forty-eight hundred workers.[20] Bravely, Vice President George Bush visited the closed plant that month, only to be met by hundreds of protesting workers. He assured the workers that President Reagan's economic policies would eventually work to turn the situation around for the industry.[21] He did not explain whether his prognostication applied to the economy of the Mon Valley or more to the steel industry broadly. The same month, the J&L subsidiary of LTV laid off most workers at its Aliquippa pipe works. Virtually overnight, tubular producers went from near-capacity production levels to "the lowest shipment level in over 40 years" during 1982.[22] One reporter summarized the declining demand for tubular products as the "steel industry's last defense starting to crack."[23]

The US steel industry only slowly began to move past denial, accepting that its growth phase had ended. At the AISI's 1982 annual meeting—held as it had been every year since 1908 in New York's Waldorf Astoria Hotel—U.S. Steel's chairman David Roderick made clear how traumatic recent history had been for the steel industry: "We have been shocked out of our complacency and smugness. We now realize that American industry has no manifest destiny to be always first, always right, always best."[24]

The dour message was still not fully accepted in Pittsburgh. Workers "had seen downturns before, and the business had always come back. They didn't realize this was a different scene."[25] Nonetheless, by 1983, regional employment in primary metals industries had dropped to under 62,000 jobs, down from over 100,000 just four years earlier. [26] The scale of decline was remarkably close to what the *Economic Study of the Pittsburgh Region* had predicted more than two decades earlier. So dire was the state of the steel industry that some considered that it might need to be nationalized to save it, the fate of the British steel industry in 1951 and again in 1967. If not outright ownership, some form of federal bailout was expected by business leaders who believed: "No way we can afford to let a vital defense industry go the way of energy in the 1970s."[27] Unlike later examples of federal bailouts of major US firms, no such federal support was on its way. Both the steel industry and the economy of greater Pittsburgh would be left to their own devices to deal with escalating levels of job destruction.

Still, at the end of 1982, local workers believed the majority of plant closings across the region were expected to be temporary. Much like in past cyclical downturns, layoffs may have been labeled indefinite, but few workers doubted they would eventually be recalled. Most plants kept skeleton crews at work maintaining equipment, ensuring operations could restart as soon as economic conditions rebounded. Pittsburgh was only beginning to realize that many of its shuttered plants would never operate again. In April 1982, Carnegie Mellon University economist Mariann O'Nan was a rare and contrary voice publicly acknowledging the region's predicament: "We're in for a period of dislocation. Carbon steelmaking in this part of the country will never be what it was. That's all over."[28]

1983 marked a decisive turnaround as the United States emerged from recession. The nation's inflation-adjusted GNP growth exceeded 7.8 percent, but decline decisively continued for the Pittsburgh region. In December, U.S. Steel announced a new wave of plant closures. The corporation planned to permanently close thirty additional facilities across the nation. In Pittsburgh, the U.S. Steel's Shiffler facility and the larger Ambridge Works—both of which had been saved from closing in 1979—were again slated to close. Also marked for shutdown was the Johnstown Works, sixty miles east of Pittsburgh. Larger layoffs were announced for the Homestead, Duquesne, and Edgar Thomson Works, but the plants were still expected to return to operation in the future.

1983 began a rapid acceleration of the physical deconstruction of Pittsburgh's industrial infrastructure. The 270-foot blast furnace at the LTV's Second Avenue Works—idled since 1979—was felled by explosives on June 15, 1983. J&L had operated the iconic blast furnace within eyesight of Downtown Pittsburgh since 1899. A former worker observing the destruction made a self-evident comment: "If you don't have a plant to work at, then you can't call the men back. This is the end of it all."[29]

Economic news for Pittsburgh was only getting worse as corporate disclosures began to catch up with the inevitable. In May, steel production at LTV's historic South Side Works ended. Still, the company briefly maintained the fiction that swing operations would be kept on to restart the plant in the future.[30] In June 1984, U.S. Steel announced plans to permanently close all of the historic Duquesne Works and not continue operation of the plant's electric furnaces as was previously announced. In July, the Westinghouse Corporation announced closure of facilities in Sharon, Pennsylvania, fifty miles north of Pittsburgh, and a nearby plant in Greenville, Mercer County. Steelmaking operations at U.S. Steel's Clairton works were shut down by the end the year, continuing only its coke-making operations. Lingering hopes for a return to past levels of steel industry employment and output became hard to justify.

1985 did not bring any reprieve. In February, LTV ceased operations at the former J&L plant in Aliquippa, where more than ninety-two hundred workers had been fully employed just two years earlier.[31] In October, U.S. Steel announced it was closing the 160-inch plate mill at its Homestead Works, the core of the plant's production since it was built on the site by the Defense Plant Corporation in World War II, shut down in 1985—effectively ending the site's long history as a fully integrated steel mill.[32]

As regional manufacturing continued to contract, news of individual plant closures was superseded by corporate bankruptcies of the firms that owned them. In April 1985, Wheeling-Pittsburgh, Pittsburgh's third biggest steel producer, filed for Chapter 11 bankruptcy. Listing debts exceeding $500 million, the company forfeited its modern steel-rail mill to the US Economic Development Administration, which it owed between $80 and $90 million. The loans were part of $161 million in federal loan guarantees the company had received to finance a series of upgrades and expansions to its plants in 1979.[33] During its bankruptcy reorganization, the company sought to void existing contracts with workers. Workers at the plant went on strike in July, the first major steel strike in Pittsburgh since 1959. The plant never operated again and closed permanently in September 1986.

In September 1985, the Armco Corporation laid off twelve hundred workers at its Ambridge pipe-making facility, which had been in operation for over seventy-two years. Limited parts of the Homestead Works continued to operate at the beginning of 1986, but the final heat of steel at the site was produced in May. The last skeleton crew departed in July—over 106 years after the site began operation.[34]

Ironically, the unemployment rate in the Pittsburgh region ended 1985 below 10 percent after having been stuck in double digits for nearly three years. The decline was attributed not to any meaningful improvement in regional labor market conditions but the escalating discouragement of laid-off workers. The standard definition of unemployment at the time was nearly identical to what it remains today. Population surveys ask jobless individuals if they are currently seeking employment. Those who want jobs but who have not been actively seeking employment are not counted among the unemployed but rather are classified as discouraged workers. With so many steelworkers seeking employment, many quickly abandoned their efforts to look for new jobs. Younger workers had the best chance to move into new occupations or industries. Regarding older industrial workers who remained in Pittsburgh, according to a *Los Angeles Times* article, "there is a whole generation of people who can't make the transition."[35] Even as the region's unemployment rate moderated, Pittsburgh would be left with a surfeit of prime working-age but discouraged workers.

Virtually none of Pittsburgh's shuttered steel plants ever recalled sizable numbers of their former workers. Though the rate of job loss slowed, industrial contraction continued through the end of the decade. Once flush with demand for tubular products, U.S. Steel permanently closed its National Works in McKeesport in 1987. The beginning of the end for the plant was a work stoppage that extended from August 1, 1986, until February 2, 1987. U.S. Steel called it a strike; the United Steelworkers called it a lockout. Three days after the dispute ended, U.S. Steel announced the indefinite closing of the mill. Two months later, it declared that the plant would never reopen.

Plant closings and mass layoffs through the 1980s were not limited to older facilities or those in heavy industries. The Pullman-Standard Company had operated a plant producing railcars in Butler County, north of Pittsburgh, since 1902. The plant shut down in 1982, leaving 2,500 workers—nearly 20 percent of Butler County's entire manufacturing workforce—without jobs. In 1987, the Westinghouse Corporation announced plans to shut down its historic East Pittsburgh plant, which had specialized in the production of electrical generators, transformers, and turbines for more than ninety-four years. Later that year, the Volkswagen Corporation announced its much newer automobile assembly plant in New Stanton would close within a year. Opened to great fanfare in 1978, the plant employed more than 6,000 workers at its peak. When the last car rolled off the production line in July 1988, the plant's remaining 2,450 workers were laid off.[36]

Corporate machinations far beyond Pittsburgh conspired to eviscerate even more of the region's economic base. In 1984, Standard Oil of California acquired the Gulf Oil Company, forming Chevron. Unfortunately for Pittsburgh, the new corporation located its headquarters in southern California. The Gulf Building in Pittsburgh was abandoned quickly, as were the expansive research labs Gulf had maintained in suburban Pittsburgh since the 1920s. More than three thousand Gulf employees worked at the corporation's headquarters Downtown as late as 1981, and an additional six hundred workers were employed at the company's research and development complex. By 1986, no sizable Gulf operations remained active in Pittsburgh.

The largest plant closings only begin to describe the economic losses that extended across the region. Pittsburgh had as mature an agglomeration of industrial output as existed anywhere in the world. The long history of manufacturing in the region resulted in extensive networks of specialized suppliers dependent on orders from the region's industrial plants. Once the massive industrial plants closed, there were unavoidable losses of jobs up and down the supply chain. Even more losses resulted from the depressed expenditures of workers permanently laid off from the only jobs many ever expected to hold. Each plant's workforce fueled an entire localized economy, as workers spent the bulk of

Major closures across southwestern Pennsylvania, 1980–1989

1982	American Bridge	Ambridge Works
1982	Pullman Standard	Butler County
1982	Crucible Steel	Midland
1982	Dravo	Neville Island shipyard
1983	American Bridge	Schiffler Plant, Lawrenceville
1984	American Bridge	Ambridge Plant
1984	U.S. Steel	Carrie Furnaces
1984	LTV (Formerly J&L)	Aliquippa Works
1984	U.S. Steel	Clairton Works (Partial)
1984	U.S. Steel	Duquesne Works
1985	Armco	Ambridge Works
1985	Gulf Oil	Downtown Headquarters/Gulf Labs (Harmar)
1986	LTV (Formerly J&L)	South Side Works
1986	U.S. Steel	Homestead Works
1986	Wheeling-Pittsburgh	Monessen Works
1987	U.S. Steel	National Works, McKeesport
1988	Westinghouse	East Pittsburgh
1988	Volkswagen	New Stanton Plant

their incomes within nearby communities. Economists call this the induced impact of economic changes, a multiplier of the direct job losses. No sector of the Pittsburgh economy was immune from the cascading economic miasma.

For all the economic losses concentrated in Pittsburgh and much of American US heavy industry, there was one major success. The Federal Reserve had beaten back inflation. Following the rebound of inflation in 1981, the Fed took its time before pulling back from its aggressive policies throttling the economy. The federal funds rate was kept above 10 percent for twenty-six months, between August 1980 and October 1982, by far the longest period it had ever remained in double digits. Lest a hint of inflation in 1983 get out of hand, the rate was briefly pushed up again to peak at 11¾ percent over the summer of 1984. No quarter was given to the ghost of inflation still lurking in the economy.

Volcker's firehose of monetary policy eventually achieved its intended goal.[37] By 1982, the nation's inflation rate had been cut in half, to 6 percent; by 1983, it had been cut in half again, to 3 percent, a low rate enabled in no small part by the extended recessions the nation had endured. The Fed's victory was complete when the inflation rate reached a multidecade low annual rate of 1.1 percent in November 1986.

At the end of the 1980s, southwestern Pennsylvania retained only a fraction of the steel production it hosted just a decade earlier. Two of the three plants that had once formed the core of Carnegie's industrial empire, the Homestead Works and the Duquesne Works, were permanently shuttered, as were ten other integrated steel plants across the Pittsburgh region. A few facilities had already been demolished, including most of the structures at LTV's steelmaking operation in Hazelwood, but actual deconstruction had not begun on most sites at the beginning of 1990. In most cases, the industrial artifacts remained in place at their former sites awaiting repurposing yet to be conceived, let alone financed.

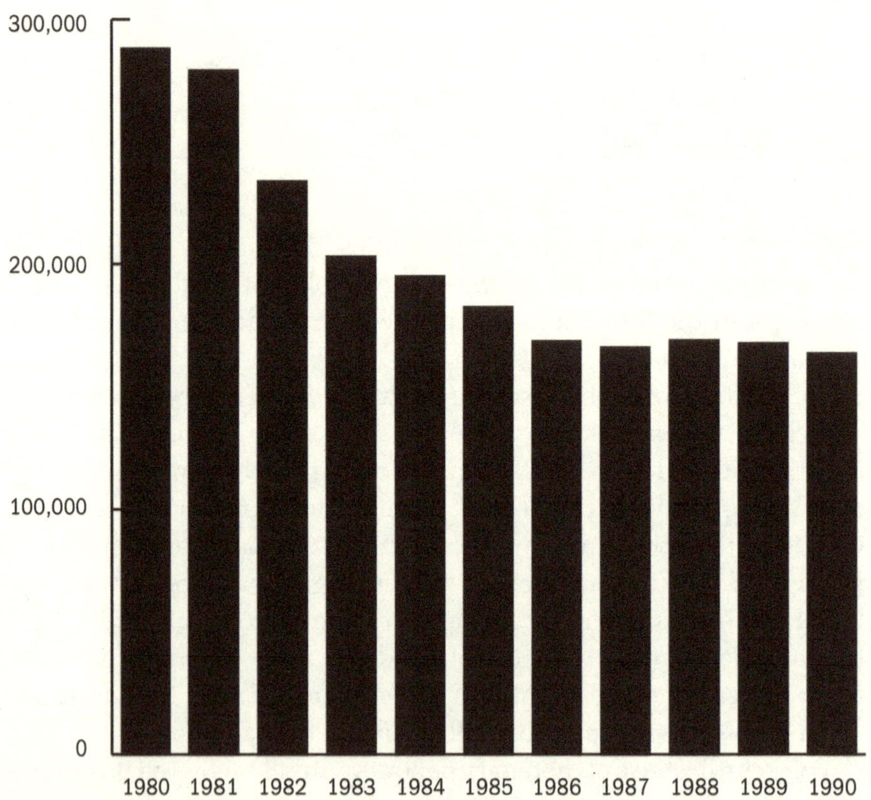

Southwestern Pennsylvania manufacturing employment, 1980–90

At mid-decade, the yet-to-be demolished structures proved to be a foil for a passing campaign theme when presidential candidate Walter Mondale said President Reagan was "turning our great industrial Midwest and the industrial base of this country into a rust bowl." Journalists soon morphed the turn of phrase into an indelible moniker: the US Rust Belt.[38]

At the beginning of the 1980s, U.S. Steel remained the largest employer in southwestern Pennsylvania, as it had been since it was formed eight decades earlier. Over the decade, the firm's local employment dropped from over thirty-six thousand workers to under seven thousand. The corporation was a fraction of the industrial behemoth created by J. P. Morgan. The Jones & Laughlin Corporation—long the largest employer in the city of Pittsburgh—virtually abandoned the region entirely by the end of the 1980s. Only the former J&L coke works in Hazelwood—the last basic steel operation within the corporate limits of the city of Pittsburgh—continued to operate at the beginning of the 1990s.

As the regional unemployment rate peaked at over 18 percent, subareas with even greater concentrations of manufacturing industries suffered

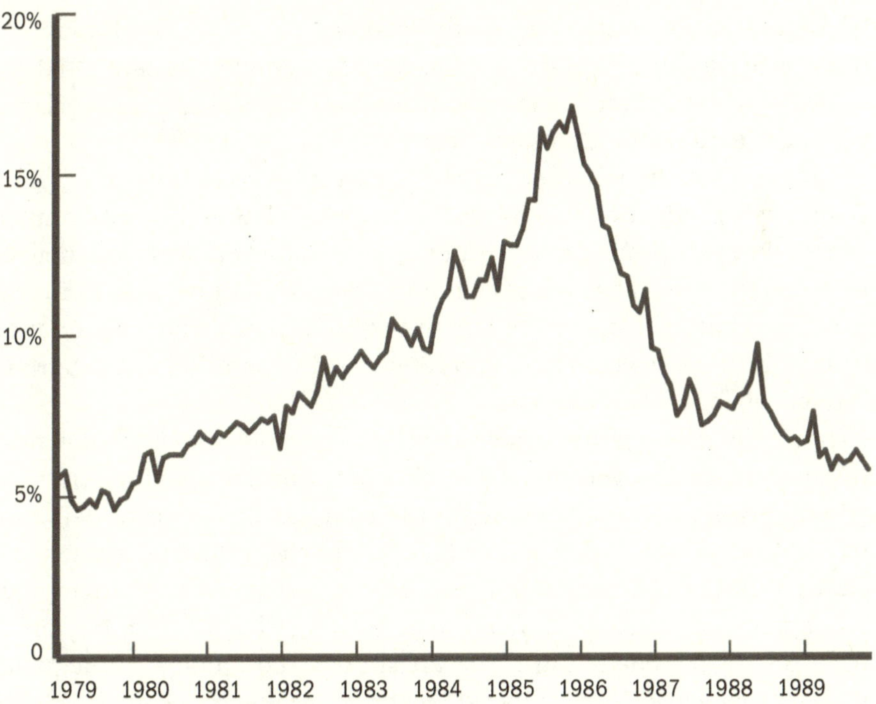

Pittsburgh Region unemployment rate, 1980–90

far higher rates. Unemployment in Beaver County—where heavy industry hugged the banks of the Ohio River—had dipped to 7.4 percent in August 1981. Just seventeen months later, in January 1983, the county recorded an unemployment rate of 28 percent, higher than most states' peak rates during the Great Depression.

Throughout the decade, cascading job losses became the primary issue facing government and community leaders across the region. Stopping the job loss, or at the very least slowing the rate of plant closures, was the universal goal of public policy. Yet few tools were available for public officials in the face of such widespread economic change. They struggled to find ways to respond to the growing joblessness. Given the dire economic conditions, most small communities could barely maintain basic services. Few had any discretionary resources to dedicate to new economic development initiatives of any kind.

Even limited measures to mitigate the economic damage being inflicted on the region proved beyond the capability of most local governments. In 1983, the city of Pittsburgh—the single largest municipality in western Pennsylvania—enacted a new municipal law requiring employers to provide public notice before mass layoffs could take effect. The legislation required 90 days' notice for layoffs of 50 to 100 employees, 180 days' notice for layoffs of between 101 and 500 employees, and 270 days' notice of layoffs of more than 500 workers. The local law was declared void in litigation later that same year.

City officials then focused on saving just 130 jobs at the Clark Candy Company's production facility on the city's North Side. The city council resorted to threatening a boycott of Clark products if jobs were not retained in the city.[39] They were temporarily saved—only because a Finnish firm purchased the operation late in 1985. The new owners abandoned its city facility two years later and remained in operation at a suburban Pittsburgh for a few more years.[40]

Local government in southwestern Pennsylvania, which has the most fragmented local government structure in the nation, had little fiscal or administrative capacity to take on the complex problems of deindustrialization. A 1986 survey of local leaders in the industrial Mon Valley showed that over 61 percent of respondents believed "local unemployment problems were too difficult to be solved by local and county organizations."[41] Outside of the city of Pittsburgh, the average municipality in southwestern Pennsylvania held fewer than eight thousand residents in 1980 and far fewer by the end of the decade. Many municipalities suffered severe fiscal distress as their former tenant industries closed and their resident workers remained unemployed. Neither municipalities nor counties had anywhere near the resources to ameliorate the suffering of laid-off workers, let alone attempt meaningful economic development to attract or retain new industries. Resources for new economic development initiatives had to come from elsewhere.

The breadth of job loss translated to severe fiscal crises for virtually all local governments across the region. Many of those boroughs, townships, and even cities were creations of the region's industrial geography. Each prototypical mill town had little or no economic diversification almost by design; they were in many ways extensions of the plants themselves. For each plant that closed, an entire community lost its economic base.

Some of the Mon Valley towns that had birthed the modern steel industry were the hardest hit. Homestead was chartered as a borough in 1880, the year ground was broken to build the future Homestead Works. Like so many other mill towns, it is unlikely the municipality would have ever existed independently for so long if not for the plant. Even before the mill shut down permanently, the continuing downturn put great stress on the municipal finances. The town's fiscal distress became dire once the plant closed for good in 1986. In August, West Homestead municipal employees were pooling donations to purchase state lottery tickets, in the hope that a payout could cover mounting municipal deficits.[42]

Official unemployment rate statistics only begin to capture the scale of distress forced on the region's former mill towns. In one Aliquippa neighborhood, a 1986 study found that 54 percent of heads of households were unemployed.[43] McKeesport—the largest municipality in the once hyper-industrialized Mon Valley—experienced an official unemployment rate of 22.8 percent in January 1983. The concentration of discouraged workers who had given up seeking work meant actual underemployment rates were incalculably higher. A 1986 study of three Mon Valley communities—Clairton, McKeesport, and Duquesne—found the suicide rate of residents twice the comparable national rate.[44]

Dour social conditions persisted long after local jobs disappeared. Maintaining basic municipal services required municipalities to raise most tax rates as corporate and property tax revenues declined. Homeowners in declining mill towns found themselves caught in a "vise of falling market prices and high prices" that made their communities even "less desirable for stable, energetic families looking for homes."[45] The spiral of decline extended depressed conditions in most former mill towns long after the nation, or even the greater Pittsburgh region, emerged from recession. Even in 1993, a decade after the peak of the regional jobs losses, a journalistic survey of conditions in the Mon Valley left little to be optimistic about: "The industrial towns that line southwestern Pennsylvania's rivers have become the region's Third World, increasingly disadvantaged and increasingly unable to take care of themselves."[46]

The shock of the cataclysmic economic losses Pittsburgh faced through the 1980s was magnified by strong economic conditions, and even more optimistic prognostications, that had preceded it. Regional wages climbed through the 1970s in both absolute terms and when compared to other metropolitan regions. The concentration of new building in Downtown Pittsburgh through the 1970s, collectively known as Pittsburgh's Renaissance II, only reinforced the casual observation that Pittsburgh's economy was strong and rapidly evolving.

Famed Hungarian American photojournalist Stefan Lorant spent a decade authoring a history of the city first released in 1968. Subsequent editions included coverage of the changes ongoing through the 1970s. In the last chapter of the third edition, published in 1980, the new developments were described with nary a premonition of what the future held for Pittsburgh: "The exuberant feeling of the first Renaissance is back. Pittsburgh is once more on the march. Its future looks golden."[47] At the time few contrary voices made themselves known.

Eventually, a new equilibrium emerged in Pittsburgh, as unemployment rates dropped and employment levels stabilized. The industrial firms that survived looked toward the future. In 1991, union negotiators pressured USX to install a modern $250 million continuous caster at its Edger Thomson Works in Braddock, ensuring its competitiveness over coming decades.[48] Pittsburgh's steel industry evolved, retaining a core of specialty steel producers, along with a professional services and consulting industry that increased its sales to steel producers globally.[49] The bulk of metal manufacturing that survived in the region at the end of the century was not in the bulk "tonnage steel" that had long concentrated in Pittsburgh but specialty steel, including titanium steel and related alloys. Still, the employment levels across all regional metals industries never reached a fraction of past peaks.

Whether steelmaking in southwestern Pennsylvania needed to collapse as rapidly as it did is an open question. That Pittsburgh had lost much of its competitiveness as a steelmaking region is undeniable. For decades, production had emerged across entirely new regions across the nation. The geographic shift was much the result of the continuing expansion of minimill-based steel production.[50] Once limited in the range of products they could produce, minimills continued to innovate. In 1989, Nucor developed a new steelmaking technology that enabled it to compete in the flat-roll carbon-sheet and strip-steel market—considered the "last bastion" of competitiveness for integrated steelmakers.[51]

No new minimill started up in Pittsburgh at any point through the 1970s or 1980s. Only in 1994 was $20 million in state funding committed to support Pittsburgh's first minimill project. The irony that public money was needed to induce steel investment in Pittsburgh was not mentioned, nor was the lack of involvement by any Pittsburgh firm. The project was undertaken not by any of Pittsburgh's historic steel firms but by a virtually unknown one: WorldClass Processing, Inc.—a small, privately held venture that had only started up as a steel fabricator two years earlier.[52] Unable to find the additional funding needed for the project, the company failed to start a new plant that had been slated to be located in Ambridge, along the Ohio River. Even if it had been built, the four hundred jobs envisioned paled in comparison to the thousands of jobs that had been lost at each of the integrated steel operations that once defined Pittsburgh.

No groundbreaking also ever took place for the new Conneaut "supermill" U.S. Steel was planning through the 1970s. A 3,331-acre portion of the site was later sold to the Mellon Foundation for donation to the Western Pennsylvania Conservancy. The Pennsylvania Game Commission took ownership of most of the site in July 1991, and the site was named, ironically, for U.S. Steel's President David M. Roderick. Roderick had been most responsible for changing U.S. Steel into the hybrid USX Corporation and had presided as chairman during the era when the firm contracted faster than ever before in its history. At the end of the twentieth century, the Roderick Wildlife Preserve, also known as State Game Lands 314, is yet mostly inhabited by deer, turkey, squirrel, pheasant, and coyote. Its position along the Lake Erie shoreline includes a two-plus-mile stretch of bluff that remains the longest piece of undeveloped Lake Erie shoreline between Toledo, Ohio, and Buffalo, New York.[53]

Decades of decline would not end hopes that Pittsburgh would see a resurgence of its steel industry. In 2014, literally three decades after the peak of job destruction in the region's steel industry, a longtime business reporter observer noted, "Steel dreams die hard, especially in the Steel City. Industry skeptics are fond of saying the only way they know a shuttered mill will never come back is if it is shredded for scrap and melted in a furnace. Sometimes, even then they can't be certain."[54]

If you wait for the steel industry to come back, you'll wait forever.

Tony McGann, Regional/ Urban Design Assistance Team, speaking in Homestead, Pennsylvania, February 27, 1988

Dorothy

August 1, 1988

Just before noon, Bob Macey stood along a busy expressway to watch the final moments of a mostly forgotten symbol of the United States' manufacturing decline. Scheduled for demolition was yet another blast furnace the steel industry had located along the banks of the Monongahela River, barely twelve miles upriver from Downtown Pittsburgh. The river and the communities of the Mon Valley had formed the core of the US steel industry for over a century. Barely a mile downriver from where Macey stood, Andrew Carnegie redefined the modern US steel industry in 1875, when the Edgar Thomson Works began operation at Braddock. Just a mile farther downriver stood the former Homestead Works, which Carnegie had acquired in 1883 and quickly integrated into his growing business.

Demolition was technically on real estate still part of U.S. Steel's Duquesne Works, though the nominal owner had virtually abandoned the site years earlier. The blast furnaces at Duquesne, along with those at Braddock and Homestead, once formed the foundation of Andrew Carnegie's industrial empire. Macey had worked at the plant for twenty years and was the fourth generation of a family of steelworkers who had worked at the Duquesne Works.[1] When "Taps" played over the public address system four years earlier, he and others wore black armbands as they finished the final shift to operate the plant's primary blast furnace, Dorothy Six.[2] Secondary parts of the plant continued to operate for a few more months, but Dorothy Six would never restart.

U.S. Steel was not the vast enterprise it had been just a few years earlier, and by 1988, the corporation was only marginally a steel company at all. The extant shell of "Big Steel," as U.S. Steel had been known since it was created by J. Pierpont Morgan eighty-seven years earlier, was merely a subsidiary on the short end of its parent company's business plan. Corporate survival instincts had induced the quintessential steel company to move decisively into entirely new industries. In 1982, U.S. Steel outbid Mobil to buy Marathon Oil, then the nation's seventeenth-largest petroleum producer. The diversified conglomerate had changed its name to the USX Corporation in 1986. In 1990, USX would formally relocate its headquarters to Houston, Texas. Rebuilding the steel production that was the corporation's century-long heritage was no longer a primary goal for the reimagined company.

The communities of the Mon Valley had decidedly different goals. Restarting steel production from the Duquesne Works was the only priority of workers, politicians, and community leaders. With USX decidedly uninterested in restarting the plant and no investors looking to acquire the real estate for any alternative use, the public was about to become the site's investor of last resort. A comprehensive deal had been worked out the year before. USX was planning to turn over the site to the Allegheny County Department of Economic Development. The formal transfer of ownership for the 254-acre site was deferred only until the scheduled demolition was complete. The real estate was then to be immediately vouchsafed to a quasi-public agency, the Regional Industrial Development Corporation (RIDC) of southwestern Pennsylvania, with a goal of transforming it into an industrial park, future tenants yet unknown.

RIDC was originally formed in 1955 but reorganized in 1962 to promote economic development across the greater Pittsburgh region.[3] For a quarter century, its primary mission had been to develop new locations for industrial development in a region so overdeveloped that economic growth was believed to be throttled by a lack of available space. Circumstances across the region had inverted, and the Duquesne Works posed an entirely new challenge. Lack of available industrial space was no longer the problem. Across southwestern Pennsylvania was an oversupply of former industrial sites lacking tenants. Any potential investors, and there were few to be found, had a growing set of choices among the vacant industrial brownfields.

Preparing the site for a future investor was not going to be a simple task. What stood in the way of a vaguely defined future was a surfeit of outsized industrial ephemera anchored in place. What the site would eventually produce was unknown, but that it would not be producing steel had become undeniable. Moving on required, at a minimum, clearing the site and starting over. Deconstruction brought down the twenty-nine-story blast furnace—named Dorothy Six since it began operation in January 1963—that dominated the site. The hope was that the demolition of the blast furnace would cauterize the economic damage its continuing presence was causing the community around it.

The demolition was not the first and would be far from the last to take place in the Mon Valley. In very recent memory, the valley had been home to the greatest concentration of industrial output anywhere on the planet. Over just a few years, the communities that hugged the river had become a collection of shuttered plants, laid-off workers, and poverty not seen in the region since the Great Depression. Yet even the Great Depression eventually came to an end. Plants that had endured years of minimal output or outright cold shutdown during the 1930s eventually returned to near full employment before the United States' entry into World War II. By August 1988, there was little expectation that history would repeat itself. Most of the valley's plants that had shut down over the recent decade were no longer being maintained in anticipation of future work. It was an inconceivable reality that so many plants, which had employed literally generations of local workers, would never recall even a small fraction of their once vast workforces.

This latest episode of industrial démontage was different. The heart and soul of the Duquesne Works was Dorothy Six, the largest blast furnace that ever operated in the Mon Valley. Shut down four years earlier, Dorothy took on an afterlife unlike any of the shuttered plants spread across the US Rust Belt. Unwilling to let corporate decisions define their future, workers, politicians, and entire communities came together to try to take control of the site and bring Dorothy Six back to life. Their battle briefly made the blast furnace a symbol of a US economy struggling to regain the self-determination it had painfully lost.

U.S. Steel showed no interest in keeping the Duquesne Works open and even less in facilitating its continued operation under a new owner. The battle to "Save Dorothy" became an entirely new type of fight. Stakeholders struggled to find a new model of capitalism to take ownership of the site and restart production. Those efforts had proceeded with frenetic intensity from the moment the plant's closure was announced but in the end only delayed the eventuality that finally came in 1988.

Timing, or fate, took from Dorothy Six its last chance to avoid destruction. A group of museum officials and preservation experts toured the Duquesne Works just a week before its demolition on August 1. The team was evaluating the many shuttered industrial sites in the Mon Valley to see which could be preserved merely as historical artifacts.[4] By noon on August 8, there was nothing recognizable left to preserve at Duquesne. Controlled explosions felled Dorothy Six before the preservationist's final report was submitted. The experts pressed on with their assigned task: identifying key historical sites before "physical evidence of Pittsburgh's steel history evaporates." They concluded that efforts should be focused on saving the remaining parts of the neighboring Homestead Works.[5]

Duquesne

In 1988, Duquesne was three years shy of celebrating its centennial. Incorporated in 1891, the municipality only came to exist because of the new steelworks and the population growth that came with it. Over the subsequent century, the fortunes of the plant and the town around it were inseparable, a symbiosis typical for most of the mill towns of the Mon Valley and beyond.

When J. P. Morgan purchased Carnegie Steel, the Duquesne Works became a core asset of the new U.S. Steel conglomerate, which continued to invest in the plant. Two more blast furnaces were added in 1909, bringing the total on site to six. Following World War I, the entire plant underwent a major reconstruction between 1918 and 1924. World War II generated additional investment at the site. A new electric arc furnace was installed in 1943, financed and technically owned by the federal government's Defense Plant Corporation until the Carnegie-Illinois Steel subsidiary of U.S. Steel repurchased the new equipment after the war.

Soon after the end of World War II, the Duquesne Works entered a period of precipitous decline. Much of the plant was placed on standby status because of aging equipment. The state of disrepair of the work's fifty-year-old open-hearth No. 1 steelmaking shop necessitated its complete shutdown in 1949. At a time when electrical power had been commonplace in the industry for decades, the mill's even older primary mill was still powered by steam. Older technologies faced nearly insurmountable difficulties complying with new state and county ordinances aimed at improving air quality in southwestern Pennsylvania. Many expected the

Duquesne Works to begin permanently winding down operations. Workers were unsurprised when plant officials told them, during a company outing at the nearby Kennywood Amusement Park in the early 1950s, that the plant might close permanently.[6]

Ironically, the Duquesne Works saw its life extended by the same environmental regulations that threatened it with closure. Allegheny County's 1949 enactment of smoke control legislation threatened U.S. Steel's ability to produce ferromanganese, a common alloy essential in steelmaking. Ferromanganese was produced at the corporation's Isabella Works in Etna, Clairton Works, and Duquesne Works. An unavoidable byproduct of ferromanganese production was a dense, pyrophoric fume that could not be entirely cleaned by the existing plants. The only way to comply with the new air-quality regulations was to build a new production facility that both cleaned the gas and sintered the flue dust into briquettes.[7] A full-scale system was built at the Duquesne Works in 1953.[8] As a result, the even older Isabella Works, which had operated since 1872, was closed. In 1958, the most complete metallurgical testing laboratory in the steel industry was built on the site, and the latest in computerized controls were installed to operate the plant. Alone among the steel plants operating in the Mon Valley, the Duquesne Works was capable of producing sophisticated steel products needed by the rapidly expanding aerospace industry.

In 1960, U.S. Steel announced an even greater reinvestment at the Duquesne Works. A new blast furnace to be built on site was slated to become the largest in the world, and the very first basic oxygen process furnace to be built by U.S. Steel. US steel producers, and U.S. Steel, in particular, had been slow to adopt the new technology which was revolutionizing steel production worldwide.

Dorothy, as the new furnace was universally known, became more than a nickname. The moniker came from Dorothy Helen Rice Worthington, wife of U.S. Steel president Leslie Worthington, who christened the furnace when it began operating in 1963. Worthington had been appointed president in November 1959, just as the corporation resolved a 116-day national strike that shuttered the vast majority of US steel production. Once the strike concluded, Worthington's task was to modernize the vast conglomerate. The corporation began closing unprofitable operations and reinvesting elsewhere.

By the 1960s, the steel industry had already begun to disinvest in plants least likely to remain profitable in the face of expanding global competition.[9] Nonetheless, new investment at the Duquesne Works was a clear sign the corporation intended to produce steel in southwestern Pennsylvania long into the future. It is easy to understand why most believed Dorothy Six symbolized Pittsburgh's continuing leadership in the industry. "We at United States Steel believe that the construction of this furnace demonstrates firm confidence Pittsburgh will continue to play a dominant role in the steel industry of this country," said Edwin Gott—then–U.S. Steel vice president for production and who replaced Worthington as president in 1967.[10]

When built, Dorothy Six was the largest blast furnace in the world, capable of producing over four thousand tons per day of raw steel. It retained that title for barely half a decade, only until the Japanese steelmaker Nippon Kokan blew in a six thousand–metric-ton blast furnace at its Hiroshima works in March 1968. The size of the Hiroshima plant "stagger[ed] the boys on the banks of the Monongahela," according to local coverage of plant's opening.[11] The Japanese plant was not just incrementally larger than Dorothy Six. The new Japanese plant was capable of producing a full 60 percent, more than what Dorothy Six could each day. New competition from both domestic and international sources spelled Dorothy's future demise.

Dorothy Six's larger place in history began on the day U.S. Steel announced its impending closure. The public reacted differently to Dorothy's shutdown, because the Duquesne Works had more than symbolic importance for the future of the entire Mon Valley. Not only was Dorothy Six considered the most advanced blast furnace in the region, but the Duquesne Works was an essential link for a large part of the Mon Valley's steel production network. Output from the Duquesne Works supplied steel ingots to the neighboring Homestead Works, which milled the raw steel into finished products. The two plants were the primary users of industrial coke produced at U.S. Steel's Clairton Works, less than ten miles upriver from Duquesne. Output from the Duquesne and Homestead Works were primary inputs to a wide network of steel fabrication businesses across southwestern Pennsylvania. It was as mature an agglomeration of steel production as existed anywhere in the world. Without Dorothy, much of that industrial ecosystem was at risk.

That Dorothy Six was still standing at all in 1988 was a testament to the tenacity of a community that fought to save it from destruction. Rumors of U.S. Steel's plan to close the Duquesne Works began circulating in September 1983. In early December, workers at U.S. Steel plants in Alabama, Ohio, and Illinois received letters demanding wage concessions in ongoing contract negotiations; the company explicitly threatened to shut down its respective plants if they did not comply. Duquesne workers viewed it optimistically that they did not receive similar letters.[12] Having accepted wage cutbacks early in 1983, Duquesne workers expected the concessions to protect their jobs. Likely, no letters were sent to Duquesne workers because the final decision to shut down the plant had already been made. On December 28, just four days after the Duquesne Works was awarded U.S. Steel's Iron Master award for beating the year's production targets, the corporation officially announced the closing of all or parts of thirty steel plants, including Dorothy and most of the remaining operations at Duquesne.

U.S. Steel provided union workers ninety days' notice of the plant's closure—as required by the industrywide basic steel contract then in force. In May 1984, 1,150 workers were laid off, and Dorothy Six went cold. Initially, the firm planned to keep the remainder of the Duquesne Works open, but in June, U.S. Steel announced it was permanently closing all operations at the site. The plant's production quota for bar products was shifted to U.S. Steel's Lorain Works, thirty miles west of Cleveland.

Workers were initially in denial that the shutdown at Duquesne was permanent. As with so many previous shutdowns, the expectation lingered that economic conditions would turn around, the plant would restart, and workers would be recalled. Those hopes were quashed in October 1984 when the demolition of the Dorothy Six blast furnace was scheduled for December, just two months in the future.

Even before U.S. Steel made public its plan to close the Duquesne Works, efforts to restart production at the plant had already begun. Local 1256 of the United Steel Workers of America (USW), representing workers at the Duquesne Works, first approached U.S. Steel in October 1983 with a proposal to transfer the assets at Duquesne to form a new employee stock ownership plan (ESOP).[13] It received no reply from the corporation. From that initial effort forward, U.S. Steel remained cool to any effort to sell the Duquesne Works to workers or any third party.

The announcement of Dorothy Six's scheduled demolition accelerated community efforts to find a way to restart operations at the Duquesne Works. A panoply of elected and union officials, activists, and community organizers crafted a dedicated "Save Dorothy" campaign. A plan to create a new public authority, the Steel Valley Authority (SVA), was at the center of a four-pronged strategy to restart operations at the Duquesne Works.

The first battle was against an owner intent on shutting it down. To keep alive any hope that Dorothy could ever be restarted, the blast furnace had to be prevented from depreciating past the point of no return.

Workers were particularly concerned the furnace would not remain viable through the rapidly approaching winter. Local 1256 workers volunteered to winterize the plant without pay. However, U.S. Steel still owned the site and remained focused on demolition, not preservation. Workers raised the $4,000 needed for basic materials to winterize the plant and an additional $16,000 to cover the insurance U.S. Steel required before the volunteer workers were allowed to reenter the site. The local raised $20,000, with a loan from its parent union.[14]

Local 1256 then organized an unprecedented effort to protect the plant's capital assets, not from potential theft or destruction but from U.S. Steel itself. Workers "set up a guard shanty across the street from the main gate of the mill." For more than six months, twenty-four hours a day, seven days a week, rotating shifts of unemployed steelworkers stood watch to ensure the company removed no vital equipment from the plant.[15]

The first victory came on November 18, 1984, when U.S. Steel announced that the scheduled December demolition was postponed until February 2, 1985. Local officials had been pressuring the corporation to delay the demolition as they sought to implement their October strategy. The short reprieve allowed just enough time for a report to be commissioned to evaluate the economic feasibility of a worker takeover of the plant. The $150,000 needed to complete the report was funded jointly by Allegheny County; the city of Pittsburgh; and Duquesne Light, the local electric utility.

The fight to save Dorothy Six soon became a national crusade. In January 1985, former presidential candidate Jesse Jackson led a protest outside the gates of the virtually empty plant. He described the decision to close the plant as an "industrial mugging" and urged the creation of an employee-owned cooperative to take possession of the site. Regional political leaders were equally invested in the plant's future. "I want to see this valley stay alive," proclaimed City of Pittsburgh Mayor Richard Caliguiri.[16]

The rapidly completed feasibility report was released on January 29, 1985, just days before the already rescheduled demolition was expected. Prepared by Locker-Albrecht Associates, Inc., a union-affiliated consulting firm based in New York City, the report concluded that there was a feasible business model where workers could both own and operate the hot end of the plant, where Dorothy Six powered the plant's output of raw steel ingots. The report assumed U.S. Steel would be a willing partner for the employee-owned plant, anticipating that semifinished output from the Duquesne Works would be milled into marketable products at nearby U.S. Steel facilities. The transition was not without considerable challenges. The report also concluded the aging plant required an immediate $24 million investment. To keep the plant economically viable, within three years, a new continuous caster, costing an additional $150 million, would also be needed.

The report did nothing to convince U.S. Steel of the plant's viability. Even though the company reported its 1984 annual profit of $483 million the same day, the corporation was not planning to reinvest at Duquesne.[17] Nonetheless, the optimistic conclusion of the Locker-Albrecht report forced U.S. Steel to delay the demolition a second time. Laid-off workers and the entire Mon Valley community were empowered by the hope that the Duquesne Works could still have a future. U.S. Steel remained equally insistent that the mill should remain closed. If Dorothy Six was ever to restart, it would have to be under a new owner, one unidentified at the beginning of 1985. Without any potential buyers making themselves known, the coalition fighting to Save Dorothy focused on taking direct ownership of the site, with or without cooperation from U.S. Steel.

Tri-State Conference

Employee ownership of a major industrial plant was not unprecedented. In 1984, workers collectively took ownership of the Weirton Works of National Steel—thirty miles west of Pittsburgh—making it the largest example of an employee-owned manufacturing plant in the nation. However, the workers at Weirton faced a fundamentally different situation than their compatriots at Duquesne. In Weirton, National Steel was a willing partner in the transfer of the plant to workers. The corporation wanted to shed responsibility for the costs it would incur if forced to shut down the plant. Not only were environmental remediation costs at the Weirton Works estimated to be prohibitive, but a large unfunded pension liability for the owners made the outright shutdown of the plant problematic.[18] National Steel encouraged a transaction that transferred away much of its potential liabilities for future pension payments and environmental remediation.

An ESOP was formed and took control of the Weirton plant in a $386 million deal, creating the nation's largest employee-owned business at the time.[19] The new plant reported a $500 million profit in 1984, $170 million of which was returned to workers in the form of profit sharing among the collective owners.[20] However, the profits were only possible because employees agreed to a 20 percent cut in pay and benefits and a six-year freeze on wage increases.

By 1985, workers in Duquesne likely would have considered similar concessions if they guaranteed the plant's continued operation, but circumstances were different for the Duquesne Works.[21] U.S. Steel was unwilling to voluntarily transfer ownership of the site to workers or any other potential buyer. An entirely different set of tactics was needed if Duquesne Works was going to be saved, tactics that would have to overpower the singular opposition of one of the largest corporations in the United States and take control of the plant by other means.

The vehicle was a new type of labor activism that had emerged in the greater steel industry corridor beyond Pittsburgh. On what was labeled Black Monday, September 19, 1977, the Lykes Corporation announced the shutdown of its Campbell Works in Youngstown, Ohio. The loss of jobs decimated Youngstown, a community long centered on steel production. The closure came after the Youngstown Sheet & Tube Company merged with the New Orleans–based Lykes Corporation in 1969. The combination proved to be an unsustainable business model built around mostly outdated plants and equipment. In an era before federal law required advance notice of major layoffs, the announcement instantly left five thousand workers unemployed. Youngstown soon faced greater job losses. In 1979, the LTV Corporation, the Texas conglomerate that had absorbed the Jones & Laughlin Company, closed its nearby Brier Hill mill. The same year, U.S. Steel wound down operations at the local McDonald Works.

Economic upheaval concentrated in Youngstown incubated a new form of labor activism. At first, an ad hoc coalition of religious, community, and union organizations protested plant closures in Youngstown and sought legal recourse to force the plants to continue operating. Ironically, the primary threat Youngstown was facing early in 1979 was not the contraction of the steel industry but U.S. Steel's plans to expand steel production elsewhere in Ohio. Jobs in Youngstown, and likely Pittsburgh, were threatened by U.S. Steel's plan to construct an entirely new supermill in Conneaut, Ohio, a port on Lake Erie at the Ohio–Pennsylvania border.

U.S. Steel had announced plans to build a massive new integrated steel plant on six thousand lakefront acres at Conneaut in 1977.[22] The colocation of steel production at a deepwater port was modeled in part on U.S. Steel's Gary Works—constructed over seven decades earlier on the shore of Lake Michigan and U.S. Steel's Fairless plant outside Philadelphia on the Delaware River—a location with direct access to international shipping. Carnegie Steel had first envisioned a Conneaut steel plant in the 1890s, but despite several public announcements that a plant would soon be built on Lake Erie, actual construction never began.[23] The plant envisioned in the late 1970s was intended to meet much of the nation's expected growth in the demand for steel.[24] Workers in Youngstown feared the new plant would make their jobs redundant.

The US Army Corps of Engineers issued a permit to build the new plant on June 18, 1979. Anticipating local jobs would be relocated there, Youngstown-area activists and workers viewed the new plant as a threat to their communities. "I believe the dream of Edgar Speer (former U.S. Steel board chairman) of building a mill in Conneaut is a nightmare for the steelworkers," said a local union official. Youngstown activism soon evolved into a formal organization. The Tri-State Conference on the Impact of Steel—described as a "Christian discussion of steel industry problems in America"—was held on July 19, 1979. On the same day, a new organization of the same name filed suit in federal court to block the construction of the plant at Conneaut. The lawsuit alleged the new plant would incur uncounted environmental and social costs in the area where it was to be built. The Conneaut site required vast new investment in what was at the time a very small town.[25] While the court eventually dismissed the legal strategy, it may have been responsible for delaying the project just long enough to prevent it from ever getting off the ground. Far from giving up, Tri-State began planning to fight against plant closures along the vector of Rust Belt deindustrialization, leading directly to Pittsburgh and the Mon Valley.

Tri-State was founded in part by attorney Staughton Lynd, who also had a PhD in history and for a time was a professor at Yale.[26] While on staff at Youngstown Neighborhood Legal Services, Lynd and his colleagues argued for collective ownership of the Lykes Corporation plants that were closing. A Youngstown planner first suggested a new legal tactic: "You know, Staughton, if you have a rundown neighborhood, abandoned homes, you can use eminent domain; why not use it for abandoned industrial facilities?"[27]

From that initial ideation, Tri-State developed a legal strategy that had previously been used primarily to seize property from individuals and small businesses. Federal, state, and local governments had long exercised the power of eminent domain to take control of real estate when necessary for new or expanded public works. With the cooperation of local governments, corporations had used eminent domain to acquire real estate when needed for major industrial expansions. Tri-State's innovation would be use eminent domain against the corporations that were trying to shut down operating plants. It was a novel and entirely untested legal strategy. There was not enough time to develop the concept to save any plants in Youngstown, but Tri-State began to publicize the possibility of using eminent domain to save factories from closing elsewhere.[28]

In the summer of 1982, the Crucible Steel Company announced plans to shut down its plant in Midland, Pennsylvania, halfway between Youngstown and Pittsburgh. Five thousand jobs were at risk. The Cyclops Steel Company wanted to buy the Crucible mill and had gone so far as to negotiate a potential contract with the local union. Yet, Crucible refused to sell. Monsignor Charles Owen Rice, a Catholic priest who had risen to prominence supporting organized labor during the 1930s, presented Tri-State's plan to seize the plant with the legal power of eminent domain. The existing Midland Redevelopment Authority could implement eminent domain, and Cyclops claimed it was willing to invest sufficient capital needed to fund the takeover. Ultimately, the Midland Borough Council would not go along with the plan, at least not in the limited time available to prevent the plant from being shut down. The untried strategy still had too many unanswered questions pertaining to the borough's financial liability, workers' pensions, and other unknowns.

Tri-State had greater success as it shifted focus closer to Mon Valley. Late in 1982, it joined a coalition of organizations working to stop the planned closing of the Nabisco Corporation's industrial bakery in Pittsburgh, which had operated in the city's east end since 1937. More than thirty religious, labor, and civic groups came together to oppose Nabisco's plan. The ad hoc coalition was called the Save Nabisco Action Coalition, giving it the apropos acronym SNAC. SNAC partnered with Tri-State to advocate for the use of eminent domain to take control of the plant. Mayor Caliguiri supported doing "whatever it takes" to keep the plant open. In the face of mounting public opposition and the threatened use of eminent domain, Nabisco backed away from its closure plans. Though the company gave no reason for its change of heart, the public perception was that its public retreat was due to Tri-State's legal posturing.

Empowered by the Nabisco success, Tri-State turned its attention to the Mon Valley, where the wave of plant closings was escalating at the end of 1982. The plan to use eminent domain in the Mon Valley was hindered by a lack of a redevelopment authority in the area. To execute a legal strategy dependent on the use of eminent domain, a new special-purpose government had to be created.

Pennsylvania law gave Tri-State the tool it needed. Section 306 of the Municipal Authorities Act of 1945 allowed local municipalities to establish public authorities specialized in economic development efforts "including, but not limited to, projects to retain or develop existing industries and the development of new industries."[29] Those powers included the power to exercise eminent domain—which allowed a local government to take private property for public uses, even without property owners' consent. Tri-State wanted to turn the statute on its head and use eminent domain to wrest control of industrial facilities away from owners trying to shut them down. In 1983, the Tri-State Conference began its plan to create an entirely new redevelopment authority, independent of existing municipal governments. In November 1985, seven municipalities in the Mon Valley, along with the city of Pittsburgh, jointly created a new redevelopment authority charged with fighting deindustrialization in the region.

The SVA was a new type of public organization. Nominally formed by a collaboration of Mon Valley municipalities and the city of Pittsburgh, it was really a collaboration of workers and the communities trying to save the industrial capacity of the region. Forming the SVA was the next step in the plan to Save Dorothy that had been set in place in October 1984. Once formally incorporated, the SVA was expected to implement the Tri-State strategy and exercise eminent domain to gain control of the Duquesne Works.

Restarting production at the plant depended on getting Dorothy Six, the "hope of Pennsylvania steelworkers," back into operation.[30] Restarting production was more than just a technical challenge. For the Duquesne Works to be a viable business, its output needed customers. Locker-Albrecht concluded there was a growing market for semifinished steel products, slabs, and other marketable shapes that were commodity outputs of steel plants and that production costs at Duquesne could be kept low enough to compete successfully with low-priced imports of foreign slabs.

U.S. Steel countered the Locker-Albrecht study by releasing its own feasibility study in April 1985. Coming to an almost opposite conclusion, the company dismissed any potential economic viability of the Duquesne Works. It estimated that $400 million in new investment was needed immediately to restart the plant, not the $24 million projected by Locker-Albrecht. U.S. Steel was not just uncooperative with efforts to restart the Duquesne Works under new ownership but it publicly lobbied against the community efforts underway. U.S. Steel's CEO, David Roderick, pointed out that if Allegheny County provided public funding to restart the plant, it would result in sizable property tax increases for all county property owners.[31]

The Locker-Albrecht analysis was more of a concept, far from a detailed business plan. At best, it was an outline of what was possible, far from sufficient to entice new investors to sign on to a new business venture. Any scenario for reopening the plant required a sizable investment. With no federal bailout expected, and given the dire financial status of most local governments in the region at the time, any significant new investment had to come from the private sector.

Soon after Locker-Albrecht released its preliminary report, the USW commissioned a comprehensive study to produce a detailed business plan for restarting the hot end of the Duquesne Works. Wall Street investment consultant Lazard Frères & Co. and the local investment firm of Russell, Rea & Zappala donated the cost of their efforts to complete the study. Originally scheduled to be completed in the fall of that year, Lazard Frères released its report in January 1986. The report's conclusions were dour and definitive: "Reopening Dorothy Six was not financially feasible." Recognizing the ongoing battle to restart the blast furnace, Lazard Frères was apologetic: "The people who worked so long and so hard to save Duquesne did not give up on Duquesne and will not give up on the steel industry."[32]

The report conclusively ended efforts to Save Dorothy and reopen the Duquesne Works. On January 9, 1986, U.S. Steel and the USW issued a joint press release announcing the end of efforts to restart production at the plant.[33] Not only were the economics of the existing Duquesne plant infeasible given current or anticipated market conditions, but the scale of investment needed to rehabilitate the plant was prohibitive.

Locker-Albrecht had been in error not so much on the technical challenges facing the Duquesne Works but on the practical reality of competing against U.S. Steel. Its initial analysis had erred in presuming that an independent Duquesne Works could operate symbiotically with the vestiges of U.S. Steel still in the Mon Valley. The report specifically assumed that the commodity steel output of the Duquesne Works could feed the rolling and finishing operations of other U.S. Steel operations still operating in the Mon Valley, a business model not far removed from how the plants had worked together for over eight decades. However, it was a model that relied on U.S. Steel's cooperation, or at least impartial business practices. Lazard Frères quickly concluded that not only was U.S. Steel not going to be a willing business partner but also that it was instead planning to be an aggressive competitor. U.S. Steel made clear that if the plant restated "they would throw everything they had at it to compete with it."[34]

The SVA was officially incorporated in January 1986, just as the release of the Lazard Frères study doomed efforts to keep the Duquesne Works open. The new SVA shifted its energy to keeping other plants in the valley operating. Its next focus was LTV's South Side Works, just six miles downriver from Duquesne.[35] As with Duquesne, the shuttered LTV site never reopened. The SVA's only formal legal effort to exercise eminent domain came in March 1986, when it filed suit in both the Court of Common Pleas of Allegheny County and federal district court in Western Pennsylvania, attempting to block the American Standard Company from closing its plant in Swissvale. The federal district court rejected the SVA's petition based on a technicality that the property in question had never been formally condemned, a legal requirement for exercising eminent domain.[36] No operating plant in Pennsylvania would ever be taken over against the will of its owner using the power of eminent domain as envisioned by Lynd and the Tri-State Conference.

Extreme efforts to keep Dorothy Six operating were not unprecedented in deindustrializing areas worldwide. For steel regions from Lille in France to Luxembourg and the Ruhr Valley of Germany, the 1980s were a painful period of restructuring. Recession, slumping demand, and increasing competition from Asian producers created nearly simultaneous recessions across all traditional steel-producing regions. Not just local municipalities but regional national governments mobilized to keep domestic manufacturing industries from shutting down. All attempted, in some form, to retain their manufacturing base in the face of daunting market conditions.

Luxembourg—a nation-state of under a million people once dominated by the steel industry—shared a long industrial history with Pittsburgh.

Nearby coal and iron ore resources made the nation an ideal location for heavy industry to develop. The iron ore mines that once enabled Luxembourg's metal industries were mostly exhausted by the 1970s. The depletion of local resources made steel production uncompetitive. The nation's last iron ore mine closed in 1981. In response to industrial decline, the small country invested the equivalent of 2 billion euros between 1975 and 1987 in a national steel plan, a series of emergency measures. Luxembourg's government invested directly in Aciéries Réunies de Burbach-Eich-Dudelange, the remaining national steel producer, taking ownership of 42.9 percent of the company by the mid-1980s. In the United States, no level of government ever provided any similar level of funding or ever took any equity ownership in any steel firm.

The Save Dorothy campaign was different because its core was a grassroots effort of workers and the communities of the Mon Valley. Local steel plants received only minimal support from federal programs. No national structural adjustment policy was in place to assist regions suffering even the most severe contractions. Mon Valley communities were left to themselves to negotiate massive economic changes that were beyond their control to alter.

In Japan, restructuring of heavy industries produced very different impacts for both workers and local communities. Nippon Steel downsized its integrated steelworks at Kitakyushu—where the government-run Yahata Steel Works dated its first production to 1901—during the 1980s. Unlike in the United States, both corporate and government efforts focused on finding alternative employment for all displaced workers. Nippon Steel reassigned them to other plants and worked to diversify its own operations. In an attempt to find alternative employment for workers, the firm went so far as to create a Space World theme park in Kitakyushu. As a result of those efforts, even in a region where steel output declined on a scale equivalent to Pittsburgh's, there were no direct layoffs of steelworkers.[37]

In Germany, workers took direct action to block plant closures in the steel industry. In Rheinhausen—a district of Duisburg in the Ruhr Valley—initial attempts to close the integrated Krupp steelworks there spawned mass protests of more than ten thousand participants at the plant gates. Wider public protests against plant closings included a sixty thousand–person human chain across the region in 1980.[38] The protests succeeded in keeping Rheinhausen open for a time.[39]

Six years later, the Krupp plant at Rheinhausen closed for good. The only palpable difference between what happened in Pittsburgh and in

Duisburg was the final disposition of the massive industrial artifacts left in each region. Across southwestern Pennsylvania, closed industrial sites were immediately targeted for demolition. Final efforts were often only delayed by the limited funding available. In Duisburg, the former abandoned steel plant remained in place as a museum and an exhibition of environmental remediation renamed Landscape Park.[40]

Duquesne faced a long timeline before it would ever be ready for any alternative use. The Regional Urban Design Assistance Team that evaluated Mon Valley industrial sites in 1988 concluded, "The Duquesne site probably presents some of the most complex problems faced in this exercise. This is due almost entirely to the vast scale of the U.S. Steel plant and its infrastructure."[41] No repurposing of land on such a vast scale could come quickly. The demolition of Dorothy Six was just the beginning of a long process at the former Duquesne Works. The remaining blast furnaces on the site were not demolished for another decade. Only in October 1995 did demolitions bring down the remaining blast furnaces there.[42]

Change came slowly to the banks of the Monongahela River. Between 1998 and 2000, the vast Homestead Steel Works was emptied of all but a few symbolic pieces of its industrial past and was remade into a vast mixed-use amalgam of retail shopping, apartment complexes, light industry, and office space. Across the river from Homestead, only the Carrie Furnace that had once supplied the pig iron to the furnaces remained as it was when shut down. Though it was slated to be the one industrial artifact preserved in the Mon Valley, no significant investment has ever been made into stabilizing the structure over the subsequent quarter century. Inside the abandoned Carrie Furnace, the only noticeable change other than depreciation has been the oversized guerilla art erected in place.

The external help that came to assist Duquesne and the greater Mon Valley in its ongoing transformation was barely a fraction of what was needed. In 1999, Vice President Al Gore came to the valley to announce Duquesne was awarded a $200,000 grant to assist in brownfield development. The amount was awarded to the still extant SVA but was to be diluted for environmental assessments across three different sites in Duquesne, Clairton, and McKeesport.[43]

Only limited commercial infill came to Duquesne after the vestiges of the former Duquesne Works had been removed. The site remained a focus of redevelopment efforts for decades. A limited number of new tenants eventually came, but cumulative employment at the site never made up even a fraction of the number of jobs lost. The most notable new tenant was a textile and mattress factory that arrived in 2003. But even those jobs did not reflect new growth for the Pittsburgh region. The factory was merely relocated to Duquesne from the city of Pittsburgh's Lawrenceville neighborhood, where it had operated since 1950.

Over the quarter century after the demolition of Dorothy Six, the greatest single source of new jobs in the Mon Valley came to neighboring McKeesport. There, in 1988, on the site of the former National Tube Works, a satellite TV business set up a massive call center. With average wages of only seven dollars per hour, the jobs paid only a fraction of what the average millworkers used to make. Still, the thousand-plus jobs created were more than welcome in a region that had few such prospects. Yet even those jobs did not last, and the McKeesport call center closed in 2009, after only eleven years, a sharp contrast from the ninety-nine years people had been employed at the Duquesne Works.

A century of industrial production made redevelopment at Duquesne difficult and expensive. A short list of contaminants at the site included polychlorinated biphenyls (PCBs) and over fifteen miles of asbestos-wrapped pipe. Most of the soil contaminants would never be removed, only covered with twelve inches of topsoil to mitigate the environmental concerns. The greater damage was to the very fabric of the communities. Best articulated during the legal battles fought in Youngstown, plant closures across the Mon Valley had much the same impact as had earlier concentrated job destruction in northeastern Ohio. When Federal District Judge Thomas Lambros declined to issue an injunction activists were seeking to prevent companies from closing down steel plants in Youngstown, he struggled to explain the basic inadequacy of the law in addressing the economic situation: "Everything that has happened in the Mahoning Valley has been happening for many years because of steel. Schools have been built, roads have been built. Expansion that has taken place is because of steel. And to accommodate that industry lives and destinies of the inhabitants of that community were based and planned on the basis of that institution: Steel."[44]

Local 1256 found itself without active members once the Duquesne Works shut down permanently, forcing it to sell its nearby union hall. The building was converted to a personal care home in 1987.[45] Mike Bilcsik, former president of local 1256 later said the "loss of a whole generation of older steelworkers who couldn't be retrained was the 'overwhelming tragedy' of the 1980s." Nonetheless, he also came to grips with the inevitability of the change that was still ongoing: "Twenty years from now, I think we'll see the '80s as the best thing that happened to the Mon Valley since the industrialism of the 1880s attracted European immigrants like my grandfather who came to Duquesne in 1910."[46]

Less than two weeks after Dorothy Six was felled, the Allegheny County Department of Economic Development announced that the demolition was expected to produce between 175,000 and 200,000 pounds of scrap steel and other materiel that could be resold. So valuable was the industrial residue that its $22 million value exceeded the $14 million cost of the demolition itself.[47] To the accountants, the public was coming out ahead.

The permanently laid-off steelworker has never had the training even to understand what these want ads mean, let alone to apply for the position.

President Ronald Reagan, National Conference on the Dislocated Worker, Pittsburgh, April 6, 1983

Diaspora

June 24, 1985

Workers were again arriving outside the U.S. Steel Duquesne Works. Even though most operations at the plant had shut down the year before, more than four hundred laid-off workers were back. None had been called back to their old jobs. Instead, they were hoping for interviews with potential new employers who had come to a job fair at a job assistance center set up directly across the street from the plant's main gate. Among others, representatives from the Texas Bureau of Corrections, the Dallas Police, and the Federal Bureau of Investigation had come to Pennsylvania to recruit from the ample supply of unemployed workers.

Most recruiters were interviewing for jobs not located in Duquesne or anywhere close to western Pennsylvania. The three law enforcement agencies were seeking candidates who knew they would have to move far from Pittsburgh for any position. Relocation was not a problem for many, and some were "ready to fly out that day."[1] The workers showing up in Duquesne were far from the only ones planning their economic futures elsewhere.

Despite ongoing efforts to restart the Duquesne Works, the undeniable reality was that most of the jobs once supported by the plant were never coming back. The concentrated job destruction extended across all of southwestern Pennsylvania. That so many laid-off steelworkers lost nearly identical jobs nearly simultaneously meant there was competition many times over for any blue-collar job openings.

The imminent failure to Save Dorothy, six months in the future, would make clear steel would never again be produced at the Duquesne Works, an eventuality replaying itself at industrial plants across the greater Pittsburgh region. Even if some factory jobs trickled back in at local plants, long union roles had a surfeit of workers with vast seniority who would be the first to be called back. Most laid-off workers, and especially younger ones, knew their chances of ever returning to their old jobs—or to similar jobs anywhere near Pittsburgh—were minimal. There was only one choice for the bulk of the unemployed mill workers. If they were going to find work anytime soon, let alone stable economic futures, they would have to look elsewhere.

Concentrated job destruction across western Pennsylvania begat an unprecedented population migration away from Pittsburgh. Between 1980 and 1990, the Pittsburgh metropolitan statistical area (MSA) contracted by over 180,000 people, the single greatest population loss for any metropolitan region that decade. The Detroit MSA—nearly twice the size of Pittsburgh in 1980—experienced a population decline only half as large as Pittsburgh's; shrinking by "only" 88,000 over the same decade. The Pittsburgh region contracted by 7.4 percent during the 1980s, far worse than the population losses in other major metropolitan regions. The Detroit region lost 2 percent of its population during the 1980s, while the Cleveland region lost 2.6 percent.

Pittsburgh was not the only region to suffer dire rates of population loss. Virtually every nearby region of western Pennsylvania, Ohio, and West Virginia suffered similar fates as jobs disappeared and workers departed. Smaller metropolitan regions close to Pittsburgh experienced even more grim rates of decline. The Wheeling, West Virginia, metropolitan area, thirty miles west of Pittsburgh, declined by over 14 percent between 1980 and 1990, while the Steubenville–Weirton region contracted by 12.6 percent and Johnstown, Pennsylvania, by 9 percent. For workers losing their jobs anywhere near Pittsburgh, no nearby region offered better employment prospects. New opportunities could only be found far from Pittsburgh.

Summary statistics of net population loss mask how many people moved away from the worst-hit regions. Through the 1980s, Pittsburgh, like the rest of the nation, continued to experience natural population gains resulting from the rate of births exceeding deaths each year. So large was the US baby boom generation, generally considered the cohort of births between 1946 and 1964, that the children of the baby

Metropolitan statistical areas with the largest population declines between 1980 and 1990

Metropolitan statistical area	Population 1980	Population 1990	Change	Percentage
Pittsburgh, PA	2,423,311	2,242,798	-180,513	-7.4
Detroit-Ann Arbor, MI*	4,752,820	4,665,236	-87,584	-1.8
Cleveland-Akron-Lorain, OH*	2,834,062	2,759,823	-74,239	-2.6
Buffalo-Niagara Falls, NY*	1,242,826	1,189,288	-53,538	-4.3
Youngstown-Warren, OH MSA	531,350	492,619	-38,731	-7.3
Davenport-Rock Island-Moline, IA-IL MSA	383,958	350,861	-33,097	-8.6
Peoria, IL MSA	365,864	339,172	-26,692	-7.3
Duluth, MN-WI MSA	266,650	239,971	-26,679	-10.0
Wheeling, WV-OH MSA	185,566	159,301	-26,265	-14.2
Huntington-Ashland, WV-KY-OH MSA	336,410	312,529	-23,881	-7.1

Notes: Metropolitan area geography based on 1983 definitions for both years.
* Consolidated metropolitan statistical area.

boomers created a secondary bubble in US demographics. By the 1980s, this demographic ripple—the beginning of what is also called the echo boom, or the millennial generation—was a primary source of population growth for most regions, even Pittsburgh.

If migration flows in and out of the region had been evenly balanced, natural population growth alone would have caused the population of southwestern Pennsylvania to increase by at least 70,000 through the 1980s. The scale of outmigration from Pittsburgh not only offset all those potential population gains but was singularly responsible for the region's unprecedented population contraction. Net outmigration from southwestern Pennsylvania over the course of the 1980s is estimated to have exceeded 227,000, nearly 8 percent of the region's population at the time.[2] Most departing workers took with them their families or their future families, as well. The children of departed Pittsburghers compounded the region's demographic loss by an additional 205,000 people between 1970 and 2000.[3] Without migration losses, the region's population in 2000 could conceivably have reached far closer to 3 million, versus the 2.35 million that the decennial census enumerated that year.

Pittsburgh's population loss was all the more traumatic because of what had been projected just before. Through the 1970s, locally produced population projections expected only benign shifts demographic trends. In 1976, the Regional Industrial Development Corporation—one of Pittsburgh's primary economic development agencies—projected regional job *growth* in both manufacturing and nonmanufacturing sectors over the coming fourteen years, growth expected to produce a net *gain* of 117,000 jobs by 1990.[4] Job growth was projected to generate modest population growth, despite that Pittsburgh's population had been slowly declining over the previous quarter century.

Local officials went out of their ways to refute any statistics that called into question even the most optimistic projections. A 1978 report sponsored by regional business leaders claimed: "Estimation technique used by the Census Bureau may underestimate the population of industrialized areas." For Pittsburgh, it claimed, "the economic growth experienced since the mid-1970s may not be fully reflected in the 1976 (population) estimates."[5] The new report even revised previous, already unrealistic, forecasts *upward*. The Pittsburgh metropolitan region was expected to generate 119,000 net new jobs between 1980 and 1990, and the regional population was projected to increase by 100,000 over the same decade.[6]

The reality about to set in was the exact opposite of projections. In March 1981, the Pittsburgh metropolitan region recorded its largest labor force ever to date, with just over 1.196 million workers employed or seeking work. At its nadir, in November 1985, the regional labor force had dropped to 1.089 million, a net loss of nearly 107,000 workers.

The scale of the region's population loss was barely conceivable even as it was happening. A survey commissioned by the *Pittsburgh Post-Gazette* in 1983—the year the regional population outmigration was reaching historic peaks—reported that Pittsburgh residents said they were less likely to move away than they had been four years earlier.[7] A 1985 news story benignly reported on the region's population loss between 1982 and 1984, noting only that "Pittsburgh lost some people, but may have gained some faces."[8] Only years later would the scale of the region's population loss be commonly described as Pittsburgh's own diaspora.[9]

Reflecting the pattern of regional job destruction, those departing were more likely to be men. So unbalanced was the flow of young workers leaving the region that a 1984 Princeton University study concluded the Pittsburgh region had the nation's second lowest proportion of single men aged twenty to fifty-nine. The study offered no explanation for the region's low ranking. Its author only conjectured, "Pittsburgh doesn't have as many [jobs] as a lot of other places. So with the large companies cutting back, people have to leave."[10]

A longer-lasting demographic impact was caused not by the number who left but by who in particular was leaving. The economic-induced outmigration taking place was very age-selective. Younger workers were the most likely to leave, while older ones and those already retired remained. As the outmigration flows peaked in the early 1980s, the Pittsburgh region was losing an estimated 4 percent of its twentysomething population each year. Over 70 percent of net migration between 1980 and 1985 is estimated to have been generated by the loss of population age twenty-nine or younger.[11]

Common advice given to young Pittsburgh workers was "get educated and get out"—which many heeded.[12] The few laid-off workers who were eventually recalled experienced sharply reduced earnings. One estimate is that male workers who returned to their former jobs earned just 75 percent of what they had expected, given previous wage trends in Pittsburgh.[13] Regional workers who remained also suffered from lower wages, reduced hours, and fewer weeks of work per year for years into the future. Overall, regional workers who lost their jobs in the 1980s saw their real wages depressed by 12.5 percent a decade into the future. Especially hard hit were regional workers without college degrees, who saw their real wages depressed by 30 percent ten years after job loss.[14] Depressed economic opportunities affected new entrants more than other workers. Nominal mean earnings for new entrants to Pittsburgh's workforce actually dropped between 1979 and 1989.[15] Migration alone caused the number of twentysomething residents of southwestern Pennsylvania to shrink by 19 percent over the 1980s.[16] In a region struggling to transform itself in the face of massive economic losses, the workers most capable of adapting to new jobs in new industries were the same workers departing en masse.

As the 1980s ended, Pittsburgh's immediate future was going to be shaped by those who remained. More likely to have stayed were older workers, including those who still had jobs and an almost uncountable number of those who did not. Just as workers were departing Pittsburgh for better opportunities elsewhere, few workers from elsewhere were moving into the region. The overhang of excess labor displaced the need for workers who might have normally moved into the region, affecting the dynamics of the region's labor market long into the future. As late as 2001, the rate at which people were moving into the Pittsburgh region was ranked second lowest among the twenty-five largest metropolitan areas that year.[17]

With the youngest cohorts of workers departing and relatively few arriving to replace them, the Pittsburgh region continued to grow older long after the worst of the job losses subsided. Many laid-off workers never worked again, dropping out of the labor force entirely but never moving away.[18] The result was a marked shift in the demographics of southwestern Pennsylvania. What was already a relatively older region at the beginning of the 1980s soon became one of the oldest in the nation. By 1990, the Pittsburgh area recorded the second highest concentration of population age sixty-five and over among the fifty largest metropolitan areas in the nation. So old was Pittsburgh by 1990 that the only major metropolitan areas to have higher concentrations of elderly residents were Tampa–Saint Petersburg and Miami. Both Florida regions were magnets for retirees from across the nation. Pittsburgh's older population, by contrast, had aged in place with many of its communities eventually described as naturally occurring retirement communities.[19]

Superficially at least, Pittsburgh's regional labor force rebounded by the end of the 1980s. The region's overall unemployment rate dropped from a peak of 18 percent in February 1982 to under 10 percent by late 1985 and averaged 7 percent in 1987. From a peak of 210,000 in 1983, unemployment rolls officially dropped to a nadir of just over 52,000 at the end of the decade. However, the drop did not represent a significant rebound in regional job growth. Total regional employment ranged between 1.0 and 1.1 million throughout the decade, with minimal sustained growth. The rapid decline of unemployment rolls was possible only due to the significant outmigration of workers and their families and the discouragement of many former workers who remained in the region but stopped looking for work.

Workforce Development

A regional workforce could not be transformed quickly, especially in a region that had remained so concentrated in a single industry for so long. Employment in the mills had long since been a family heritage in many communities. In 1951, the U.S. Steel Corporation estimated there were four thousand father-son pairs of workers at its Homestead plant alone and that active third-generation workers were not uncommon.[20] Homestead, like many of Pittsburgh's historic mills, had provided virtually guaranteed opportunities for not just years but generations. Many workers expected they could work their entire careers at the mills. When the mills seemed a permanent part of the regional economy, workers had little incentive to acquire training that could provide them new opportunities or the flexibility to move into other occupations, let alone other industries. Once mills closed permanently, most workers were ill-prepared to face new economic circumstances.

Despite the obstacles, getting former mill employees back to work became the primary goal of economic policy across southwestern Pennsylvania. For most workers remaining in the region, the only viable path was to find jobs in new occupations, occupations that required new sets of skills. The challenge of retraining unemployed steelworkers brought President Ronald Reagan to Pittsburgh on April 6, 1983. Arriving early in the afternoon, the president delivered a speech at an ad hoc national conference dedicated to the plight of the "Dislocated Worker" that was being held at the Hilton Hotel adjacent to Gateway Center in Downtown Pittsburgh. The conference featured not only the president but also the secretary of labor and Pennsylvania governor, Richard Thornburg.

The president noted how different were the skills required for the jobs being created in the economy. As an example, he read one local classified ad looking for a "Systems Programmer-Large Scale IBM, VTAM, TSO/SPF, ACFII, CICS, OS/MVS." Many of the unemployed workers concentrated in Pittsburgh had begun their careers before the advent of digital computing, now the predominant source of regional jobs going unfilled. The president's remarks acknowledged the difficulty of retraining of workers to fill the technical jobs then in the most demand: "The permanently laid-off steelworker has never had the training even to understand what these want ads mean, let alone to apply for the position."[21]

Reagan's speech highlighted improving economic conditions nationally and the recently signed Job Training Partnership Act (JTPA). Though the national recession had officially ended six months earlier, Pittsburgh had shown little sign of moving beyond its enduring economic morass. The president's message was not well received. Despite a cold spring rain, more than four thousand unemployed steelworkers protested outside the luxury conference hotel.[22] The protest was, ironically, staged on the purposely designed thoroughfares adjacent to Point State Park and Gateway Center, the highlighted success of Pittsburgh's postwar renaissance.

Reagan concluded his trip to Pittsburgh with remarks at a local corporation contracted to train 120 unemployed workers in computer installation, maintenance, and repair.[23] One trainee, a soon-to-be-famous Ron

Bricker, boldly interrupted the president during his speech: "Mr. President, I've been looking for a job for a year, and I can't find one."[24] He then walked up to the president and handed him a résumé. The event concluded the half day the president spent in Pittsburgh, and by dinnertime, the president was back in Washington.

Critics noted the jobs Reagan highlighted during his visit were some of the most specialized occupations that had only recently come into existence. "Reagan fails to read between the lines," read the page one headline the following day. The classified advertisement he quoted made clear that most of the unfilled jobs required advanced training, college degrees, and levels of experience that virtually no laid-off steelworker possessed nor could acquire anytime soon.

Ron Bricker's bold move initially appeared to have paid off. Within a week, the publicity not only landed him an interview on NBC's *Today Show* but also generated a new job repairing computers at Radio Shack. His pay of $6.50 an hour worked out to half what he had been making previously.[25] For a moment, he was a rare example of a former steel industry worker who had successfully transitioned to an entirely new industry. Nonetheless, Bricker quit his new job and within a few weeks was called back to his former job at a local steel warehouse.[26]

Through the worst of the region's job destruction, only limited federal programs were in place to directly address the ballooning need for worker retraining. At the beginning of the 1980s, the primary federal program supporting retraining efforts was the Comprehensive Employment and Training Act (CETA), which had only been in place since 1973. It had replaced the Manpower Development and Training Act (MDTA), originally passed in 1962. The original legislation creating the MDTA had been sponsored by Pennsylvania's Senator Joseph Clark and Congressman Elmer Holland, the latter of Pittsburgh.

Holland was a member of the United Steelworkers of America. In December 1960, he had compiled a report for President-elect Kennedy on the impacts of increasing automation on the US workforce.[27] Presaging the wider effects of technology on labor force productivity, Holland pointed out: "30,000 New York elevator operators and 40,000 telephone operators have lost their jobs as a result of automation." The report he presented to Kennedy counted 4 million US jobs expected to be eventually replaced by increased uses of automation.[28]

Holland was not portending mass layoffs. What he foresaw was depressed hiring as businesses chose not to replace workers as they retired:

"When new mechanical or electronic devices are installed, assurances are given to workers in many industries that they will not be hurt or fired. However, when they leave—due to retirement or resignation—no one is hired to replace them."[29] Early federal workforce programs were, at best, designed to address that slowly evolving shift within the nation's labor force, not the mass layoffs of concentrated job destruction.

The recession of 1982–83 quickly created a need for worker retraining far beyond the tools available under MDTA and later CETA. Existing programs were ill-suited for the massive dislocation of manufacturing workers in Pittsburgh or in any other heavily industrialized regions. Even before the recession set in, the instability of CETA was criticized, after it had been amended eight times in twelve years.[30] Then, in the midst of its greatest challenge, CETA was superseded by JTPA, passed in October 1982. The new federal program was barely getting off the ground as the need for worker retraining was reaching its apogee in Pittsburgh.

Unlike CETA, JTPA was not intended to be a comprehensive structural adjustment program. Rather, it was a highly decentralized program, more a distributor of funding than a national workforce strategy. In 1991, a Government Accounting Office report estimated JTPA program funds went to six hundred different local organizations.[31] The devolution of program administration was intentional and was supposed to lead to better targeting of worker retraining efforts. Decentralization also isolated the federal government from taking on a more comprehensive role in regional restructuring. For Pittsburgh or any other Rust Belt region, there would be no intervention on the scale of the Tennessee Valley Authority to assist newly unemployed workers.

No matter the scale of job losses located there, Pittsburgh received no disproportionate federal aid to help displaced workers. JTPA efforts were spread out geographically across the nation by statute. Funding was then required to be distributed across multiple policy goals. Through JTPA's first eight years, an estimated $28 billion was expended across the nation. A substantial amount, but the average of $3.5 billion a year had built in statutory requirements that required the funding to be divided across all states and programs. Dislocated workers were only one focus of JTPA programs. Title IIA of the JTPA legislation targeted economically disadvantaged youth and adults, while Title IIB focused exclusively on programs for youth. Only Title III focused on dislocated workers. In 1983, at the very peak of Pennsylvania's manufacturing-centric job destruction, the entire state was allocated a total of $1.8 million under JTPA's

Title III program for dislocated workers.[32] In February, the state's total unemployment count officially peaked at over 708,000, so the division of funds works out to $2.30 per unemployed worker. In comparison, five years earlier the Commonwealth of Pennsylvania had provided the Volkswagen Corporation with an estimated $78 million in public incentives to support the anticipated creation of just four thousand jobs—or roughly $19,500 per job.

The limited funding that eventually made it into worker retraining programs had only minimal effects in the face of so many workers seeking new employment opportunities. A 1986 *Pittsburgh Press* investigative series concluded that local JTPA efforts were "mired in a bureaucratic tangle that throws millions of dollars into dead-end training programs."[33] One participant in an electronics training program complained, "There was never enough equipment to work on, and most of the equipment was from 1969."[34] Additional criticism was that in Pittsburgh, 96 percent of JTPA funds were being spent on classroom instruction, with few resources dedicated to hands-on training that would have been more appropriate for the bulk of the mostly blue-collar unemployed workers.[35]

By 1984, JTPA programs in Pittsburgh had been attended by a total of seven hundred workers, with only two hundred completing programs and only seventy-five finding new jobs upon completion. A token result when the Pittsburgh region's official unemployment level averaged 128,000 that year, not counting the region's expanding corps of discouraged workers. "The retraining effort is a mess," said Jim Cunningham, a University of Pittsburgh professor of social work, in April 1984.[36]

Only later in the 1980s did new federal workforce policies emerge. In 1988, Congress passed both the Economic Development and Worker Adjustment Assistance Act (EDWAA) and the Worker Adjustment and Notification Retraining Act (WARN). EDWAA amended Title III of the JTPA to provide additional funds to states targeting worker retraining programs. WARN required larger employers to provide notice sixty days in advance of covered plant closings and covered mass layoffs. Both programs were only marginally supported by the executive branch, with cursory implementation by the Department of Labor. The Reagan administration had actively opposed the WARN legislation and allowed the bill to become law without the president's signature.[37]

New efforts were too little, and certainly too late, for the bulk of workers who by 1988 had been pushed out of their industrial jobs for several years or longer. Problems identified in regional worker retraining efforts persisted. A 1989 RAND Corporation study on worker retraining programs in the Pittsburgh region concluded, "Little is systematically known about the performance of parts of the system." RAND noted that a more fundamental problem undermining the effectiveness of worker retraining efforts was the continued depressed state of Pittsburgh's labor market. With insufficient demand for jobs and an excessive supply of unemployed workers, most Pittsburgh employers "had little difficulty in finding the workers they need," and thus little incentive to invest in retraining efforts.[38]

Where there was success, worker retraining programs were rarely on a scale necessary to affect the economic course of the region as a whole. One program focused on the nascent robotics sector emerging in Pittsburgh and elsewhere. The Community College of Allegheny County, in close cooperation with the Westinghouse Corporation, developed a robotics installation and repair program especially for displaced steelworkers.[39] The program trained small classes of displaced workers in robotics, with promising results, but only three twenty-person classes ever completed it. [40]

At the end of the 1980s, the effectiveness of worker retraining efforts had not improved much beyond its state a decade earlier. A 1990 study of worker training programs in Pittsburgh concluded bluntly: "The multiplicity of actors, the disparate problems that each faces, and the lack of political bodies that encompass the entire region all make it difficult to identify points for intervention. Further, existing organizations that cross jurisdictional boundaries do not have education and training as their mission and tend to be weak by design."[41]

The lack of both organization and resources dedicated to worker retraining remained a problem for years. In 1993, a *New York Times* article on the state of Aliquippa, Pennsylvania, seven years after the closure of LTV's plant there, summarized the failure of retraining programs for former workers. "The trouble is that there's not enough training to really upgrade people's skills and not enough high-tech jobs available even if they get the training," one student-trainee observed, adding, "The United States lags way, way behind other industrial countries in providing new opportunities for workers where plants are shut down."[42]

In the early 1960s, the comprehensive *Economic Study of the Pittsburgh Region* (*ESPR*) predicted Pittsburgh's difficulty adapting to change, decades before change was forced upon it. It long presaged the workforce challenges that came to Pittsburgh: "The adaptability of workers and of business firms to new tasks and opportunities is less when a high proportion of those workers and firms have been doing substantially the same thing for a long time and have acquired a large stake in the status quo, and when there is a relative dearth of new and young entrants to the labor force and the business community who are prepared to take up new and unfamiliar functions."[43]

By the end of the 1980s, few regions had a bigger dearth of "new and young entrants to the labor force" than Pittsburgh. The impact was exactly as had been predicted in the *ESPR*. Limited successes of worker retraining in Pittsburgh came only in decidedly nonindustrial programs. In 1989, the JTPA gave its annual Presidential Award to the Generations Together program at the University of Pittsburgh, the only such JTPA award to a group based in southwestern Pennsylvania. Generations Together was recognized for its efforts in retraining older female workers—unlikely to have ever been steelworkers in Pittsburgh—in child care.[44]

Women in the Workforce

As Pittsburgh looked to build a new economy, not just a lack of younger workers, or even ineffective worker retraining programs, stood in the way. The region had to quickly evolve beyond its labor force's most enduring characteristics. The manufacturing industries that long defined the region had long hired a disproportionate number of men and generated far fewer job opportunities for women. For decades, Pittsburgh had underutilized women in its workforce, further limiting the pool of human capital needed to rebuild economic competitiveness.

In aggregate, the worst of the Pittsburgh labor force declines abated by the middle of the 1980s and began a slow march forward through the end of the decade. However, the mill workers were not returning to their old jobs, nor even to other jobs in the region. Regional job losses of the 1980s were mostly men, reflecting the male-dominated workforces of the heavy industries declining the fastest. In 1980, just under 40 percent of all workers in Pittsburgh were women. A decade later, men still made up the large majority of regional workers, but the trends presaged bigger shifts to come. In 1990, men working in the Pittsburgh region numbered 630,000, still down over 70,000 from 703,000 male workers counted there in 1980. Yet, the number of women working in the region expanded by 64,000, from 461,000 to 525,000, over the same decade.

The surge of women coming into the labor force was in part a necessity of circumstances. There were fewer jobs in the traditional heavy industries employing men, and the need for multiple wage earners in a typical household to compensate for the lost income forced many women into the workforce. Lost manufacturing jobs meant many households lost their primary wage earners for extended periods. Even those former mill workers who stayed in the region and eventually found new jobs, few ever regained the previous wage levels.

For generations, women had remained relatively absent from the Pittsburgh workforce. Not only had heavy industry long been a male-dominated workforce, but what made Pittsburgh different was the diminished role of women even in occupations likely to include women and slower growth in female labor force participation than in the rest of the nation. The mill jobs employing men paid well enough that second wage earners were less essential than for households with wage earners in other industries or in other regions. Also, most millwork was shift work, which typically meant employees were moved between different work periods in a recurring rotation. Dynamic schedules made it difficult for second wage earners, especially in households with dependent children, to hold jobs.

The lack of women in the labor force was not surprising in postwar Pittsburgh, but the extreme lack made Pittsburgh stand out. As far back as the 1946, the Econometric Institute's "Long Range Outlook for Pittsburgh" highlighted the problems posed by Pittsburgh's extremely low rate of female labor-force participation. The region's growth would be stunted unless there was growth in firms "employing women or engaged in the production of consumer goods."[45] For such a statement to be made in 1946, long before gender equity in the workforce was commonly noticed, let alone addressed, marked how abnormal was Pittsburgh's workforce.

Pittsburgh's industries were particularly hostile to the employment of married women. In 1950, the labor force participation rate of white married women in Pittsburgh measured only 12.4 percent, compared to 53.4 percent for single white women and over 79 percent for white men.[46] At the time, an estimated sixty-five thousand female workers would have been present in Pittsburgh's labor force if local labor force participation rates matched what was common elsewhere in the nation.[47] The disparity in married women in the workforce was not an accident but often enforced by industry rules and in some cases civil law. Soon after the war, most women were let go from manufacturing jobs because Pennsylvania state law explicitly banned them from any form of shift work. After

June 28, 1946, the Carnegie Steel Corporation formally banned employment of married women unless they were widows or the wives of disabled mill workers or veterans.[48] The relative absence of women in the workforce was noted as the explanation for Pittsburgh having one of the lowest rates of labor force participation at the beginning of the 1960s.[49]

As late as the 1970s, Pittsburgh newspaper job want ads were listed by gender. Jobs "for men" were listed independently from jobs "for women" long after the practice had ended in most other regions. A 1972 case brought before the Pittsburgh Commission on Human Relations took issue with the way classified advertisements were separated by gender. Even though the practice had faded in most major papers across the nation, the *Pittsburgh Press* continued it, going so far as to defend the practice "as a convenience to the readers." The *Press* only stopped separating its ads in 1973, after the US Supreme Court conclusively ruled against its appeals.[50]

As long as the region was dominated by manufacturing industries, Pittsburgh remained a less than welcoming place for women seeking professional employment. It is not surprising that the area significantly lagged in providing some core infrastructure to support women in the workforce. A 1983 report commissioned by the Carnegie Endowments in New York concluded, "Pittsburgh has very little infant and toddler care, afterschool care, sick childcare, night and weekend care, employer support of childcare or educational opportunity for childcare specialists."[51] Lacking such support, it was difficult for women to enter or reenter the labor force.

As the 1980s began, the rate of female labor-force participation in the Pittsburgh region still palpably trailed the nation.[52] Only the concentrated job destruction over the decade began a trend that would eventually balance Pittsburgh's labor force. From the period of peak job destruction forward, the rate of female labor-force participation and the sheer number of women working in Pittsburgh steadily increased. In 2009—the year the G20 summit came to Pittsburgh—the number of men working in the seven-county Pittsburgh Metropolitan Statistical area averaged 554,284. Likely for the very first time in history, that number was exceeded by the 555,720 women at work in the region.[53]

Border Guard Bob

In a region unable to forget past population losses, efforts continued to try and fight the flow of workers leaving after the flow itself had dissipated. In 1998, a newly formed economic development organization, the Pittsburgh Regional Alliance (PRA), intended to address the population loss as one of its first major initiatives. The PRA developed a multimillion-dollar advertising campaign aimed to dissuade younger workers in Pittsburgh from moving away. The campaign centered on a character named Border Guard Bob, who would deliver TV, radio, and newspaper advertising aimed at younger workers explaining why Pittsburgh was an attractive place to live.[54]

The campaign was not designed to attract new residents. Instead, it was going to focus on selling Pittsburgh to Pittsburghers. The planned advertising campaign was all the more quixotic in that the rate of out-migration from Pittsburgh had slowed precipitously since the early 1980s. The campaign was developed shortly after statistics were released showing a period between 1992 and 1993, when more people were moving into the Pittsburgh region than were departing. If Pittsburgh had a population problem, it was not the rate of people leaving but the continued low rates of people moving into the region. Border Guard Bob was preparing to fight the last demographic battle of the region's previous economic war.

The perceived loss of younger workers and the need to retain them continued to be a concern decades after the loss of workers subsided. In 2000, Richard Florida, the Heinz Professor of Regional Development at Carnegie Mellon University, completed a series of small focus groups talking with students.[55] His questions focused on whether the soon-to-be young professionals were looking to remain in Pittsburgh after graduation and what could entice them to stay. Florida concluded that the most sought-after benefits were natural, recreational, and lifestyle amenities. The students still considered Pittsburgh similar to traditional industrial regions such as Cleveland and Detroit and less like leading high-technology places such as Austin, Seattle, and Denver. Echoing the goals of the never-implemented Border Guard Bob campaign, one focus group participant commented: "Pittsburgh is trying to appeal to the people who grew up here. If the city was to try to appeal to people going to college here and realize what backgrounds they come from, they could do a better job keeping people here."[56]

The small project was the genesis of Florida's broader research, which eventually developed into his work on the impact of "creative-class" workers. The distilled message of Florida's emerging thesis—as gestated in Pittsburgh—was that the clustering of specialized workers was a crucial driver of regional economic competitiveness. The message that people, not firms, were the key to Pittsburgh's future was not new. The *ESPR* had reported much the same nearly four decades earlier. Remarking on the anticipated decline in Pittsburgh's core industries and prospects for future regional growth, the report concluded in 1963: "The Pittsburgh region's future depends to such a major extent upon retaining and attracting highly qualified and professional and technical people and business enterprisers, who are in demand everywhere and who command a high standard of residential amenity and cultural and professional opportunities."[57]

As conventional as those words may seem a half century later, in the middle of the twentieth century they were a radical deviation from the accepted thought and practice that economic development rarely focused on more than infrastructure. Edgar M. Hoover and his team who compiled the *ESPR* wanted to know what competitive factors would influence the growth and decline of regions long into the future. After dissecting virtually every aspect of how regional industries were changing—and were projected to change in the future—their ultimate conclusion was that "people rather than physical geography will play the leading part in shaping the region's future."[58]

For much of history, there had never a question of whether workers would move to wherever there was economic growth. Such it was that even in the explosive growth years of industry and jobs in southwestern Pennsylvania in the decades just before and after the turn of the nineteenth century, workers arrived to fill the need, no matter how fast it came. The jobs were fixed by geography, first by the proximity of local coal and the tremendous importance of rivers in early transportation networks. No matter how fast the regional steel industry grew, if workers were not available from elsewhere in the nation, waves of international immigrants filled the gap.

An emerging economic debate centers on whether people really do follow jobs or whether jobs follow people. The factors that determine regional growth are never so simple, but if the balance in that equation has even begun to shift it would alter the way practitioners think about economic development. The nature of Florida's message, if taken to its logical conclusion, is that workers are becoming the determinative factor that will shape regional competitiveness and growth or decline in the long run. The *ESPR*'s key conclusion morphed into the "war for talent" that is a ubiquitous topic today.

Still, the legacy of Pittsburgh's lost generation of workers continued to shape the economy of the region long after the worst of its job losses subsided. In the mid-1990s, public and private leaders in Pittsburgh again came together to form a new economic strategy for the future. The Working Together Consortium set an explicit goal for the Pittsburgh region to create a hundred thousand net new jobs between 1995 and 2000.[59] Progress was tracked by an ongoing Regional Economic Revitalization Index. The employment goal represented a modest 9 percent increase over the region's total employment of 1.1 million in 1995. The region only needed to sustain annual job growth of less than 2 percent a year to achieve that predetermined goal.

The Working Together Consortium's final report noted that jobs in the Pittsburgh region had only increased by seventy thousand, an average annual growth rate of less than 1.5 percent. Further, most of the new jobs had been in the health and education industries, which had not been the program's primary goal. The reality was that even such a moderate economic goal had to face inexorable demographic trends set in place a decade earlier. In the mid-1990s, Pittsburgh began to experience a new drag on its population and in turn on its economy. In 1995—just as the consortium began its new initiative—Pittsburgh became the first major US metropolitan region to experience natural population decline as the number of deaths surpassed the number of births. Even if Pittsburgh had experienced no loss of population due to migration, the region's population was contracting.

Population decline produces its own unavoidable job destruction. Two thirds or more of a typical regional economy is fueled by the consumer purchases of goods and services generated by local residents. Demographic aftershocks of the Pittsburgh's spasm of job destruction would extend far into the future. Moving beyond the demographic impact of steel's decline proved to be a much longer challenge for all of southwestern Pennsylvania.

Beyond

10

All of the studies seem to be indicating that smokestack chasing doesn't work.

Raymond Reaves, Allegheny County planning director, September 1986

Beyond Smokestack Chasing

May 1981

In early 1981, Pittsburgh appeared to have weathered the short but severe national recession that was later officially dated to extend between January and July 1980. The most substantial regional economic development effort then underway was an $800,000 advertising campaign jointly sponsored by the Allegheny Conference for Community Development (ACCD) and Penn's Southwest, a nonprofit focused on attracting industry to southwestern Pennsylvania. In May, advertisements were placed in national publications, beginning with the *Wall Street Journal*, to tell "the Pittsburgh Story." Acknowledging no economic weaknesses, regional business leaders believed Pittsburgh merely had "a bad rap nationally," a problem that a marketing campaign could fix. One of the new advertisements, titled "Dynamic Pittsburgh," matched with a picture of the region's top business leaders, a group of thirty older white men. The marketing campaign highlighted the region's quality of life, but for a very targeted audience. One of the prototype ads highlighted how business executives who relocated from elsewhere have unique opportunities to purchase large homes in rural Pittsburgh suburbs, where they could become "gentleman farmers."[1]

By July 1981, a new national recession was emerging, and the ACCD was beginning a three-year project to develop a new strategic economic plan for the Pittsburgh region. The project had its genesis four years earlier, when Allegheny County Commissioners asked the Pittsburgh business community to help modernize county operations. In response, an ad hoc group of local business leaders formed the Committee for Progress in Allegheny County (ComPAC). One ComPAC subcommittee was charged with addressing the county's economic development practices. In its first major report, the economic development committee asked: "Is it adequate to focus on the economic development requirements of Allegheny County alone?" Should economic development be pursued "on a countywide basis or, rather, from a regional perspective?" Concluding the latter, the report called for the ACCD to "begin planning for the region's long-term economic development."[2]

In 1981, the ACCD assumed ComPAC's mantle and began work on a new strategic plan for Pittsburgh's economic future. Eighteen of the region's top corporate executives led a reformed economic committee that was expected "to chart the region's economic development for the next two decades."[3] The new project brought together economists from the city's major banks, executives from the region's corporations, and contracted specialized consulting help from the Stanford Research Institute, a consulting firm later known as SRI International. What had begun as an informal committee was soon made into a permanent organization under the ACCD's auspices. Fletcher Byron, the CEO of the Koppers Company—an industrial coke company—was named committee chairman. Hiram Milton stepped down after fourteen years as the director of the Regional Industrial Development Corporation (RIDC)—one of the region's oldest economic development organizations—to become the committee's fulltime director. Robert Pease, who had been the executive director of the ACCD since 1958, said the new committee was preparing not just a study but a comprehensive "strategy for economic growth" for greater Pittsburgh.

Since the end of World War II, the ACCD had been the institutional core of Pittsburgh's hybrid public–private civic leadership. The success of the region's postwar renaissance has been attributed in no small measure to the partnership of Richard King Mellon, who helped form the ACCD in 1943, working with City of Pittsburgh Mayor David Lawrence. Mellon and his proxies led the newly formed ACCD through its first decade and beyond. After Mellon's passing, whoever served as chairman of the ACCD was his de facto successor as the leader of Pittsburgh's business community.

Recently retired Gulf Oil CEO Jerry McAfee was serving as ACCD chairman in the fall of 1982. McAfee was a natural choice for the position.

Not only was Gulf Oil one of Pittsburgh's largest corporations, but it was originally a Mellon family business, located in Pittsburgh since its early-twentieth-century incorporation. When an early outline of the three-year economic committee study was presented at the ACCD's annual meeting in November 1982, McAfee was recuperating from an operation that prevented him from attending. His prepared remarks were delivered by his successor, current Gulf Oil Chairman and CEO James E. Lee, who would succeed McAfee as ACCD chairman within a year. Lee emphasized that the new economic development committee was "one of the Conference's most significant undertakings since the first Renaissance," no minor characterization given the breadth of ACCD projects through its first three decades.[4]

Much had changed in Pittsburgh's corporate leadership since Gulf Oil was formed in 1907, and even more dramatic change for the company was imminent. Over the next twelve months, Texas oilman T. Boone Pickens acquired over 11 percent of Gulf Corporation stock. Gulf's stock price had begun to collapse as energy prices declined from their peaks of the previous decade. The prototypical corporate raider, Pickens aimed to take full control of Gulf, which he argued was undervalued, and to force the corporation to divest its oil and gas assets. The dispute between Pickens and Gulf's board of directors evolved into one of the biggest corporate proxy fights in history. Gulf held off Pickens's effort at its November 1983 annual meeting, but takeover threats did not go away. The company was forced to seek a corporate white knight willing to acquire the company on more agreeable terms. In March 1984, less than eighteen months after Lee's speech at the ACCD's 1982 annual meeting, Gulf announced it had agreed to be acquired by the Standard Oil Company of California.

The corporate sleight of hand had immediate and existential consequences for Gulf's Pittsburgh operations. The combined company was renamed Chevron and consolidated its headquarters in southern California—effectively ending Gulf's long history in Pittsburgh. At the beginning of the 1980s, Gulf was one of the world's largest oil companies and the seventh-largest US corporation with extensive operations around the globe, all of which were based in Downtown Pittsburgh in the art-deco skyscraper that bore the company's name.[5] Founded by the Mellon family, led by William Larimer Mellon—cousin of Richard K. Mellon—nearly eight decades earlier, Gulf was central to the city. McAfee's and Lee's top roles at the ACCD symbolized Gulf's importance to Pittsburgh's civic leadership. Despite the bulk of its energy being business located far from western Pennsylvania, Gulf had deliberately retained its worldwide headquarters in Downtown Pittsburgh. For thirty-eight years, until supplanted by the U.S. Steel Building in 1970, the iconic forty-four-story Gulf Building was the tallest skyscraper in the city.

Less than a year after it was acquired by Standard Oil, Gulf's formal presence in Pittsburgh evaporated. James Lee was its last CEO, as the company disappeared permanently from the economic landscape of southwestern Pennsylvania. Lee's service leading the ACCD was just one example of why Gulf was considered Pittsburgh's quintessential corporate citizen. Gulf's leadership had long been a bedrock of the region's corporate community, but the corporation's expansive philanthropic efforts made it a civic force far beyond the boardroom. Gulf's lightning evacuation from Pittsburgh was feared to affect "everyone from the Boy Scouts to the local hospitals."[6]

Gulf's rapid decoupling from Pittsburgh created a void in the region's corporate leadership precisely when leadership was needed most. Economic circumstances already dire in late 1981 had devolved unabated through 1982. Yet the five business areas the ACCD economic committee prioritized were, at best, vague ideas for future study: first, expanding and diversifying Pittsburgh's industrial base; second, helping business sectors that supply services that can be "exported" to other areas, including financial services, engineering, and healthcare; third, developing international markets, fourth, attracting high-technology businesses; and fifth, reinforcing the city as a center for corporate headquarters.[7] The five vectors did not signify as great a shift from the past as they may have appeared. Hiram Milton, director of the committee that was preparing the report, made this clear publicly: "The intent is not to go to a quick high-tech fix," and "there is still a primary metals manufacturing industry here that is important to the area."[8] Milton's remarks emphasized that Pittsburgh was going to stick to its knitting and was far from ready to move away from its legacy industries. More troubling was that the preliminary report lacked specifics about implementing its recommendations. For example, the report concluded there was a significant need for worker retraining in the region. Still, when asked where funding for worker retraining programs could come from, the committee's chairman only vaguely speculated, "I imagine it will have to be a combination of federal, state, and local sources."[9] What those potential funding sources could be was left unidentified.

There was growing criticism of the structure of the ACCD economic committee, which was composed almost entirely of business leaders. Little or no participation was invited from local institutions of higher education or elected officials.[10] Amid the economic turmoil, a different coalition of regional economic leadership was beginning to emerge. In June 1983, Wesley Posvar, the University of Pittsburgh chancellor, sponsored a three-day summit to address Pittsburgh's regional development Strategy for the 1980s and 1990s. With more than eighty attendees, the conference brought together not only industry leaders but university, government, and nonprofit leaders from across southwestern Pennsylvania. It produced thirty-five distinct recommendations. One of these was to coordinate efforts with those of the existing ACCD Economic Development Committee, but only as part of an expanded leadership for the region. The summit's main recommendation was for the Pittsburgh region to form an entirely new leadership group where "all community interests should be represented."[11]

In late 1984, the ACCD finally presented its final 220-page *Strategy for Growth,* three years in the making. Described as "a call to action and a plan for action," the full report itemized over 100 distinct proposals.[12] The new plan was called "a major disappointment" because so little effort went into implementing any of its recommendations. "They presented a plan. . . . And you don't hear any more about it," said Jim Roddey, Port Authority chairman and future Allegheny County chief executive. Three years after its release, Carnegie Mellon University President Richard Cyert called the 1984 report "basically a flop," describing most of its recommendations as "sort of superficial, like 'Let's get better advertising for the city.'"[13]

Strategy 21

Faced with historic rates of job destruction, unemployment, and outmigration—and with most local governments under severe fiscal distress due to escalating economic collapse—the public was increasingly looking to state government for relief. Receiving myriad funding requests, state officials faced a daunting problem in trying to prioritize among them given the limited funding that could be allocated—a process that was more economic triage than strategic planning. In 1984, then–State Representative Tom Murphy—a future mayor of Pittsburgh—persuaded city and county officials to coordinate funding requests to state government.

The collaborative process that resulted became a new public–private coalition, one that included not only representatives of city and county governments but also private corporations, the Pennsylvania Economy League, Carnegie Mellon University, and the University of Pittsburgh. The group, and plan, came to be known as Strategy 21.

Strategy 21 issued its priority list for public investment across southwestern Pennsylvania in 1985. In sharp contrast to the ACCD's recent effort, the new report was conspicuously coauthored not by business leaders but by Mayor Richard Caliguiri and collectively the incumbent Allegheny County commissioners, along with Cyert and Posvar. The report became a new blueprint for the Pittsburgh region's economic development strategy as it attempted to deal with unabated deindustrialization. Still fealty, its manufacturing core was not being abandoned. Strategy 21's stated goals were to first reinforce the region's traditional economic base as a center for the metals industry and international corporate headquarters; then convert underutilized land, facilities, and labor force components to new uses, especially those involving advanced technology; enhance the region's quality of life; and, finally, expand opportunities for women, minorities, and the structurally unemployed.

The largest and highest priority funding request was $97 million to construct a new midfield terminal at the Greater Pittsburgh International Airport—described as "one of the projects most important to the successful economic transition of the Pittsburgh region." The document also specified an additional $76 million requested from the state for a Southern Beltway highway project to connect the relocated airport terminal with the arterial Parkway West extended to Downtown Pittsburgh. The combined request of $173 million for airport-related projects made up the largest part of the $425 million list.[14]

Other than airport-related projects, the next largest itemized request was $38 million to rehabilitate Three Rivers Stadium and its environs, a project envisioned to include the development of an adjacent science center, hotel, and additional commercial developments along Pittsburgh's riverfronts.[15] Further down the list was $14 million for converting the former LTV steelworks along Second Avenue in close proximity to Downtown Pittsburgh into an office complex optimistically later named the Pittsburgh Technology Center.

Still lacking was a strategy to move the region away from its concentration in manufacturing industries. What materialized from Strategy

21 was largely concentrated on physical renewal projects and remained "silent on the subject of renovating the region's secondary industrial sector along modern lines."[16] Ther report also enumerated an additional list of unranked needs. Other than the request for funding the new airport terminal, the lack of prioritization was arguably a deliberate tactic to keep the broad coalition authoring the report intact; each participant was free to focus on specific projects they most supported.[17]

The Strategy 21 report shaped the bulk of public funding coming to Pittsburgh from state government at the peak of the region's economic distress. When the Commonwealth of Pennsylvania's 1986–87 budget was finalized, it authorized the full amount requested for the midfield terminal. In addition, the state fully funded the construction of the connecting Southern Beltway, a highway project essential to the relocation of the new terminal. Also closely following the priorities of the Strategy 21 request, the next largest earmark in the state's budget went toward projects on Pittsburgh's North Shore near Three Rivers Stadium.

Plans for reinvestment at Pittsburgh's principal airport were far from new in 1985. When the airport began regular commercial operations in 1952, its newly constructed passenger terminal was briefly the second-largest in the country, but it saw little expansion over subsequent decades. By the 1970s, exponential growth in commercial air transportation left the terminal behind the times. A new passenger terminal was first envisioned in 1969. That year, concept drawings for a futuristic six-story building connected to six-passenger "docks" were unveiled.[18] The plan was approved in principle but could never source funding for the project. Then–County Controller Frank Knox voiced opposition: "The total cost of this disturbs me. Who's going to pay for what?"[19]

A new $250 million concept, combining a relocated landside and an entirely new midfield terminal, was proposed in 1978.[20] Costs were inflated by the need for the multiple buildings central to the redesign as well as the need for an expensive and automated underground people-mover between the landside and airside terminals. Again, the revised proposal struggled to obtain funding. In 1982, an updated budget estimated the total cost for the midfield terminal concept had risen to between $379 and $644 million, forcing a design revision that cut nearly a third of the cost.[21] Even the scaled-back proposal was anticipated to cost $289 million. US-Air—the renamed dominant air carrier in Pittsburgh—publicly rejected the concept due to its high cost. The airline disputed the notion that the existing terminal was overcrowded. Its CEO, Ed Colodny, described the east dock of the existing terminal as "totally underutilized . . . you could shoot a cannon and not hit anybody."[22]

Colodny consistently argued that the airport's and USAir's competitiveness would be "jeopardized unnecessarily by increased costs of doing business."[23] The airline refused to commit to a long-term lease at the airport unless the Commonwealth of Pennsylvania provided at least $100 million in direct funding.[24] The long-deferred project would likely have remained an unfunded concept if it had not been redefined as key to Pittsburgh's postindustrial transformation. No longer framed as a solution for overcrowding at the existing decades-old airport terminal, a new midfield terminal was marketed as something that "could restore Pittsburgh's economic base" and somehow "help counterbalance the loss of the Mon Valley steel industry."[25] Pushing for funding to complete the project, Allegheny County Commissioner Tom Foerster argued: "At stake is the whole future of the region—southwestern Pennsylvania, eastern Ohio, West Virginia, and our ability to keep jobs and attract new ones." Inordinate hopes were being placed on a refurbished airport terminal becoming a catalyst for the entire regional economy.

Commissioner Foerster, who cochaired the committee that drafted the Strategy 21 proposal, ardently supported the midfield terminal project. His backing facilitated the priority given to its construction in the funding request sent to the state, but state leaders readily jumped on the bandwagon. In a July 1986 visit to Pittsburgh, Governor Richard Thornburg echoed Foerster's enthusiasm and called funding for the new terminal "the No. 1 priority in this region." Thornburg emphasized that the new terminal was the key to transforming the region from "the economic base of today to the economic base of the future."[26] Political action was still running ahead of the airline industry's support for the project. USAir had yet to agree to the long-term lease, which was the core justification for the new terminal.

Shifts within the national airline industry did not dampen support for the project. Portending later corporate machinations, in March 1987, Carl Icahn led an effort by TWA to buy USAir for $1.4 billion. This eventually failed, but had the acquisition gone forward, the potential consolidation of the two airlines would have likely obviated much of the economic justification for the new terminal. The potential downsizing of the airport's largest airline, an airline critical to the plan for the new terminal, did not deter public officials. Despite Icahn's ongoing efforts, county commissioners vowed to proceed with the construction, and initial construction contracts for were approved in 1987, even before Allegheny County signed a crucial long-term agreement with USAir. Commissioners explained they were proceeding despite the risk because the project was "too important to the region" to allow any delay in the construction schedule.[27]

When the projected cost of the new terminal increased to $550 million, even the additional state funding was insufficient to ensure the project could proceed. USAir continued to balk at the costs it would inevitably bear directly or indirectly through increased landing fees long into the future. Only in 1988 did the airline finally agree to a new long-term contract with the county. In addition to state funding for the terminal and the Southern Beltway, the US Federal Aviation Administration provided $51.6 million for the new terminal, while Allegheny County provided an additional $42.3 million and a supplemental $4.2 million came from the Pennsylvania Department of Transportation.[28]

Construction of the new midfield terminal commenced in 1988. In addition to financial support for the new terminal, Allegheny County allocated $150 million in public funds to refurbish the airport's runways, and $190 million in public money would be spent building the Southern Beltway expressway needed to provide access to the relocated terminal. Direct subsidies were in addition to $524 million raised by Allegheny County bonds issued in 1988 to fund the new airport projects, bonds guaranteed by revenues collected from airlines extending until the year 2019.[29] Nearly five years of construction culminated in the opening of new landside and airside terminals in 1992, together hailed as "the single greatest economic generator this area has seen."[30] Despite its earlier misgivings, US Airways agreed to a thirty-year lease, obligating the airline to use fifty-three of the airport's seventy-six new gates through 2022—a date that would extend far past the corporation's lifespan.

Renaissance Cities and Mehrabian Report

Despite the funding provided for Strategy 21 priorities in Pennsylvania's 1986–87 budget, pressure continued for additional state support to address deteriorating economic conditions elsewhere. Pennsylvania state government was criticized for being slow to assist the state's most distressed areas. Governor Thornburgh at first opposed funding many such locally focused efforts but instead favored the broader strategies that could improve the state's industrial competitiveness. Relenting to public pressure, the Thornburgh administration authorized $95 million in 1986 for an omnibus Renaissance Communities program aimed at helping some of the most depressed communities, including the Mon Valley, Beaver County, and the Shenango Valley, all in western Pennsylvania.[31]

Hope persisted that regional steel plants could be restarted. The Renaissance Cities package included $12 million for highway improvement but also a specific earmark for report to study the future of steel manufacturing in the Pittsburgh region.[32] In 1988, Allegheny County channeled the state funding into a "steel retention study." Management consulting firm Arthur D. Little and Hatch Associates, a specialized firm with expertise in industrial facilities, completed the study. Hatch Associates had recently provided an optimistic report that concluded the closed Duquesne Works could be viable as an employee-owned enterprise. The contracted purpose of the new steel retention study was to "guide public investment in support of private efforts to retain those portions of the local steel industry that can be competitive in the foreseeable future." The report evaluated the potential to restart four shuttered steel plants, including LTV's South Side Works, USX's Homestead Works, LTV's Aliquippa Works, and Wheeling–Pittsburgh's Monessen Works. It concluded that only LTV's South Side Works could be economically viable, and only if a new $200 million continuous caster was installed on the site. Private-sector interest in restarting steel production at the site never materialized, and other priorities more than spoke for public-sector funding. Through the 1980s, none of the various efforts to retain heavy industry in the region achieved lasting success.

Steelworkers, in particular those in the steel communities outside of the city of Pittsburgh, expected no immediate relief from the efforts to build a new airport terminal nor from most of the longer-term projects prioritized by Strategy 21. On the ground in the former mill towns, the only redevelopment efforts that mattered were those that could result in restarting shuttered factories. Any more fundamental transformation was not on the agenda. "I don't want to see my valley waiting five to 10 years for new industry to be developed," said Homestead Councilwoman and future Mayor Betty Esper in March 1988. "We can't eat grass," she explained, responding to a report by international experts recommending that part of the closed Homestead Works be converted into an International Garden Festival.[33]

In 1987, the Federal Reserve Bank of Cleveland issued a report looking at the deindustrialization still unfolding in Pittsburgh. So fast was the industrial collapse that the concentration of manufacturing industry employment in Pittsburgh had already dropped to the lowest among in the district's four largest cities, including Cleveland, Cincinnati, and Columbus. Economist Randall Eberts, too, attributed the scale of Pittsburgh's decline to the resistance to change that had come earlier. Prosperity in steel "didn't leave much room for the new areas of potential success." For Pittsburgh and other regions, the study concluded, "a prerequisite for future growth is the ability to break with the apparent security of the past and a willingness to assume the risks of the future."[34] The observation mirrored the warnings of the past.

Through the end of the 1980s, efforts to retain existing steel employment proceeded alongside nascent strategies aimed at shifting the structure of the regional economy. Conflicted goals fostered confusion in the region's economic leadership and difficulty in translating Strategy 21's success into ongoing cooperation and coordination. A 1988 editorial lamented that Pittsburgh needed "some agency, some institution, to step forward and take charge of the region's destiny."[35]

In 1993, the ACCD commissioned another analysis of Pittsburgh's economic competitiveness, conducted by a committee chaired by Carnegie Mellon University President Robert Mehrabian. The 1994 White Paper highlighted the area's economic resilience but also its "failure to successfully compete for economic growth with other regions." The report bluntly criticized the region's collective leadership: "After years of intense debate without a conclusion, the region is adrift. Our economic problems have reached crisis proportions." Addressing inaction in the face of such dire needs, the report concluded that Pittsburgh's "economic development civic structure is beset today by increasing factionalism, fragmentation and overlapping agendas which divert attention from solving real problems."[36] So adversarial had economic development efforts within the region become that a 1996 report looking at Allegheny County government recommended that a regional nonaggression pact be instituted between counties in southwestern Pennsylvania.[37]

Yet the Mehrabian report still did not push for abandoning Pittsburgh's legacy industries. It emphasized a "renewed emphasis on manufacturing" and went so far as to question the emphasis on alternative redevelopment efforts in the 1980s, which were seen as having prioritized the promotion of high-technology and service-sector industries. Reflecting a continuing article of faith, the report concluded, "Nothing has yet replaced manufacturing as the region's engine of growth and prosperity."[38]

The Mehrabian report recommended a nine-month task force be formed to develop a set of initiatives to improve Pittsburgh's economy. The Working Together Consortium (WTC), as the new effort was labeled, sought to bring focus to the myriad objectives of overlapping economic development organizations. Toward those goals, the Pittsburgh Regional Alliance was formed in 1995. The new organization was intended to be an umbrella organization for several of Pittsburgh's largest economic development organizations, including the Greater Pittsburgh Chamber of Commerce, Penn's Southwest Association, the RIDC of southwestern Pennsylvania, and the World Trade Center of Pittsburgh.[39]

The WTC again made it a priority to build on the region's strengths, which it clearly identified as a historic concentration of metal industries but now also chemicals, health systems, and biomedical, information, and communications products. A new industry supplying environmental products and services was seen as a growth sector in southwestern Pennsylvania in no small part due to the ongoing brownfield cleanup required of shuttered industrial facilities. In 1995, the WTC emphasized the goal of rebuilding the region's manufacturing sector by titling its last public report *Investing in the Future: Strategies for Strengthening Southwestern Pennsylvania's Regional Core and Restoring Its Manufacturing Base.*[40] By 1994, employment in all primary metals industries in the Pittsburgh region had dropped to under 30,000 jobs, a sizable number, but far from the region's top industry sector.[41] Steel was no longer dominant even within the region's manufacturing sector, which had dropped to 120,000 jobs by the middle of the 1990s, a full third smaller than 180,000 in the region's expanding health and education sectors.

The belief that the Pittsburgh region could rebuild its past industrial strength had yet to disappear. In 1995, continuing support for Pittsburgh's historic manufacturing core came from Ray Christman, the president and CEO of the Southwestern Pennsylvania Industrial Resource Center (SPIRC)—one of the region's leading economic development agencies: "The prevailing attitude I detect today is that manufacturing is a part of our past, not our future. While this is an understandable reaction, it is not based on fact. Manufacturing is still central to the Pittsburgh regional economy. Our ability to recognize this asset and take advantage of it will ultimately determine—more than any other factor—how well we compete with other regions of the country."[42]

Antagonism between SPIRC and other regional economic development organizations, including the Ben Franklin Initiative, continued through the decade.[43] There remained no consensus on what economic strategies the region should be pursuing, nor on which individual or organization was taking the lead in economic development efforts.

Even the newest parts of Pittsburgh's manufacturing agglomeration faced insurmountable challenges sustaining growth. When the Volkswagen plant closed, efforts immediately focused on finding a new owner. Little thought went into converting the site into something other than a future manufacturing facility, though what industry was undetermined. Local officials predicted industrial output would soon return: "I just can't believe a plant this modern, with this location, will long go unused. . . . I think we may go back to seeing 5,000 workers in that facility."[44] The number of workers at the site would never approach past peaks.

In 1990, the Sony Corporation of Japan was enticed to bring new investment to the site, with the help of $40 million in state incentives, mostly provided by the Commonwealth of Pennsylvania.[45] Beginning in 1992, Sony assembled televisions on the site and later expanded operations to include an integrated state-of-the-art glass factory. Talk of a new electronics cluster for southwestern Pennsylvania was often repeated while the plant was operating. For a period in the 1990s, Pittsburgh's manufacturing employment stabilized, but it was not because the loss of jobs in traditional industrial sectors had abated. Growth in jobs at the new Sony plant offset continuing declines across older manufacturing subsectors.[46] Yet again, the enterprise had a relatively short existence, compared to the long tenures of any of western Pennsylvania's former steel plants. Changing technology soon made the new plant obsolete. A decade after it opened, retrenchment in the global market for consumer electronics forced Sony to consolidate its international operations and permanently close its Westmoreland County operations.

Likewise, public investment in a new airport terminal did not have the catalytic economic impact envisioned. USAir's 1989 merger with Piedmont West expanded the use of Pittsburgh as a major hub of the larger airline through the 1990s. Pittsburgh-based employment at the firm expanded, and briefly the airline was the largest private-sector employer in the region. A merger with United Airlines was in the works in 2000, but negotiations broke down before it was discerned whether the combination would have received federal approval.

Already struggling financially, the airline faced ever greater problems following industrywide declines after September 11, 2001. Less than a year later, in August 2002, US Airways filed for Chapter 11 bankruptcy and entered bankruptcy again in 2004 and 2005. Most of the long-term leases the airport had negotiated with Allegheny County and its successor, the Allegheny County Airport Authority, would be abrogated in the course of bankruptcy proceedings. Bankruptcy also begat the airline's rapid shift away from its Pittsburgh-based operations. Following a merger with America West in 2005, the airline's need for Pittsburgh as a hub dissipated further. A merger with American Airlines in 2014 would bring about the closure of a consolidated flight operations center, along with the loss of six hundred jobs that had been based in Pittsburgh. From 2002 through the end of the decade, daily traffic through the airport declined by nearly two-thirds from the peak of US Airways hub operations there. The legacy costs of the midfield terminal persisted, pushing up fees for other airlines.

The midfield terminal, and the hub operations it was purposely designed for, was expected to build a new post-steel industry cluster for Pittsburgh. So important was that goal that it absorbed the large bulk of public funding the region mustered for economic development in the 1980s. Much of the impact of that spending was fleeting.

Hazelwood

Hopes to reindustrialize Pittsburgh had not faded late in the 1990s. At the time, the last basic steel plant operating within the corporate limits of the city was the LTV Coke Works at Hazelwood, once just one part of the much vaster steelworks of Jones & Laughlin. In March 1997, the EPA filed a notice of violation against LTV for exceeding particulate emissions from combustion stacks for more than 18,000 of the 29,400 hours the plant operated from May 1 through December 1, 1996. By July, LTV announced it could not keep the operation in Hazelwood open, claiming over $500 million investment was required to correct operating and environmental problems.[47] Just shy of its sesquicentennial of nearly continuous coking operations within the city, the plant ceased operation in 1998, but efforts to bring coking back to the site had already begun.

Within months, the city of Pittsburgh proposed a financial incentive package using tax increment financing (TIF) to lure a new operator to restart coking operations on the same site. A TIF allowed local taxing bodies to borrow money to finance site improvements. It would pay back the loans from the higher property tax revenues collected in the future. The Sun Coke Company took the bait and proposed not just restarting the existing coke works but building a new larger coking facility on the same site, a plant that would have been 50 percent larger than the LTV plant.

Bringing a new coke plant to the city of Pittsburgh immediately became a singular priority for virtually all of the region's political and business leaders. Sun's proposal had nearly universal support of local unions and county officials, along with the wholehearted backing of both the Republican governor of Pennsylvania, Tom Ridge, and city of Pittsburgh's Democratic mayor, Tom Murphy.[48] Even local media headlines obsequiously supported the consensus effort. "Sun Coke plant sets a shining example," shouted a local news article.[49] The potential of new industrial jobs superseded all other concerns in a region desperately hoping to bring back lost industries.

Despite the unified front, the region's economic priorities were not as monolithic as they once were. Community-based opposition to the proposed coke works reemerged to oppose the wide coalition supporting

LTV Coke Works, Hazelwood, City of Pittsburgh, 1998 (Photography by Ken Kobus / Ken Kobus Collection, 1980–2008, AIS.2006.18, Archives & Special Collections, University of Pittsburgh Library System)

the project. Many who lived in close proximity to the site did not see the benefits of the new plant but feared a return to emissions that would be hard to prevent in a new coke works. Just beyond the environs of the Hazelwood neighborhood were some of the more prosperous and stable neighborhoods of the city of Pittsburgh. Nearby residents were far more likely to be employed in education or healthcare—which had sustained steady growth as the region's manufacturing sectors contracted—than in any other industry.

Community opposition to the proposed new coke works focused on its potential impact on air quality. As long as the former coke works had operated, sulfur dioxide emissions measured in Hazelwood had sustained levels far above what was measured in Downtown Pittsburgh.[50] Between January and June 1973, the Allegheny County Health Department reported that Hazelwood only had "good air" 6.2 percent of the time and typically recorded the worst air quality in the county.[51] Past emissions from the shuttered coking operation had inevitably spread over much of the city of Pittsburgh's east end. Routine smells spreading across the city were characterized as everything from banana oil to burnt mothballs.[52] The 1998 closing of the coke works had immediately improved air quality for the downwind residents.[53] Continuing a role it had created for itself over a quarter century earlier, the Group Against Smog and Pollution filed motions to intervene in the legal case brought against LTV and organized community opposition to the new plant.[54] Stark clashes between nearby residents and potential workers played out in the political debate over proposed tax incentives offered to Sun.[55]

The new coke plant would likely have been built, if not for the critical role of publicly funded incentives that were an integral part of the deal. In addition to the TIF, the site was set to be designated one of Pennsylvania's twelve Keystone Opportunity Zones. The state designation would have made the made income generated from operations at the site tax-free for twelve years. Allegheny County commissioners had approved the TIF, and Pittsburgh's city council had given a preliminary vote in support of the Keystone Opportunity Zone designation. Residential opposition focused on the governing board of Pittsburgh School District. The school district is a separate local government, and the public incentive package required the school board's approval. In December 1998, the school board did what was once unthinkable in western Pennsylvania: it voted against the potential of new industrial jobs in Pittsburgh. By a vote of 5 to 4, the board voted against the opportunity zone designation. The result eliminated the potential tax abatements, effectively killing the project. Early in 1999, Sun Energy abandoned its efforts to rebuild a coke works in Pittsburgh.

No follow-on industrial development came to the former LTV site. If the site were the only large industrial brownfield needing redevelopment in the region, it would have been a major challenge to remediate and repurpose. However, by the 1990s, the former coke works in Hazelwood was just one of many such behemoth industrial brownfields. What emerged across southwestern Pennsylvania was a set of new environmental challenges created by the shuttered plants that remained in place long after the jobs they once hosted had departed.

11

There are some 40 miles of abandoned industrial riverbank in the Monongahela Valley alone: blast furnaces stand rusted and silent like gaunt sculptures; railroad spurs lie hidden in tall weeds, waiting for the scrap merchants. And on the hillsides above are the communities of the unemployed steelworkers, where the psychological damage is every bit as great as the economic.

David Lewis, Remaking Cities Conference, Pittsburgh, 1988

How Now Brown Town?

October 29, 1986

For three weeks in the fall of 1986, Hollywood came to western Pennsylvania, but not for a reason regional marketers wanted to advertise widely to potential investors. Production crews for a major film slated for release the following summer had come to greater Pittsburgh because of the vacant industrial sites uniquely available there. Movie producers needed a site to represent a dystopian future industrial landscape. Though the setting was intended to represent Detroit, greater Pittsburgh provided more than a few surrogate locations. Thus, the shuttered Monessen Works of the bankrupt Wheeling–Pittsburgh Steel Company was briefly the set for the 1987 movie *Robocop.*

The steel complex began operations in 1902, and within just a few years it became a fully integrated steel plant stretching nearly two miles along the Monongahela River. Like so many other mill towns in the Mon Valley, the fate of the city and its coterminous steelworks were inseparable. The massive plant monopolized all of Monessen's riverfront access, which had been an industrial center from its incorporation as a municipality. The municipal name was a combination of the Monongahela River and the German steelmaking center of Essen in the heavily industrialized Ruhr Valley. Three blast furnaces, fifty-six byproduct coke ovens, a basic oxygen process shop, and a range of finishing mills were all collocated on the site, making it one of the largest steelworks even among the massive industrial operations clustered in southwestern Pennsylvania. As mature as the industrial complex was, it nonetheless represented some of southwestern Pennsylvania's most modern steelmaking capital. Before it merged with Wheeling Steel in 1968, Pittsburgh Steel had undergone a costly Program for Profits reinvestment plan in the 1960s, including installing the latest basic oxygen process blast furnaces. Then, in 1978, the Carter administration, through the US Economic Development Administration and the Farmers Home Loan Administration, guaranteed 90 percent of a $150 million loan that was used to construct a new rail mill and the rebuilding of two batteries of coke ovens.[1]

The loan guarantee was the largest in the development agency's fifteen-year history and a rare provision of federal support for the steel industry or any of southwestern Pennsylvania's legacy industries. Even though steel rail was the product that fueled the expansion of Pittsburgh's steel industry at the end of the nineteenth century, Monessen's new rail mill was the first built in the United States since 1921 and had been deliberately constructed with the most advanced Japanese technology. Finally, the company invested in a modern five-strand continuous bloom caster—made with the latest German and Japanese technology—completed on the site three years earlier, in 1983.[2]

In the face of the national recession, the recent investments made little impact, and the steel industry's historic contraction was well underway as the last new investment came to the Monessen Works. Federal funding complemented the company's own debt-financed investments at the plant. The company found it difficult to service its debt as the demand for steel and steel prices collapsed amid the recessions of the early 1980s. In April 1985, Wheeling–Pittsburgh became the first major US steel producer to seek court protection from its debtors.[3] Once industrial operations shut down, the abandoned site proved attractive for the movie producers.

The Los Angeles–based firm crew described the site and the economic conditions it represented: "Everything you see here tells you it was really dangerous, dirty work. And some of these guys put in 30 or 40 years here, and look what they got—nothing."[4] The former steelworks encompassed over three hundred acres, monopolizing most of Monessen's prime riverfront locations. It was left to the public sector to find new uses for the sprawling site, uses that could only come once intensive environmental remediation had been completed. The Westmoreland County Industrial Development Corporation was tasked with redeveloping the site, heavily contaminated with lead, arsenic, cadmium, polychlorinated biphenyls (commonly known by the abbreviation *PCB*) oils, coal tar, and coke oven gas residues, among other contaminants.[5]

Monessen was an exception to the typical fate of most industrial operations in southwestern Pennsylvania, in that it partially restarted some of its legacy operations, albeit intermittently. In 1988, Wheeling–Pittsburgh sold the coke works and continuous caster on the site to Sharon Steel, a company that was itself in bankruptcy at the time. Environmental problems with the coke battery kept the company from restarting operations. Eventually, the works was sold to Koppers, one of the oldest coking companies in Pittsburgh, which operated the coke ovens until 2008, when it sold them to ArcelorMittal, a Luxembourg-based multinational steel company, for $160 million.

On May 5, 2009, just three weeks before the White House announced Pittsburgh as the site of the May 29 G20 summit, Arcelor announced the shutdown of the remaining coking operations at the Monessen site.[6] Pittsburgh's economic transformation was going to be highlighted during the G20 summit, while the rump of the region's heavy industry continued its historic contraction. The announcement was just the latest setback for the industrial suburb of Monessen. Two days earlier, the Associated Press described it as Pennsylvania's emptiest town.[7] The coke works remained shuttered for five years, but in 2014, a rebound in the international market for metallurgic coal prompted the company to invest $50 million to restart Monessen's coke batteries. The new investment brought back less than two hundred jobs—an almost inconsequential fraction of the eight to ten thousand that had once been employed on the site—and the coke produced was no longer part of a Pittsburgh-centered agglomeration of steel production. Output from the restarted coke works was directed to supply steel plants the Luxembourg-based company operated near Cleveland.[8]

The coke works used just 45 acres of the former integrated plant, leaving over 250 acres for other uses. No new employers ever employed more than a small fraction of the site's former workforce. Thirty years after Wheeling Steel declared bankruptcy, residents still looked back at the former steelworks. "We're dying rather than letting something new grow and move forward," said a local small business owner, continuing: "older residents know that steel is not coming back, but they cannot imagine anything else. Everybody is just defeated."[9] The challenge was that the vacant and contaminated site was not an anomaly but the modal legacy left by the steel industry along all of the rivers of southwestern Pennsylvania.

Brownfields

Through the 1980s, hopes lingered that shuttered industrial operations could eventually restart, but at the end of the decade, few plans existed to reopen any of them. By 1990, a vastly incomplete inventory of vacant industrial sites in proximity to Pittsburgh included both the massive Homestead Works and Duquesne Works of U.S. Steel along with the corporation's National Tube Works in McKeesport, most of the former Monessen Works, Westinghouse's East Pittsburgh Plant, most of LTV's steelworks along both sides of the Monongahela River within the city of Pittsburgh (still operating was LTV's coke works in Hazelwood), and all of its Aliquippa Works along the Ohio River, twenty miles from Downtown Pittsburgh. Each site was among the largest former industrial sites, or brownfields, ever to need redevelopment.

The largest industrial sites were the most glaring challenges, but they were only the most visible part of the region's cumulative problem. Innumerable smaller sites, once active parts of Pittsburgh's industrial heritage, were also left vacant as heavy industry contracted. Land use across the region had conformed over a century to industrial uses rapidly vanishing. Disused industrial sites, large and small, had concentrated environmental degradation that required remediation before any reuse was possible. Environmental remediation costs made most former industrial sites economically unviable for private-sector investors. The costs to clean up an industrial brownfield and prepare it for reuse far exceeded the costs to invest at an unused greenfield location, unencumbered by the price of environmental remediation. Environmental cleanup at each site was a singular challenge, but cumulatively the environmental challenges extending across southwestern Pennsylvania had no precedent in the United States.

One of the first major redevelopment projects undertaken in the region was at the industrial brownfield closest to Downtown Pittsburgh: the former Eliza Works of the Jones & Laughlin (J&L) Company. The corporation's operations, which stretched over a mile along Second Avenue, had been used exclusively by heavy industries since before the

Civil War. In 1977, the company announced it would close major parts of the site and dispose of nearly 178 acres close to Downtown Pittsburgh.

The last blast furnace to operate on the site, named Ann, had been in operation since 1899. Workers believed sheer age was the main reason steel production was shutting down, not that it was the harbinger of any wider regional or national contraction in the steel industry. A *New York Times* headline from later in 1979 declared "LTV's Steel Operations Prospering After Merger," referencing the company's recent acquisition of the Lykes Corporation and highlighting LTV operations in nearby Aliquippa.[10] In 1980, J&L executives were adamant: "There is nothing else in the Pittsburgh category. We have no other major shutdowns up our sleeve.'"[11] Nonetheless, Pittsburgh officials faced their first major challenge: repurposing an abandoned industrial site.

The city of Pittsburgh initially considered purchasing the site for a new public parking garage serving Downtown Pittsburgh. Allegheny County considered a warehouse on the site for conversion into an annex for its existing Downtown jail. The mayor's office resisted a city council proposal to purchase the entire site; "There isn't that kind of money" was the paraphrased response of a top city official.[12]

Pittsburgh Councilwoman Michelle Madoff, who had been instrumental in founding the Group Against Smog and Pollution a decade earlier, pushed for the city to acquire the bulk of the site for a proposed garbage-to-steam refuse plant. Pressing environmental issues included what to do with ever-increasing amounts of solid waste sent to landfills. A nonprofit corporation had been formed to create a garbage-to-steam plant in Pittsburgh that could recycle two thousand pounds of refuse daily to produce steam and electricity. Support for the project waned as opposition emerged from local landfill operators fearing competition while dropping energy prices in the 1980s decreased the potential value of energy to be produced at the plant.

In 1981, the Park Corporation—a Cleveland-based company specializing in industrial salvage—purchased forty-nine acres of the former plant from LTV, intending to clear and remarket it for alternative uses. Park purchased the site after local economic development leaders failed at finding a buyer they hoped would continue to use it as a steel strip mill, the very use J&L was abandoning.[13] Park initially intended to remarket the site for industrial uses, citing the same advantages that once applied to many of the region's large steel mills: direct access to the river and rail lines. The salvage company considered locating its machinery division in a building previously used as a galvanizing plant. Still, plans remained to clear the site and find new industrial tenants as of 1982.[14]

Economic conditions were rapidly deteriorating in Pittsburgh just as Park took ownership of the site. While in 1981 it might have seemed reasonable to prepare the site for new industrial uses, by 1983, the possibility of bringing new industry into the region had faded. In November 1993, the Urban Redevelopment Agency (URA) of Pittsburgh paid Park $3.4 million for the entire site. As part of the agreement, the Park Corporation agreed to complete the demolition of the site's remaining structures.[15] Midday on June 15, 1983—and without advance public notice—its last two standing blast furnaces were felled in a planned demolition.

The former industrial site was optimistically named the Pittsburgh Technology and Industry Park, but in 1983, plans for it were preliminary, vague, and mostly unfunded. Investing in the site was far from the top priority in a region searching for an economic strategy to address the deindustrialization being forced on it. The 1985 Strategy 21 plan that the Pittsburgh region used to prioritize state funding for redevelopment efforts included a specific request for $14 million to support converting part of the former J&L into an office park, a small fraction of the $97 million requested to build a new midfield terminal at the Pittsburgh International Airport and the additional $76 million for a new highway segment to connect to the new terminal.[16]

Construction of the first building at the Pittsburgh Technology Center began in 1991, but redevelopment efforts faced nearly immediate challenges because of environmental concerns that originated far back in Pittsburgh's industrial history. Though the site had been covered with fresh fill to a depth of several feet, preconstruction testing found traces of ferrous cyanide on the site, later identified as coming from a tar storage tank, part of the coal-gas plant that had operated there more than a century earlier. This discovery resulted in the delay of major construction for more than two years and required Carnegie Mellon University to relocate its planned research building fifty feet downstream from the property line of the former gas plant.[17]

Redevelopment of the Second Avenue site required both collaboration and funding from nearly all of the economic development organizations in Pittsburgh. URA became the owner of the site but vouchsafed site clearance and planning to the Regional Industrial Development Corporation. The state of Pennsylvania's Department of General Services agreed

Pittsburgh Technology Center, 2023

to purchase two buildings to be constructed on the site, which were to be leased to the University of Pittsburgh and Carnegie Mellon University.

Funding came from a myriad of sources, including state appropriations. The Pennsylvania Department of Commerce invested $10 million in the project, and the state's Department of Community and Economic Development allocated $8.3 million, while local philanthropic foundations provided $300,000. A tax increment financing district (TIF) was created at the site—the city of Pittsburgh's first use of a TIF—allowing the URA to borrow against future property tax revenues for additional investment required for site preparation.

Finding new technology-based companies to become tenants at the new Pittsburgh Technology Center was another challenge. The city's two major universities were the first tenants. Belying the site's technology moniker, the first commercial tenant was actually one of Pittsburgh's oldest industrial companies. Union Switch and Signal—a railway signaling company originally founded by George Westinghouse in 1881—relocated its research operations to the new center in 1995. The company received $16 million in state incentives to relocate its local operations from suburbs north of Pittsburgh, and not move to South Carolina, where the company had moved its headquarters in 1992.[18] Sixteen years had passed from the time steel was last produced on the site. Nonetheless, ongoing development eventually brought more tenants than originally projected, and the bonds issued as part of the original TIF package were fully repaid by 2001.[19]

When redevelopment efforts began on the former LTV site along Second Avenue, the vast bulk of Pittsburgh's heavy industry was still operating. By the time the first private-sector tenants moved in, a cascade of industrial plants across western Pennsylvania had permanently shut down, each requiring equally extensive environmental remediation. Among the new industrial brownfields requiring redevelopment was U.S. Steel's former Homestead Works. In operation since 1881, the plant had been absorbed into Andrew Carnegie's early steel empire by 1883 and then consolidated into U.S. Steel when the conglomerate was formed in 1901. Steel production ceased on the site in 1986, amid the wave of plant shutdowns.

The Park Corporation, which had initially sought to redevelop LTV's Second Avenue site closer to Pittsburgh, purchased 270 acres of the former Homestead Works in 1988. In 1983, Park had purchased the assets of the bankrupt Mesta Machine Corporation adjacent to the Homestead Works. Instead of selling off Mesta's machinery and clearing the site, Park kept it operating. Eventually, other steel companies were merged with Mesta to form the West Homestead Engineering and Machine Co., or WHEMCO. But there was never any similar effort to keep the massive former Homestead Works open. Eight years was required to clear the site of nine hundred thousand tons of scrap and more than 1 million tons of concrete from over 10 million square feet of building space.[20]

Again, redevelopment relied on a myriad of funding sources and collaboration among a wide range of local government and public agencies. Located outside the city, the Allegheny County Department of Economic Development took a lead role in site development. Over $30 million in public investment for the site was raised through the creation of a TIF that was a collaboration of three distinct municipalities and the coterminous Steel Valley School District. The TIF allowed money to be borrowed against the future real estate value expected to be created by the new development.[21] The first new tenants on the site moved in by 1999—thirteen years after U.S. Steel ended steel production there. Construction on the mixed-use site, now made up of residential, shopping, and light industrial operations collectively named the Waterfront, continued over the subsequent decade.

Pittsburgh's postwar Renaissance, and the later construction boom known as Renaissance II in the late 1970s, both depended primarily on private-sector investment. Gateway Center, the centerpiece of Downtown Pittsburgh's redevelopment, was only possible with investment by New York's Equitable Life Assurance Society. In the 1970s, the construction of PPG Towers and five other major Downtown construction projects were all primarily financed by private-sector investments. The situation the region had faced less than a decade later could not have been more different. Little private-sector investment was looking to redevelop the brownfields that proliferated across southwestern Pennsylvania. Public investment was required to offset the additional costs of investing at an industrial brownfield compared to greenfield development. Yet the same economic contraction creating unprecedented need for economic development funding was also putting nearly insurmountable

Former Homestead Steel Works site, 1998

strains on government revenues at all levels. Escalating needs to address mountng social service needs doubly strained public resources as jobs disappeared and unemployment soared. With public funding stretched thin across so many competing needs, there was little choice but to seek creative new ways to finance redevelopment efforts.

At the end of the 1980s, the largest industrial brownfield within the city of Pittsburgh was the former South Side Works of LTV Steel. As LTV headed into bankruptcy in 1986, the corporation permanently shut down its South Side Works, across the Monongahela River from the Pittsburgh Technology Center. Redevelopment efforts were initially focused on plans to reinvest in, and restart, steel production. An Allegheny County report identified the South Side Works as the most likely of the county's former industrial sites that could restart steel production.[22] Only after efforts to find an industrial tenant exhausted themselves, the site was remarketed as a potential base for riverboat gambling, not yet legal in Pennsylvania. In 1993, the URA purchased the site intending to develop a riverboat gambling and entertainment complex. A private development company looking to lease the riverfront real estate in the future loaned the URA money for the purchase.[23] Neighborhood resistance stalled passage of enabling legislation required to legalize riverboat gambling in the state, eventually ending the plan.

Mirroring the Waterfront redevelopment in Homestead, the former South Side Works was eventually redeveloped into a mixed-use residential, retail, and shopping district. This project, too, had to overcome severe environmental remediation costs and funding compiled from a range of state and local sources. Also mirroring the long timelines of other major brownfield projects, the first new tenants on the site only arrived in 2002, almost two decades after its industrial operations concluded. Eventually, the reincarnation of the South Side Works would include not only a mix of retail and residential development but the University of Pittsburgh McGowan Center for Artificial Organ Development, a new $20 million regional headquarters for the Federal Bureau of Investigation, a training field and sports performance center for the Pittsburgh Steelers and University of Pittsburgh football teams, and a 125,000-square-foot training facility for the International Brotherhood of Electrical Workers.

Both the scale and speed of redevelopment efforts in Pittsburgh faced funding limitations that did not hinder redevelopment efforts in other nations facing concentrated deindustrialization. In Germany's Ruhr

Valley—a region suffering a comparable contraction of its historic core of coal and steel industries during the 1980s—a federal initiative called Zukunftsinitiative Montanregionen, or the Initiative for the Future of Coal and Steel Regions, was begun in 1987 to assist local redevelopment efforts. The regional government of North Rhine–Westphalia created a "super fund" with the equivalent of over $250 million ($750 million in 2025) for industrial redevelopment projects. Economic development efforts were not hindered by a lack of funding so much as a lack of ideas of what to do with former industrial sites.[24]

The funding available in the heart of the Ruhrgebeit, as the integrated industrial region was known, was only one part of a far larger public investment focused on the environmental reclamation of former industrial sites. Over the course of the decade between 1989 and 1999, the regional North Rhine–Westphalia government invested an additional $2 billion in environmental reclamation and redevelopment projects. While most brownfield redevelopment efforts in western Pennsylvania were pursued independently of each other, the much larger German public investments were part of an integrated plan to address legacy environmental issues across nineteen municipalities.

The IBA Emscher Park Initiative (Internationale Bauausstellung Emscher Park) was an omnibus strategy to reclaim more than five thousand acres of industrial brownfields across Germany's Ruhr Valley.[25] The largest redeveloped sites included a former steelworks in the city of Duisburg and the conversion of the Zeche Zollverein coal mine and coke works in Essen—once the largest coal mine in Europe—which was converted into an art gallery and later declared a UNESCO World Heritage Site in 2001. Other projects included the revitalization of the inner harbor of the city of Duisburg, a city much like Pittsburgh—one of Europe's largest inland ports because of the shipment of coal, coke, and steel once concentrated there. Over 125 individual projects included 25 dedicated to revitalizing housing in the region and efforts to retrain and reemploy former industrial workers displaced by deindustrialization. Significant funding was focused on the renaturalization of the Emscher River, which had been mostly used as shunt for industrial sewage through much of the twentieth century—all problems that had stark similarities to the problems facing Pittsburgh and its environs.

Comprehensive regional efforts for land reclamation were needed in both Pittsburgh and the Ruhr Valley because the environmental impacts of industry spread far beyond the industrial sites and extended across municipal borders. Just over the river from the Homestead Works, but resting within the city of Pittsburgh, was a twenty-story artificial mountain containing an estimated 269 million cubic feet of industrial slag.[26] The open-hearth steel production that dominated Pittsburgh through the first half of the twentieth century generated enormous amounts of slag, an industrial byproduct mostly made up of limestone but infused with a range of contaminants. Over 72 million tons of industrial residue had accumulated at the one site between 1922 and 1972, when dumping operations at the location were discontinued. The 238-acre artificial landscape had also filled much of the valley of the Nine Mile Run waterway. When the URA purchased the real estate in 1995, the site was described as "desolate moonscape."[27] The purchase price of $3.8 million was only the initial cost of a far more significant investment required to first clean and then find a new use for the site.

In the late 1990s—nearly three decades after the site had ceased being an active dump location—the city of Pittsburgh formulated a plan to convert it into a new residential neighborhood. Reversing policies from the 1950s, when several city neighborhoods were intentionally razed for industrial expansion, new housing stock was created from formerly industrial real estate. The acquisition was the largest in the history of Pittsburgh's Urban Redevelopment Authority and later encompassed the largest stream restoration in the United States by the US Army Corps of Engineers.[28] Lacking precedent, a major challenge was meeting entirely undefined environmental standards for such a project. A significant part of the time and cost of the project were multiple, often redundant, levels of environmental oversight to ensure compliance with yet-to-be-codified environmental standards.[29] When completed, the residential neighborhood, named Summerset, was the first neighborhood-scale expansion of residential housing within the city since World War II.

Like the Emscher River in Germany, concentrated industrialization had dire consequences for regional waterways across western Pennsylvania. Slag deposited across from the Homestead Works had virtually obliterated the Nine Mile Run waterway still feeding into the Monongahela River. Long since devoid of life, because of the concentration of industrial waste, the waterway had been envisioned as a new city park by renowned architect Frederick Law Olmsted in the 1920s. Though in 1928 the site was designated to become a city park, industrial needs took priority, and the real estate was instead sold to the Carnegie Slag Company, whereupon it became a dumping ground for industrial slag from at least three different steelworks in the Mon Valley. Efforts to renaturalize the creek only began in 2003, when the city of Pittsburgh invested $2.7 million, matched by more than $5.5 million from the US Army Corps of Engineers, to restore the aquatic ecosystem.

The challenges at Summerset and Nine Mile Run were endemic to the greater problem of early brownfield redevelopment that had to proceed before there was clear legal guidance on what standards must be met before former industrial sites could be converted to new uses. Early redevelopment efforts were challenged by "uncertainties over contamination and its potential legal impacts."[30] From the peak of plant closures in the mid-1980s, a decade passed before Pennsylvania passed some of the first legislation to address the many legal unknowns that impeded redevelopment of former industrial sites. A package of laws known as the Pennsylvania Land Recycling Program attempted to clarify the legal requirements that applied to the remediation of former industrial sites.[31] The new laws included the Pennsylvania Land Recycling and Environmental Remediation Standards Act of 1995, which defined cleanup standards and, more importantly, ended future liability when cleanup standards were achieved. Later, the federal Small Business Liability Relief and Brownfields Revitalization Act of 2002 was modeled after Pennsylvania's legislation.[32]

Riverfronts

The geography of industrial facilities in western Pennsylvania was never spread out evenly across the region. Most steel production crowded into narrow industrial corridors, taking up virtually all of the region's accessible river valleys. Once freed from industry's century-long monopoly, Pittsburgh slowly found new uses for its formerly blockaded riverfronts. Reclaimed industrial sites opened up new possibilities for the rivers that once gave Pittsburgh its unique advantage as a center for transportation, trade, and industry.

Using rivers as recreational assets was not an entirely new strategy. The postwar Pittsburgh Renaissance included efforts to create a new Point Park at the head of the Ohio River, a project only completed when its iconic 150-foot water fountain became operational in 1974. Postwar flood-control efforts had begun to tame the unruly rivers that had routinely flooded, making many alternative uses of riverfronts difficult or impossible. With the completion new sewage processing facilities, water quality began to improve, and the use of the rivers for water-based recreation began to increase.[33] Still, the 1959 *A Master Plan for Riverfronts and Hillsides in the City of Pittsburgh* criticized "one serious omission" in the priorities of the Pittsburgh Renaissance: "To date the conservation and use of the riverfronts and hillsides for recreation has been rare and generally incidental." For long Pittsburgh's "rivers themselves, and the adjacent land had been neglected in all but one aspect, serving industry and commerce." The report was conflicted in stating first, "Our city is awakening to the recreation and aesthetic value of its rivers and hillsides as its greatest natural asset." Yet it also emphasized that "the flat land adjacent to the rivers must continue to be occupied by the industry and commerce which support the City."[34]

Once industrial plants closed, the newly accessible rivers faced their own environmental challenges. Industrial concentration along the banks of the Monongahela River, along with the vast networking of mining operations that supported it, left the waterway far from healthy by the middle of the twentieth century. Abandoned mines across the vast riversheds generated acidic mine runoff contaminated with toxic levels of iron, zinc, manganese, lead, and mercury, just to begin. Compound sources of pollution had eliminated what had once been a diverse ecosystem; no fish were found living in the river into the late 1960s.[35] Though ample water supplies were an economic advantage for the industries of Pittsburgh, irregular surges in river acidity were even a recurring problem for regional steel plants.[36]

As heavy industry receded, the potential for other uses of the rivers was beginning to emerge as key to a broader strategy for a region. In 1987, the American Institute of Architects sponsored its first Remaking Cities Conference in Downtown Pittsburgh. The conference came to Pittsburgh to address the ongoing economic challenges facing the region. The keynote speaker and honorary chairman of the conference was Great Britain's heir apparent, Prince Charles. [37] The conference was held at the original David Lawrence Convention Center, built in 1981, during Pittsburgh's Renaissance II construction boom, but it was a mostly windowless hall that made little attempt to connect with the Allegheny River just outside.

The conference also brought to Pittsburgh a Regional/Urban Design Assistance Team (R/UDAT), which was comprised of architects and planners who presented a new vision of the city that looked to the rivers as a source of regional revitalization. For generations, the heavy industries of southwestern Pennsylvania had virtually monopolized the rivers, blocking alternative uses by mill towns and their residents. The visiting planners believed economic transformation required that the communities of southwestern Pennsylvania regain access to the region's abundant natural amenities. Recommendations included extending street patterns of Mon Valley municipalities through former industrial real estate to reach the riverbanks and creating a "greenway-amenity river walk" to improve quality of life for residents, a priority that had long since lagged behind the needs of industry.[38]

Water quality in the region was as decimated as the air had been. Promoting alternative uses for the rivers remained a secondary priority through Pittsburgh's postwar renaissance. Industry had long used the major rivers and their tributaries as industrial inputs to be consumed, with little concern for water quality. The steel industry needed large quantities of water, as did ancillary coking operations. Extensive coal mining across the vast watersheds of the Allegheny and Monongahela Rivers had particularly detrimental impacts on the rivers. As far back as the 1930s, the Pittsburgh station of the Bureau of Mines had been sealing abandoned coal mines in attempts to prevent acidic coal byproducts from seeping into regional rivers and streams.[39]

Improving water quality proved far more intractable than many other environmental problems facing southwestern Pennsylvania. The national energy crisis of the 1970s set back efforts to clean Pittsburgh waterways, as many formerly closed coal mines across the watersheds of the Monongahela and Allegheny Rivers were reopened. Increasing mine runoff again pushed up the waterways' toxic acidity. Inadequate reinvestment meant that antiquated water and sewer infrastructure across the region routinely overflowed into the rivers, contributing to one region's major environmental problems. As late as 2001, Pittsburgh rivers were declared unfit for human contact 50 percent of the days during the summer recreational season.[40]

Efforts to use the region's rivers and riverfronts began to take a new priority only at the end of the twentieth century. A trail advocacy group, Friends of the Riverfront, was founded in 1991 and accelerated efforts to convert riverfront real estate into quality-of-life assets. The river-focused vision described by the R/UDATs for the municipalities of the Mon Valley was extended for a broader swath of the region extending from the city's core. Development of riverside trails for biking and pedestrian use leveraged riverfront real estate transitioning away from industrial uses. Efforts accelerated after a new Riverlife Task Force was formed in 1999 by an amalgam of Pittsburgh's public, private, and philanthropic leadership to develop a vision and master plan for Pittsburgh's riverfronts. Completed in 2000 by Harvard professor and urban planner Alex Krieger, a new Waterfront Master Plan focused on thirteen miles of riverfront in close proximity to the city of Pittsburgh. The re-visioned purpose for Pittsburgh's rivers excluded any plan for reindustrialization or return to an industrial past, their primary use for over two centuries.

Three years before the G20 arrived in Pittsburgh, *The Economist* profiled the ongoing change in the city by asking: "How now brown town?" The centerpiece of the region's transformation was how Pittsburgh was "doing its best to reshape old land, by cleaning up former mining and industrial sites for uses that suit the modern economy." The article emphasized the impact cleaner air, land, and water had on the economic prospects for the city and region. In the new economy, the region's quality of life was central to attracting the workers needed to foster transformation. The article highlighted the role of major brownfield redevelopments in Pittsburgh's transformation. It noted how enhanced riverfront amenities had the potential to "improve Pittsburgh's appeal to creative or knowledge-intensive workers—and those who employ them."[41] It is unlikely the author knew of the proscription of the *Economic Study of the Pittsburgh Region* more than four decades earlier—that the region's future would indeed depend on its ability to improve its quality of life to attract workers.

Plant closures in western Pennsylvania extended long after the spasm of deindustrialization concentrated in the 1980s. In 2012, the Horseheads zinc plant in Monaca, Beaver County, announced plans to cease operations. First built in 1931, zinc smelting at the site continued until 2002, after which it continued as a processor of secondary zinc feedstock, until it was fully closed in 2013. The vacant site may have presented local economic development officials with yet another contaminated brownfield needing redevelopment and tremendous environmental remediation because of its specialized use over eight decades. Surprisingly, the site was destined for another future and was about to become one of just a few former industrial sites near Pittsburgh ever to find a new industrial tenant. In 2015, the land was sold to Shell Chemical Company to erect a new ethane cracker, the latest development in yet another energy revolution emanating from Pittsburgh.

12

What accounts for the differences between cities? Arriving as strangers, we usually sense the "something" that marks the character of a place. Take Pittsburgh. The essence of Pittsburgh is energy.

From the film *Pittsburgh*, 1959

Energy Burgh

October 20, 2004

On quiet farmland twenty miles southwest of Downtown Pittsburgh, over a million gallons of water were being pumped deep into the ground. A Texas exploration company was testing a new mining technique in Pennsylvania for the first time. The injection of water, sand, and chemical additives was being forced into a deep layer of shale to create microfractures in the underground rock. If the process was successful, the sand would hold the cracks open and free commercially viable amounts of natural gas.

The existence of untapped natural gas reserves throughout northern Appalachia was well known. A 2003 government report estimated that natural gas resources across the Appalachian Basin could exceed 70 trillion cubic feet of undiscovered gas, over three times the nation's annual consumption of the fuel at the time.[1] The vast bulk of natural gas underneath Pennsylvania was trapped within layers of shale and other rock formations that extended as far as three miles underground. Conventional wisdom held that the extraction costs of northern Appalachian shale gas were too expensive for the method to ever be commercially viable, but one company was playing a hunch. Range Resources, Inc. believed the application of hydraulic fracturing ("fracking")—an unconventional mining technique that was stimulating new oil and gas production in Texas—could also work in Pennsylvania.

Fracturing underground rock to release natural gas was not a new technology. Hydraulic fracturing had been developed in the oil and gas industry during the 1940s and was a standard, but limited, technique used to enhance the production of existing wells. In the 1980s, the Texas exploration company Mitchell Energy began applying hydraulic fracturing to develop natural gas in the Barnett Shale gas field in northcentral Texas.[2] In 1991, the Department of Energy subsidized an experiment conducted by that company utilizing horizontal drilling techniques in natural gas exploration.[3] Little came from these efforts until 1997, when engineers adjusted the mix of fluids being pumped into the shale. The shift, coupled with the experimental horizontal drilling techniques, soon made the Barnett Shale not only a productive field but the single biggest new source of natural gas within the continental United States in decades. Exploration firms believed the same techniques could be applied elsewhere, sparking a national search for the next big shale play.

The test bore that initiated a new energy boom in Pennsylvania almost never happened. Range Resources had come to the Renz farm a year earlier, not planning to apply fracking to the site. Traditional bores into the Oriskany sandstone and Lockport dolomite geologic layers below the farm in 2003 had tapped a layer of natural gas that briefly appeared promising but had quickly exhausted themselves. By 2004, the wellhead was being prepared for abandonment and land reclamation.[4] Only after core samples from the site were reexamined back in Texas did the company decide to redrill on the same site, this time using the most advanced slick-water fracking that had proven successful in Texas.[5]

Southwestern Pennsylvania was an obvious place to test new shale-gas extraction techniques. Over a sixteen-year period beginning in 1976, the Department of Energy expended $92 million exploring the potential of fracturing and horizontal drilling techniques to extract natural gas from Appalachian shale gas reserves. Initiated by the Morgantown Energy Research Laboratory just south of Pittsburgh, the Eastern Shale Gas Reserves program eventually wound down by 1992, but the program paved the way for future exploration efforts. It advanced several of the technologies that later catalyzed unconventional shale gas production and documented the shale gas potential of Appalachia.[6]

Four days later, flow tests confirmed that significant amounts of natural gas could be extracted from the Marcellus Shale. Quietly, the company began expanding its acquisition of land across Pennsylvania to exploit the discovery, but the potential of shale gas across Pennsylvania could not be hidden for long. Soon not just Range Resources but dozens of oil and gas exploration companies came to Pennsylvania and rapidly expanded land acquisition and drilling operations. By the end of the first decade of the twenty-first century, the Renz #1 well was joined by more than five thousand other new wells drilled across Pennsylvania and a growing number in adjacent areas of West Virginia and Ohio. In 2010, natural gas production from the Marcellus Shale exceeded output from the Barnett Shale. New drilling activity was affecting the economy of communities across Pennsylvania, but Pittsburgh became the gateway for much of the investment flowing into the state. So large was the new supply of natural gas that the resulting energy boom immediately began reshaping energy economics for the nation. For Pittsburgh, though, fracking was yet another chapter in a recurring story of extractive industries emerging in the region. A new Pittsburgh was being faced with an economic catalyst it knew far too well.

Few regions can claim to be the nexus of so many different energy booms, across so many different eras, as western Pennsylvania. In 1850 Samuel Kier, a partner of Benjamin Franklin Jones in several central Pennsylvania iron foundries, constructed what is believed to be the first oil refinery in Pittsburgh, a one-gallon still he operated on Seventh Avenue in Downtown Pittsburgh. Kier discovered a method to distill crude oil into fuel for lighting and semimedicinal uses that were common in the era. At the moment of invention, the uses for Kier's product remained limited, as did the supply of crude oil, usually a byproduct of salt mining or flowing at the surface from natural seeps.

Kier's engineering became exponentially more important once another energy source was successfully developed in the state. The modern oil industry traces its roots to the discovery of oil at a site less than a hundred miles from Pittsburgh just before the Civil War. When Edwin Drake spudded the first commercial oil well in Venango County in 1859, a new economic boom descended on western Pennsylvania. Though the Drake well was eighty miles north-northeast of Pittsburgh, the city of Pittsburgh was the largest major city nearby. The Allegheny River and its tributaries provided a ready means of transporting the new commodity to Pittsburgh. Oil was brought the city first in barrels floated downriver and later via dedicated pipelines that connected the new oil fields with industrial users. The city quickly became the world's largest refining center, with fifty-eight local oil refineries operating by 1867.[7] Pittsburgh benefited as the center of finance commerce for the new industry, but its most lasting impact likely came from the oil-generated wealth of which Pittsburgh-based investors, including a young Andrew Carnegie, disproportionately took advantage. Carnegie's investment in stock of the Columbia Oil Company provided him the capital he would later reinvest in iron, bridge, and steel ventures.

Well before hydraulic fracturing reinvigorated the industry, natural gas had a long history in southwestern Pennsylvania. In fact, the modern natural gas industry traces its roots to a town twenty miles east of Pittsburgh in 1878, when brothers Michael and Obediah Haymaker accidentally discovered natural gas. Their neighbor, Josh Cooper, had been using a natural seep of gas along the nearby Turtle Creek to boil down sap for maple syrup. The Haymaker brothers thought the gas was an indicator of undiscovered oil that could be commercially developed far closer to Pittsburgh than the vast oil fields around Titusville, Pennsylvania, ninety miles north. They leased land and erected a derrick near the borough of Murrysville in search of the nation's next big oil discovery. Instead, as the well reached a depth of fourteen hundred feet on November 3, 1878, their bore dipped into a gas-rich layer of sand and brought a tremendous flow of natural gas to the surface.[8]

The nascent refining industry began shifting away from western Pennsylvania within the first decade of commercial production from Drake's first well. With the expansion of oil pipelines, the geography of refining shifted eastward. Oil boomed in Pennsylvania until the early fields began to show exhaustion and faded in importance once far greater discoveries in Texas and the Gulf Coast emerged early in the twentieth century. The shallow vertical wells that fueled Pittsburgh's natural gas boom of the 1880s, and a much more sedate 1919 boomlet in nearby McKeesport, all faded in importance as regional supplies were exhausted.

What remained through all eras was a virtually limitless quantity of coal available across southwestern Pennsylvania and its environs. Pennsylvania coal remained the primary fuel of the second industrial revolution in North America. By 1899, Pennsylvania produced nearly 80 percent more coal than all other states in the nation combined. The Consolidated Coal Company based in Pittsburgh grew to become the world's second largest coal company.[9] Pittsburgh, once defined by the iron and glass industries, had transformed into the nation's center of coal and steel. At its peak in 1914, over 82,000 jobs were generated by the coal industry within just the Pittsburgh region.[10] Based on the central role of coal alone, southwestern Pennsylvania had a resource-based economy through most of its settled history. Without coal, Pittsburgh would likely have evolved as a major trading center, due to its location at the head of the Ohio River, but the region's defining industrial history could never have emerged.

Through the middle of the twentieth century, the Pittsburgh district remained the nation's primary supplier of metallurgic coal used to make industrial coke.[11] Coal has yet to exhaust itself in southwestern Pennsylvania, but inevitable technologic advances eventually eroded the region's once dominant advantages in coal supplies. The shift from small-scale beehive ovens to largescale byproduct ovens expanded the pool of usable coal supplies for coke production. When coke was produced in a multitude of small-scale beehive ovens, the low sulfur coal of Connellsville was virtually the only coal suitable for the manufacture of industrial coke for blast furnaces. Increased demand during World War I spurred the development of much larger industrial-scale byproduct coke ovens. The larger coke works could source coal from a far wider range of fields in southern West Virginia, Kentucky, and Virginia, obviating advantages of coal from southwestern Pennsylvania. Increasing efficiencies in the steel industry further depressed demand for metallurgic coal. As a result, coal production in the region dropped by a third, from its peak of 76 million tons in 1918 to 51 million in 1928, even as regional steel production expanded.[12]

Decades later, as World War II ended, the decline in demand for coal accelerated as entire industries shifted toward the use of other fuels. Coal-fueled steam power was rapidly being displaced by diesel engine technology in railroad and water transportation. Diesel, like gasoline, was commonly produced as a distillate of petroleum. Across the nation, more than 35,000 coal-powered locomotives were still in operation in 1950, but that number dropped to fewer than 350 by 1954.

Rapidly declining use of coal in the years immediately after the war was an economic threat to Pittsburgh, where 66,000 regional workers were still directly employed in mining industries.[13] The coal industry desperately sought new innovations that would reinvigorate demand. For a brief moment, it looked like the coal industry might develop into a growth sector once again in Pittsburgh, with new growth to be generated by the promise of yet another energy revolution on the verge of emanating from the city.

On March 25, 1947, an above the fold headline in the *Pittsburgh Press* announced the "biggest story in the history of coal."[14] The day before, the Pittsburgh Consolidation Coal Company, then the nation's largest coal company, in partnership with the Standard Oil Company of New Jersey,

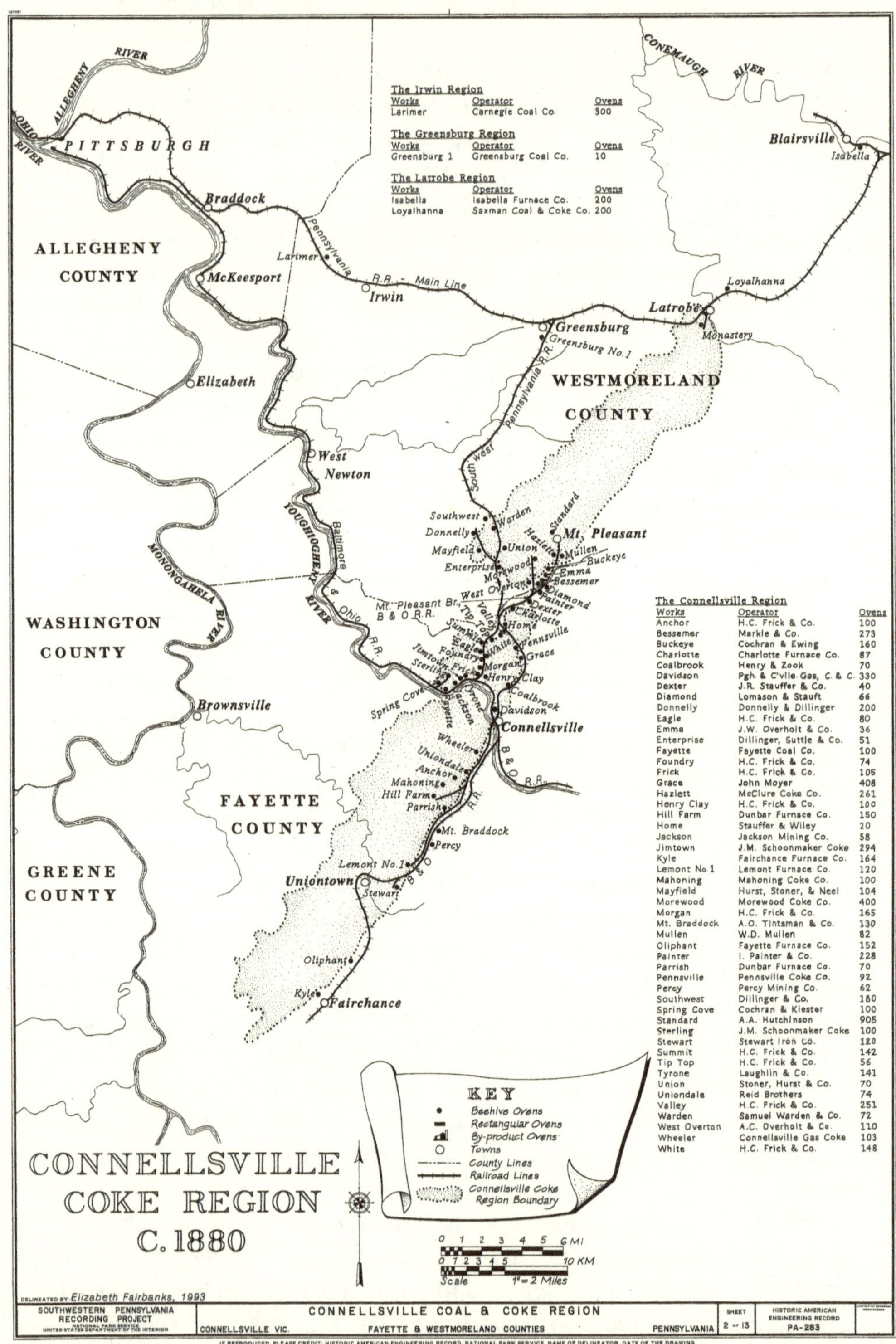

Connellsville coal and coke region, Fayette County, Pennsylvania

the nation's largest oil producer, announced plans to construct a $120 million coal liquefaction plant twenty-five miles south of Pittsburgh. Commercial-scale production of liquefied coal promised not only to revolutionize the coal industry but to create new competitive advantages for the energy-intensive manufacturing industries that remained concentrated in Pittsburgh. Suggesting no hyperbole, the project promised, "A vast industrial miracle is coming to Pittsburgh," When completed, the project was expected to "affect everyone in Western Pennsylvania, bringing them new prosperity and a cleaner place to live."[15]

The excitement over a technology still in development was due to the compound implications it had for Pittsburgh. Coal liquefaction held the potential of giving back to coal a competitive advantage it was rapidly losing to petroleum-based fuels. With coal reserves underneath northern Appalachia still effectively limitless after more than a century and a half of continuous extraction, any new economic advantage for the coal industry was a strength for Pittsburgh. Foreshadowing promises for an ethane cracker to be built in the region a half century in the future, local coal executives and Allegheny County officials pointed out, "Sizable employment gains are visualized for the areas selected for the locations of such large plants." The plant envisioned for Pittsburgh would generate sixty-five hundred regional jobs.[16]

Despite the region's oversupply of coal, energy was the biggest threat to Pittsburgh's economy in the years after World War II. Localized natural gas shortages forced Pittsburgh utilities to ration supplies to industries during the winter of 1946–47. The hundred largest industrial consumers of natural gas faced a nearly 100 percent curtailment of supplies through February 1948.[17] More than fifty thousand regional workers were temporarily laid off because of the fuel shortage, and Pittsburgh was increasingly seen as uncompetitive as a location for new industrial investment because of insufficient fuel supplies. Cost-effective and industrial-scale coal liquefaction appeared to be a fortuitous solution, expected to simultaneously solve several of the most glaring problems threatening Pittsburgh's economic future. The new technology was anticipated to provide "the first effective challenge coal has given oil in the 20th century."[18] For greater Pittsburgh, the technology promised to "assure coal a continued high place in the business sun," "insure full success of the smoke control program," "build up the area as an oil center," and "attract new industries."[19] With no hint of hyperbole, Park Martin, executive director of the

Allegheny Conference for Community Development, declared the new plant "the best shot in the arm Pittsburgh has ever had."[20]

The joint venture between Consolidated Coal and Standard Oil was just a part of what appeared to be a rapidly emerging new synthetic fuel industry cluster in Pittsburgh. In May 1948, the US Bureau of Mines dedicated its Pittsburgh-area facility in Bruceton, Pennsylvania, to coal gasification research. The following month, the Gulf Oil Company and the Koppers Company announced a cooperative private-sector research effort to develop coal gasification technologies. In preparation for the larger plant, Consolidated Coal stood up a $300,000 experimental plant in November 1948. The full prototype plant was projected to be in operation for a year to obtain required baseline data before construction of the larger $120 million plant could begin, expected as early as 1949.

Mentioned only in passing was the caveat that scientists and engineers needed to "iron out the wrinkles of the not-fully-completed project."[21] Construction of the full-scale plant never began, as the economic necessity of the potentially disruptive technology quickly evaporated. By the end of 1948—barely seven months after his company's coal-gas project had been announced—Consolidated Coal President George H. Love acknowledged, "At present there is no apparent economic justification for investment of large sums in commercial facilities to convert coal into gasoline."[22] For Pittsburgh, an entirely unanticipated shift in the region's fuel supplies—an indirect impact of World War II exigencies and a battle waged across the North Atlantic ocean years earlier—curtailed the need for alternative energy sources.[23]

Pipelines

Immediately after the United States declared war on Germany, on December 8, 1941, the commander of the German navy's U-Boat fleet began planning extensive operations against US shipping. Admiral Karl Dönitz's original plan for Operation Paukenschlag (Drumbeat), was to immediately deploy virtually the entire German submarine fleet off the North American coast, but this was scaled back because the warships were needed elsewhere. Starting with just five submarines that crossed the Atlantic in January 1942, by May the German navy had sunk 233 ships, including nearly 22 percent of the US fleet of tankers, in the North Atlantic approaches to US ports. At the beginning of the war, northeastern states received over 95 percent of their oil supplies from the Gulf Coast via oceangoing tankers.[24] Beginning as early as January 22, 1942, the shocking success of U-boats against the civilian tanker fleet immediately forced gasoline rationing all along the east coast. To safely get oil to the eastern United States, the federal government began a crash program to construct two fourteen-hundred-mile pipelines—the largest projects of the war other than the Manhattan Project and the Alaska Highway.

Completed in just eleven months, the "Big Inch" was a twenty-four-inch diameter pipeline that transported oil from East Texas oilfields to Illinois and then to eastern Pennsylvania, where the line split to bring product to refineries in both New Jersey and Delaware. The complimentary "Little Big Inch" was a twenty-inch pipeline that delivered refined products including gasoline, heating oil, diesel, and kerosene. Built for less than their predicted cost of $95 million, the pipelines were sold as surplus after the war for $146 million. The Texas Eastern Transmission Corporation was incorporated in early 1947 to purchase the pipelines and immediately converted them to transport natural gas eastward. It was only an accident of fate, and the geology of the Appalachian Plateau, that the two pipelines passed through southwestern Pennsylvania just south of Pittsburgh along the Pennsylvania–Maryland border. Once the conversion was completed, and new secondary lines extended to Pittsburgh, regional industries had access to a vast new fuel supply.

Pennsylvania regulators initially tried to block the conversion of the pipelines to transport natural gas by refusing to grant necessary permits allowing fuel other than oil to be shipped across rivers within the state. Pipeline officials blamed the coal industry, and its fear of new competition in northeast energy markets, for the opposition.[25] Only when the Pittsburgh region faced dire shortages of natural gas, in the winter of 1947, did Pennsylvania regulators agree to permit limited gas supplies to be shipped via the pipeline into the Pittsburgh region, and they later approved the full pipeline for natural gas transmission across the state. Before the war, oil companies had proposed construction of a dedicated pipeline to move excess natural gas from Texas to the East Coast, but the Texas senators, who saw it as inhibiting industrial development in Texas, opposed the project.[26] Once the pipeline was built, Texas's potential economic loss was clearly Pittsburgh's gain. It benefited more than any other region could from access to the new fuel network.

Expanded natural gas supplies immediately shifted the economics of energy across southwestern Pennsylvania and inverted the normal relationship between increased environmental regulation and business costs. New pipeline supplies immediately deflated the price of natural gas. Despite the region's unvanquished coal supplies, by the end of 1948, natural gas was decidedly cheaper than bituminous coal per BTU in the Pittsburgh market.[27] Regional industries needed little regulatory prodding to rapidly convert from more expensive smoke-producing coal where they could. The need for synthetic coal gas or liquified fuel derived from coal evaporated before the technology could be commercially developed.

Just as the prospects of a new synthetic fuel industry faded before it began, another new energy industry was incubated in Pittsburgh. Atomic energy emerged as an entirely new growth as the new technology was harnessed for the production of commercial power. Nuclear power was not based on any natural resource close to western Pennsylvania, and its path to Pittsburgh far from accidental.

Nuclear Power

In 1946, the US Navy's Captain Hyman Rickover and a team of navy engineers were sent to the federal laboratory in Oak Ridge, Tennessee—which had been set up to support research and development for the Manhattan Project—for a year's study of the potential of atomic energy for power production.[28] Argonne National Lab in Illinois, one of the centers of the federal government's nuclear power research, managed Oak Ridge. Staffed primarily by academic scientists, the lab had been spun out from the Metallurgical Laboratory of the University of Chicago, where Chicago Pile 1—the world's first self-sustaining atomic reactor—went critical in December 1942. Rickover's team recommended that the navy immediately begin construction of a nuclear-powered submarine. The navy set up a new Naval Reactors Branch at Argonne, and expectations were that the existing federal laboratory would take the lead in efforts to design and build a practical power plant.

Rickover had served during most the war as head of the electrical section of the navy's Bureau of Ships, a position that put him in close contact with defense industries and certainly the Westinghouse Corporation, dominant in the production of both electrical power and maritime propulsion systems. Believing the project was more an engineering than scientific challenge, Rickover insisted that the Westinghouse Corporation be incorporated into the navy's contract for the development of a maritime nuclear power plant. Rickover wanted a joint venture in which the Argonne National Lab would share design responsibilities with Westinghouse, which would build the reactor itself.[29] Following Rickover's proposal, Westinghouse was contracted to build the S1W atomic reactor that was the prototype for the power plant the company built for the USS *Nautilus,* the world's first nuclear-powered submarine.

The Atomic Energy Commission (AEC) and the US Navy set up a joint atomic power research laboratory at new facilities near Bettis Field, once the primary airport serving Pittsburgh. The joint Navy/AEC atomic power laboratory was spun off into the Bettis Atomic Power Laboratory, managed by Westinghouse for five decades. Additional spinoffs related to nuclear energy were anticipated. In 1959, Westinghouse set up a dedicated Astronuclear Laboratory to study the potential applications of nuclear power in space.

When the AEC sought proposals for a private-sector partner to operate the nation's first civilian power plant, Pittsburgh's Duquesne Light Company beat nine other competitors to win the contract. Even though the AEC underwrote over 90 percent of the initial construction costs, Duquesne's bid offered $5 million in support and, more importantly, guaranteed to purchase electricity generated by the plant for five years at a rate of 8 cents per kilowatt-hour, a rate well above the 3.5 cents/kWh that was the company's comparable cost to produce electricity from conventionally fueled power plants. The winning bid was estimated to represent a total contribution of $30 million toward the project, well above the estimated $24 million value of the second highest bid, from Philadelphia Electric.[30]

Duquesne's unprofitable bid was made possible by Pittsburgh's much longer industrial history. When Duquesne Light responded to the AEC request for proposals, the company was coming off a series of highly profitable years. After a brief postwar recession, industrial output quickly picked up in the Pittsburgh region and was later pushed higher by industrial expansion the result of the Korean War. High rates of industrial utilization increased demand for electricity, and revenue for electricity suppliers. In November 1953, the AEC sought a utility to partner with it in the construction of the first civilian nuclear power plant. Duquesne Light had sustained 8 percent annual revenue increases in income between 1950 and 1955, a growth spurt the company had not experienced since the 1920s. Boosted profits enabled the company to submit the money-losing bid to manage the new nuclear power plant, expanding the nuclear industry cluster forming in the region and generating secondary economic impacts for Pittsburgh. The reactor for the new civilian power plant was designed at the Bettis Laboratory and built by Westinghouse while the reactor portion was constructed by the Pittsburgh firm Dravo. At the peak of construction, more than eighteen hundred workers were employed building the plant.[31]

From the 1950s forward, Pittsburgh was as dominant in the nascent nuclear power industry as it had ever been in the coal, oil, and natural gas industries. Westinghouse alone supplied eight reactors to seven different countries during the 1960s.[32] Domestic growth included Duquesne Light's 1967 decision to join a consortium of Pennsylvania- and Ohio-based utilities in plans to build seven new nuclear power plants. Only three plants would ever be built, but two of these were located in the Beaver Valley in proximity to the plant at Shippingport—fifteen miles northwest of Downtown Pittsburgh.

By the middle of the decade, the Westinghouse Corporation faced an entirely unexpected and nearly existential problem that threatened the economics of the entire civilian nuclear power industry. As part of its construction contracts for civilian nuclear reactors worldwide, Westinghouse had entered into turnkey fixed-cost contracts that incorporated complementary long-term contracts to supply new nuclear power plants with uranium. As the multifaceted energy crisis of the 1970s accelerated, Westinghouse faced increasing uranium prices, which jumped eightfold—from just $5 per pound in 1972 to over $40 per pound by 1975.[33] At the higher prices, the long-term contracts were not just economically unviable but impossible to meet. Before mid-decade, the company was projected to lose over $2 billion if it provided uranium as promised. In September 1975, the company unilaterally declared it could not meet its commitments to supply uranium to the utility companies operating the plants it had built. Most of the affected utilities sued Westinghouse for breach of contract. So serious was the crisis that Westinghouse CEO Robert Kirby delegated his day-to-day duties managing the massive corporation to one of his deputies so he could devote all of his time to addressing the danger uranium prices posed to the company's future.[34]

Westinghouse claimed spiking prices were the deliberate result of an international cartel of producers scheming to corner the uranium market and raise prices above their fair market prices. Most of the alleged participants in the cartel were international corporations, many wholly owned by national governments. Westinghouse sued Gulf Oil, the only

US company named in Westinghouse's lawsuit, due to the participation of its wholly owned Canadian subsidiary, Gulf Minerals of Canada Limited, in the consortium.[35] The lawsuit pitted two of Pittsburgh's most prominent corporate citizens against each other. Though the case was settled just before it was scheduled to come to trial in 1981, the legal machinations had rattled potential consumers and was one factor that arrested expected growth for the industry.[36] Coupled with the partial meltdown at one of three reactors at the Three Mile Island power plant near Harrisburg in 1979, many of the nation's plans for new civilian power plants in the United States were curtailed.

Corporate trauma at Westinghouse prompted a process that begat a greater transformation for the corporation and for Pittsburgh. In 1980, Westinghouse paid $664 million to acquire the Teleprompter Corporation, one of the nation's largest cable television companies. The acquisition was the beginning of a deliberate shift away from the company's industrial legacy that stretched back over a century. The corporate metamorphosis reached its ultimate conclusion when Westinghouse acquired the media giant CBS for $5.4 billion in 1995. In 1997, the company went farther and renamed itself CBS. Transformation into a media company was a precursor to Westinghouse's divestment of its industrial units. Unable to find a unitary buyer, the company abandoned early efforts to spin off its legacy industrial operations whole and began to sell off its industrial divisions piecemeal. One of the last such units to be spun off, the Westinghouse nuclear power division was sold to British Nuclear Fuels Limited in 1999.

Machinations within the nuclear power industry had broader spillover impacts across other industrial sectors in Pittsburgh. Four of the seven new nuclear power plants planned by Duquesne Light and its partners were canceled by the end of the decade. Duquesne had already invested $34.7 million in the unbuilt plants, and Penn Power of New Castle, Pennsylvania—forty-five miles north of Pittsburgh—had expended over $9.6 million. The utilities petitioned the Pennsylvania Public Utility Commission (PUC) to recoup their lost investment with higher rates on its customers amortized over a ten-year period. The PUC initially approved the increases in 1982, which added to the relatively high electricity costs throughout western Pennsylvania. Though Pennsylvania legislation later prohibited the recoupment of costs for the unbuilt plants, the legacy costs of energy infrastructure built for an industry mostly shuttered would remain a drag on Pittsburgh's ability to attract and retain new industries.

Despite Pittsburgh's roles at the inception of so many diverse energy industries, at the end of the twentieth century, energy prices were a major obstacle in the region's continuing efforts to retain what was left of its industrial base. Across a range of manufacturing industries, but especially for the steel industry, energy costs inhibited heavy industry from rebuilding. Regional coal and coke sources remained plentiful and price-competitive, but coal's role in the modern steel industry was entirely different from the era when Andrew Carnegie and his competitors had built most of the region's integrated steel plants.

Pittsburgh's industrial history was arguably the cause of its new energy challenges. As western Pennsylvania emerged from the 1980s, the region's existing power infrastructure had been built to support what was expected to be a much larger industry, leaving behind a legacy of past investment costs that needed to be paid by current consumers. Thirty years earlier, industrial expansion had pushed regional utilities to expand their generating capacity. Net new demand prompted the region's largest electric utility, Duquesne Light, to initiate the largest expansion program in the company's history. Six new electricity-generating plants had been built near Pittsburgh following World War II. Postwar expansion culminated in the construction of the 310-megawatt coal-powered Elrama generating unit along the Monongahela River near Elizabeth in 1952, at the time the company's largest generating unit.[37] Already relatively high electricity costs in western Pennsylvania were pushed even higher during the 1980s, when for a period regulators allowed higher rates recoup the costs of canceled nuclear power plants.

With electricity costs uncompetitive, there was little chance new steel minimills—built around electric arc furnaces—would ever come to southwestern Pennsylvania. Only one abortive attempt to build a minimill in the Pittsburgh region was ever announced in 1994, but the project was abandoned before construction began.[38]

As late as 2006, U.S. Steel executives regularly complained before the PUC that "the electricity prices in the Mon Valley were among the highest in the six states where U.S. Steel facilities are located. The current cost of electricity in southwestern Pennsylvania presents a competitive disadvantage to U.S. Steel and other large commercial and industrial customers located in that area."[39]

Natural Gas Redux

In 2004, prospecting on the Renz farm, let alone the potential for unconventional natural gas across the region, was still unknown to most of the public. After nearly two centuries of economic growth shaped by a succession of energy industries centered in western Pennsylvania, Pittsburgh was facing an economic future not built on a competitive advantage in energy production or distribution. The coke-powered integrated steel plants that remained in the region were mostly legacies of investments dating back over a century, with little new capacity projected. The region was dependent on natural gas imported from elsewhere, and the civilian nuclear power industry was primarily being employed providing service and maintenance to the existing base of reactors, with little growth expected in the foreseeable future.

Just as energy appeared to have finally played out its long history generating long waves of economic growth for Pittsburgh, history repeated itself with the expansion of shale-gas exploration and production. The shale-gas revolution that began at the Renz farm brought to Pittsburgh not just new investment but a need for specialized workers not to be found anywhere in the regional workforce.

On September 25, 1998, an earthquake moderate by global standards struck northwest Pennsylvania. Registering 5.2 on the Richter scale, the seismic event was the largest in state history and affected a broad area in proximity to Pymatuning Lake, eighty miles north of Pittsburgh. No injuries were recorded, but minor damage was reported in several nearby towns. The earthquake's most significant impact only became apparent over the following week as residents of up to 120 nearby homes discovered that their wells had gone dry, leaving them without water.

The earthquake is believed to have created cracks in underground shale deposits, causing water to drain from higher pools that had fed the residential wells for decades. The affected wells were still viable but needed to be redrilled to lower depths. Even though the scale of the geologic event was limited, the demand for the workers capable of drilling wells quickly exceeded the limited supply of the specialized workers available locally. Local retired workers with expertise in drilling were recalled to redrill wells and restore water supply to affected homes. The state was soon in need of several orders of magnitude more workers with even more specialized expertise in deep underground drilling.

Statewide, just 12 wells were completed in the Marcellus Shale in 2006, a number that jumped to 59 in 2007, 167 in 2008, and then to over 400 in both 2009 and 2010.[40] Thousands of additional permits for new natural gas sites were approved, presaging additional investment that was only limited by critical shortages in workers and resources. As a result, shale-gas-generated employment growth across Pennsylvania was ramping up just as it was announced the G20 was coming to Pittsburgh in the spring of 2009. Workers experienced in such unconventional new mining technologies were in short supply not just in Pennsylvania but in oil regions in the southwest. Each well required boring down vertically nearly three miles, whereupon specialized equipment extended the bore in multiple horizontal directions. Then a combination of oil, sand, and specialized chemicals under pressure created cracks in the shale to release trapped gas. The techniques were far more complex than the shallow vertical wells that had come to Pennsylvania in the nineteenth century.

With increases generated mostly by new natural gas activity, employment in Pennsylvania oil and gas industries expanded by 15,000 workers between 2007 and 2012, a 259 percent increase over earlier levels.[41] Projections at their peak anticipated the state could experience net new job creation of just under 212,000 workers by the year 2020 due to shale-gas exploration and production.[42] The economic impact of new gas prospecting was magnified because a panoply of competing energy firms were investing in the Marcellus Shale play simultaneously, compounding the speed of investment and the cumulative need for workers.

Like the Pennsylvania oil boom that began nearly a century and a half earlier, much of the new drilling activity was located far from Pittsburgh. However, fracking-induced employment included not only the workers directly involved in exploration and development but a range of supporting industries, many of which were concentrated in southwestern Pennsylvania. Pittsburgh was again one of the largest cities in proximity to most of the new mining activity, making the city and region a central hub for new jobs generated by shale-gas investment across the state.

Much of the natural gas being produced by the Marcellus, and later the Utica Shale plays were "wet" gas that had valuable liquid hydrocarbons, including ethane. Ethane is a feedstock for the production of ethylene, an input for a wide range of industrial products. Ethane generally needs to be extracted from wet gas before transmission over long distances via pipeline. The region became an obvious choice for the location of new ethane cracker facilities that could convert the ethane into ethylene. Proposals for new ethane crackers began to emerge almost as soon as production from the Marcellus shale began. In June 2011, the Shell Chemical Company announced it was considering plans to build a world-scale facility in Beaver County.

Once again, natural resources began to reshape Pittsburgh's economy. Technology and other service sectors emerged in the face of national, even global, competition. However, the new unconventional gas industry, was as fixed in geography as Pittsburgh Seam coal. Hopes again emerged that new shale gas supplies could lead to a broad reindustrialization of a region still coming to terms with what it had lost decades earlier. One of the largest developers of the Marcellus Shale play advertised in Pittsburgh that "drilling is just the beginning," all but promising a resurgence of manufacturing jobs.[43]

But Pittsburgh in the twenty-first century was different. Its economy had evolved in the decades since the collapse of heavy industry in the region. By 2007, total manufacturing employment in Pittsburgh had dropped below 100,000 workers and was continuing to decline. Indeed, Pittsburgh was selected as host for the 2009 G20 Summit because of an economic transformation that had been emerging for decades, and before the full scale of the fracking-induced natural gas buildout was known. Slow and steady growth across education and healthcare, and academic research associated with both sectors, had given greater Pittsburgh an economic stability that it had long lacked its manufacturing era, when structural and cyclical shifts were magnified in the region. If shale gas was going to catalyze new manufacturing employment in Pittsburgh, it would do so alongside a very different set of industries were finally emerging, industries that had been incubating in the region for decades.

While Pittsburgh used to be called "Steel Town," you need to call it "Knowledge Town."

President George W. Bush, February 2002

Knowledge Town

August 25, 1954

From its headquarters in Downtown Pittsburgh, the U.S. Steel Corporation announced it was planning to take delivery of a new "electronic brain" at the McKeesport offices of its National Tube Works.[1] The UNIVAC was the commercial successor of the ENIAC—the world's first general-purpose digital computer—developed at the University of Pennsylvania during World War II. The two engineers leading the team that built the ENIAC, John Mauchly and J. Presper Eckert, left the university in 1946 in order to build a commercial version of the device. The Remington-Rand Corporation bought Mauchly and Eckert's company in 1949 and funded the development of what became the UNIVAC.

When Remington-Rand began selling the UNIVAC in the early 1950s, each device was a room-sized installation, measuring twenty-five by fifty feet and weighing upward of twenty tons. Nonetheless, UNIVAC represented the state of the art in the new field of digital computing. The very first clients to take delivery of the industrial-scale contraption were large government agencies with specialized research needs, including the Census Bureau, the US Air Force, and the Atomic Energy Commission. In 1954, private-sector clients began purchasing similar devices. The installation in McKeesport was the first major commercial installation of the UNIVAC anywhere in the world.[2] By the end of the year, it would be joined by a nearly identical machine delivered to the Westinghouse Corporation's East Pittsburgh plant.[3] Pittsburgh corporations Alcoa and Pittsburgh Plate Glass both acquired their own

UNIVACs before Remington-Rand ended sales of the computer in 1958. With the sole exception of the much larger New York City region, nowhere in the country had more commercial installations of the UNIVAC than Pittsburgh. In addition, Westinghouse in the 1950s was the largest customer of Burroughs Corporation, an early competitor of Remington-Rand, and in 1955 Mellon Bank in Pittsburgh became one of the first banks to install an IBM Electronic Data Processing System.[4]

Each of the four Pittsburgh-based corporations that took delivery of UNIVACs was among the largest corporations in the nation. A century of economic growth had culminated in making mid-twentieth century Pittsburgh one of the major corporate centers of the nation, if not the world. An early cluster of digital computing was just one artifact of the commercial success that had accumulated in the region.

Digital computing was just one of many new advances in technology spurred by the war. Firms and regions that were slow to adopt new technologies risked slower growth, but Pittsburgh appeared well prepared for new challenges. Regional industries had just proven themselves capable of rapid transformation when necessary. Less than a decade had passed since the industries of Pittsburgh had rapidly adjusted to wartime demands, even when it meant shifting into entirely new product lines on short notice. Westinghouse itself was a worldwide leader in analog computing and control systems. In becoming an early adopter of emerging digital technology, Pittsburgh showed as much potential to take advantage of postwar technology revolutions as any region in the nation.

Research

Pittsburgh had a large role in shaping the evolution of commercial research in the United States. Westinghouse created a dedicated research division in 1906 with six fulltime employees, and in 1916 a new research center was built in Forest Hills, a close-in suburb of Pittsburgh. The dedicated research center was a hub of activity in both basic and applied research. Westinghouse's investment in research brought into the corporation a critical mass of technical experts who pushed the company to expand into new fields unimagined by Westinghouse during his lifetime.

In 1937, twenty-three years after George Westinghouse passed away, his namesake company's engineers constructed a 5 million–volt Van de Graaff generator. The device used a mechanical belt and a hollow sphere to create extremely high electrical voltages. The particle accelerator powered by the generator created nuclear reactions by bombarding target atoms with a beam of high-energy particles, making it the world's first atom smasher. More than a technical feat, the decision to build the oversized generator was remarkable in that the device had no known commercial application when it was constructed. More than a decade passed before Westinghouse began related work in the development of nuclear reactors for maritime propulsion.[5] The company had embarked on a program in pure research with faith that practical commercial applications would follow. It was an investment in basic research few US corporations of the era attempted, let alone sustained over decades. Westinghouse systemized a process of technology commercialization, catalyzing innovations as diverse as the formation of the commercial radio industry, nuclear power, and even the electric water heater.

The institutionalization of corporate research was common among major firms located in Pittsburgh, not the least of which was the Gulf Oil Company. Gulf was different from most of the wildcat oil companies of the day. The investment made by William Larimer Mellon—nephew of Secretary of the Treasury Andrew Mellon—in the Spindletop well near Beaumont, Texas, had returned sizable profits, leading to the 1907 incorporation of the Gulf Oil in Pittsburgh. From its earliest days, Gulf was a pioneer in applying the most advanced scientific methods to oil exploration. Gulf Oil's subsidiary, the Gulf Production Company in Texas, became one of the first oil exploration companies to apply geophysics on a large scale, with much of that research emanating from Pittsburgh.[6] In 1927, the physicist Paul. D. Foote left the US Bureau of Standards, then the nation's preeminent research center, to accept a Gulf Corporation fellowship at Pittsburgh's Mellon Institute for Industrial Research.

The hybrid Mellon Institute was founded in 1913 with funding from Andrew and Richard Mellon. Originally formed as the Department of Industrial Research at the University of Pittsburgh, the institute was spun off as an independent nonprofit research center in 1927. Unlike most academic labs of the time, research at the Mellon Institute was funded by industry to address specific applied problems.[7] Novel was the operating model that funders retained the ownership of resulting innovations—presaging a partnership model between industrial and academic research that would not become more common until later in the century.

Foote's energy-focused fellowship expanded so much that by 1930 his work was spun out to become a new research department for the Gulf

Corporation. Continued expansion led his department to be reorganized as an independent Gulf Research and Development Corporation in 1933, with Foote named director of research and vice president.[8] In 1935, the outsized complex moved to a suburban location in Harmarville, just outside Pittsburgh along the Allegheny River. With 221 employees by 1934, Gulf maintained one of the largest corporate research staffs dedicated to energy research.[9]

The geographer Patrick Vitale has documented the cluster of corporate research concentrated in corporate campuses surrounding Pittsburgh in the decades following World War II.[10] During the early decades of the Cold War, major regional corporations consolidated and expanded their preexisting research complexes within the region.[11] Expansion of Gulf Oil Company's Pittsburgh laboratories after the war was matched by Westinghouse's 1955 expansion of its central research laboratories at a new research and development campus in Churchill, just outside of Pittsburgh. Alcoa's corporate laboratories in New Kensington, just northeast of Pittsburgh, were kept busy by the ever-increasing demands for aluminum in the expanding aerospace industry. Private-sector research was buttressed by public-sector efforts at the Department of the Interior's Bruceton Research Center south of Pittsburgh.

By the early 1960s, the *Economic Study of the Pittsburgh Region* (*ESPR*) identified forty-one major research facilities in Pittsburgh, and clearly identified the "nation's fastest-growing industry today" as "one whose chief product is not tangible goods but the intangibles which make progress in the production of goods and services possible: information, decisions and new knowledge."[12] At midcentury, the bulk of research activity taking place in Pittsburgh was within the confines of large corporate, government, and, to a lesser extent, academic and public institutions. Ominously, smaller firms were generating few innovations, most likely a reflection of how underrepresented small and even medium-sized businesses remained in Pittsburgh's economy.

Pittsburgh enviable research infrastructure notably failed to provide much competitive advantage to the region's industrial base, still concentrated in heavy industries. By the end of the 1950s, the plethora of mostly corporate research complexes nurtured in Pittsburgh were concentrated in suburban enclaves, isolated not only from each other but almost intentionally "isolated from the immediate demands of manufacturing plants and corporate headquarters."[13]

Palpably deficient in Pittsburgh in 1960 was the scale of entrepreneurial activity, and the corresponding rate of new business creation, expected for a region of its size. Benjamin Chinitz, associate director of the *ESPR*, pointed out that Pittsburgh had an abnormally high concentration of large firms, which dominated the economy of southwestern Pennsylvania. Not only was Pittsburgh's corporate success concentrated within a few industries, but it comprised primarily a small number of larger firms. Chinitz hypothesized that the concentration of large industrial firms actually worked to inhibit the normal process of firm creation: "You do not breed as many entrepreneurs in families allied with steel."[14] An eerily similar comment made decades later was that "starting your own company was not a very popular or socially acceptable thing to do around Pittsburgh."[15]

Equally foreboding was Chinitz's observation that Pittsburgh decisively trailed in the commercial spinoff activity that normally resulted from commercial research and development. At midcentury, the *ESPR* identified the Westinghouse Corporation as virtually the sole source of the few new firms being spun off from corporate research activity in the region. From other firms, the report ominously concluded, "no other such spinoffs have occurred."[16]

Even as corporate research activity in Pittsburgh was expanding, the nexus of cutting-edge research was changing. Where research and development had long been concentrated in private-sector industrial labs or the hybrid Mellon Institute, the development of new technology was evolving a new symbiosis with academic research. In 1947, the University of Pittsburgh's School of Medicine recruited Jonas Salk to an associate research professor of bacteriology. His work over the next seven years culminated in successful field tests of a safe and effective vaccine preventing polio, then one of the world's most deadly diseases. As seminal as the research was for society, it did not have a complementary commercial impact on Pittsburgh. Such was the nature of academic research at the time: the polio vaccine was not patented by either Salk or the university.

By the 1950s, the University of Pittsburgh began efforts to consolidate its medical and health schools. Support from the A. W. Mellon Educational and Charitable Trust enabled the creation of a new School of Public Health in 1949. In 1952, the university created a vice chancellor for the health sciences position and gave it purview over its five health-related schools. The new position was part of a larger plan to create a comprehensive university medical system. An internal University of Pittsburgh report concluded the same year, "There is a unique opportunity to build a complete medical center for all the health professions in one integrated building, and this in physical continuity with the major teaching hospital."[17]

The region's second-largest institution of higher education was rapidly evolving at the same time. In 1949, Carnegie Tech hired Herbert Simon, an assistant professor at the Illinois Institute of Technology, to help start a new Graduate School of Industrial Administration (GSIA). The school was created with a substantial bequest from William Larimer Mellon, who had founded the Gulf Corporation a half century earlier. Simon was hired as dean of undergraduate business education in the new school, but his impact would soon expand far beyond that initial appointment.

GSIA was formed as a different type of academic business school, which at the time mostly concentrated on teaching. It would be built with a greater emphasis on research. The original plans for the new school included dedicated space for a statistical computing lab, not yet a common feature of academic business schools.[18] Within just a few years of GSIA's founding, the growing concentration of computer expertise in Pittsburgh was just one factor that led Simon to create the school's Computation Center in 1956. Before the new center acquired its own computer, an early agreement allowed it limited access to an IBM computer Pittsburgh's Mellon Bank had acquired the year before.

Panther Hollow

Through the 1950s, the University of Pittsburgh continued to transform its research infrastructure. Though much older than Carnegie Tech, with roots dating back to 1787, in the early 1950s, Pitt in was primarily a regional teaching institution. In 1955, it hired Cornell University Business School Dean Edward Litchfield. The University of Pittsburgh's board of directors recruited Litchfield to make Pitt "one of the world's great universities."[19] In his inaugural address to the university in 1957, the new chancellor emphasized a "more systematic attention to the creation of research institutes in all of our schools and colleges."[20] It was a vision far from reality at the time. The year Litchfield was hired, total research contracts with the federal government amounted to just under $2.5 million, an amount that would grow fivefold over his tenure.[21]

Litchfield's strategy evolved into a more comprehensive plan for Pittsburgh's future. In May 1962, Chancellor Litchfield proposed a major new collaborative research center be established in the city. He argued that a new omnibus research park was critical to "ensuring the diversification of industry which has become essential to our economic progress." The plan was explicitly modeled on the prototypical academic-corporate research collaborations at the Stanford Research Park, in Palo Alto, California, and the Research Triangle Park in North Carolina.[22]

An essential part of Litchfield's concept was not to place the new research center in a suburban campus—similar to the location of the region's many corporate research centers at the time and where land was readily available. He believed the crucial factor in the success of similar research centers was location in proximity to established research universities, and in Pittsburgh, those institutions were in the city center. Instead, he proposed a new research park be built in the city's Oakland neighborhood, literally between the city's two largest educational institutions, the University of Pittsburgh and the Carnegie Institute of Technology. The challenge was that Oakland was already densely packed and lacked space for any major new development, let alone an expansive new research park. The solution was the innovative concept of placing the new research center within the Panther Hollow ravine that ran through the neighborhood and separated the University of Pittsburgh and Carnegie Tech. The early design was to literally place a roof over much of the milelong ravine with a multistoried construction effort, transforming it into "the world's greatest research park."[23] Litchfield created the Oakland Corporation, a private development company, to pursue the ambitious project.

The full project was expected to take a decade to complete, with an initial cost of over $250 million, the equivalent of nearly $2.6 billion in 2025, making it at the time one of the most ambitious developments ever proposed by an academic institution.[24] If the entire project were built out as Litchfield envisioned, projected costs reached as high as $750 million. The "Valley of Tomorrow"—as the Panther Hollow project was called—was projected to eventually include a nuclear reactor as well as a computing center and computer data bank, all to be used collectively among both academic and private-sector tenants.[25] As visionary as the envisioned geotechnical engineering was, the greater leap was in the connection being made between sheer technical talent and regional prosperity. Litchfield believed that "scientists need—and insist on—close contact with academic institutions and other cultural resources."[26] With Panther Hollow, the chancellor aimed to "unite all the research facilities in the Oakland area . . . to help solve Pittsburgh's economic problems."[27] Unclear is how much of Pittsburgh's business community believed it had any fundamental problems to be solved.

The plan for the Panther Hollow Research Park proved too ambitious to implement. It was only one part of a costly expansion of research infrastructure at the University of Pittsburgh, which led to budget crises that compounded later in the 1960s.[28] Coupled with tepid support among regional business and academic leaders, these difficulties meant the scheduled inauguration of the project was deferred. Eventually, operating deficits at the university proved difficult to overcome, a factor that contributed to Litchfield's resignation as chancellor in 1965.

Nonetheless, the seeds for a far greater academic research enterprise had been planted. However, at the end of the of the 1960s, the bulk of advanced research being conducted in Pittsburgh still resided in corporate or government labs. The 1968 Department of Labor report on Pittsburgh's economy, requested by Congressman Elmer Holland, highlighted the "lack of a scientific community attached to the University of Pittsburgh or any other independent agency or institute which would serve as a magnet for the modern so-called growth industries."[29] Also in 1968, a report from the Regional Industrial Development Corporation (RIDC) concluded that Pittsburgh was "emerging as one of the nation's most important research and development centers."[30] Still, the research that RIDC highlighted was almost entirely in the private sector. Little mentioned was any ongoing academic research.[31] Nonetheless, Pittsburgh's academic institutions continued to expand their research activities. Simon's experimental computing lab grew steadily, leading to Carnegie Tech's 1965 formation of one of the first academic computer science departments. The University of Pittsburgh followed in 1967 by offering a master's degree in computer science. By 1979, Carnegie Mellon University—formed by the merger of Carnegie Tech and the Mellon Institute in 1967—established its Robotics Institute.[32] In 1978, the RIDC's annual report again stressed the role of scientific innovation in the region's economy but emphasized the cooperation between local universities and industries, along with a need to commercialize research activity and generate commercial products. Yet the explicit goal of promoting research remained its potential to strengthen regional manufacturing sectors. If successful, "research and pilot development products can lead to full-scale production facilities and the region can hope for a share of the facilities which emerge."[33]

Only at the end of the 1970s did state governments begin new efforts promoting advanced technology as a means of generating economic growth. Until then, most state and local economic development efforts were defined by "first stage" economic development policies, which focused mostly on attracting manufacturing facilities, and little effort was spent trying to attract or grow smaller firms or firms in other industries. For Pennsylvania in the late 1970s, the very recent success bringing the new Volkswagen plant to Westmoreland County had only reinforced such "smokestack chasing," or manufacturing-centric policies. Deindustrialization would provide a catalyst for new strategic thinking in how to promote economic growth.

Walt Plosila—appointed the state's director of policy development when Pennsylvania Governor Dick Thornburgh took office in 1977—later explained that "issues about talent, the role of higher education, the building of entrepreneurial cultures and related issues deemed more important today were rarely considered."[34] Plosila has been credited with engineering a national shift of state policies toward more technology-based economic development programs.[35] In February 1981, the Thornburgh administration proposed the creation of the Ben Franklin Partnership Challenge Grant Program for Technological Innovation. State officials believed "government action is important for encouraging and facilitating increased investment and technology advancement in existing Pennsylvania firms and development of new high-growth businesses."[36] Pennsylvania appropriated $1 million for the new program in the 1982–83 fiscal year. In 1983, Pennsylvania State Representatives Tom Murphy—later a mayor of Pittsburgh—and Rick Geist proposed additional legislation promoting high-technology industries across the state. Their legislation would be incorporated into Pennsylvania's Ben Franklin Partnerships, a new program with a novel focus on commercializing university research.

The new program was one of the first "second stage" economic development policies implemented by state governments. Even marginally shifting away from manufacturing-centric policies was not easy in a region that had been dominated for so long by heavy industry. At the beginning of the 1980s, not just private-sector investment but motivation to support smaller high-technology firms was clearly lacking across western Pennsylvania. Mirroring the region's corporate structure, highly concentrated in large and established firms, little of Pittsburgh high technology was being generated by smaller or startup firms. One of the few venture capitalists in Pittsburgh, Stephen Banks of the Hillman Company, lamented as late as 1981: "I feel if we don't get ourselves into the new game, there isn't much left in the old game. Wringing our hands about the steel industry isn't going to do much good. . . . I doubt the steel industry is going to be able create those jobs."[37]

The creation of the new Ben Franklin program and similar ones in other states patterned off of Pennsylvania's efforts coincided with even broader shifts in federal research policies. Criticism had been building of the low rate of commercial spinoffs being generated by federally funded research. A seminal catalyst for university-based research came from the enactment of Bayh-Dole legislation in 1980, sponsored by Senators Bob Dole of Kansas and Birch Bayh of Indiana. Prior to this act, the federal government retained exclusive ownership of virtually all federally funded intellectual property. With university-based research activity heavily sponsored by federal agencies, there had long been little incentive on the part of universities or industry to commercialize technology. The new legislation fundamentally shifted the incentives of academic research by giving ownership of new intellectual property to the institutions where the research was completed. The simultaneous expansion of state policies aimed at promoting technology-based economic development created an entirely new role for research-based universities as partners in regional technology-based economic development.[38]

As it began, opposition to the Ben Franklin program was surprisingly acute. State support for new high-technology businesses was perceived to be at the expense of established firms and long-established industries. In 1984, a spokesperson for the Pennsylvania Department of Commerce admitted publicly, "High technology is a dirty word around here."[39] Within the private sector, commercial firms already engaged in research saw the new program as publicly funded competition. "The program 'opens up' the university's facilities for outside users at rates substantially lower than would be available from for-profit taxpaying firms," complained the president of a private-sector research laboratory. The Ben Franklin program "constitutes unfair competition against firms already proving such services."[40]

Unrealistic expectations begat early criticisms of the Ben Franklin initiative, initially funded with just $1 million split across three areas within Pennsylvania. A report compiled in 1983, barely a year after the program had formally kicked off, prematurely concluded that that the program "has not been successful in substantially increasing the percentage of Pennsylvania jobs in the advanced-technology industries."[41] Among its criticisms was that research activities in Pennsylvania "have not sparked the kind of economic boom that in the 1970's exploded around the university research facilities of Massachusetts and California."[42]

Other technology-based or entrepreneurial-focused efforts were expanding in Pittsburgh at the same time. Though a shadow of what had been envisioned in the Panther Hollow project two decades earlier, the Enterprise Corporation was a 1983 joint venture bringing together Carnegie Mellon University and the University of Pittsburgh and local philanthropies to support firm incubation and the commercialization of academic research. The hybrid nonprofit venture capital fund was created with funding from the R. K. Mellon Foundation by Jack Thorne. Thorne was a Carnegie Tech grad active in California's aerospace industry whom Carnegie Mellon University President Dick Cyert had recruited in 1972 to come back to Pittsburgh to teach a course in small-business entrepreneurship.[43]

Also in 1983, the Pittsburgh High Technology Council was formed, and its first executive director came aboard the following year. The new industry organization stood in sharp contrast to Pittsburgh's existing business ecosystem. Long dominated by large and historic firms, the new organization focused on smaller technology-based startups and the promotion of entrepreneurship. One of the council's first projects was a joint venture with the Enterprise Corporation to create a CEO Venture fund in Pittsburgh to promote tech startups.[44] Then in 1984, a $3.34 million state grant founded Pittsburgh's Advanced Technology Center, a joint university partnership between the University of Pittsburgh and Carnegie Mellon University.

Even at the end of the 1980s, there was no universal belief that newer technology-based industries would supplant Pittsburgh's heavy industries. Soon after he succeeded Richard Thornburg as governor of Pennsylvania in 1987, Governor Robert Casey prioritized more traditional economic development projects, including the construction of a major highway through the Mon Valley to spur reindustrialization.[45] Pittsburgh's evolution away from heavy industry would proceed; however, it would come not from any rapid shift into new industries but the continuation of slow and steady growth in sectors once considered more as support for the region's industrial core.

Healthcare

By the mid-1980s, what was indisputably moving ahead was the scope and scale of university-based research activity in Pittsburgh. In 1984, Carnegie Mellon University was awarded a $104 million contract from the Department of Defense to start up its new Software Engineering Institute. The new institute was just one part of a vast expansion of research activity in Pittsburgh's Oakland neighborhood, which housed not only the region's two largest universities, but a concentration of major health institutions, including Presbyterian Hospital, Montefiore Hospital, and the Eye and Ear and Falk Clinics.

In 1965 those health institutions joined with the University of Pittsburgh to form a new consolidated institution: the University Health Center of Pittsburgh. Until the 1980s, the individual hospitals operated independently, and Pittsburgh's School of Medicine was still mostly "a regional institution with modest research activity."[46] In 1982, the university appointed Tom Detre as senior vice chancellor for health services, a role in which he oversaw the university's medical school but also the Western Pennsylvania Institute for Psychiatry (WPIC), a state institution the university had assumed management of in 1949. Detre was a psychiatrist who had been recruited from Yale in 1972 with the assistance of an endowed chair funded by the Richard K. Mellon Foundation.[47] He was charged with revamping WPIC and the university's psychiatry program. During his first decade, WPIC dramatically turned around both financially and as a research center. Once on the verge of takeover by state officials concerned with the operation of the facility, it had become one of the nation's top recipients of competitive research funding. Detre was promoted to university vice chancellor to replicate that same success across its broader health activities.[48]

The 1980s saw rapid expansion of university medical research, especially in the new field of transplantation services. Thomas Starzl, who had performed the first successful liver transplantation in 1967 at the University of Colorado, was recruited to the University of Pittsburgh in 1981 and oversaw what was still mostly experimental research in organ transplantation. The university invested $230 million to expand its transplantation program and a rapidly expanding center for cancer research. That funding, and Starzl's discovery of antirejection therapies, catalyzed the rapid expansion of transplantation services based in Pittsburgh. By the end of the 1980s, Pittsburgh was the largest center of organ transplantation in the United States, almost all of which was taking place in Oakland. The University of Pittsburgh performed 2,090 primary liver transplants between 1984 and 1990.[49] A 1988 study estimated that the median charge for these transplants at the time was $145,776.[50] Revenues generated from the near monopoly on early transplantation efforts fueled consolidation of the region's healthcare system. In 1990 the Presbyterian–University Health System, the parent of Presbyterian Hospital, acquired the debt and management control of adjacent Montefiore Hospital. The same year the university's health system was reorganized and named the University of Pittsburgh Medical Center, later renamed UPMC.

Technology

Some of the most successful technology-based economic development efforts were collaborations with local universities. In 1986, the University of Pittsburgh in partnership with Carnegie Mellon University and the Westinghouse Corporation successfully won a federal contract for the creation of the Pittsburgh Supercomputer Center. The following year, the new center became the first customer to order the most advanced Cray Supercomputer, even before the computer came into production. Similarly, the two universities agreed to become the initial tenants of the former LTV Works along Second Avenue, renamed the Pittsburgh Technology Center, in close proximity to Downtown Pittsburgh.

Still, efforts to catalyze commercial spinoffs from university-based research lagged. One continuing weakness was a lack of venture financing for new startups. A 1989 survey of major venture capital firms across the nation identified only fourteen such firms with offices in the Pittsburgh region, just eleven of which were actually based in Pittsburgh. Few had long track records, and only one of these had been formed before 1982: Hillman Ventures, Inc., was founded in Pittsburgh in 1976 but had just moved its headquarters to California in 1988.[51] Even the minimal public funding funneled through the Ben Franklin programs was not sustained through its first decade. In 1989, state funding for the program was slashed, especially the allocation for western Pennsylvania.[52]

Also lacking was development of a connection between emerging technology-based employment and employment opportunities for the workers most severely affected by the contraction of the region's heavy industry. Over more than two decades there were hopes that a new magnetic levitation, or maglev, transportation industry in Pittsburgh would spur reindustrialization across the region. In 1985, the Pennsylvania High-Speed Intercity Rail Passenger Commission voted 5–4 to study the possibility of a high-speed magnetic levitation transit system to connect Pittsburgh and Philadelphia. The vote dropped from consideration slower, but more conventional, high-speed upgrades to existing rail service. From its earliest conception, proponents knew that any development of maglev in Pennsylvania depended on significant public investment.[53] In June 1990 a local firm, Pittsburgh Maglev Inc., received $250,000 from private-sector Japanese investors to study the concept. The investment was rare private funding for the project. Over the next two decades, continued funding would primarily come from a mix of public and philanthropic support.

As the 1990s began, health-related research and employment continued to expand in Pittsburgh. A 1992 Pennsylvania state government initiative, Operation Jump Start, expended over $2 billion to stimulate the state's economy. $470 million went to institutions of higher education, of which University of Pittsburgh received $69.1 million to further expand the university's medical center.[54] Growth in transplantation technology spurred research into tissue engineering as a way to overcome a chronic shortage of viable organs. The Pittsburgh Tissue Engineering Initiative was created in 1994 to build a network and promote expansion of the core of tissue-engineering firms that had already started in the region.

State oversight of the Ben Franklin program waned at the very end of the twentieth century. In 1998, the lauded Ben Franklin Center for Western Pennsylvania was rocked by allegations of fund mismanagement. Its top officers, including the CEO and COO, would be forced out and convicted of felonies. The turmoil fostered not only turnover but rapid reorganization of the technology-focused economic development programs in Pittsburgh. By the end of the year, the Ben Franklin Partnership of southwestern Pennsylvania was forced to merge with the Enterprise Corporation to create Innovation Works, which subsumed the goals of the two organizations in promoting technology-based startups.[55]

State funding of local technology-based investment slowed and became narrowly focused as the twentieth century came to close. One of the largest new investments came from the state of Pennsylvania's support for Project Renaissance. Much of the project's funding went to one Pittsburgh-based technology company, Cadence Systems, in an effort to induce the creation of a chip industry cluster in the Pittsburgh region. In 1999, Project Renaissance became the Pittsburgh Digital Greenhouse, charged with continuing the effort. The publicly stated goal was to create fifteen hundred jobs within three years. One of its major successes was the decision of the Sony Corporation, which had occupied the former Volkswagen plant in Westmoreland County with a TV assembly operation in 1998, to locate a small design team in Pittsburgh's east end.

In 2001, the Pittsburgh Digital Greenhouse reported that it had been responsible for the creation of 661 jobs over its first two years of operation. But those gains were questioned in news accounts that noted that six of the twelve firms already had presences in the region before the program was initiated and only two of the remaining six attributed their presence in Pittsburgh to any funding provided by the program. In 2004, five years after the program began, only 230 jobs were created among thirty-five chip-design firms then in existence in the region, far below initial goals to create at least 1,500 regional jobs. Cumulative state funding over those five years was estimated to be $25.3 million.[56]

Sony abandoned even its small research operation in the City of Pittsburgh in 2002, after occupying its east end location for only nine months of a five-year lease. Its chip-design staff was consolidated with operations in California, and Sony laid off or transferred out of the region the six employees who had briefly worked in Pittsburgh. Sony's landlord filed suit against it for departing long before the lease ended. Regarding where he expected to find new tenants, the landlord was adamant that in Pittsburgh "tech is dead" and that financially sound high-technology tenants were "few and far between."[57]

Yet another hybrid organization, the Pittsburgh Life Sciences Greenhouse (PLSG) was formed in 2002 as a collaboration of the state of Pennsylvania with Carnegie Mellon University, the University of Pittsburgh, and the UPMC health system. PLSG functions as an early-stage seed funder and an incubator of medical firms in the region. Also in

2002, the National Center for Defense Robotics was formed to persuade major defense contractors to build design centers and manufacturing facilities in the Pittsburgh area. In 2005, the Pittsburgh Digital Greenhouse merged with the Robotics Foundry to create a new organization, the Technology Collaborative.[58]

Fitful starts and incomplete successes at generating commercial spinoffs did not thwart steady expansion of academic research activity in Pittsburgh. In 2010, annual research expenditures at Pittsburgh universities exceeded $1 billion for the first time and continued to grow over the following decade.[59] Coupled with the region's health sector, "eds and meds" was touted as a touchstone of Pittsburgh's economic transformation during G20 meeting in Pittsburgh in 2009. While not the only pole of growth, the combined regional employment of health and education industries numbered 240,000 workers by 2010, nearly three times the 88,000 employed in regional manufacturing industries that year.

Yet, growing commercial technology-based industries remained elusive at the beginning of the twenty-first century. The reasons continue to be difficult to pin down, but the low rate of entrepreneurial ac-

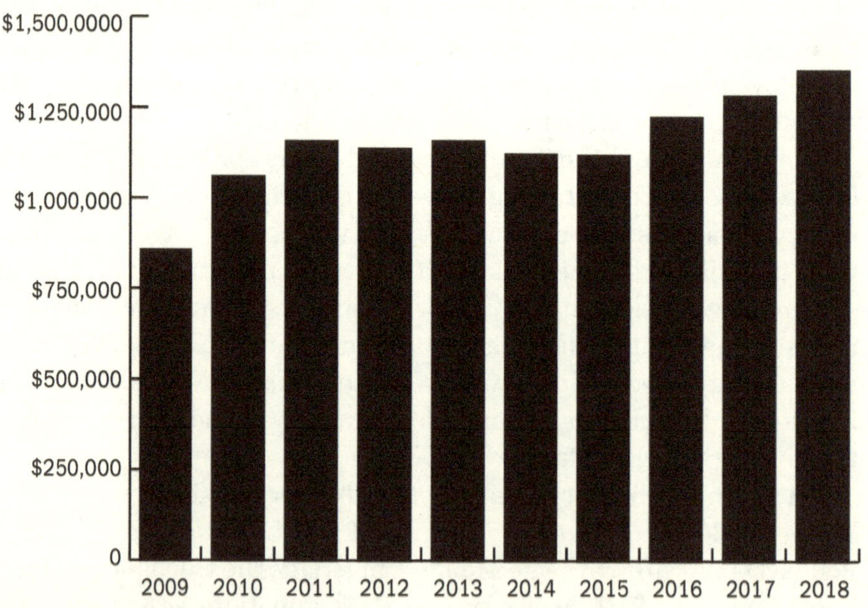

Southwestern Pennsylvania manufacturing employment, 1980–90

tivity mirrored observations that had been made about Pittsburgh for decades. One of the region's most experienced venture capital funders commented in 2007: "I think probably our greatest shortcoming is we don't have the critical mass of experienced entrepreneurs that you see in Boston or the Bay Area."[60]

That Pittsburgh maintained, let alone grew, a core of research is remarkable given the scale of contraction that the region's research infrastructure endured in conjunction with the decline of heavy industry. Gulf and Westinghouse had collectively formed the core of Pittsburgh technology production for most of the twentieth century. Both corporations saw their regional presence collapse by the 1990s, taking with them most of their preexisting research enterprises. The collapse of the two companies also took from Pittsburgh the annual cohort of young engineers they recruited to Pittsburgh each year.

Pittsburgh fared badly at the incubation of technology-based firms and often failed to retain the few technology firms that started there. One major corporate spinoff that began in Pittsburgh was Lycos, an early internet search engine that evolved out of a National Science Foundation-funded project at Carnegie Mellon. Expected to experience rapid growth in the future, the project spun out as a private company in 1994, but the new firm would not stay in Pittsburgh long after it separated from the university. The new Boston-based owners announced they were moving the young company to that city in 1996.[61] For a period, Lycos kept a presence in Pittsburgh solely because of the terms of its acquisition agreement with Carnegie Mellon University. The company peaked at approximately three hundred Pittsburgh employees.[62] Lycos briefly was the dominant internet search engine and anticipated rapid growth. Why did it leave Pittsburgh? Its departure was blamed on a lack of available local workers, despite the concentration of tech graduates coming from its universities.[63]

Even if Lycos truly believed it could not grow a Pittsburgh-based workforce in the 1990s, other tech-based companies enjoying success and growth in Pittsburgh at the same time did not face the same problem. One of the largest examples of a technology-based firm that organically grew from Pittsburgh was Fore Systems, a producer of computer-networking and communications equipment formed in 1990 by a group of Carnegie Mellon University researchers. The company continued expansion through the decade, eventually employing over a thousand workers at its headquarters in a suburb north of Pittsburgh. It was not workers

Pittsburgh lacked as much as active venture capitalists. The funders who purchased Lycos explained it was "only a short plane ride from Boston to Pittsburgh, but it was almost the equivalent of oceans between us because you're not able to walk down the corridor and say, 'Hello. What can we do next?'"[64]

Despite the region's concentration of research activity, Pittsburgh barely participated in the dotcom boom of the 1990s. Only near the end of the 1990s did the produce one of the last major information technology initial public offerings (IPO) that had defined the era: Freemarkets, Inc. listed on Nasdaq in 1999. The company was formed to implement novel reverse online auctions, focused on the business-to-business and government services markets. Freemarkets began in Pittsburgh in the mid-1990s and grew to over a thousand employees by the end of the decade. When the company completed its IPO, it briefly had a market capitalization greater than that of U.S. Steel.

Few of the new technology companies in Pittsburgh had the lasting impacts that technology firms in Silicon Valley sustained. The UK General Electric Company would acquire Fore Systems for $4.5 billion in 1999, and Freemarkets merged with its Silicon Valley competitor Ariba in 2004.[65] Neither company retained sizable Pittsburgh workforces, nor the rapid follow-on growth generated by technology industry "gazelles" concentrated elsewhere.[66]

Industrial workers also failed to benefit from the expansion of research activity in the region. At the beginning of the twenty-first century, hopes faded that maglev technology could spur Pittsburgh to become the center of a new advanced transportation industry and generate new blue-collar jobs. The closest the project came to fruition was in 2001 when the US Department of Transportation narrowed the potential sites for a new demonstration maglev project to one proposed in Pittsburgh an alternative for the Baltimore–Washington rail corridor. Pittsburgh seemed to gain an advantage when interest in moving forward waned in Maryland, but instead of defaulting to Pittsburgh, the Department of Transportation expanded the potential pool of regions for the novel technology.[67] Eventually, alternative routes from Las Vegas to Los Angeles and Atlanta to Chattanooga emerged as new competition for federal funding.

In 2003, Pittsburgh Maglev Inc. opened a fabrication facility in McKeesport, in the heart of the Mon Valley. A draft environmental impact statement for potential maglev routes was completed in 2005. As late as of 2009, the Federal Railroad Administration awarded a $28 million grant for preliminary work on the long-planned Pennsylvania High-Speed Maglev project.[68] Yet, the firm was unable to obtain required nonfederal matching funds. By 2011, Pittsburgh Maglev Inc. declared bankruptcy, after having exhausted all grant revenues and without ever having attracted any substantial private investment: "They didn't have any projects, they didn't have any revenue. . . . All of their money to date has been grant money and it has pretty much dried up under the current economic conditions."[69] The firm's remaining assets, mostly office equipment and supplies, were auctioned off in 2012.

In the first quarter of the twenty-first century, the core of Pittsburgh technology-based economic growth has come from industries and institutions with long legacies in the region. Efforts that attempted to grow entirely new industries usually fared worse than those with links to Pittsburgh's historic industries or institutions. Academic research expertise in healthcare, robotics, and computer technologies all derive from investments initiated decades earlier. Herb Simon's early efforts at expanding computer-based research at Carnegie Tech extend to the later success Carnegie Mellon University had in becoming a world leader in several fields of digital technology. The departure of Jonas Salk, who left Pittsburgh to help found the Scripps Institute in San Diego, nonetheless spurred the expansion of health-based research in Pittsburgh that built momentum in subsequent decades.

None of Pittsburgh's emerging technology-based industries ever benefited from the artificial protections basing point pricing once afforded Pittsburgh's steel agglomeration. Pittsburgh's near monopoly on transplantation services was eroded by the end of the twentieth century as the capacity to perform even the advanced procedures rapidly diffused across the nation.[70] Enviable expansion of research in information technology in Pittsburgh, including robotics, failed to displace dominant centers of comparable technology in Northern California or Boston, and growing academic life sciences research spurred few sizable new commercial firms.

The economic advantages of industrial Pittsburgh had been generated by the region's rivers and geographic proximity to the high-quality metallurgic coal of Connellsville. New economic advantages were being spawned by proximity to the region's largest universities, and the core of the academic research they had built up over decades. Universities were generating a new advantage for Pittsburgh, a core of technical workers and expertise that wanted to stay in the region.

In 1999, the first of several of the nation's largest technology firms located branch operations in Pittsburgh. Seagate—the world's largest producer of computer hard drives—started a research division in Pittsburgh. Carnegie Mellon University Professor Mark Kryder, an electrical engineer, motivated the firm's decision to invest in Pittsburgh.[71] The new office included investment in a state-of-the-art electronics clean room in a former warehouse on Pittsburgh's South Side. Private developers had acquired the building—just a few blocks from the site of the former Jones & Laughlin South Side Works—and had remarketed it as a hub for high-technology firms. In 2001, Seagate made additional investments in the region with a new $40 million research laboratory in the Strip District, adjacent to Downtown Pittsburgh.

Seagate was the precursor of a string of similar investments over the subsequent decade made by some of the largest technology companies in the nation. Apple Computer set up a regional office in Pittsburgh in 2005, clearly intending to collaborate with academic research at local institutions. The new offices were in a building managed by the RIDC—one of Pittsburgh's oldest economic development organizations—but on the Carnegie Mellon University campus. The building was part of a new Keystone Innovation Zone, a program set up by the state of Pennsylvania enabling tax incentives to encourage new business activity. The new zones were a logical successor to Pennsylvania's decades-old Ben Franklin initiative and required partnerships with universities, research institutions, or hospitals to foster technology transfer and commercialization. The internet commerce giant Amazon established a branch office on Pittsburgh's South Side in 2011. Few of Pittsburgh's new technology establishments were formed by companies incubated in Pittsburgh, but the nation's largest tech firms were coming to Pittsburgh nonetheless.

There might be no better microcosm of Pittsburgh's fight between its past and its future than the fate of the former Nabisco Factory in Pittsburgh's east end. When industrial operations ended there in 2004, the plant had been the target of repeated public efforts over decades to keep it in operation as a commercial producer of cookies and crackers. Architect Albert G. Zimmerman designed the plant's 1914 structure as one of several that would "act as shining models of modernity to the communities in which they stood."[72] Nabisco attempted to shut down operations there in the early 1980s but backed down in the face of concentrated community opposition and a threat from activists and the city of Pittsburgh to take over the plant via eminent domain. Nabisco closed the plant in 1998, but a public-private partnership was formed to restart it as an independent commercial bakery, which continued operations until its 2004 bankruptcy.[73] After the plant closed, the city of Pittsburgh resorted to an old economic playbook. In 2006 declared the site was declared blighted, enabling the Urban and Redevelopment Authority to acquire it by its inherent power of eminent domain, six decades after the legal tactic was pioneered in the redevelopment of Downtown Pittsburgh. An early plan to convert the site into 250 residential lofts failed to materialize, because of concerns that that the local apartment market in Pittsburgh's east end was overbuilt.[74] Later, $1 million in state subsidies, along with $10 million of tax increment financing, backstopped with private investment that resulted in a mixed-use site for offices, retail space, and a new hotel. The first tenants of the newly developed space included the University of Pittsburgh, along with Google, which came to dominate the internet search industry after Lycos failed to capitalize on its earlier start.

University of Pittsburgh Chancellor Edward Litchfield had once envisioned Pittsburgh's economic future as dependent on the research activity that he argued could best be catalyzed in close proximity to universities. That roadmap would only begin to play itself out after more than a half century passed. By the first decade of the twenty-first century, the expansion of technology-based employment inside academic institutions and the attraction of national technology firms in the city were generating jobs, increasing incomes, and transforming entire neighborhoods. However, the region's new vectors of economic growth were mostly divorced from the firms, workers, and communities that had benefited the most from Pittsburgh's past dominance in heavy industry.

Success at technology-based economic development had unanticipated secondary impacts for Pittsburgh. Where the city was once vaunted as a model of civic cooperation, the more fragmented entrepreneurial economy did not fit well into the model of consensus that had long defined the leadership of industrial Pittsburgh.

14

Pittsburgh has its own particular genius. . . . It has its own directions.

Adolph Schmidt, president of the A. W. Mellon Educational and Charitable Trust, 1964

Cooperation and Fragmentation

January 1946

Within weeks of taking office, Pittsburgh's newly elected mayor hosted an informal meeting that brought together two of the city's most disparate, and yet most powerful, leaders. Each was already at the pinnacle of their respective careers in business and politics, yet the two achieved their greatest legacies by a partnership that was only just beginning. David Lawrence had long been the party boss and de facto leader of the Democratic machine that coalesced its power over the city more than a decade earlier. He was elected Pittsburgh's mayor in the fall of 1945 and took office on January 6, 1946. His visitor was Richard King (R. K.) Mellon, nephew of former Secretary of the Treasury Andrew Mellon and scion of the Mellon financial empire gestated in Pittsburgh.

Andrew Mellon's accumulated capital was both a catalyst for and an artifact of Pittsburgh's period of explosive economic growth that spanned the decades immediately before and after the turn of the twentieth century. Judge Thomas Mellon, R. K.'s grandfather, arrived in western Pennsylvania at age five with his family from County Tyrone in Ireland. Upon graduating from the Western University of Pennsylvania (later the University of Pittsburgh), he began a successful law career. In 1869, he resigned after a decade of service as a judge on the Allegheny County Court of Common Pleas to found T. Mellon & Sons Bank. Judge Mellon later observed that any man who could not get rich within ten years in Pittsburgh was a fool, and he proved he was no fool.[1] The bank formed the basis for future wealth that spread across a panoply of industries and would be passed down through generations of the Mellon family. By the middle of the twentieth century, Thomas Mellon's heirs redefined what wealth meant in an already affluent United States. When *Fortune* magazine ranked the wealthiest US citizens for the first time in 1957, R. K. Mellon was individually listed in the top eight, and so was his sister Sarah Mellon Scaife, along with his cousins Ailsa Mellon Bruce and Paul Mellon.

After being mustered out of active service in the US Army during World War II, in 1948 Mellon returned family's financial empire, in which he held multiple roles, but also to his position as the de facto leader of Pittsburgh's business community. Lawrence's background could not have been more different. Raised in the slums of Downtown Pittsburgh, he had long been a journeyman of the city's Democratic Party machine. Over the previous decade, he had risen to become Pennsylvania state chairman of the Democratic Party before being elected mayor in the fall of 1945.

Despite their differences, the meeting was the beginning of a partnership at the core of Pittsburgh's postwar transformation. The series of civic initiatives known as the Pittsburgh Renaissance—later referred to as Renaissance I in a region repeatedly searching to reinvent itself—became a model for urban renewal across the nation. More than anything else, Pittsburgh came to symbolize the collaboration between business and public sectors, collaboration entirely only possible because of the tacit cooperation between Lawrence and Mellon. In 1943, Mellon was almost singularly responsible for the formation of the Allegheny Conference for Community Development (ACCD), which institutionalized the collaboration between Pittsburgh's public and private sectors. At the same time, Lawrence reshaped the economic development apparatus of city government by creating the Urban Redevelopment Authority of Pittsburgh (URA), which became the public sector's vehicle for implementing the signature projects of the Pittsburgh Renaissance.

The two new organizations, along with the existing Pittsburgh Regional Planning Association (PRPA), which R. K. Mellon served as president, became enduring instruments of change in the region. The URA enabled a greatly expanded use of the power of eminent domain, which facilitated government acquisition of real estate for major projects championed by the ACCD. *Time* described the new ACCD as a "new experimental form of capitalism," a rare acknowledgment that it strayed from capitalism as many would have defined it at the time.[2] There is a certain irony that civic leaders encouraged support for the coalition by "framing the Renaissance as a response and an alternative to communism"—irony in that many of the key decisions shaping Pittsburgh's future were deferred to the parsimonious leadership of the ACCD, a central committee that operated independently with "no allegiance to anyone but itself."[3]

Early successes in addressing flood control and smoke abatement, a URA creation, and the construction of Gateway Center in Downtown Pittsburgh all encouraged the ACCD to address an even wider range of public policy issues. In its second decade, the ACCD focused on county-wide transportation and public transit challenges. Responding to the fiscal challenges of mostly private transit operators, the ACCD began promoting the consolidation of existing bus and trolley companies into a new public authority.[4] In 1956, the Pennsylvania legislature authorized the creation of the Port Authority of Allegheny County to oversee development for the inland port facilities so important to industrial Pittsburgh, which morphed into a public transit agency in 1959.

The new institutions of Pittsburgh were truly hybrid organizations, operating outside the normal boundaries of either the public or private sectors. Like the URA, the repurposed Port Authority was granted the power of eminent domain, typically used to acquire blighted land for public purposes. The Port Authority extended the scope of eminent domain and used it to condemn not just real estate but private businesses. Pursuant to the goal of creating a unified transit authority, most preexisting bus and trolley companies voluntarily sold their assets to the Port Authority, but the county's largest transit operator, Pittsburgh Railways, resisted. After the Port Authority completed acquisition of thirty other bus and trolley lines and began operation as an integrated transit agency at the beginning of 1964, the authority formally condemned the assets of the recalcitrant company. Pittsburgh Railways filed suit, but the state supreme court dismissed the petition by July the same year.[5]

Through the 1950s, the ACCD continued its urban redevelopment agenda, which still concentrated on Pittsburgh's central core. By the end of the decade, construction had begun on a new public auditorium, with a novel retractable roof, in the Lower Hill District, directly adjacent to the central business district. Following the pattern that worked in the construction of Gateway Center, the City of Pittsburgh declared the bulk of the neighborhood blighted, after which it was acquired by the URA and subsequently razed. The area housed more than eight thousand residents—mostly African American families. Little effort was spent on finding new living arrangements for the displaced households.

The Pittsburgh Renaissance undeniably shaped the city's physical revitalization, but it had a far more limited effect on the broader Pittsburgh region and even less impact generating cooperation or consensus across the region's innumerable local governments. For much of the twentieth century, the extreme fragmentation of local governments across southwestern Pennsylvania stood in sharp contrast to structure of the region's core industries. Nearly every industrial plant had spawned an independent local municipality, the virtual antithesis of the region's oligarchic corporate leadership.

Though any region's economy is almost always defined at metropolitan scale, the Pittsburgh region has long been governed by an amalgam of fiefdoms resistant to any proposal for political consolidation. A 1929 referendum had come closest to merging all the municipalities within Allegheny County. Its results documented overwhelming support for the proposal, which failed to be implemented solely because of legislative legerdemain in the Pennsylvania state capital.[6] Proponents of regional consolidation were left asking if an unofficial metropolitan Pittsburgh was a "Legal Fiction or Economic Reality?"[7] Few efforts to reorganize regional government have ever succeeded—leaving a void that has been left to private-sector organizations such as the PRPA and the ACCD, and their innumerable auxiliaries, to try and fill.

Seeking a more formal regional mandate, in 1961 the executive director of the PRPA, Patrick Cusick, proposed the creation of a new Southwestern Pennsylvania Regional Planning Commission (SPRPC) to empower planning efforts across a six-county region centered on Pittsburgh. The commission was created the following year and briefly operated in parallel with the PRPA, the two organizations initially sharing offices and staff. Confirming the new organization was an extension of existing leadership coalitions, Mellon aide and proxy Adolph Schmidt was named the first chairman of the SPRPC. In 1968, SPRPC began crafting an official development plan for the Pittsburgh region.[8]

SPRPC took on much of the local planning activity once sponsored by the PRPA and would later acquire quasigovernmental responsibilities for regional transportation planning. The Federal-Aid Highway Act of 1962 required the "establishment of a continuing and comprehensive transportation planning process carried out cooperatively by state and local communities."[9] The planning process became a requirement for receiving federal highway funding, and SPRPC was formally designated the metropolitan planning organization (MPO) for southwestern Pennsylvania in 1974. As the gatekeeper for federal transportation funding, SPRPC shepherded financial resources that the PRPA could never provide.

Cooperation between government and corporate leaders eroded through the 1960s as the new institutions of Pittsburgh's Renaissance were forced to continue without the influence of their founding principals. Longtime Pittsburgh Mayor David Lawrence passed away in January 1966, during his first term as governor of Pennsylvania. R. K. Mellon retired as chairman of the PRPA in 1965 and then as chairman of Mellon Bank in January 1967, before passing away in 1970. Neither left a successor who commanded similarly dominant roles in their respective spheres of influence. At the end of the decade, the challenge of maintaining consensus was highlighted by the failure to develop the Skybus transit system.

Throughout the 1970s, high-profile civic efforts mostly reverted to an older playbook concentrating on physical redevelopment of the region's urban core. Most successful was the series of Downtown real estate developments collectively named Renaissance II. The centerpiece of the new development was a new Downtown headquarters for the PPG Corporation, one of Pittsburgh's oldest companies. In addition to PPG Place, new projects collectively described as part of Pittsburgh's Renaissance II included One Oxford Center, Liberty Center, Riverfront Center, CNG Tower, Two Chatham Center, and One Mellon Bank Center, all of which began construction between 1977 and 1981. At the same time, Port Authority Transit, or PAT, regrouped following the collapse of plans for a Skybus transit system and began construction of a more limited and conventional new light-rail system to replace some of the county's older trolley routes.

It remains a debate as to whether the 1970s spurt of real estate development in the city was the result of concerted civic leadership or the city's unique tiered property tax. In 1916. modeled on the proposals of nineteenth-century economist Henry George, the city implemented a tiered tax that set a property tax rate on the value of land twice that of the tax placed on built structures. In 1977, a proposal from city of Pittsburgh councilor, and later congressman, Bill Coyne increased the ratio of the city's tax on land to that of structures to 5 to 1, greatly enhancing the incentives to more densely develop real estate within the city.

Most of the Renaissance II projects were completed just as Pittsburgh faced the contraction of the region's heavy industries. The new forty-two-story PPG Place was dedicated in April 1983, only a few months after the region's unemployment rate reached over 18 percent. The economic crisis bore down hardest on the manufacturing industries that remained concentrated in Pittsburgh but posed an even greater threat to the region's civic leadership. Many of Pittsburgh's largest firms faced existential battles that took priority over all nonbusiness concerns. Gulf's departure added to the escalating job destruction facing Pittsburgh and was a singular loss to the region's civic-minded corporate leadership. Most of the region's largest corporations were undergoing similar existential shifts. U.S. Steel was beginning an acquisition strategy aimed at transforming itself into an energy company that would move its headquarters to Texas, while Westinghouse was making investments in media ventures that eventually led to it absorbing the CBS corporation and shifting its headquarters to New York City in the 1990s. Virtually all of Pittsburgh's leading companies were forced into survival mode, which distracted from any civic projects. As one Pittsburgh CEO honestly explained at the time, "survival strategies leave little room for sentiment... or social assistance."[10]

Devolution of Pittsburgh's corporate leadership was escalating just as the region's economic challenges were becoming more complex. Soon after he retired in the mid-1980s, former Gulf CEO James Lee described how different the economic challenges of the 1980s were for Pittsburgh: "If you go back to the early days of the [Allegheny] conference, they were dealing with problems that could be solved with engineering, technology, and money." The newer problems of job creation, unemployment, and economic transition are "not the kind of problems that can be easily solved." [11] An emergent opinion was that the model of the Allegheny Conference "must be redesigned to meet the new challenge."[12] Many of its initiatives focused on the physical renewal of the city of Pittsburgh, specifically the city's central business district. The same model proved difficult to effect change across the many mill towns spread across southwestern Pennsylvania. Lacking were not just funding but the tools necessary to revitalize entire communities. One criticism was that the existing leadership structure "had little experience in grappling with the social and economic problems of the surrounding region."[13]

A major challenge was the scale of funding required for initiatives large enough to have a palpable impact on the region's economic trajectory. Early initiatives of the postwar Pittsburgh renaissance required minimal locally sourced public funding. The ACCD's critical support for early flood-control efforts was in lobbying political support in Congress and the Pennsylvania legislature for a series of projects that were eventually funded almost entirely by the federal government. The new supplies of natural gas brought into the region by the conversion of the wartime "Inch" pipelines in 1947—which at an optimal moment made natural gas less expensive than coal—heavily incentivized smoke control efforts in Pittsburgh. Mitigating the structural economic adjustments at a regional scale required far greater levels of funding precisely at a time when the regional businesses community had minimal resources to divert to public revitalization efforts.

Renewed cooperation between Pittsburgh's public and private leadership during the years of Renaissance II did not fully heal the rifts that had emerged in the previous decade. Lingering acrimony put additional pressure on the region's ability to generate new funding for economic development initiatives. In March 1987, the Supreme Court of Pennsylvania ruled that Duquesne Light, western Pennsylvania's largest electric utility, had to refund nearly $32.7 million it had collected in rate hikes originally approved to pay for canceled nuclear energy projects. While $28 million was to be refunded directly to customers, the remainder was earmarked for community development projects. The civic-minded, but nonetheless private-sector ACCD was initially designated as the organization to disburse the funds. So acrimonious had the relationship between political and business leaders become that unanticipated criticisms to the ACCD role derailed the plan. State Representative Tom Murphy led a group of legislators to reassign the funds to the Pittsburgh Foundation, which received $1.5 million of the remaining funds for redistribution to local projects. Murphy, later elected mayor of the city of Pittsburgh, sharply critiqued the region's business leadership in 1987: "When this region faced its toughest times, they did not play the role they could have played."[14]

No longer was the ACCD, nor any other single organization, the nexus of regional economic strategy. By 1984, a common perception was that "development efforts in the region are being driven not by coordinated planning, but by independent and sometimes contradictory efforts of more than 10 different organizations and agencies."[15] If not the ACCD, what institution could fill the role it once played? In the 1970s, there was an emerging public debate over whether SPRPC, which had evolved from the older PRPA, should "remain a passive planning agency or become an active political force," while sharper critiques argued that a "regional approach can't work" in southwestern Pennsylvania.[16]

Regional leaders looked for alternative institutions to spearhead new initiatives and push back against the impacts of rapid deindustrialization. For decades the ACCD acted "primarily in a planning and facilitating capacity, identifying critical issues that needed attention and then bringing together the appropriate public, private and nonprofit organizations to remedy the problems"; and rarely would the organization operate any program itself. Many entirely new nonprofit organizations were formed to address the unmet needs being created by widespread economic disruption across the region.[17]

In 1991, the federal government designated SPRPC as the gatekeeper for federal funding of major transportation projects across a broad region of southwestern Pennsylvania. The recently passed Intermodal Surface Transportation Efficiency Act of 1991 required regional transportation projects be prioritized by a local metropolitan planning organization. The following year, SPRPC sponsored the creation of a parallel organization, the Southwestern Pennsylvania Regional Development Council (SPRDC), which soon began clashing with existing economic development organizations and local governments.[18] The expanded development roles for SPRPC/SPRDC competed directly with some of the efforts previously spearheaded by the ACCD but also overlapped with efforts by Penn's Southwest, an economic development organization established in 1973 that focused on nine counties across southwestern Pennsylvania.

There was to be no consensus that SPRPC would shepherd economic development efforts for the region still reeling from a decade of industrial contraction. In the early 1990s, a fight emerged between SPRPC and the southwestern Pennsylvania Industrial Resource Center (SPIRC), over which organization would administer a small business program funded by the Appalachian Regional Commission (ARC). Relations between the two economic organizations "turned ugly," placing further stress on developing a regional economic strategy.[19]

SPRPC became the physical hub of regional collaboration when in 1997 the Alcoa Corporation announced plans to move its headquarters out of its iconic aluminum-clad skyscraper in Downtown Pittsburgh to an entirely new building on the north shore of the Allegheny River. Alcoa's CEO and future US Treasury secretary, Paul O'Neill, made an unusual offer to Pittsburgh's civic leadership. Instead of selling its former headquarters, he offered it for free for use as a new Regional Resource Center that could be used to co-locate all of the myriad economic development organizations in the region—the complexity of which was described as a "spider web or a diagram of the internet."[20] SPRPC, renamed the southwestern Pennsylvania Commission (SPC) in 1998, assumed ownership of the repurposed skyscraper. SPC relocated its offices there, as did the ACCD, along with many of the region's civic organizations, which became tenants in the renamed Regional Enterprise Tower.

Early in the 1990s, efforts focused on reorganizing the institutions central to Pittsburgh's civic leadership. The Western Division of the Pennsylvania Economy League partially merged with the Allegheny Conference in the spring of 1992, facilitating more coordinated efforts aimed at reforming local government. The Pittsburgh Regional Alliance (PRA) was created in 1995 to become the umbrella for several major economic development organizations, including the Greater Pittsburgh Chamber of Commerce, Penn's Southwest Association, the Pittsburgh High Technology Council, the SPIRC, the Regional Industrial Development Corporation (RIDC) of southwestern Pennsylvania and later incorporated the World Trade Center of Pittsburgh.

Parallel efforts focused on reforming local government and funding major civic amenities, which had long relied on resources provided by the city. As population dispersed within the region, so did fiscal capacity. By the 1970s, the city of Pittsburgh was challenged to sustain financial support for institutions such as the Pittsburgh Zoo, local museums, and major parks. The Pennsylvania Economy League (PEL) highlighted the growing issue in a 1985 report: *Pittsburgh: A Regional City with a Local Tax Base.*[21] By the 1990s, little had changed, and increasing stresses on city finances were becoming acute. The ACCD led a coalition that lobbied for an additional sales tax to be levied across Allegheny County.[22] In 1993, the Pennsylvania General Assembly overwhelmingly passed legislation creating a regional asset district for Allegheny County. Beginning in 1994, the Allegheny County Regional Asset District began collecting a supplemental 1 percent countywide sales tax, with half of the new revenues distributed across a broad range of local cultural institutions. The other half was divided among local municipal governments, with two-thirds of those funds designated for reductions of local taxes. The ACCD described the new tax as "a truly historic achievement for southwestern Pennsylvania" and "the most significant improvement in the structure of our government in 40 years."[23]

Additional efforts focused on restructuring Allegheny County government. Without a dominant government partner to work with, the ACCD attempted to create one. Concentrating first on the governance of Allegheny County, two major initiatives in the 1990s significantly altered the structure of county government. Sponsored by the Pennsylvania Economy League, the 1996 Committee to Prepare Allegheny County for the 21st Century (ComPAC 21) report advocated for "total change in the economic development activities of Allegheny County government" and a major shift in the structure of Allegheny County leadership.[24] A three-commissioner board had exercised a combined executive and legislative leadership of Allegheny County since the 18th century. In 1999, a county referendum narrowly approved a home rule charter that implemented many recommendations from the ComPAC 21 report, including the creation of a single county executive and a complementary parttime legislative council.

Emboldened by the successes at creating the regional asset district tax and passage of the Allegheny County Home Rule Charter earlier in the decade, the ACCD and Pittsburgh's civic leadership pushed for more expansive reforms that could have created the framework for a more formal regional government. A new Regional Renaissance Initiative (RRI) was proposed in the mid-1990s. The plan evolved into referendum seeking approval of a supplemental half-percent sales tax, projected to raise $700 million over seven years.

The RRI was nominally focused on funding replacements for Three Rivers Stadium and the original David Lawrence Convention Center, built in 1981 but considered undersized and outmoded barely a decade later. If adopted, the plan would have required the creation of a new multicounty special-purpose government, to be named the Regional Renaissance Authority, to oversee and distribute funds received from the supplemental tax. Of the anticipated revenue, 56 percent was to be directed to the construction of new stadiums and a new convention center in the city of Pittsburgh. Though the coalition in support of the new tax included almost all factions of Pittsburgh's business and civic leadership, opposition proved difficult to overcome. The RRI required approval of voters in a multicounty referendum. The enabling legislation for the referendum passed both chambers of the Pennsylvania General Assembly by large margins, reflecting the broad consensus among Pittsburgh's civic leaders.[25] While this was clearly intended to be a referendum held in Allegheny County and just nine contiguous counties of southwestern Pennsylvania, cartographic confusion caused the referendum to be held in eleven counties.[26]

Business leaders joined with a broad coalition of civic leaders in support of the new RRI, with U.S. Steel Chairman Tom Usher leading the advocacy efforts. Over $4 million was raised for a regional marketing campaign in support of the RRI—most of which was revealed to have been provided by the city's two largest sports teams, the Pittsburgh Pirates and the Pittsburgh Steelers.[27] The marketing message focused on how the new amenities would be transform Pittsburgh, with one television advertisement arguing, "We can continue to live in the shadow of the past and go downhill, or we can change and make our region strong again."[28] Proponents spent nearly forty times more than a much smaller campaign opposing the referendum. Opponents successfully labeled the supplemental tax a "stadium tax" but also played off fears of "regionalism" harking back to criticism of "Creeping Metropolitanism" that had persisted over decades in the region.[29] When the referendum took place in November 1997, voters from all counties decisively rejected the plan. Surprisingly, even a majority of Allegheny County voters opposed the plan, even though the common perception was that the region's core would benefit more than any other county. Allegheny County voters rejected the referendum by 42–58 percent. Only 8 of the county's 128 municipalities gave majority support to the proposed plan. More shocking was that the referendum was even rejected by voters in the city of Pittsburgh, where the margin was 47–53.[30] The lopsided results were said to "set regional cooperation back a decade."[31]

Lofty plans for the PRA were also unraveling at the same time. The vision that the new organization could bring focus to economic development efforts, much in the way the ACCD had a half century earlier, proved too difficult to implement. Three years after it was formed, the planned merger of Pittsburgh's major economic development organizations under a single executive director had yet to be implemented. Turf wars between the legacy organizations, and demoralization following the failed RRI referendum, effectively ended the PRA's goal to become the apex of a new grand coalition.[32] The PRA refocused on a more practical mission of regional marketing and even lost its nominal independence. In 2000, the ACCD entered into a formal agreement to subsume three other economic organizations—the Western Division of the PEL, the PRA, and the Greater Pittsburgh Chamber of Commerce. The CEO of the ACCD was designated to oversee all four organizations, effectively repatriating the overarching role once envisioned for the PRA.[33]

In the end, the Regional Enterprise Tower, which had emerged as a symbol of a renewed cooperation in Pittsburgh's civic leadership, became a greater sign of the region's enduring fragmentation. Costs to maintain the building overwhelmed the revenues raised from the primarily nonprofit tenants. As the G20 came to Pittsburgh in 2009, the building was already losing tenants, deepening the financial crisis it was causing for its owner, SPC. By 2011, the building was forced into foreclosure, and most of Pittsburgh's civic leadership, including both ACCD and SPC offices, was forced to relocate. The building was eventually sold via bankruptcy and later redeveloped for residential use.

The common narrative of civic leadership in Pittsburgh inevitably harkens back to the model defined by the unique partnership of David Lawrence and R. K. Mellon in the decade following World War II. In reality, there was little static about how that leadership worked at the time and less in how it has evolved since. The uniqueness of the economic circumstances Pittsburgh faced as it emerged from the war did not extend long into the future. Since then, the unspoken reality is that Pittsburgh's civic partnerships have been more defined by ongoing change, with no era ever again emulating the model that facilitated Pittsburgh's original Renaissance.

What emerged in Pittsburgh was another pole of leadership distinct from the political, academic, and business coalitions that had long been the core of the city's civic leadership. The burst of entrepreneurial activity that had emerged in Pittsburgh in the latter half of the nineteenth century had transformed into concentrated corporate capital in the first half of the twentieth. Theough the latter half of the century, a further transformation morphed the same corpus of wealth into an enviable concentration of private philanthropy assets. The scale of charitable giving and a growing activism in how that giving was targeted grew in Pittsburgh even more than it was growing nationally.

Expansive philanthropy was not new to Pittsburgh. Andrew Carnegie pioneered a career in "big philanthropy" while he was still actively leading the steel empire he had created. The "retail" phase of his philanthropic career focused on the sponsorship of local libraries and, in particular, new institutions near Pittsburgh. Between 1886 and 1896, Carnegie's donations provided for new libraries in five Pennsylvania communities: Allegheny City, Braddock, Johnstown, Homestead, and the city of Pittsburgh and, anomalously, one in Fairfield, Iowa. Subsequently, during the "wholesale" phase of his philanthropic career, he systematically took requests for donations, eventually supporting more than two thousand new libraries across the country.

By the middle of the twentieth century, much of the region's accumulated corporate wealth began a transformation into the investment corpus of private foundations. Ailsa Mellon Bruce founded the Avalon Foundation in 1940. In 1941, the Howard Heinz Endowment was formed, upon the death of its namesake. That same year, Paul Mellon created the Old Dominion Foundation and the Sarah Mellon Scaife Foundation began operations. In 1945, the Union Trust Company formed the Pittsburgh Foundation, a community foundation based on the nation's first community foundation which had been operating in Cleveland since 1914. The Richard King Mellon Foundation was created in November 1947. Many other fortunes had been made in Pittsburgh and were also making a similar transition. The Claude Worthington Benedum foundation started in 1944 with profits Michael Benedum had generated in the oil and gas industries through the first half of the twentieth century. In 1951, the Hillman Foundation was chartered, followed in 1952 by the Alcoa Foundation.

Remarkable also are the number foundations currently based elsewhere in the United States but nonetheless spawned from wealth generated in Pittsburgh. The Pew Charitable Trusts, with over $7.5 billion in assets as of 2024, grew from Pittsburgh native Joseph Pew's success in Pennsylvania oil and gas industries and later in founding Sun Oil, renamed Sunoco in 1998. In 1969, the Avalon Foundation and the Old Dominion Foundation merged to create the New York City–based Andrew W. Mellon Foundation. Even the relatively smaller Arthur Vining Davis Foundation was closely linked to both Pittsburgh and the Mellon Family. Vining was the very first employee of the Pittsburgh Reduction Company, later Alcoa, after A. W. Mellon and Captain Alfred Hunt founded the company in Pittsburgh in 1888. Rising to become CEO in 1910, Vining remained with the company until 1957 and left the bulk of a $400 million estate to his namesake Florida-based foundation.

A complete list is too long to itemize here, but charitable giving by both individuals and foundations has been instrumental at seminal points in the modern history of many Pittsburgh institutions. William Larimer Mellon funded the creation of the Graduate School of Industrial Administration at the Carnegie Institute of Technology in 1949. Mellon family donations were crucial to the creation of the Graduate School of Public Health at the University of Pittsburgh and enabled consolidation of the University Medical Center in Oakland. The Mellon Foundation later funded the creation of the position that brought Tom Detre to the University of Pittsburgh to rejuvenate the Western Psychiatric Institute and Clinic, then run under contract by the University of Pittsburgh, and later to be appointed vice chancellor of the University of Pittsburgh.

In the 1960s, philanthropic efforts in Pittsburgh were informally coordinated by separate groups of corporate leaders and private foundation leaders. Leaders in the two spheres eventually came together to form the Pittsburgh Contributions Group. Local foundations began an evolution into a more formal and distinct force amid the economic turmoil of the 1980s. At the beginning of the decade, most local foundations maintained only modest staffs. The Howard Heinz Endowments and the Pittsburgh Foundation—two of Pittsburgh's largest private foundations—operated with a combined staff of two, only adding a third staff member in 1980.[34] In 1983, the Contributions Group evolved into Grantmakers of Western Pennsylvania, formally incorporated in 1985.[35]

As the region emerged from the depths of the economic contraction of the 1980s, the nation entered into an extended period of economic growth. Only broken by what has been called the dotcom bust and a relatively mild national recession between March and November 2001, the nation's expansion continued until the onset of the Great Recession in 2007. Economic growth fueled unprecedented stock markets gains. Between 1987 and 2000, the Standard & Poor's (S&P) 500 Index increased by over 230 percent, with the fastest appreciation coming in the latter half of the 1990s. The economic boom translated into significant asset gains for most institutional investment holdings, to include the assets of major charitable foundations. Each of Pittsburgh's major foundations experienced sustained gains in its core investment portfolios. Assets held by the R. K. Mellon Foundation—Pittsburgh's largest private foundation—grew from under $438 million in 1984 to over $1 billion in 1993 and reached just under $1.5 billion by 1997. Similar appreciation came to other major private foundations. By 2007, the fifteen largest foundations based in or active in Pittsburgh held combined assets exceeded $7 billion, with charitable distributions nearing $350 million annually, an amount slightly less than the total annual tax revenues of the city of Pittsburgh—the largest municipality in western Pennsylvania—and far greater than the economic development budget of any economic development agency across southwestern Pennsylvania.

Expanding investment portfolios were changing not just the scale but the structure of charitable giving. The traditional form of charitable giving has been mostly in the form of outright grants. Private foundations typically separated their grantmaking activities from the management of the core investment assets. What was expanding both in Pittsburgh and nationally were hybrid philanthropic efforts that included the targeted investment of their much larger investment trusts. Program-related investments (PRIs) leveraged the portfolios held by large philanthropic institutions by targeting investments into projects that aligned with their institutional missions. PRIs could come in the form of loans, loan guarantees, and even equity investments. PRIs were enabled by tax law changes that not only permitted the wider use of investment capital but also allowed PRI expenditures used be counted as part of foundations annual minimum payout as required by tax laws to retain their nonprofit status.

Nationally, philanthropies' use of PRI was not new. The Ford Foundation—one of the nation's largest private foundations, with over $12 billion in assets in 2024—pioneered the use of PRI and was active in lobbying for new laws to codify their legality. The Ford Foundation lobbied for changes implemented in the Tax Reform Act of 1969, which codified the expanded use of investment assets though the new law did not eliminate ambiguity in the scope of permissible PRI. In 1972, the IRS issued a limited list of nine examples of permissible PRI. In 2002, the MacArthur Foundation submitted an expanded set of nineteen additional examples of program related investments for consideration.[36] Though the IRS would not formally promulgate an expanded list of permissible PRI examples until 2012, the nation's largest foundations, and especially the foundation community in Pittsburgh, were taking on larger and more collaborative projects, taking advantage of their growing investment portfolios.

Prior to the 1980s, major philanthropic efforts in Pittsburgh, had mostly been pursued independently or in limited collaborations for larger projects. In the late 1960s, the transformation of former Loew's Theater in Downtown Pittsburgh into a new home for the Pittsburgh Symphony was mostly an effort of H. J. Heinz II and primarily funded by the Heinz Endowments and the A. W. Mellon Charitable Trust. In an early example of PRI, two affiliated foundations—the Sarah Mellon Scaife foundation and the A. W. Mellon Charitable Trust—worked together to quietly acquire Downtown real estate to support the unrealized Skybus transit system in the early 1970s. Greater collaboration came in 1984, when the nonprofit Pittsburgh Cultural Trust was formed with collaborative funding provided by the Heinz Endowments, the Richard King Foundation, and the Benedum Foundation. Adjacent to Heinz Hall, a $43 million project redeveloped the former Stanley Theater, renamed the Benedum Center, which opened in 1987 and continued efforts focused on creating a contiguous cultural district Downtown. Combined foundation funding was essential to execute land acquisition at the core of the Cultural Trust's strategy.

Acquisition of the former LTV site in Hazelwood would become the largest example of PRI in Pittsburgh. Previous and ongoing redevelopment efforts in the city had put significant strains on resources available for brownfield redevelopment. As a former coke works, the site presented significant environmental remediation costs. Either a lack of resources immediately available when LTV finally abandoned the site or the excessive remediation costs anticipated may have played a role in the URA not immediately pursuing ownership of the site.[37]

In 2002, four of Pittsburgh's largest foundations: the R. K. Mellon Foundation, the Heinz Endowments, the McCune Foundation and the Benedum Foundation, came together to purchase the former site of the former LTV coke works. The purchase was a significant departure from public-led models of brownfield development efforts that had come before. The URA of Pittsburgh had been the principal player in redevelopment efforts for two of the region's largest brownfields: the former LTV steelworks along Second Avenue (to become the Pittsburgh Technology Center), and the South Side Works, directly across the Monongahela River. In coordination with the RIDC, Allegheny County had led the redevelopment of the former Homestead Works into the Waterfront complex. The RIDC or other county governments had taken the lead in major brownfield redevelopment efforts elsewhere in the Pittsburgh region.

The consortium taking ownership of the site initially renamed it Almono, for the region's three major rivers: the Allegheny, the Monongahela, and the Ohio. There would be no effort to bring heavy industry back to the site. The new owners wanted redevelopment of the vast property to support of a broader set of goals than had governed earlier brownfield projects. The major brownfields already been developed had not necessarily benefited adjacent communities. At the end of the twentieth century, Hazelwood was one of Pittsburgh's poorer neighborhoods. At the time, criticisms were mounting that nominally successful redevelopment of the former U.S. Steel Homestead works had failed to deliver meaningful positive impacts for the residents of the adjacent municipality, which remained a distressed community subject to Pennsylvania's Act 47 oversight.[38] At over 170 acres, the Almono site was the last major brownfield site left undeveloped within the city of Pittsburgh, and foundations were looking to "take full advantage of the site's location along the riverfront."[39] By taking ownership of the former coke works, foundations were taking a new and vastly larger role in shaping the city's ongoing economic development.

As with other redevelopment projects of similar scale, change would not come quickly. An initial master planning process for the site was completed over the three years. In 2005, the site remained so desolate that it was used as a testing landscape simulating barren desert conditions. Researchers at Carnegie Mellon University began using the semicleared site to test highly customized sport utility vehicles as they navigated driverless in preparation for a competition sponsored by the Defense Advanced Research Projects Agency.[40] In 2016, the site became an indirect link between Pittsburgh's industrial past and future, when Silicon Valley–based Uber began construction of a simulated city road network on the expansive site. Pending its redevelopment, the site was used to simulate a road network to test self-driving robotic cars. Renamed Hazelwood Green,

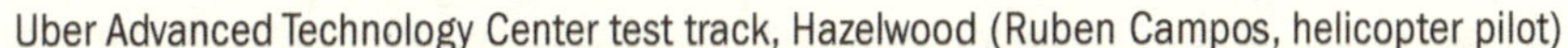

Uber Advanced Technology Center test track, Hazelwood (Ruben Campos, helicopter pilot)

the site is the location of new university projects focused on robotics, advanced manufacturing, and life sciences.

Efforts to find a new model for redevelopment in Hazelwood reflect an enduring challenge across Greater Pittsburgh. For every story of success in building a "new" Pittsburgh that is the result of new investments in new industries, there remains an enduring core of communities that have yet to participate in any postindustrial transformation. Some of the region's oldest economic development challenges remain.

Leveling Up

15

We were taught how the pioneers went into the west.
They opened their eyes, and made up what things could be.
A long time ago, things got broken here, people got sad and left.
Maybe the world breaks on purpose, so we can have work to do.
People think there aren't frontiers any more.
They can't see how frontiers are all around us.

Video advertisement for the Levi Strauss Company, 2010

Left Behind

May 28, 2007

An announcement from the Pennsylvania secretary of education explained that the only high school in the Duquesne City School District would not open in the coming fall.[1] Facing unresolved fiscal crises, the school district had effectively been taken over by the state of Pennsylvania in October 2000, but even under the control of a state oversight board it had yet to engineer a path to fiscal solvency. With over 53 percent of resident children living in poverty as of 1999, the school district faced the compound challenges of insufficient fiscal capacity to raise revenue and excessively high costs given the economic circumstances of its students and heightened legacy costs of its depreciated infrastructure.

Once such a large and thriving municipality that the Commonwealth of Pennsylvania designated it a third-class city—unlike the boroughs and townships that surrounded it—Duquesne was no longer able to provide an education for students in grades 9 through 12. Three years later, the school district ceased instruction in grades 7 and 8. Local students were essentially abandoned to neighboring school districts, which were forced to take them in pursuant to an order from the Pennsylvania Department of Education.[2] The closure decisions were not voluntary but imposed on Duquesne residents by a state bureaucracy. The fiction of local governance in the Mon Valley was reaching a dystopian conclusion.

The school district and its coterminous municipality, the city of Duquesne, hosted the massive Duquesne Works for almost a century.

When operating, the steelworks anchored much of the Mon Valley's steel-based economy. Without it, Duquesne was unable to provide its residents with the most basic public services. Given the district's ongoing fiscal plight, the unprecedented decision was almost inevitable. In many ways, the question is why such a drastic eventuality had taken so long to arrive, given that steel production had ceased in Duquesne over two decades earlier.

Shortly before the plant was closed, the plant generated half of Duquesne's municipal budget.[3] When the plant closed in 1984, the USX corporation promised the city and school district annual payments for seventeen years to make up for lost tax revenues, payments that ran out before alternative revenue streams emerged. A failing school system made Duquesne even less desirable to potential new residents, begetting further population decline. By 2023, the municipality, which once counted over twenty-one thousand citizens, had dropped to a total population of less than fifty-one hundred. Four decades after the Duquesne Works closed, half of all Duquesne children remain in poverty, just under 30 percent of the city's housing units are vacant, and there is still no concrete vision for when or how such disparities will be alleviated in the future.

Braddock

Pittsburgh's success in moving beyond steel is far more nuanced when evaluated in comparison to other communities within southwestern Pennsylvania. Corporations can jettison their pasts much more readily than can the workers or the municipalities that once relied on them. For all the stories of postindustrial transformation, the region's most glaring failure has been in how unevenly that transformation has extended across western Pennsylvania.

Moving on from steel continues to prove hardest for the individual mill towns created around individual steel plants: cities, boroughs, and townships that had virtually no history prior to the erection of the production plants they once hosted. By most any sociodemographic metric, the former steel communities of southwestern Pennsylvania continue to be left behind even as economic transformation elsewhere makes headlines. A particular pathology is that the worst blight remains in the communities that still hang on to the remaining vestiges of steel production in the Mon Valley. At the beginning of the twenty-first century,

Andrew Carnegie's original steel plant at Braddock was the last blast furnace U.S. Steel continued to operate in Pennsylvania. U.S. Steel's other operations in Allegheny County included a coke works at Clairton and a rolling mill in West Mifflin, but the blast furnaces in Braddock stood alone producing raw steel.

Continuing production at the Edgar Thomson plant, the lynchpin of U.S. Steel's consolidated Mon Valley Works, generates little prosperity for the borough. Much like the broader Pittsburgh region, the fate of the steel industry had long diverged from Braddock's. Braddock has contracted from a peak of over twenty thousand residents in the 1920s to under seventeen hundred by 2023. Once hosting one of the most vibrant retail districts in the state, the Braddock Avenue thoroughfare is today mostly filled with vacant storefronts and empty lots. A few of the formerly grand buildings along the thoroughfare have been repurposed, but some, like the former home of Braddock's First National Bank, remain vacant because there are no plans for their redevelopment nor any resources to pay for their demolition. Yet, if you stand on any corner along Braddock Avenue today, you will soon see a five-ton pickup truck leaving the still-operating plant, likely its cargo of still off-gassing slag being hauled away for disposal.

Like the declines of many other mill towns, Braddock's began long before the apogee of the regional steel industry. Most of the fragmented mill towns of southwestern Pennsylvania were incorporated in an era before commuting by car or public transit became routine. Workers and their families had little choice but to cluster in close proximity to their work sites. Residential locations near the behemoth plants and their industrial discharges were less than ideal. As workers' incomes and transportation options increased, mill towns de-densified; workers and their families moved away from the industrial sites, even if they kept the same jobs. For most blue-collar workers, there were never practical employment alternatives, certainly none that offered comparable wages. Population decline began early in the twentieth century and for many municipalities has yet to abate. The contraction of heavy industry in the 1980s only compounded municipal decline and distress, often taking from local governments the revenue sources they relied on to provide their remaining residents the most basic public services.

In 1988, the State of Pennsylvania declared Braddock's municipal government fiscally distressed and forced it to enter into its Act 47 program, state receivership akin to bankruptcy. In 2000, the borough's largest employer shut down: a branch hospital of the region's largest healthcare system, itself a fractional remnant of the once independent Braddock General Hospital. The closure made U.S. Steel's Edgar Thomson plant the town's largest job center again, but very few local residents were employed by U.S. Steel. The modern municipality of Braddock persistently ranks among the very poorest Pennsylvania communities, with an older and declining population.

All of the municipalities immediately adjacent to Braddock—including Rankin, East Pittsburgh, and North Braddock—would eventually be declared distressed and likewise involuntarily taken into Pennsylvania's Act 47 program. State oversight wrestled significant control from local elected officials yet provided minimal financial resources to support individual communities. For Braddock and most of its Mon Valley neighbors, there was no substantial funding dedicated to blunting ongoing decline, let alone rebuilding new jobs or new industries. Even the smallest municipalities were left to fend for themselves, without even the barest fiscal capacity necessary to address the structural economic decline being imposed on them by economic forces far beyond their control. Even larger county governments in Pennsylvania lacked the resources to substantially alter the economic trajectory of former mill towns, and state government resources were highly diluted across so many areas needing assistance.

Brownsville

Just as Pittsburgh's industrial geography extended far from the city center, so did the impacts of deindustrialization. Brownsville, Pennsylvania—thirty miles south-southeast of Downtown Pittsburgh—brackets the far end of the once hyper-industrialized section of the Monongahela River. Once the intersection of the National Pike and the Monongahela, the town was a center for intermodal commerce long before the modern steel industry emerged. Migrants moving westward often first reached the navigable tributaries of the Ohio River at Brownsville. The borough became an early boatbuilding center and home to the first nail factory west of the Alleghenies by 1798. Soon into the nineteenth century, demand for nearby Connellsville coal generated growth and sustained a modicum of prosperity for a century. Nearby coking operations and extensive railyards were all deeply connected to a vast steel industry supply chain across southwestern Pennsylvania.

Like so many of its Mon Valley neighbors, Brownsville had no alternative economic base to fall back on as legacy coal and steel industries declined. The pathology of extreme deindustrialization meant that local real estate lost most of its value once industry departed. So devalued was real estate in Brownsville that a single undercapitalized developer could accumulate virtually all of the borough's commercial property in the early 1990s, including most of its once-thriving main street business district. Over a hundred commercial properties and, by default, the borough's economic future, were purchased by a single developer with little experience and insufficient resources to complete any meaningful redevelopment. Promised investments included a floating casino, to be docked along the river—similar to a competing project once planned for the former South Side Works in the city of Pittsburgh—along with a new recreational wharf and marina. As mythical as such proposals were, local officials were more than willing to support any offers that came to rebuild economic opportunities. There were few alternatives.[4]

None of the promised investments ever materialized, and local properties were left to depreciate. In 2001, the local volunteer fire department declared most of the borough's main street real estate too unsafe to enter under any circumstances. Legal machinations kept the real estate portfolio in legal limbo for more than a decade, even though the nominal owners had long since stopped paying property taxes. Devoid of revenues, the municipality of Brownsville was forced to lay off all but a single worker in 2006.[5] Only in 2009—over a quarter century after the collapse of heavy industry in the region—did legal actions begin to repatriate properties from the absentee landlords who had virtually abandoned them.

Across southwestern Pennsylvania, but especially along the entire breadth of the Mon Valley, municipal boundaries were originally formed to circumscribe the communities centered around industrial plants now permanently closed—a political geography long since overcome by economic shifts. In 1988, the University of Pittsburgh sponsored a conference titled "Mill Towns: Despair, Hopes and Opportunities." A major recommendation to emerge from this was to merge most Mon Valley communities into a single municipality to facilitate economic development efforts. It was not a sentiment shared by many community residents. Even though a study the year before had predicted most of the municipalities in the Mon Valley would be insolvent by 1989, "each individual community still has its pride and respect, a sense of identity and a desire to be their own town." No consolidation of any southwestern Pennsylvania municipalities would ever take place.[6]

One of the steel industry's most indelible legacies across southwestern Pennsylvania has not been lost jobs but a persistent fragmentation of governments and regional leadership, which made it virtually impossible for many communities to participate in the transformation taking place around them. The disconnect between political and economic borders was so severe that late in the 1990s regional politicians began advocating for the outright disincorporation of former mill towns, which was not even permitted in Pennsylvania law.[7] Many former steel communities and their residents remained trapped in an industrial past that no longer existed.

Mon-Fayette Expressway

When economic development policies focused on Mon Valley communities, these were rarely to build a postindustrial future based on encouraging investment in new industries and far more likely to look backward. Over decades, the most consistent economic development efforts in the Mon Valley have been plans to build a new major highway through the area, today named the Mon–Fayette Expressway. When completed, the highway is intended to connect Morgantown, West Virginia, and the Pennsylvania Turnpike, a route that takes it through the heart of the Mon Valley. The "whole purpose" of the yet-to-be-completed project remains "to spur redevelopment efforts and reindustrialize the Mon Valley area."[8] Other redevelopment efforts and future industries are most often left un-itemized.

Most of the steel plants of southwestern Pennsylvania had been constructed before the modern highway system had even been conceived, one of the reasons that locations along navigable rivers were once so vital to industrial Pittsburgh. In contrast, almost all modern manufacturing industries rely on a national highway infrastructure that has been built out over the last century. The lack of a major highway through the Mon Valley had long been seen as an economic weakness for the region's existing industrial plants and an even larger competitive liability for attracting new investment.

The roadway currently named the Mon–Fayette Expressway was first included in development plans for southwestern Pennsylvania at least since World War II, if not earlier. Even in 1965, Washington County commissioners issued a proclamation urging "the Governor of the Commonwealth of Pennsylvania to give top priority to the proposed Monongahela Valley Expressway as part of the Appalachia Program for Pennsylvania."[9] Ground was broken for the first section of the new highway in 1973, when then Governor Shapp called the new highway a "new lifeline . . . carrying economic development and hopes for continued future growth."[10] In 1983, California University of Pennsylvania's president, John Watkins, declared that the new highways was "essential and critical to the economic survival of the valley."[11] Even as industry contracted, inertia continued to push the yet to be completed highway project forward.

As Pittsburgh faced its peak deindustrialization, questions began to be raised about the need for the new highway. The Strategy 21 proposal included a section for "Mon Valley Highways" but only advocated a series of improvements to existing highway links, even arguing against any "massive, new and unaffordable expressway construction."[12] It was not a fatal setback for the multidecade project. The construction of the roadway remained a singular priority to those who believed it could bring industrial operations back to the Mon Valley's brownfields. Some segments have been built, but the full roadway remains uncompleted. Until it is finished, the highway can provide only a limited catalyst for new industrial development, and it remains unclear what new investment will come even if it is completed. If anything, development in many municipalities along the route has been dampened by the lingering prospects of future construction. It makes little sense to make significant investments in any real estate likely to be subsumed by eminent domain for future roadway construction. That uncertainly has only been compounded by changing routes planned for the highway over its long history.[13]

Even when alternative economic development visions for the future of the Mon Valley have been conjured, they have rarely received the minimum funding or support to even begin implementation. A 2004 comprehensive economic development strategy report sponsored by Allegheny County bluntly said that the entire Mon Valley was still "caught in a downward development spiral" and that the region "does not need economic development, it needs RADICAL economic development." To achieve a shift in the region's trajectory, the report recommended revitalization efforts in the Mon Valley be concentrated at five community hubs: Hazelwood in the city of Pittsburgh; McKeesport; Duquesne; Clairton-Elizabeth; and the Carrie Furnace site, one of just a few industrial artifacts that remained standing in the region. The vision included enhanced public transit connecting the Mon Valley with Downtown

Former Carrie Furnace, 2024

Pittsburgh and the creation of a dedicated Mon Valley Economic Development organization.[14] Released with great fanfare, little came of the proposals over the subsequent two decades. No new transit links have come into the Mon Valley, and only in 2023 did the first phase of construction at the Carrie Furnace site even begin.

Gentrification

Even, or especially, where Pittsburgh's postindustrial transformation has been most successful, the secondary impacts of economic change have created new pockets of distress. For nearly half a century after World War II, the city of Pittsburgh suffered compound population losses, driven not only by concentrated deindustrialization but by the suburbanization of population away from the region's urban core. Though it remained the largest municipality in western Pennsylvania, the city of Pittsburgh had seen little territorial expansion since the 1930s, remaining a relatively small part of the greater Pittsburgh metropolitan area. Comprising the region's urban core, the city declined from a peak of over 676,000 in 1950 to just over 300,000 in 2010. Population loss begat greater concentrations in poverty and urban blight, as higher-income households were most likely to move to the suburbs or out of the Pittsburgh region.

During the region's industrial heyday, steel production and the jobs it created stretched far away from the city center. For postindustrial Pittsburgh, new investments have been far more concentrated within the city proper. By 2010, the city of Pittsburgh's population stabilized for the first time after declines stretching back nearly eight decades. Though the city's population has yet to show significant growth, stability in aggregate levels belies far greater changes in the characteristics of the city's resident population, changes that have had consequences for many of the city's older communities.

In the first decade of the twentieth century, the city of Pittsburgh saw its Black population peak and then start an accelerated decline. Between 2010 and 2020, the city's Black population declined by 7 percent, despite the its total population remaining nearly even over the decade. The city's Black residents—who had mostly arrived a century earlier as part of the Great Migration of southern workers into northern industrial centers—were moving by either choice or economic displacement into more areas outside of the city. The communities experiencing the largest increases in the number of Black households were primarily in the former industrial municipalities of the Mon Valley. The housing stock of many former mill towns had suffered decades of disinvestment and blight. Their lack of revitalization continued to suppress real estate prices, making residences in these areas some of the most affordable housing options in proximity to the city of Pittsburgh.

Demographic shifts have been even more dramatic for certain city neighborhoods. As late as 2000, the concentration of elderly residents of the city of Pittsburgh's Lawrenceville neighborhood was so high that it was commonly described as an extreme example of a naturally occurring retirement community.[15] By 2009, the influx of much younger residents into Lawrenceville became one reason the *Financial Times* described Lawrenceville as a "Diamond in the Rust."[16] Over less than a decade, the neighborhood shifted from one of the oldest across southwestern Pennsylvania to one of the youngest, as households of young professionals replaced residents who had aged in place in the neighborhood for decades.

Change within Pittsburgh has been the most dramatic where postindustrial shifts have been concentrated. Today, the city's East Liberty neighborhood is routinely touted as the center of gravity of new technology-based investment in the region. When Google expanded its Pittsburgh presence in the neighborhood's Bakery Square development, it catalyzed population and employment growth that soon displaced the bulk of existing residents and businesses. East Liberty had been a majority Black neighborhood since the early 1970s, when the displacement of residents from redevelopment in Pittsburgh's Lower Hill District forced many to move into the city's east end.[17] Between 2000 and 2023, the neighborhood's concentration of Black residents dropped from 68 to 34 percent. Among young adults between the ages of twenty-five and thirty-four, the percentage of Black residents dropped even more precipitously, going from 68 to 9 percent over the same period, a trend that appears to be continuing. Neighborhood housing prices have jumped even as East Liberty has attracted a disproportionate concentration of Pittsburgh's new housing development and investment dedicated to rehabilitating older housing. So dramatic is the change to the neighborhood that controversy erupted when in 2017 a local artist put up a billboard declaring simply, "THERE ARE BLACK PEOPLE IN THE FUTURE."[18]

Any success at generating new jobs or attracting new technology-based investment has yet to result in significant improvement in deep and persistent racial disparities in Pittsburgh. A 1995 study showed that Black men in Pittsburgh aged twenty-five had the lowest rates of labor force participation among the fifty largest metropolitan areas in the United States.[19] While Pittsburgh has received multiple accolades for having a highly ranked quality of life, it is clear that the benefits do not apply to all equally.

Postindustrial Pittsburgh has likewise yet to rebuild much of the workforce protections that had been codified in the past by decades of collective bargaining. While many of the new jobs generated in Pittsburgh—to include continuing growth of jobs in education, health services, financial services, and technology-based industries—are well paying, fewer and fewer regional workers are union members. Where once a majority of Pittsburgh's manufacturing-centric workers were covered by collective bargaining protections, by 2014 less than 10 percent of all private-sector workers in the Pittsburgh metropolitan statistical area were unionized.[20] Historian Gabriel Winant has recently chronicled the distinct transformation and new challenges of labor management relations in a modern Pittsburgh workforce that has little in common with its industrial past.[21]

Pittsburgh's challenges are not unique, either within the United States or globally. Urbanist Alan Mallach has chronicled the challenge many cities in the United States face as they seek equitable redevelopment policies. He has called out Pittsburgh's urban resurgence based on growth of an "eds and meds" or technology-based employment but has also noted the lack of spillover impact on its middle-class or lower-middle-class neighborhoods.[22]

In the United Kingdom, persistent disparities between prospering regions and former industrial regions like the Mon Valley led a Conservative Party government to propose a national Level-Up campaign in 2019. The British government would go so far as to create a national Department of Leveling Up, focused entirely on addressing chronic inequality between regions in the nation. Greater priority for place-based economic development policies have emerged because persistent geographic equalities are having impacts far beyond the left-behind communities themselves. Economic disparities between regions are seen as driving the national Brexit campaign, which resulted in the United Kingdom formally ending its forty-seven-year membership in the European Union in 2020.[23] There is growing research into how local and regional disparities have affected political divides globally and in particular how "prolonged economic decline of regions is fueling populism both in Europe."[24]

Economists have long generally preferred person-based economic development programs over place-based ones because investing directly in individuals—through education, training, or income support—offers greater efficiency and flexibility.[25] Investments in human capital can be more precisely targeted to those who need support, but they can also work against the goal reviving declining areas, as often individuals seeking their best opportunities move away from the most depressed areas. Place-based economic development policies have experienced a resurgence, in no small part due to the persistence of extreme disparities.[26]

So severe remains the concentrated blight of the Mon Valley that persistent poverty has evolved into a new type of status symbol. Nine months after the G20 summit concluded in Pittsburgh, filming began in Braddock for Levi Strauss's multimillion dollar "Go Forth and Work" advertising campaign.[27] The producers crafted an image of hardscrabble, self-reliant residents that belied the starker reality that even the few local jobs remaining in the borough were disappearing. Five months before the advertising campaign debuted in July, Braddock's largest employer and local hospital permanently shut down. Even though U.S. Steel's Edgar Thomson plant continues in operation, few places remain as left behind as Braddock and its Mon Valley neighbors.

National advertisers had come to Braddock because of the most unlikely of totems. Soon after he was elected mayor in 2007, John Fetterman almost immediately took on a new role as a symbol of unvanquished rustbelt decline.[28] The new mayor tattooed Braddock's zip code on his forearm and then began adding tattoos of the dates Braddock residents were killed by violence during his tenure.[29] Much forgotten about for decades, Braddock had emerged in a series of national media stories almost entirely because of its iconic mayor. Braddock's ultimate legacy to Pennsylvania may be in catalyzing an unlikely political career, as Fetterman was elected lieutenant governor of Pennsylvania in 2018 and US senator in 2022. His would be a political career entirely divorced from any steel history. Fetterman had first come to the Pittsburgh region as an AmeriCorps volunteer in 1996 and moved to Braddock in 2004 to work with an antipoverty program. He had no connections to the borough's deep industrial roots other than eventually taking up residence across the street from the still operating Edgar Thomson Works. Literally in the shadow of Andrew Carnegie's first steel plant, persistent blight was forging an entirely new history for Braddock a generation after the bulk of the steel industry Carnegie invented collapsed across southwestern Pennsylvania.

If people are looking for hope, it's here.

Sabina Deitrick, *New York Times,* January 2009

Termination Shock

1999

The post-Soviet economy of modern Russia continued a difficult transition at the beginning of the twenty-first century. For more than six decades, recurring five-year plans had dictated the economic specializations of entire cities and guaranteed demand for all that they were required to produce. When faced with competition for the first, many regions throughout Russia and other former states once part of the USSR were left with anachronistic industrial bases.

Soviet planners had required industries to concentrate into large and specialized agglomerations called моногорода, or monotowns. A 1999 Russian government report identified 467 Russian cities and 332 smaller towns with economies so lacking in diversification that they were classified as monotowns. Especially for commodities such as steel, economies of scale function much the same in command economies as they do under capitalism—decreasing per-unit costs as production levels increase. Soviet economic doctrine argued the concentration of production was far better than what it saw as the chaotic and wasteful patterns of production in the West. A 2010 report from the World Bank concluded that the system only "worked as long as relative prices were controlled to reflect domestic planning priorities" and "collapsed in the face of market realities when prices were liberalized."[1]

No central plan ever assigned the production of steel to southwestern Pennsylvania. Yet, no deliberate federal effort could have produced a more specialized economy than the century-long imprint of steel on greater Pittsburgh. Andrew Carnegie championed the business model of integrated steel production on a scale that dwarfed all of his early competitors. The unprecedented economies of scale he achieved were the core of his early success in the steel industry. Then at the beginning of the twentieth century, J. P. Morgan and Elbert Gary consolidated the industry on an even larger scale, allowing them to establish market control and centralized management to such a degree that made it hard to distinguish from the national-scale central plans that were only codified later in the century.

Pittsburgh's industrial core long had similarly been protected from unfettered market forces but collapsed decades before the final five-year plan of the Soviet Union was promulgated. Thus, many regions have looked to Pittsburgh for lessons on how to deal with unexpected economic shocks and build new futures. Indeed, the very same 2010 World Bank report on Russia's post-Soviet economy gave a targeted shoutout to Pittsburgh as "a model for other regions coping with industrial decline."[2]

For all the examples of a very incomplete revitalization within the region, Pittsburgh's transformation remains a remarkable story of resilience. Persisting economic challenges only highlight how far all of Greater Pittsburgh had to go to dig itself out of after the region's spasm of deindustrialization. Literally every corner of western Pennsylvania suffered from the massive job loss that materialized over just a few years in the early 1980s. Historic levels of job loss and outmigration compounded the region's economic decline, making transformation far more difficult than it appeared, and it appeared very stark. The greatest threat to future prosperity was that declining job opportunities made Pittsburgh a very unattractive place for young workers. Unable to attract workers with the most cutting-edge skills, how could Pittsburgh rebuild the industries that fostered new growth? It was not inconceivable that the feedback loop of deindustrialization and depopulation would spell the demise of Pittsburgh as a major metropolitan region.

No matter the required caveats, change happened and the region's downward spiral eventually abated. Pittsburgh's rebound is all the more remarkable given that the region's core of manufacturing jobs never returned, as Seattle's manufacturing base did in the decade after the Boeing Bust of the early 1970s. Economic transformation was based on growth that occurred across a number of industries that had been secondary or supporting industries during Pittsburgh's industrial heyday. It was without a burst of growth in any dominant industry that Pittsburgh persisted in rebuilding a new prosperity, based not just on new industries but on entirely new competitive advantages.

Maybe because it lacked any singular story of change, Pittsburgh's rebirth remained mostly unnoticed in January 2009—just four months before Pittsburgh was announced as a future location of the next G20 summit—when an assessment of Pittsburgh appeared on the front page of *The New York Times*. My colleague Sabina Deitrick was quoted in the article: "If people are looking for hope, it's here. You can have a decent economy over a long period of restructuring."[3] The Pittsburgh story was being noticed across the nation. Perhaps White House planners read *The New York Times* and thought outside the box when searching for the next location to host world leaders.

Nothing in the story of Pittsburgh's turnaround happened overnight. Mythical inflection points usually reflect when the world notices change long percolating. Change had long been underway before the G20 ever arrived in Pittsburgh, or there would have been no rationale to showcase the city. What Pittsburgh exhibited at the onset of the Great Recession was the stability the world was seeking, a stability it had not experienced over most of the twentieth century.

Indeed, Pittsburgh fared better through the Great Recession than most other metropolitan US regions. As the national recession worsened, Pittsburgh's employment remained stable. Particularly hard hit in the deepening trough were some of the same industrial regions that had suffered more than others in the 1980s. Detroit's unemployment rate peaked at over 18 percent in January 2008, while Pittsburgh only briefly reached half that during the worst of the recession. Pittsburgh's unemployment rate dipped below the comparable national level at the beginning of 2007 and then remained there for the following eight years. During the decade between 2010 and 2020, the Pittsburgh metropolitan area experienced a modest population gain for the first time since the 1950s, a decade when the national baby boom bestowed unearned population gains across most regions of the United States.

Much changed for Pittsburgh over the half century following World War II, when Pittsburgh's economy was subsumed whole into the nation's mobilization efforts. Pittsburgh's postwar renaissance remains an example of how much a city and metropolis can be changed by sheer community will. Urban land was repurposed on a massive scale, visible smoke reduced, flood control implemented, and novel civic organizations formed to guide the region's ongoing transformation for decades into the future. Still, as much as the collaborative efforts of civic leaders deliberately altered Pittsburgh's urban form, Pittsburgh's dependence on heavy industry remained virtually unaltered, arguably reinforced by the same collective efforts. That Pittsburgh would always be a manufacturing center remained an article of faith until such optimism proved too unrealistic to cling to. Just short of two decades after the war, the early 1960s' *Economic Study of the Pittsburgh Region* (*ESPR*) summarized the conflicted legacy of the postwar renaissance on the Pittsburgh economy: "In the area of facelifting, of improving the Region's physical appearance and improving the physical, educational and cultural services it offers the population, Pittsburgh's pioneering efforts stand as a model for the entire nation. But where activities specifically destined to attract new industry are concerned, the regional record as a whole has until very recently been uncoordinated and inadequate."[4]

No matter how much the region's economic competitiveness as a manufacturing center drained away, Pittsburgh insisted on remaining dependent on steel. Few incentives were ever developed to even begin shifting the region away from the core industries that had first concentrated there in the nineteenth century. Limited exceptions, such as efforts to spur the development of Skybus or more quixotic attempts to provide public funding to develop a magnetic levitation transportation system, typically failed before they ever really began, even as disinvestment continued unabated for Pittsburgh's legacy industries. More successful but short-lived efforts, such as Volkswagen's investment in Westmoreland County in the 1970s or Sony's in the 1990s, were still manufacturing-centric investments, and neither left a lasting impact on Pittsburgh's economy after they shut down.

There has emerged an idea that Pittsburgh somehow pushed a public policy version of the "easy button" and collectively decided to create a technology-based regional economy once the local steel industry collapsed. Any such success did not emerge overnight, and real change only came in the face of recuring opposition. As my colleague and law professor Mike Madison has written, the revisionist idea "that Pittsburgh somehow planned for the end of steel is historically inaccurate."[5] Where limited economic transformation came to Pittsburgh, it was despite an almost insurmountable inertia pushing back against change.

Why were, or are, more fundamental economic changes so difficult for Pittsburgh? The goal could not have intimidated the region's civic leaders. The projects that the Allegheny Conference deliberately tackled during Pittsburgh's postwar renaissance were among the most difficult challenges. However, where there was nearly universal agreement that flood control, smoke abatement, and urban blight should be addressed, there was a visceral pushback against any suggestion that the region's core industries were in decline. Repeated analyses concluding that Pittsburgh's decreasing competitiveness as a location for steel production were repeatedly met with cognitive dissonance, if not outright denial.

Sociologist Sean Safford has contrasted the different trajectories of communities that are willing to separate themselves from their economic past and those which are not. In *Why the Garden Club Couldn't Save Youngstown,* he contrasts the recent history of two historic steel regions, Youngstown, Ohio, northwest of Pittsburgh, and Allentown, Pennsylvania, the largest city in the Lehigh Valley steel region of eastern Pennsylvania. He compared Youngstown, with a civic infrastructure unwilling to move past steel, with Allentown, which more readily moved beyond its steel history.[6] The two former steel regions have faced starkly divergent histories since the 1980s, with Youngstown's population declining by 47 percent between 1980 and 2020, while Allentown has grown by 22 percent.

Like Youngstown, greater Pittsburgh's historic problem was separating its economic past from any vision of its future, producing an antipathy to change that pervaded much of the region's business and civic leadership. The region developed an almost institutionalized opposition to entrepreneurship and the economic evolution new industries should generate. With an economy built on sheer engineering might, Pittsburgh should have been well placed to take advantage of the technological revolutions that arrived after World War II. Yet, through the whole of the twentieth century, Pittsburgh found it difficult even to take advantage of new technologies fostered within the region's industries and academic institutions. At the beginning of the twenty-first century, a team led by Harvard Business School Professor Michael Porter completed a comprehensive study of Pittsburgh's economic competitiveness. The report's conclusions echoed assessments from the past:

> The main assets in Pittsburgh business environment are its numerous specialized research and training institutes and high levels of R&D spending. However, slippage in knowledge commercialization limits the impact these research centers have on the economy. Furthermore, the environment for startups is challenging, due to a lack of networking, lack

> of mentorship opportunities, lack of experienced entrepreneurial talent and limited VC [venture capital]. Perhaps the most important challenge in the business environment involves the lack of collaboration across diverse groups in the region.[7]

Pittsburgh's difficulty in moving beyond the contraction of the steel industry was in no small part made even more challenging by the limited external support the region received when it was needed the most. Only modest federal funding was ever available for regional economic development efforts, and no meaningful structural adjustment policies even existed in the United States. Nations suffering from underinvestment and decline can be supported by a range of structural adjustment policies managed by organizations such as the World Bank or the International Monetary Fund. Within the European Union, targeted nations are allocated economic adjustment funds to promote economic transformation, and many nations have long had dedicated programs to address slow-growth subregions. When Pittsburgh needed such assistance the most, only limited federal programs existed to support regional economic restructuring.

The policy vacuum was just one artifact of the US aversion to federal intervention in the private sector of the economy, but that has not been a consistent proscription. There have been many periods when rapid economic change forced the federal government into expanded roles. The Great Depression catalyzed a broad range of federal interventions in private markets, interventions that included direct spending through new federal agencies such as the Works Progress Administration, but also comprehensive federal regulation of markets through the National Recovery Administration. Wartime exigencies through World War II brought even greater federal oversight of all aspects of the economy through rationing, price controls, and comprehensive federal control of industrial markets which persisted until peace returned.

Regionally focused federal interventions were not unprecedented, but rare to nonexistent for Pittsburgh as it faced the collapse of its steel industry. During the Great Depression, the Tennessee Valley Authority (TVA) was created to build up the economic infrastructure a multistate region stretching across Tennessee and including portions of Alabama, Mississippi, Kentucky, Georgia, North Carolina, and Virginia. The federal corporation was explicitly chartered to modernize the mostly rural economy of its targeted geography. TVA implemented flood-control programs, built power plants, and even engaged in industrial targeting efforts promoting fertilizer production—collectively the most comprehensive federal involvement in regional economic planning within the United States.

A more limited effort to support regional economic development came when Congress passed the Area Redevelopment Act in 1961. The act was the result of over six years of legislative efforts by economist and Illinois Senator Paul Douglas, who wanted to channel federal resources to revive "chronically depressed areas" of the country.[8] The act created a new experimental Area Redevelopment Authority (ARA) in 1962. Senator Douglas specifically intended the ARA to assist "well-to-do mature, but distressed" areas, a definition applied explicitly to Pittsburgh in the 1960s.[9] However, the new agency's minimal funding was primarily channeled into southern states, with little available for redevelopment efforts in legacy industrial regions.[10] Defunded by 1965, the agency's lasting legacy was spurring the creation of the Appalachian Regional Commission, the first regional commission envisioned by Title V of the Public Works and Economic Development Act of 1965. The ARA's broader mission was subsumed into a new and permanent Economic Development Administration (EDA) created at the same time. The EDA was also charged with assisting economically troubled regions but was never empowered or funded on a scale provided the TVA.

Two decades later, there was no effort to create a TVA-like response to assist even the hardest-hit manufacturing regions of the 1980s. Building criticism of the TVA during the 1960s presaged fundamental shifts within the US political system, shifts that directly shaped the federal response to the emergence of the US rust belt. The most strident criticism of TVA came from an unlikely source, Ronald Reagan, then General Electric spokesman. In the 1950s, Reagan had moved on from his career in Hollywood to become the host of *General Electric Theater* and goodwill spokesman for the General Electric Company—then the nation's largest company.

Reagan's boilerplate message began focusing on the TVA by 1960, attacking the quasi-public organization as a singular example of federal government overreach. So strong were Reagan's fulminations that federal officials threatened revocation of $50 million in government contracts General Electric was receiving at the time.[11] The company canceled its sponsorship of the program, effectively ending Reagan's role as corporate spokesman. Reagan's battle with the TVA was central his transformation from actor and corporate spokesperson to politician. A seminal point in

Reagan's biography came when he endorsed Republican Barry Goldwater during his 1964 presidential campaign against Lyndon Johnson. Just two years later, Reagan was elected to his first term as governor of California and was soon talked about as a future presidential candidate.

Reagan was elected president in the fall of 1980, on the precipice of the industrial decline that would soon be concentrated in Pittsburgh. "Government is not the solution to our problem; government is the problem," declared the new president in his inaugural address on January 20, 1981.[12] Even as federal monetary policy all but ensured the rapid contraction of the United States' historic core of manufacturing—a contraction that came faster than any industry and in particular any region could adjust to—the new president made clear the federal government was not going to intervene in any significant way to assist industrial regions struggling to mitigate the unavoidable consequences.

Even the modest scope of the EDA—which had evolved out of the Area Redevelopment Administration and in the 1980s was the primary federal agency charged with assisting regional economic development—ran afoul of the Reagan administration. Within his first month in office, President Reagan forcefully argued for terminating the entire federal agency.[13] Congress did not go along with this, but the Reagan administration proposed elimination of the EDA every subsequent year of its tenure.[14]

Precisely when Pittsburgh needed federal assistance the most, little was forthcoming—which is not to say federal funding has never been available for regions facing sharp economic declines. Detroit's economic history was altered in 1979, when federal loan guarantees prevented the bankruptcy of the Chrysler Corporation. In the fall of 2008, the financial conglomerate AIG received a staggering $85 billion in federal loan guarantees to prevent it from declaring bankruptcy. The following year, the federal government became an equity investor in General Motors, investing $50 billion to keep the automaker operating through its 2009 bankruptcy. The same year, Detroit benefited again when federal funding facilitated the takeover of the still-extant Chrysler by the Italian carmaker Fiat.

In contrast, the direct or even indirect federal support the legacy industries of Pittsburgh received was barely measurable and even less effective. Plants shut down, entire firms declared bankruptcy, and few industrial assets were repurposed by new owners. Few if any regional jobs were ever saved by any federal program or expenditure. Without any of the dedicated help that other regions received to ease their transitions,

Pittsburgh shaped its economic future on its own, a process that could not happen quickly.

For many regions, there comes a point where change becomes inevitable. Moving forward requires at least being able to consider that legacy industries will not rebound. Equally dangerous has been a corrosive mythos that some singular industry could replace what was lost. Pittsburgh may be an extreme example, but it is far from alone in how it fought against its future. An observation from Germany's Ruhr Valley in the 1980s is applicable to all regions facing structural economic change: "Many in the Ruhr Valley are under the 'illusion' that a new industry will replace the old one.... That's a mistake."[15] The same belief persisted in Pittsburgh long past the worst of steel's regional contraction in the 1980s, even though it is hard to imagine any industry ever replicating Pittsburgh's steel cluster in size. For much longer than later revisionism will admit to, "Pittsburgh wished and waited for another largescale industry to arrive and restore the region, for a substitute to be found to replace US Steel as an oligopolistic but reliable and stable anchor."[16] The reality is that the circumstances that first cast Pittsburgh as the nation's center of steel production will likely never be repeated for any industry, in any region.

More than any other single factor, the rich Pittsburgh Seam coal determined the agglomeration of heavy industry in the region. Steel provided a degree of separation from mining, but the economy remained an artifact of the ample coal supplies nearby. Economies based on extractive industries are theorized to suffer from the paradox of the resource curse, also known as the Dutch Disease—a name coined during the period of natural gas discoveries in the Netherlands during the 1950s that has been applied more broadly. The paradox is more hypothesis than theory, asserting that regions endowed with enviable reserves of extractable resources typically fail to grow as fast as regions without such resources. The mechanism, and for some even the existence of the paradox, remains in dispute. If any causality exists, the negative impact of natural resource–based wealth likely comes from the displacement extractive industries have on other economic sectors that are more likely to generate long-run growth.[17] In retrospect at least, it is clear that carbon-based steel production displaced much of the economic dynamism that Pittsburgh could have nurtured.

Almost from the moment the metallurgic coal of southwestern Pennsylvania surrendered its advantages in the production of industrial coke,

Pittsburgh faced decline it would not admit to until it was far too late to avert. The region's loss of competitiveness was compounded by the expansion of rail and highway transportation networks that mitigated heavy industries' reliance on river transportation. While Pittsburgh was described as one of the greatest entrepreneurial regions in the nation at end of the nineteenth century, few new industries emerged there from the 1920s forward. Entrepreneurialism is almost by definition a product of human capital, but entrepreneurs will seek the best opportunities where they present themselves. Pittsburgh provided few opportunities once the region was locked into its steel destiny.

Thus, the conundrum remains for regional policymakers: Do people follow jobs, or do jobs follow people? Pittsburgh provides conflicting answers. In the first decade of the twentieth century, the region experienced a new resource-based economic boom driven by rapid expansion of unconventional natural gas development. New mining activity meant not only new investment but new workers induced to move to the region because of the many companies simultaneously seeking to exploit the new shale-gas play. As has long been the accepted paradigm, people moved to where job opportunities were being created.

Simultaneously, Pittsburgh provides an extreme example of how jobs are indeed moving toward concentrations of human capital, especially for knowledge-based industries, a phenomenon observed in regions globally.[18] Since the industrial contraction of the 1980s, little of Pittsburgh's technology-based job growth has come from entrepreneurial-driven growth or new business formation. Pittsburgh's twenty-first-century technology cluster has followed a distinctly different path. New technology investments were being generated by the concentration of technical talent that had survived the region's industrial contraction, mainly within the confines of academic research. Where technology-based job growth was being generated outside of institutions of higher education, it was not being generated by entrepreneurial firm creation but mostly from national firms setting up local enclaves seeking to take advantage of the concentration of technical talent in the region.

A very stark example of Pittsburgh's atypical path to technology-based growth came in 2015 when yet another national technology firm arrived in Pittsburgh. Based in San Francisco, the transportation company Uber was disrupting the local travel industry by disintermediating the role taxi companies had once played. Looking to develop future taxi services that self-driving vehicles could provide, the company did not initiate research and development efforts from scratch. In the spring of 2015, Uber hired the bulk of researchers at Carnegie Mellon University working on unmanned autonomous vehicles, or driverless cars.[19] But it did not relocate its newly hired workforce to San Francisco or any other location; instead, the new employees formed the core of a new Uber Advanced Technology, initially located in Pittsburgh.

It was unlikely that such a new large technology venture would have located in Pittsburgh long before Uber came. Only in the twenty-first century had Pittsburgh's technology workforce built up enough scale to be a place young professional workers would choose over other regions. Younger technology workers based their employment decisions not just on immediate job offers but on prospects for future employment. Building a competitive workforce is an unavoidably elongated process for any region, and was an even longer process for Pittsburgh, which had lost not only the bulk of its younger workforce in the 1980s but most of the firms that had for decades been the region's principal recruiters of young technical workers.

Why has Pittsburgh failed to follow Silicon Valley's model of technology-based growth sooner or more forcefully than it has, despite Ed Litchfield's research-based strategy of the early 1960s? AnnaLee Saxenian of Stanford attributes the core of Silicon Valley's success to a "decentralized industrial structure" that was "embedded in a social structure which supports a complex balance of cooperation and competition."[20] If true, Pittsburgh's diametrically different economic history explains why the region singularly failed to capitalize on its otherwise enviable technology infrastructure.

At the edge of the solar system, the distant boundary where the influence of the sun is equally matched by the solar wind blowing through the interstellar expanse is called the termination shock. The *Voyager I* spacecraft was launched from Earth in 1972 and set out on a long trajectory to escape the sun's gravity. The spacecraft took thirty-three years to reach the edge of the solar system and termination shock. Only from 2005 forward would it no longer be pulled by the gravity well of the distant sun.[21] Likewise, Pittsburgh required a full career-span of time before its economic fate was no longer determined by the concentrated job destruction and outmigration that came to a head in the early 1980s.

Past the termination shock lies the less understood heliosphere, where the spacecraft's future path becomes less predetermined, as indeed is the case for Pittsburgh's economic future.

Through eras of extended booms and busts, Pittsburgh's economy has been defined by the extremes of growth and decline. Across multiple eras, the region's leaders have attempted to deal with the economic volatility forced upon them. Recurring chapters of Pittsburgh's long renaissance have been responsible for many palpable successes in transforming the city and its greater region. The greatest successes have been in improving quality of life, a critical factor as the importance of attracting and retaining a competitive workforce becomes vital. Navigating the inevitable structural economic changes has been less successful. If anything, Pittsburgh's civic leadership more often than not abetted the region's insistence on remaining dependent on steel and associated industries, to the detriment of all other paths. Industrial concentration provided palpable benefits when times were good but gave the region little to fall back on in times of cyclical change and led to a catastrophic contraction when structural change eventually came to those industries. For far too long, the unwillingness to even believe change was coming made regional transformation nearly impossible, and Pittsburgh paid a steep price.

Denial emanates from excessive boosterism. The painful truth is that marketing cannot obviate the effects of disruptive technologic changes within industries. Little evidence can support that public messaging alone has shifted Pittsburgh's economic trajectory in any era. The image Pittsburgh presented to the world evolved in reaction to how its core industries were faring, not the other way around. Through periods of growth and decline, fundamental changes in the region's economic competitiveness explain the economic history that followed. When the multivolume *ESPR* was completed in 1964, the Pennsylvania secretary of commerce said civic leaders "must resolutely, and without boosterism, address these problems," a recommendation that mainly went unheeded.[22] Two decades later, the project's director, Edgar M. Hoover, indirectly passed judgment on Pittsburgh's unwillingness to prepare for the economic future his project had so accurately predicted. Hoover remained in Pittsburgh through the remainder of his career and in the final edition of his widely used 1984 textbook on regional economics, he opined, "Pure boosterism is truly narcotic, producing first euphoria, then addiction, and eventually decay."[23]

Without doubt, the challenges Pittsburgh faced in the past will return as future industries face unanticipated disruptions. The competition between regions that has been accelerating is unlikely to abate. Successful regions will not be those best positioned for any one industry or any singular opportunity but places most able to adapt and change nearly continuously. Pittsburgh remains an extreme example of a major US region that has had to remake itself following radical decline in its sustaining industry, an industry it clung to far longer than seems possible in retrospect. It is unlikely that any industry the size or scale of steel will remain concentrated in any single region for as long as the metals industry was dominant across southwestern Pennsylvania. It is possible no future industry will even exist anywhere near as long as steel was the dominant industry in Pittsburgh. Again, as the Hoover-led reports concluded in the early 1960s, compared to the past "capital, enterprise, and business know-how are transferred far more readily from one region to another in response to shifting opportunities." With fewer natural advantages providing individual regions with clear comparative advantages, regions need to encourage "flexibility, modernity, and receptiveness to change."[24] For Pittsburgh at least, the challenge has never been in attracting new investment but overcoming fierce resistance to change.

If you wait for the steel industry to come back, you'll wait forever.

Tony McGann, Regional/Urban Design Assistance Team, Homestead, Pennsylvania, February 27, 1988

EPILOGUE

Paris

October 30, 2019

The day before Halloween, Pittsburgh Mayor Bill Peduto "kicked over a hornet's nest among the region's business and political class" by announcing his opposition to a potential new petrochemical plant in southwestern Pennsylvania.[1] A decade into the fracking boom across northern Appalachia, new natural gas supplies were coming unabated from the region. Natural gas from the Marcellus Shale formation deep undergrown was particularly valuable because of the rich content of liquids trapped within the gas. A multibillion-dollar chemical refinery under construction just thirty miles downriver from Pittsburgh was an almost inevitable secondary impact of new natural gas production across Pennsylvania.

The new plant was designed to extract hydrocarbon liquids, particularly ethane, from the gas and convert it first into ethylene, a valuable feedstock for the plastics industry, and finally into plastic *nurdles*—small plastic pellets used to make products like bottles, bags, and foam containers. The refining process had the added benefit of making natural gas safer and easier to transport. The state of Pennsylvania had offered the Shell Chemical Company an estimated $1.6 billion in public incentives, mainly in tax abatements, to build the plant in Beaver County. That scale of public investment had become the norm since Pennsylvania had outbid all other states to bring a Volkswagen plant to Westmoreland County four decades earlier. Whether the financial incentives were needed to encourage Shell to build the plant will remain an unknown counterfactual. If anything, the state's tribute likely only ensured that the plant was constructed within Pennsylvania and not just a few miles further down the Ohio River, potentially at a nearby location in either Ohio or West Virginia.

Mayor Peduto was actually not speaking out against the enormous ethane cracker nearing completion in Beaver County. Given the scale of the new natural gas being produced in proximity to Pittsburgh, just one multibillion-dollar ethane cracker was not enough The mayor was expressing opposition to several more petrochemical refineries potentially coming to the region. His words resonated with his audience, which had gathered for the Pittsburgh Climate Action Summit, a foundation-sponsored umbrella organization of climate activists and environmentalists. Whatever economic benefits the new plant was expected generated, some in Pittsburgh feared the environmental consequences of a new petrochemical industry cluster in the region.

Reactions to the mayor's remarks were immediate. Beyond the construction jobs at the site, public and private leaders had routinely hyped the potential of the new refinery to reindustrialize western Pennsylvania. Many believed the plant would spark the expansion of the region's chemical industry and were less concerned about the environmental consequences. Betraying chronic intraregional divisions, Beaver County political leaders decried the mayor's statement, making clear that "Pittsburgh isn't located in Beaver County."[2] Even the Allegheny County chief executive found it necessary to denounce the mayor's stance.[3]

The schism that had erupted was not just a split between city and suburbs but was making transparent deeper divisions over visions for Pittsburgh's future. A week earlier, a regional energy company had publicly announced that it was withdrawing its membership in the Allegheny Conference, an unprecedented move for a major Pittsburgh corporation. The president of the natural gas exploration company CNX complained of growing opposition to mining investments: "To view energy and manufacturing as 'old economy' or simply a necessary evil and short-term bridge to something better is not only wrong but insulting to thousands in this region."[4] Divergent views on Pittsburgh's future were not new but were becoming ever more irreconcilable.

Divisions over alternative visions of Pittsburgh's economic future had taken a global context two years earlier when then-President Donald Trump justified plans to withdraw the United States from the international Paris Climate Agreement by declaring: "I was elected to represent the citizens of Pittsburgh, not Paris." The president's remarks implied that a decade after the G20 summit came to Pittsburgh, or more than three decades after the peak of the region's deindustrialization, the city and region remained defined by its legacy industries. The following year, a documentary on climate change titled *From Paris to Pittsburgh* turned that theme on its head.[5] Michael Bloomberg, a former New York City mayor, sponsored the documentary, which highlighted a distinctly nonindustrial future for Pittsburgh. The world was conflicted over what defined Pittsburgh's economy and its future, but so were Pittsburghers.

The repeated reference to the French capital was not as novel as it seemed. A full decade earlier, a popular book by local columnist Brian O'Neill had described Pittsburgh as the *Paris of Appalachia.*[6] The curious analogy evoked much older tensions in Pittsburgh, which has been the largest metropolitan region within the formal geographic boundaries of the Appalachian Regional Commission since that organization was formed in 1965. Pittsburgh was indeed a major urban center, once one of the nation's largest urban agglomerations of people and industry, yet geography placed it squarely within the broader Appalachian region that had chronically suffered from underdevelopment and lagging economic growth. Modern Pittsburgh was not facing a new debate over its future but was being reminded that old battles had never been adjudicated.

In an odd coincidence of fate, the debate over a new industrial chemical plant had erupted just as U.S. Steel made a decision that may presage its exit from carbon-based steel production. On October 1, 2019, just a few weeks before the mayor's remarks, U.S. Steel announced it had entered into an agreement to purchase an electric arc furnace steel minimill in Big River, Arkansas. The decision was a half century past when it would have first made the most business sense and long past when it could have helped the firm retain its dominant role in the US steel industry. Still, the acquisition could be the harbinger of the corporation's intent to fully divest itself from the Pittsburgh region a century and a half since Andrew Carnegie first produced steel at Braddock.

Challenges to newer poles of growth in the Pittsburgh region arrived far more quickly than they did for steel. The rapid buildout of unconventional gas across Pennsylvania had almost counterproductive results. So prolific was the new source of natural gas that it oversupplied markets that had been expected to be in dire shortage. The resulting collapse in prices had a more predictable result. Growth in employment and investment in the Marcellus Shale first stabilized and then sharply contracted by the mid-2010s. Also, despite the leading Marcellus Shale developers promising "drilling is just the beginning" and despite completion of the ethane cracker in Beaver County, few secondary industries have yet been spurred to locate nearby.

Likewise, the prospects for a rapid expansion of a technology-based regional economy have faced obstacles. The 2015 creation of Uber's Advanced Technology Center in Pittsburgh jump-started the region's private-sector commercialization of academic research. Within just a few years, a fleet of driverless vehicles was continuously traversing the city. Innumerable media articles projected further expansion of the region's autonomous vehicle industry cluster. However, in 2020, Uber shuttered most of its local research operations and sold off its Pittsburgh operations. Newer technology-based firms continued to grow in the region, but none would come close to having the oligopolistic power over any industry the way U.S. Steel once dominated the steel industry.

Pittsburgh's steel history achieved a certain closure via an unlikely press release. On November 22, 2024, the Texas-based conglomerate Conoco-Phillips announced it had completed the acquisition of the Ohio-based energy company Marathon Oil.[7] The multinational energy company had spent $22 billion to fold Marathon into its much larger energy portfolio. Consolidation in the global energy business was almost built into the industry's DNA, so the transaction in itself was not out of the ordinary. The end of Marathon Oil marked the end of a long corporate history in the oil industry dating back more than a century, but legally the merger concluded a large part of Pittsburgh's even longer steel heritage. If you were to call up the CUSIP number—a nine-digit number assigned by the Committee on Uniform Securities Identification Procedures—for Marathon Oil stock, you would notice that it matched that of a company formerly known as USX.

U.S. Steel—the vast corporation founded by J. P. Morgan in 1901—purchased Marathon Oil in 1982, and in 1986, the combined company renamed itself USX while shifting its headquarters to Houston. Through the end of the century, U.S. Steel operations in Pittsburgh were a wholly owned subsidiary of the Texas conglomerate. In 2001, the corporation renamed itself again, taking on the name of the now-defunct Marathon Oil. At the same time, it spun off an entirely new company comprising its remaining assets engaged in steel production. The spinoff was named U.S. Steel. The renamed Marathon Oil continued in operation for twenty-three more years before it was acquired by a much larger rival. The end of Marathon Oil marked the definitive end of the corporate entity created by J. P. Morgan that once dominated the steel industry.

Acknowledgments

It goes without saying that all scholarship is derivative, and all compiled here is merely a reordering of past work by a panoply of researchers, journalists, and writers. In particular, little of what is written here would exist without the work of those at the Bureau of Business Research at the University of Pittsburgh, Charles Roos and staff of the Econometric Institute, and the work of Ben Chinitz and Edgar M. Hoover in shepherding the *Economic Study of the Pittsburgh Region* (*ESPR*) in the early 1960s, among many others. If memory holds, Patty Beeson first mentioned to me the existence of Edgar Hoover and Ben Chinitz's work on the *ESPR*. Unraveling the mystery of what happened to the *ESPR* and what came before and since provided the outline for this project.

Over many years, many others at the University of Pittsburgh contributed to my understanding of Pittsburgh's economic history, including Jack Ochs, Vijai Singh, Frank Giarratani, Sabina Deitrick, and innumerable others. Just a few of the many more recent colleagues and friends who have been part of longer and ongoing conversations that I am sure have voices distilled in these pages include Mike Madison, Colby King, David Passmore, and the inimitable John Hoerr.

Certainly, many thanks to the staffs of the Detre Library and Archives at the Senator John Heinz History Center, the University of Pittsburgh Archives Service Center, the Pennsylvania State Archives, the Pennsylvania State Library, and, despite its difficult recent history, the staff at the Carnegie Library of Pittsburgh for making available resources held in the Oliver Room archives. Ron Gaydos provided both knowledge and references on recent Mon Valley redevelopment efforts.

Many have helped improve the final version of this book. My wife, Heidi, and Kate Lindholm attempted to improve my grammar and prose before others were subjected to any of the content here. My wife has also suffered the most from the opportunity cost of the hours I diverted from the many other potential uses of time to work on this manuscript.

Ruben Campos, Michael Stewart of the Brady Stewart Studio, and Ken Kobus were kind enough to make available some of the photos included here. Miriam Meislik of the University of Pittsburgh Archives and Special Collections assisted in acquiring photography permissions.

Friends and colleagues who have provided comments or encouragement along the way include Bill Lafe and Hunter Smith. Also appreciated are the comments of anonymous reviewers who have provided comments to the last and previous versions of this manuscript. I even extend a note of thanks to at least one anonymous comment on a long-ago blog post, which I know contributed to one point included here.

Thanks to all of the staff of the Kent State University Press, most certainly editor Mary Young and Erin Holman, who heroically copyedited the entire manuscript, but also all who have worked to get this project to its final form. Finally, many thanks to Derek Krissoff at the Kent State University Press for his past and hopefully future interests in the vast Rust Belt story. Derek gave new life to what was a dormant project and was a source of encouragement and advice that made this book a reality.

Notes

Preface

1. John P. Hoerr, *And the Wolf Finally Came: The Decline of the American Steel Industry* (Univ. of Pittsburgh Press, 1988).

2. William Serrin, *Homestead: The Glory and Tragedy of an American Steel Town* (Vintage Books, 1993); Judith Modell, *A Town Without Steel: Envisioning Homestead* (Univ. of Pittsburgh Press, 1988); Patrick Vitale, *Nuclear Suburbs: Cold War Technoscience and the Pittsburgh Renaissance* (Univ. of Minnesota Press, 2021); Allen Dieterich-Ward, *Beyond Rust: Metropolitan Pittsburgh and the Fate of Industrial America* (Univ. of Pennsylvania Press, 2015); Gabriel Winant, *The Next Shift: The Fall of Industry and the Rise of Heath Care in Rust Belt America* (Harvard Univ. Press, 2021).

Introduction

1. Press briefing by Press Secretary Robert Gibbs, May 28, 2009, available at the President Barack Obama website, https://obamawhitehouse.archives.gov/the-press-office/briefing-white-house-press-secretary-robert-gibbs-5-28-09.

2. *Time* magazine went so far as to observe the reporters in attendance "broke out laughing." See Dan Fletcher, "Why Is the G-20 Being Held in Pittsburgh?," *Time*, Sept. 23, 2009, http://content.time.com/time/nation/article/0,8599,1925535,00.html.

3. Derek Thompson, "Why in the World Is the G20 Meeting in *Pittsburgh?*," *Atlantic*, May 2009, https://www.theatlantic.com/business/archive/2009/05/why-in-the-world-is-the-g20-meeting-in-i-pittsburgh-i/18503/.

4. David Jackson, "Obama Will Host Next G20—in Pittsburgh," *USA Today*, May 28, 2009.

5. Thompson, "Why in the World Is the G20 Meeting in Pittsburgh?"

6. Pittsburgh Regional Planning Association, *At the Forks,* vol. 4 of *Economic Study of the Pittsburgh Region* (Univ. of Pittsburgh, 1964), i-19.

7. Pittsburgh Regional Planning Association, *Region in Transition,* vol. 1 of *Economic Study of the Pittsburgh Region* (Univ. of Pittsburgh Press, 1963), 52; Pennsylvania Dept. of Labor and Industry, Bureau of Employment Security, Labor Market Letter, Pittsburgh Area, Office of Commonwealth Libraries, State Library of Pennsylvania, Harrisburg.

8. Sheldon Russell, "Industrial Shifts in Western Pennsylvania," in *The Western Pennsylvania Region in Economic Transition,* ed. Andrew R. Blair et al. (Univ. of Pittsburgh, Graduate School of Business, 1983), 30.

9. Wilbur Richard Thompson, *A Preface to Urban Economics* (Published for Resources for the Future by Johns Hopkins Univ. Press, 1965), 24.

10. Dick Conway, "A Hard Fall," *Seattle Business,* Dec. 30, 2009, https://seattlebusinessmag.com/article/hard-fall.

11. Greg Lange, "Billboard Reading: 'Will the Last Person Leaving SEATTLE—Turn Out the Lights' Appears Near SeaTac International Airport on April 16, 1971," June 8, 1999, *Historylink.org,* http://www.historylink.org/index.cfm?DisplayPage=output.cfm&File_Id=1287.

12. Rick Boyer and David Savageau, *Places Rated Retirement Guide: Finding the Best Places in America for Retirement Living* (Rand McNally, 1983).

13. John Landis and David Sawicki, "A Planner's Guide to the Places Rated Almanac," Working Paper (Institute of Urban and Regional Development, Univ. of California, Berkeley, Aug. 1987), 3.

14. For one example of analysis of Savageau's work see Richard A. Becker et al., "Analysis of Data from the Places Rated Almanac," *American Statistician* 41, no. 3 (1987): 169–86.

15. Kathy Wilhelm, "Pittsburghers React to Life at the Top," Associated Press, Feb. 28, 1985.

16. J. Kenneth Evans, "Almanac Co-Author Refuses Key to City," *Pittsburgh Post-Gazette,* Mar. 5, 1985.

17. Loftus argued that the aggregation technique used by Savageau violated a version of the Weber-Felchner law, a theory dating to the nineteenth century. The sociological theorem asserts that the value of achieving a higher ranking diminishes as the actual rank gets lower. In other words, too much significance was placed on Pittsburgh's consistent moderate results, breaking out near the top in few categories. See Geoffrey R. Loftus, "Say It Ain't Pittsburgh," *Psychology Today,* June 1985, 8.

18. Pittsburgh Regional Planning Association, *At the Forks,* vi-37.

19. Richard L. Florida, *The New Urban Crisis: How Our Cities Are Increasing Inequality, Deepening Segregation, and Failing the Middle Class—and What We Can Do About It* (Basic Books, 2017).

20. Pittsburgh Regional Planning Association, *At the Forks,* vi-28.

21. Pittsburgh Regional Planning Association, *At the Forks,* vi-37.

22. Mel Seidenberg, "Look Ahead 25 Years," *Pittsburgh Post-Gazette,* July 30, 1961.

1. Hell with the Lid Off

1. Kenneth Warren, *Big Steel: The First Century of the United States Steel Corporation, 1901–2001* (Univ. of Pittsburgh Press, 2001), 18–19.

2. Ron Chernow, "The Deal of the Century," *American Heritage*, July 1998, http://www.americanheritage.com/content/deal-century.

3. Chernow, "Deal of the Century."

4. H. N. Eavenson, "The Pittsburgh Coal Bed: Its Early History and Development," *American Institute of Mining and Metallurgical Engineers Transaction* 130 (1938): 6.

5. Eavenson, "Pittsburgh Coal Bed," 13–14.

6. George Thornton Fleming, *History of Pittsburgh and Environs: From Prehistoric Days to the Beginning of the American Revolution* (American Historical Society, 1922), 490.

7. The view of Pittsburgh's fate being as cast as manufacturing center is defined by Richard C. Wade's *Urban Frontier.* A contrary idea, to a degree, is from Edward K. Muller—that Pittsburgh retained its role as a commerce center through the first half of the nineteenth century. See Richard C. Wade, *The Urban Frontier: The Rise of the Western Cities, 1790–1830* (Univ. of Illinois Press, 1996); Edward K. Muller, "Was Pittsburgh's Economic Destiny Set in 1815?," *Indiana Magazine of History* 105, no. 3 (Sept. 2009): 203–18.

8. "Pittsburgh—Its Influence on the Navigation of the Ohio," *Magazine of Western History* 2 (1885): 264.

9. Weston Arthur Goodspeed, *Standard History of Pittsburg, Pennsylvania* (H. R. Cornell & Company, 1898), 200.

10. Francis G. Couvares, *The Remaking of Pittsburgh: Class and Culture in an Industrializing City 1877–1919* (State Univ. of New York Press, 1984), 10.

11. John N. Ingham, *Making of Iron and Steel* (Ohio State Univ. Press, 1991), 28.

12. James Parton, "Pittsburg," *Atlantic Monthly*, Jan. 1868, 17–21.

13. For more on puddling as it was practiced at the end of the nineteenth century, see James J. Davis, *The Iron Puddler: My Life in the Rolling Mills and What Came of It* (Bobbs-Merrill, 1922).

14. National Park Service, "The Eads Bridge," Historical American Engineering Record, Apr. 1984, 14, available at the Library of Congress website, https://tile.loc.gov/storage-services/master/pnp/habshaer/mo/mo0300/mo0361/data/mo0361data.pdf.

15. Pittsburgh Regional Planning Association, *Region in Transition*, vol. 1 of *Economic Study of the Pittsburgh Region* (Univ. of Pittsburgh Press, 1963), 271.

16. "Value of Natural Gas, Its Use Clarifies the Atmosphere at Pittsburg," *New York Times*, Oct. 18, 1885.

17. Joshua Benjamin Freeman, *Behemoth: A History of the Factory and the Making of the Modern World* (W. W. Norton, 2018), 93.

2. Basing Point Pittsburgh

1. United States Steel Corporation, 8 F. T. C. 1 (1924).
2. George W. Stocking, *Basing Point Pricing and Regional Development* (Univ. of North Carolina Press, 1954), 62.
3. "Welfare Talk Only at Steel Dinner," *New York Times,* May 18, 1912.
4. "Pittsburgh's Future Is Declared Secure by President Farrell," *Gazette Times* (Pittsburgh), Aug. 11, 1911.
5. "Real Efficiency," *Town Development,* Nov. 1916, 80.
6. Rebecca C. Shoemaker, *The White Court: Justices, Rulings, and Legacy* (ABCCLIO, 2004), 116.
7. John Leland Mechem, "TRADE REGULATION: The 'Pittsburgh Plus' Case," *American Bar Association Journal* 10, no. 11 (1924): 806.
8. Marc Winerman and William E. Kovacic, "Outpost Years for a Start-Up Agency: The FTC from 1921–1925," *Antitrust Law Journal* 77, no. 1 (2012): 184.
9. US Congress and House, *Annual Report of the Federal Trade Commission for the Fiscal Year Ended June 30, 1924* (GPO, 1925).
10. Robert P. Rogers, *An Economic History of the American Steel Industry* (Routledge, 2009), 66.
11. Louis Galambos, "The American Economy and the Reorganization of the Sources of Knowledge," in *The Organization of Knowledge in Modern America, 1860–1920,* ed. Alexandra Oleson and John Voss (Johns Hopkins Univ. Press, 1979), 276.
12. Janet T. Knoedler, "Market Structure, Industrial Research, and Consumers of Innovation: Forging Backward Linkages to Research in the Turn-of-the-Century U.S. Steel Industry," *Business History Review* 67, no. 1 (1993): 109–11.
13. Richard Boeckel, "The Iron and Steel Industry," *CQ Researcher* 2 (1930).
14. "A Live Question for the Castings Trade," *Industrial World* 44 (Oct. 30, 1911): 1302.
15. Charles Cheape, "Tradition, Innovation and Expertise: Writing the Steel Code for the National Recovery Administration," *Business and Economic History* 25, no. 2 (1996): 70.
16. Michael Bernstein, *The Great Depression: Delayed Recovery and Economic Change in America, 1929–1939* (Cambridge Univ. Press, 1989), 196.
17. "Giant New Irvin Works to Be Dedicated Today," *Pittsburgh Post-Gazette,* Dec. 15, 1938.
18. "Ingot Center Moves East—Historic Trend Is Reversed," *Milwaukee Journal,* Aug. 6, 1937.
19. Memorandum on a Program for Community Planning in the Pittsburgh District, Bureau of Business Research, Univ. of Pittsburgh, July 22, 1935, 4, box Y, folder 216, Pittsburgh Regional Planning Association Archives, Oliver Room Archives, Carnegie Library of Pittsburgh.

3. Arsenal

1. Joel Sabadasz, "Pittsburgh Industrial District—World War II Structures," *Historic American Engineering Record* (National Park Service, 1991), 6.

2. Tim Colton, "Dravo Corporation, Pittsburgh, PA—Ships/Boats," *Shipbuilding History*, most recent update, Sept. 14, 2014, http://shipbuildinghistory.com/shipyards/large/dravoboats.htm.

3. Stephanie Vincent, "Flipping the Plate: Changing Perceptions of the Shenango China Company, 1945–1991" (PhD diss., Kent State Univ., 2016), 28.

4. Leslie A. Przbylek, "Supplying the Battlefront," *Western Pennsylvania History* 98, no. 1 (2015): 32.

5. James Duffy, *Target—America: Hitler's Plan to Attack the United States* (Lyons Press 2004), 34.

6. Sabadasz, "Pittsburgh Industrial District," 30.

7. Rogers, *An Economic History of the American Steel Industry* (Routledge, 2009), 90.

8. Frederick H. Gareau, "Morgenthau's Plan for Industrial Disarmament in Germany," *Western Political Quarterly* 14, no. 2 (1961): 531

9. Milton Gilbert, "The Impact of War on Commodity Prices," *Survey of Current Business* 19, no. 10 (1939): 14.

10. Keith E. Eiler, *Mobilizing America: Robert P. Patterson and the War Effort, 1940–1945* (Cornell Univ. Press, 1997), 184.

11. Michael G. Carew, *Becoming the Arsenal: The American Industrial Mobilization for World War II, 1938–1942* (Univ. Press of America, 2010), 51

12. S. Burton Heath, "Shortage Blamed for Vision Circle of Delay in War Goods Production," *Pittsburgh Press*, June 26, 1942.

13. Eiler, *Mobilizing America*, 183.

14. Sabadasz, "Pittsburgh Industrial District," 10.

15. Associated Press, "Steel to Be Off Market Soon," *Pittsburgh Post-Gazette*, May 12, 1941.

16. Steven Fenberg, *Unprecedented Power—Jesse Jones, Capitalism, and the Common Good* (Texas A&M Univ. Press, 2011), 356.

17. S. Burton Heath, "Shortage Blamed for Vicious Circle of Delay in War Woods Production," *Pittsburgh Press*, June 26, 1942.

18. "Steel for Victory Pledges Given," *Eugene (OR) Register-Guard*, July 2, 1943.

19. Sabadasz, "Pittsburgh Industrial District"; US Civilian Production Administration, *Industrial Mobilization for War, History of the War Production Board and Predecessor Agencies, 1940–1945* (GPO, 1947), 663.

20. Peter Kaskell, "Production Under the Controlled Materials Plan," *Cornell Law Review* 37, no. 4 (1952): 4.

21. David Novick and George A. Steiner, "The War Production Board's Statistical Reporting Experience," *Journal of the American Statistical Association* 43, no. 242 (1948): 220.

22. Sabadasz, "Pittsburgh Industrial District," 11.

23. "MESTA 160-Inch Plate Mill," *Historic American Engineering Record* (National Park Service, Department of the Interior, n.d.), 11.

24. United States v. County of Allegheny, 322 U.S. 174 (1944).

25. "Giant New Furnaces Pour Steel," *Pittsburgh Post-Gazette,* June 15, 1943.

26. Curtis Miner and Paul Roberts, "Engineering and Industrial Diaspora: Homestead, 1941," *Pittsburgh History* 72, no. 1 (1989): 7.

27. Associated Press, "Boost Fund to Increase Steel," *Gettysburg Times,* June 30, 1945.

28. Sabadasz, "Pittsburgh Industrial District," 16.

29. FTC v. Cement Institute 333 U.S. 683 (1948).

30. Earl Latham, "The Politics of Basing Point Legislation," *Law and Contemporary Problems* 15, no. 2 (1954): 272.

31. Pittsburgh Regional Planning Association, *Region in Transition,* vol. 1 of *Economic Study of the Pittsburgh Region* (Univ. of Pittsburgh Press, 1963), 267–68.

4. Rhapsody of Steel

1. Associated Press, "US Offers Plants Here for Sale," *Pittsburgh Post-Gazette,* Oct. 20, 1944.

2. "Realtors Studying Industry in Relation to Postwar Era," *Reading (PA) Eagle,* Aug. 9, 1942.

3. "Where We Live: Our Population Shifts South and West; War Spurs Peacetime Trend," *Wall Street Journal,* June 4, 1944.

4. "US Will Develop 5 Strategic Areas," *Montreal Gazette,* Aug. 31, 1941.

5. "Defense Plant Capacity Cited," *Pittsburgh Press,* Aug. 23, 1940.

6. Byron Fairchild and Jonathan Philip Grossman, *The Army and Industrial Manpower* (Office of the Chief of Military History, Dept. of the Army, 1959), 102.

7. Ralph E. Lapp, "Industrial Dispersion in the United States," *Bulletin of the Atomic Scientists* 7, no. 9 (1951): 256–60.

8. "Navy Sets Up System to Terminate Contracts; Won't Cut Buying Now," *Wall Street Journal,* July 22, 1944.

9. Dale McFeatters, "1944 Proves Year of All Time Records in the Pittsburgh Area," *Pittsburgh Press,* Dec. 31, 1944.

10. UP, "Report Warns State to Fight Plant Closings," *Pittsburgh Press,* Oct. 20, 1944.

11. Art Preis, "Historic Battles with Steel Kings Inspires Pickets," *Militant,* Feb. 2, 1946, as quoted in Joshua Freeman, *Behemoth: A History of the Factory and the Making of the Modern World* (W. W. Norton, 2018), 234.

12. "United States Steel's Westward March: A Chain Reaction of Concentration," *Stanford Law Review* 1, no. 1 (1948): 108–25.

13. Dale McFeatters, "Pittsburgh's Position as No. 1 Steel Center Menaced, Weir Warns," *Pittsburgh Press,* Aug. 7, 1945.

14. "National Affairs: Ghost Town," *Time,* Oct. 28, 1946.

15. T. E. Lloyd, "Pittsburgh Seen Losing Position of World's Steel Center," *Iron Age,* May 16, 1946, 92.

16. Kenneth Austin, "Pittsburgh Expected to Remain Leading Center of Steel Industry," *New York Times,* Aug. 25, 1946.

17. "Steel Exodus Just Bogey Expert Says," *Pittsburgh Post-Gazette*, Aug. 26, 1946.

18. "Local Post-War Group Adopts Wide Program—Budget of $315,000 for Study, Research Tentatively Approved," *Pittsburgh Post-Gazette*, June 17, 1944.

19. Dale McFeatters, "Communities Urged to Begin Mapping Post-War Jobs Now," *Pittsburgh Press*, May 18, 1944.

20. Rachel Balliet Colker, "Gaining Gateway Center: Eminent Domain, Redevelopment, and Resistance," *Pittsburgh History* 78, no. 3 (1995): 135.

21. Memorandum on Release of Econometric Report to Pittsburgh Newspapers, Oct. 31, 1946, box Z, Pittsburgh Regional Planning Association Archives, Oliver Room Archives, Carnegie Library of Pittsburgh.

22. Olav Bjerkholt, "Ragnar Frisch and the Foundation of the Econometric Society and Econometrica," Statistics Norway Research Department, Oct. 1995, https://www.ssb.no/a/histstat/doc/doc_199509.pdf; see also Robert Loring Allen, *Opening Doors: The Life and Work of Joseph Schumpeter* (Transaction, 1991), 269.

23. Joseph A. Schumpeter, *Capitalism, Socialism, and Democracy* (Routledge, 2013), 83.

24. Econometric Institute, "Long Range Outlook for the Pittsburgh Industrial Area," Feb. 12, 1947, box 3, folder 9, Allegheny Conference Archives, Archive of Industrial Society, Univ. of Pittsburgh Archives.

25. Memorandum on Release, 2.

26. "Final Report of the Special Committee to Study the Econometric Institute Report," Dec. 6, 1946, 1, box Y, Pittsburgh Regional Planning Association Archives.

27. Kemp G. Fuller, Andrew Irwin, and Francis McQuillin, "Report of the Conference Subcommittee Assigned to Review Section I, Chapter 2 of the Econometric Institute Report," Allegheny Conference on Community Development, Oct. 31, 1946, 3, box Z, Pittsburgh Regional Planning Association Archives.

28. Econometric Institute, "Long Range Outlook," 25–27.

29. "City Needs Reshaping to Assure Progress, Chamber Survey Shows," *Pittsburgh Post-Gazette*, Nov. 7, 1946.

30. "Econometric Institute, "Long Range Outlook."

31. "Redevelopment Study Revealed for First Time," *Pittsburgh Press*, Feb. 14, 1954.

32. Benjamin F. Fairless, *Some Problems of the Steel Industry in Pittsburgh* (U.S. Steel Corp., 1948), 7, 11.

33. Associated Press, "Steel Mogul Urges Postwar Liquidation of Federal Industry," *Evening Standard* (St. Petersburg, FL), Jan. 21, 1944.

34. Robert D. Fletcher, "The Donora Smog Disaster—A Problem in Atmospheric Pollution," *Weatherwise* 2, no. 3 (1949): 56.

35. Berton Roueché, "The Fog," *New Yorker*, Sept. 30, 1950, 33.

36. Devra Lee Davis, *When Smoke Ran Like Water: Tales of Environmental Deception and the Battle Against Pollution* (Basic Books, 2002), 18, 29.

37. "U.S. Health Service Moves into Donora to Probe Fatal Smog," *Pittsburgh Post-Gazette*, Dec. 1, 1948.

38. "Tax Bars New Steel Plants, County Warned," *Pittsburgh Press,* May 29, 1950.

39. "J&L Takes Over Scotch Bottom," *Pittsburgh Press,* Nov. 20, 1952.

40. "J&L to Put $25,000,000 on Expansion," *Pittsburgh Press,* Oct. 1, 1952.

41. W. L. Russell, "J&L Spending in Half Year Doubles Profit," *Pittsburgh Press,* Sept. 14, 1948.

42. "Moreell Sees Steel Users Moving Here," *Pittsburgh Post-Gazette,* July 17, 1948.

43. McFeatters, "1944 Proves Year of All Time Records in the Pittsburgh Area," 12.

44. U.S. Steel advertisement, *New York Times,* Jan. 2, 1951.

45. Office of the US High Commissioner for Germany Office of Public Affairs, Public Relations Division, APO 757, US Army, "West German Steel Industry," *Information Bulletin,* Sept. 1950, 65–71.

46. Toshiyasu Ito, "Reconstruction of Hiroshima Industry 1945–1960," *Regional Economic Research* 26 (2015): 5n4.

47. Thomas E. Mullaney, "Steel: One of the Vital Materials in the Building of the Nation's Defenses and in Its Civil Economy: One of Spectacular Phased of Steel Making," *New York Times,* Sept. 6, 1951.

48. "Progress Plan Opens New Era of Operations," *Pittsburgh Post-Gazette,* Apr. 29, 1954.

49. Pennsylvania Dept. of Labor and Industry, Bureau of Employment Security, Labor Market Letter, Pittsburgh Area, Office of Commonwealth Libraries, State Library of Pennsylvania, Harrisburg.

50. "Pittsburgh Doubtful on Seaway," *Youngstown Vindicator,* June 18, 1956.

51. Nicolas P. Maffei, "Selling Gleam: Making Steel Modern in Post-War America," *Journal of Design History* 26, no. 3 (2013): 304–20.

52. Sara Anne Gooch, "Mediating the Mill: Steel Production in Film" (PhD diss., Univ. of Iowa, 2012), 111.

53. "City Told Co-Operation for All Is Essential to Prosperity," *Pittsburgh Post-Gazette,* Oct. 9, 1962.

54. "Diversification of Industry Mostly Talk," *Beaver Valley Times* (Aliquippa, PA), Oct. 30, 1957.

55. "U.S. for Shift of Plants to Turnpike Area—Plan of Defense against A-Bombs," *Pittsburgh Press,* Sept. 19, 1948.

56. Leland R. Johnson, *The Headwaters District: A History of the Pittsburgh District, U.S. Army Corps of Engineers* (Pittsburgh District, U.S. Army Corps of Engineers,1979), 226.

57. Benjamin Chinitz, "Contrasts in Agglomeration: New York and Pittsburgh," *American Economic Review* 51, no. 2 (1961): 279–89.

58. Frederick Shaw, "Edgar M. Hoover and Raymond Vernon. Anatomy of a Metropolis: The Changing Distribution of People and Jobs Within the New York Metropolitan Area," *ANNALS of the American Academy of Political and Social Science* 330, no. 1 (1960): 139.

59. Pittsburgh Regional Planning Association, *Region with a Future,* vol. 3 of *Economic Study of the Pittsburgh Region* (Univ. of Pittsburgh Press, 1963), 138–39.

60. Pittsburgh Regional Planning Association, *Region with a Future,* 142–43.

61. Regional Economic Analysis Policy Group et al., *Policy Statement Based on the Economic Study of the Pittsburgh Region* (Allegheny Conference on Community Development, 1964), 6.

62. "The Lesson the Steel Strike Taught," *Business Week,* Jan. 8, 1960, 104.

63. Benjamin Chinitz, "Pittsburgh: The Anatomy of a Recovery," Jan. 19, 1965, 4, Papers of Elmer J. Holland, Archives of Industrial Society, Univ. of Pittsburgh.

64. Chinitz, "Pittsburgh," 6.

5. Disruption

1. Regina Gordon, "Nucor Corporation: A Study on Evolution Toward Strategic Fit" (MA thesis, Univ. of Pennsylvania, 2006), 5–9.

2. John, Stubbles, "The Minimill Story," *AISTech 2006 Proceedings,* Cleveland, OH, Oct. 2006, 27, https://www.brimacombecourse.org/pdf/2006_Stubbles.pdf.

3. The Association for Iron & Steel Technology, "Nucor Steel–South Carolina Turns 50," *Steel News,* accessed May 1, 2025, https://www.aist.org/nucor-steel%E2%80%93south-carolina-turns-50.

4. United States and Richard M. Duke, eds., *The United States Steel Industry and Its International Rivals: Trends and Factors Determining International Competitiveness: Staff Report of the Bureau of Economics to the Federal Trade Commission* (GPO, 1977), 75.

5. United States and Duke, *United States Steel Industry and Its International Rivals,* 483.

6. Bernard Elbaum, "How Godzilla Ate Pittsburgh: The Long Rise of the Japanese Iron and Steel Industry, 1900–1973," *Social Science Japan Journal* 10, no. 2 (2007): 258.

7. United States and Duke, *United States Steel Industry and Its International Rivals,* 12.

8. Pennsylvania, Bureau of Employment Security, Labor Market Letter, Pittsburgh Area, various dates, Hillman Library Storage, Univ. of Pittsburgh.

9. United States and Duke, *United States Steel Industry and Its International Rivals,* 70.

10. Joel B. Dirlam and Hans Mueller, "Import Restraints and Reindustrialization: The Case of the U.S. Steel Industry," *Case Western Journal of International Law* 14, no. 3 (1982): 422.

11. Pittsburgh Regional Planning Association, Pittsburgh Regional Planning Association, *Region in Transition,* vol. 1 of *Economic Study of the Pittsburgh Region* (Univ. of Pittsburgh Press, 1963), 444n41.

12. "Now Included in Records—Mini-Mills to Power 2 Million Steel Tons," *Pittsburgh Post-Gazette,* May 11, 1970.

13. Clayton M. Christensen, *The Innovator's Dilemma: When New Technologies Cause Great Firms to Fail* (Harvard Business School Press, 1997), xi.

14. Kenneth Warren, *Big Steel: The First Century of the United States Steel Corporation, 1901–2001* (Univ. of Pittsburgh Press, 2001), 311.

15. "U.S. Steel to Widen Realty Operations," *New York Times,* Mar. 3, 1969.

16. "U.S. Steel Fabricates Rooms for Florida's Disney World," *Cornell Hotel and Restaurant Administration Quarterly* 11, no. 4 (1971): 53–59.

17. George W. Jernstedt and Tom K. Phares, *Give the City Back to People: New Mobility Can Make Our Cities a Joy Again,* 1st ed. (Cityscope & Mobility, 1994), 44.

18. Morton Coleman, David Houston, and Edward K. Muller, *Skybus: Pittsburgh's Failed Industry Targeting Strategy of the 1960s,* rev. ed. (Univ. of Pittsburgh, Center for Industry Studies, 2012), 10.

19. Jernstedt and Phares, *Give the City Back to People,* 46.

20. "Skybus Complete Transit Expressway 1967," posted Nov. 13, 2011, by doug brendel, YouTube, https://www.youtube.com/watch?v=1--s_oTG8jE

21. Coleman, Houston, and Muller, "Skybus: Pittsburgh's Failed Industry Targeting Strategy of the 1960s," 18.

22. Jonathan Williams, "Mellons Out $8.6 Million on Skybus," *Pittsburgh Post-Gazette,* July 27, 1977.

23. "Federal Transit Administration History," Federal Transit Administration website, May 1, 2025, https://www.transit.dot.gov/about/brief-history-mass-transit.

24. Jonathan Williams, "Civic Leaders Constant in Faith in Skybus Plans," *Pittsburgh Post-Gazette,* Aug. 20, 1969.

25. Coleman, Houston, and Muller, "Skybus," 40n79.

26. Jernstedt and Phares, *Give the City Back to People,* 64–65.

27. Coleman, Houston, and Muller, "Skybus," 40n83.

28. Jonathan Williams, "Mayor 'Detouring' Plans—PAT Hunts City Depot for Skybus," *Pittsburgh Post-Gazette,* May 22, 1973.

29. "U.S. Funding Assured—PAT's Early Action Okayed by SPRPC," *Pittsburgh Post-Gazette,* May 22, 1973.

30. Pennsylvania, Bureau of Employment Security, Labor Market Letter.

31. US Department of Labor, "Pittsburgh: A Study of a Static Economic-Area Situation," Report Prepared for Congressman Elmer J. Holland, Feb. 2, 1968, box 290, Papers of Elmer J. Holland, Archives of Industrial Society, Univ. of Pittsburgh.

6. Twilight

1. William Allan, "Steel Industry Has Record Year," *Pittsburgh Press,* Jan. 18, 1970.

2. At the time, he Pittsburgh metropolitan area was considered a four-county region consisting of Allegheny, Beaver, Washington, and Westmoreland Counties. See Pennsylvania Dept. of Labor and Industry, Bureau of Employment Security, Labor Market Letter, Pittsburgh Area, Oct. 1953, Office of Commonwealth Records, Pennsylvania State Library, Harrisburg.

3. Pennsylvania, Bureau of Employment Security, Labor Market Letter, Pittsburgh Area, 1969, Hillman Library Storage, Univ. of Pittsburgh.

4. United States and Richard M. Duke, eds. *The United States Steel Industry and Its International Rivals: Trends and Factors Determining International Competitiveness: Staff Report of the Bureau of Economics to the Federal Trade Commission* (GPO, 1977), 70.

5. The National Bureau of Economic Research is considered the arbiter of US business cycle dates. Prior to 1979, the bureau did not issue contemporaneous formal announcements of new business cycle dates defining recessionary periods.

6. Judith Stein, *Running Steel, Running America: Race, Economic Policy, and the Decline of Liberalism* (Univ. of North Carolina Press, 1998), 223.

7. "The Enforceability of the No-Strike and Interest Arbitration Provisions of the Experimental Negotiating Agreement in Federal Courts," *Valparaiso Law Review* 12, no. 1 (1977): 57–89.

8. Mary E. Deily, "Wages in the Steel Industry: Take the Money and Run?," *Industrial Relations: A Journal of Economy and Society* 37, no. 2 (1998): 153–77.

9. Stein, *Running Steel, Running America,* 239.

10. Jack Markowitz, "Speer: Steel's Best Recession Ever," *Pittsburgh Post-Gazette,* May 3, 1975.

11. Kenneth Warren, *Big Steel: The First Century of the United States Steel Corporation, 1901–2001* (Univ. of Pittsburgh Press, 2001), 299.

12. Byron Yake, "Steel Is Pittsburgh's Hedge on Recession," *Lewiston Daily Sun,* Jan. 27, 1975.

13. Deily, "Wages in the Steel Industry," 153.

14. Background Materials RE: Ad Hoc Committee On Economic Development of ComPAC, Mar. 10, 1980, H John Heinz Archives, Carnegie Mellon Univ., https://digitalcollections.library.cmu.edu/node/105171?search_api_fulltext=%E2%80%9CBackground%20Materials%20RE%3A%20Ad%20Hoc%20Committee%20on%20Economic%20Development%20of%20ComPAC%2C%E2%80%9D%20

15. Warren, *Big Steel,* 2001, 299.

16. Warren, *Big Steel,* 302; Associated Press, "Steel Officials Optimistic," *St. Joseph (MO) News-Press,* Nov. 28, 1977.

17. Dennis W. Alexander, "Local Government Action in the Control of Environmental Pollution in the Commonwealth of Pennsylvania," *Villanova Law Review* 16, no. 5 (1971): 906.

18. "Interview with William Ruckelshaus," *Frontline,* Apr. 21, 2009, http://www.pbs.org/wgbh/pages/frontline/poisonedwaters/interviews/ruckelshaus.html.

19. On May 18, 1987, the ad appeared in both the *Pittsburgh Post-Gazette* and the *Pittsburgh Press.* On the history of the Allegheny County Variance Board, see James Longhurst, *Citizen Environmentalists* (Tufts Univ. Press, 2012), 112–29.

20. Charles O. Jones, *Clean Air: The Policies and Politics of Pollution Control* (Univ. of Pittsburgh Press, 1978), 11.

21. "About Big Steel's 'Mistake,'" *Pittsburgh Post-Gazette,* May 19, 1976.

22. "U.S. Steel Signs Accord to Curb Plant's Fumes," *New York Times,* Oct. 12, 1976; Geoffrey Tomb, "Clairton Coke Accord Reached," *Pittsburgh Post-Gazette,* Oct. 12, 1976.

23. Samuel P. Hays, "Beyond Celebration: Pittsburgh and Its Region in the Environmental Era-Notes of a Participant Observer," in *Devastation and Renewal: An Environmental History of Pittsburgh and Its Region,* ed. Joel A. Tarr (Univ. of Pittsburgh Press, 2004).

24. UPI, "Pittsburgh's Role as Steel Center Diminishing—Speer," *Beaver County Times* (Beaver, PA), June 21, 1978.

25. Gene Smith, "US Steel Reported Planning Ohio Plant," *New York Times,* June 26, 1976.

26. "Last City Blast Furnace Shuts," *Pittsburgh Post-Gazette,* June 22, 1979.

27. U.S. Steel had also closed twelve open-hearth blast furnaces in Clairton in 1962, but continued to operate the large coke works on the site.

28. David H. Wollman and Donald R. Inman, *Portraits in Steel: An Illustrated History of Jones & Laughlin Steel Corporation* (Kent State Univ. Press, 1999), 201.

29. Gerald H. Anderson, "The Steel Trigger Price Mechanism," *Federal Reserve Bank of Cleveland, Economic Commentary,* May 17, 1982.

30. Lydia Chavez, "The Rise of Mini-Steel Mills," *New York Times,* Sept. 23, 1981.

31. Frank Giarratani, Ravi Madhavan, and Gene Gruver, *Steel Industry Restructuring and Location* (Center for Industry Studies, Univ. of Pittsburgh, 2012), 10–11.

32. Adrian Lee, "How We Almost Lost the Volkswagen Plant," *Observer-Reporter* (Washington, PA), Jan. 24, 1979.

33. UPI, "State's Offer Sold VW on New Stanton," *Beaver County Times* (Beaver, PA), May 29, 1976.

34. William Beaver, "Volkswagen's American Assembly Plant: Fahrvergnugen Was Not Enough," *Business Horizons,* Dec. 1992, 19.

35. Terry P. Brown, "Chasing the Rabbit," *Wall Street Journal,* Apr. 22, 1976.

36. Ron Chernow, "The Rabbit That Ate Pennsylvania," *Mother Jones,* Jan. 1, 1978.

37. Brown, "Chasing the Rabbit."

38. Chernow, "Rabbit That Ate Pennsylvania," 20. The full-page ad appeared in the *Wall Street Journal* on March 1, 1976.

39. David Aviel, "Volkswagen's Investment in the United States: A Pacesetter for Foreign Investment?," *Fletcher Forum of World Affairs* 4, no. 2 (1980): 175.

40. Associated Press, "No Regrets in Pennsylvania Over VW Deal: Officials Sanguine After Car Maker Jilted Plant," *Los Angeles Times,* Dec. 2, 1987.

41. Jack Markowitz, "How Chrysler Came to New Stanton I: Firm Eyes Western Pennsylvania for Major Growth?," *Pittsburgh Post-Gazette,* Nov. 4, 1968.

42. "Farm Area to Get Plant of Chrysler," *New York Times,* Sept. 29, 1968; Jack Markowitz, "How Chrysler Came to New Stanton II—West Penn Pennsy Gets Yesses," *Pittsburgh Post-Gazette,* Nov. 5, 1968.

43. "Foreign Trade Zone Approved for Pittsburgh," *Pennsylvania International Trademark* 5, no. 10 (1977): 8.

44. Beaver, "Volkswagen's American Assembly Plant," 21; "VW Unit, Pennsylvania Sign Pact on New Plant," *Wall Street Journal,* Sept. 16, 1976.

45. Martin Tolchin and Susan J. Tolchin, *Buying into America: How Foreign Money Is Changing the Face of Our Nation* (Times Books, 1988), 61.

46. Ira Fine, "Labor Fights to Get VV Plant—Leaders Back New Stanton Incentives," *Pittsburgh Press*, July 7, 1976.

47. *The Federal Role in State Industrial Development Programs* (Congressional Budget Office, 1984), 51.

48. Adam M. Zaretsky, "Are States Giving Away the Store? Attracting Jobs Can Be a Costly Adventure," *Regional Economist*, Jan. 1994.

49. Yanek Mieczkowski, *Gerald Ford and the Challenges of the 1970s* (Univ. Press of Kentucky, 2005), 134.

50. Jimmy Carter, presidential address, Oct. 24, 1978, transcript available at *The American Experience*, http://www.pbs.org/wgbh/americanexperience/features/primary-resources/carter-anti-inflation/.

51. Edward Nelson, "The Great Inflation of the Seventies: What Really Happened?," Federal Reserve Bank of St. Louis, Jan. 2004, https://fraser.stlouisfed.org/title/great-inflation-seventies-1188.

7. Démontage

1. David E. Lindsey, Athanasios Orphanides, and Robert H. Rasche, *The Reform of October 1979: How It Happened and Why*, Finance and Economics Discussion Series (Divisions of Research & Statistics and Monetary Affairs, Federal Reserve Board, 2004), 20.

2. Lindsey, Orphanides, and Rasche, *Reform of October 1979*, 24.

3. Mike Moyle, "Job Rate Sets Record in District," *Pittsburgh Post-Gazette*, Feb. 1, 1979.

4. "Staying Put," *Pittsburgh Post-Gazette*, May 30, 1983.

5. Carl E. Walsh, "October 6, 1979," Federal Reserve Bank of San Francisco website, Dec. 2004, https://www.frbsf.org/research-and-insights/publications/economic-letter/2004/12/october-6-1979/.

6. GNP was the most commonly cited macroeconomic indicator at the time. In 1990, gross domestic product became more commonly referenced. Both statistics are reported quarterly but represent annualized rates of change.

7. "Quanex, Hunt Join in Tube Mill Project," *Pittsburgh Post-Gazette*, Nov. 17, 1981.

8. John P. Hoerr, *And the Wolf Finally Came: The Decline of the American Steel Industry* (Univ. of Pittsburgh Press, 1988), 139.

9. Jennifer Lin, "Falling Star—Drop in Oil, Gas Drilling Means Layoffs in Tube Mills," *Pittsburgh Post-Gazette*, Mar. 19, 1982.

10. Lorna Strauss, "U.S. Steel Posts Higher Profits, Raises Dividend," *Pittsburgh Post-Gazette*, Jan. 28, 1981.

11. Associated Press, "Pittsburgh Steel Business Better," *Youngstown Vindicator*, Feb. 16, 1981.

12. *Steel at the Crossroads: One Year Later* (American Iron and Steel Institute, 1981).

13. Marvin Goodfriend, "Inflation Targeting in the United States," in *The Inflation-Targeting Debate,* ed. Ben Bernanke and Michael Woodford (Univ. of Chicago Press, 2004), 317.

14. Patricia Moore, "Steel Layoffs: Workers Pick up the Pieces," *Pittsburgh Press,* Nov. 8, 1981.

15. Jennifer Lin, "Steel Layoffs Rise as Slump Gets Deeper," *Pittsburgh Post-Gazette,* Dec. 31, 1981.

16. Lorna Doubet, "How U.S. Steel Built Its War Chest," *Pittsburgh Post-Gazette,* Nov. 20, 1981.

17. Robert J. Cole, "U.S. Steel Moves to Buy Marathon," *New York Times,* Jan. 7, 1982.

18. Mark Potts, "Mobil May Seek Marathon Oil via Buying U.S. Steel," *Chicago Tribune,* Dec. 10, 1981.

19. Hoerr, *And the Wolf Finally Came,* 141.

20. Hoerr, *And the Wolf Finally Came,* 140.

21. Michael Workman, "U.S. Steel National Tube Works," *Historic American Engineering Record* (National Park Service, Department of the Interior, circa 1990), 4.

22. "U.S. Steel Corp. Said Tuesday It Will Reduce Dividend," *UPI,* Oct. 26, 1982, available at the UPI Archives, http://www.upi.com/Archives/1982/10/26/US-Steel-Corp-said-Tuesday-it-will-reduce-dividend/9081404452800/.

23. William H. Wylie, "Steel Industry's Last Defense Starting to Crack," *Pittsburgh Press,* Mar. 19, 1982.

24. Dave Mayfield, "Steel Conference Outcry: Imports," *Beaver County Times* (Beaver, PA), May 30, 1982.

25. Hoerr, *And the Wolf Finally Came,* 142.

26. "Changes in the Wind," *Pittsburgh Post-Gazette,* May 30, 1983.

27. Nicholas Knezevich, "1979 Shocker: District Began Its Slide," *Pittsburgh Press,* Mar. 21, 1982.

28. "Big Steel Saddled with Big Problems," *Beaver County Times* (Beaver, PA), Apr. 6, 1982.

29. "Final Blast—Last Two Furnaces Leveled at J&L's Hazelwood Mill," *Pittsburgh Post-Gazette,* June 16, 1983.

30. Tony Locy, "Bottom Falls Out for J&L Workers," *Pittsburgh Press,* May 23, 1984.

31. Associated Press, "Armco Will Close Pipe Plant; Imports Blamed," *Los Angeles Times,* Sept. 28, 1985.

32. Associated Press, "U.S. Steel Plans Plate Mill Closing," *New York Times,* Oct. 4, 1985.

33. "Wheeling-Pittsburgh Steel Corporation: Briefing Paper," Mar. 7, 1979, Digital Collections, Carnegie Mellon Univ., page discontinued as of May 2, 2025, http://digitalcollections.library.cmu.edu/awweb/awarchive?type=file&item=497749.

34. Associated Press, "Armco Will Close Pipe Plant."

35. James Risen, "The Struggle to Rebuild After Big Steel Moved Out: A

Whole Region Was Almost Ruined When the Mills Closed," *Los Angeles Times,* Sept. 27, 1989

36. Tom Hundley, "Tough Lessons Taught in VW Plant's Closing," *Chicago Tribune,* July 14, 1988.

37. Edward Nelson, "The Great Inflation of the Seventies: What Really Happened?" Federal Reserve Bank of St. Louis, Jan. 2004, https://fraser.stlouisfed.org/title/great-inflation-seventies-1188.

38. Richey Piiparinen, "Midnight in the Rust Belt," *Belt Magazine,* Sept. 21, 2013, https://beltmag.com/midnight-in-the-rust-belt/.

39. Bob Dvorchak, "Pittsburgh Talking Sweetly," *Beaver County Times* (Beaver, PA), Dec. 18, 1985.

40. Associated Press, "Pittsburgh Fights to Retain Clark Bar Plant," *New York Times,* Dec. 25, 1985.

41. James V. Cunningham and P. Martz, eds., *Trouble in Electric Valley: Local Leaders Assess the Difficult Future of East Pittsburgh and Turtle Creek* (River Communities Project, School of Social Work, Univ. of Pittsburgh, 1986), 80.

42. Bob Drogin, "'We're Just in Trouble': Steel Towns' Mettle Tested as the Industry Staggers," *Los Angeles Times,* Aug. 10, 1986.

43. Jim Cunningham and Cathy Cairns, *Aliquippa Update: A Pittsburgh Milltown Struggles to Come Back, 1984–86* (River Communities Project, School of Social Work, Univ. of Pittsburgh, Aliquippa Alliance for Unity and Development, Univ. Center for Social and Urban Research, 1986).

44. J. Corbett, "A Study of Unemployment in the Mon-Yough Valley and Its Impact on Social and Psychological Functioning," Mon-Yough Community Mental Health and Mental Retardation Center, McKeesport, PA, July 1980; Felicia L. Mason, "Suicide Rate High in Mon Valley," *Pittsburgh Post-Gazette,* July 25, 1985.

45. Cunningham and Cairns, *Aliquippa Update,* 30.

46. "Valley Towns' Fortunes Decline Steadily," *Pittsburgh Post-Gazette,* Nov. 28, 1993.

47. Stefan Lorant, *Pittsburgh: The Story of an American City* (Authors Edition, 1980), quoted in James P. DeAngelis and Sabina E. Deitrick, "The Regional Economic Development—Bibliography and Data Base (TRED/Biblio) Final Report," 8, prepared for a Subcommittee of the City of Pittsburgh and Allegheny County Service Consolidation Task Force on Economic Development, Univ. of Pittsburgh, Dec. 1994.

48. Jim McKay, "USW Local Presidents Vote 38–4 to Approve Pact," *Pittsburgh Post-Gazette,* Jan. 19, 1987.

49. Carey Durkin Treado, "Pittsburgh's Evolving Steel Legacy and the Steel Technology Cluster," *Cambridge Journal of Regions, Economy, and Society* 3, no. 1 (2010): 105–20.

50. Frank Giarratani, Ravi Madhavan, and Gene Gruver, "Steel Industry Restructuring and Location," Center for Industry Studies, Univ. of Pittsburgh, 2012.

51. "Minimills, Maxiprofits: Nucor and Chaparral," *Time,* Jan. 24, 1983.

52. Steven Rushen, *Competitiveness of the Steel Industry in the Pittsburgh Region* (Univ. Center for Social and Urban Research, Univ. of Pittsburgh, 1996), 5; Stephen Baker, "'This Is Like My Baby Child That These Guys Have Stolen,'" *Bloomberg,* June 3, 1996, https://www.bloomberg.com/news/articles/1996-06-02/this-is-like-my-baby-child-that-these-guys-have-stolen.

53. Stephen Ostrander, *Great Natural Areas in Western Pennsylvania* (Stackpole, 2000), 50.

54. Len Boselovic, "Heard off the Street: Dreams of Steel Minimill Come to End," *Pittsburgh Post-Gazette,* Sept. 14, 2014.

8. Dorothy

1. "Shutdown Prompts Memories," *McKeesport Daily News,* undated clipping, Slusher Papers, Heinz History Center Archive, Pittsburgh.

2. Bob Dvorchak, "Dorothy Six," *Beaver County Times* (Beaver, PA), May 26, 1984.

3. Peter Bradley, "Labor Dollars Voted to Aide RIDC Startup," *Pittsburgh Press,* Jan. 5, 1962.

4. Linda S. Wilson, "Preservation Pressed as Mills Topple," *Pittsburgh Post-Gazette,* Aug. 4, 1988.

5. Historical Society of Western Pennsylvania, "Final Report on Steel Historic Site Evaluation," circa 1988, H. John Heinz Archives, Carnegie Mellon Univ.

6. Joel Sabadasz, "U.S. Steel Duquesne Works," *Historic American Engineering Record* (National Park Service, Department of the Interior, 1991), 28–29.

7. W. L. Russell, "Duquesne Works Reduces Smoke," *Pittsburgh Press,* July 16, 1953.

8. C. H. Good, "The Ferro-Manganese Gas Cleaning Installation at Duquesne Works," *Air Repair* 4, no. 4 (1955): 183.

9. Mary E. Deily, "Investment Activity and the Exit Decision," *Review of Economics and Statistics* 70, no. 4 (1988): 595–602.

10. "Big Project Slated for Duquesne; Largest Setup in Area Due for Completion in '62," *Pittsburgh Post-Gazette,* July 28, 1960.

11. William Allan, "World's Biggest Blast Furnace Keeps Hiroshima Skies Red," *Pittsburgh Press,* Mar. 21, 1968.

12. Associated Press, "US Steel May Close 3 Plants," *Beaver County Times* (Beaver, PA), Dec. 9, 1983.

13. Michael Schroeder, "USW Local Eyes Duquesne Works Buyout," *Pittsburgh Post-Gazette,* Oct. 10, 1983.

14. Earl Brown, "Steelworkers Volunteer Time, Money to Save Vintage Furnace," *Beaver County Times* (Beaver, PA), Dec. 19, 1984.

15. Mike Stout, "Remembering Pittsburgh," *Unbound: Harvard Journal of the Legal Left* 7, no. 45 (2011): 53; Dana Scarton, "Workers Watch Mill from Trailer Outpost," *Pittsburgh Press,* Feb. 15, 1985.

16. Associated Press, "Jackson Urges Employee-Union Takeover," *Washington Observer-Reporter* (Washington, PA), Jan. 19, 1985.

17. Jim McKay, "Roderick Doubtful About Duquesne," *Pittsburgh Post-Gazette*, Jan. 30, 1985.

18. Staughton Lynd, "Why We Opposed the Buyout at Weirton Steel," *Labor Research Review* 1, no. 6 (1985): 42.

19. Robert E. Deans Jr., "The Cinderella Steel Town That Found Its Princes at Home," *Christian Science Monitor*, Nov. 19, 1984, 34.

20. John D. Russell, "Lessons from the Recent Failure of Weirton Steel's ESOP," *Labor Notes*, Apr. 30, 2004, http://www.labornotes.org/2004/04/lessons-recent-failure-weirton-steels-esop.

21. Weirton Steel remained in operation as an ESOP until May 2003, when the firm declared bankruptcy.

22. National Academy of Engineering et al., *The Competitive Status of the U.S. Steel Industry: A Study of the Influences of Technology in Determining International Industrial Competitive Advantage* (Univ. of Michigan Books on Demand, 1996), 51.

23. Kenneth Warren, *Big Steel: The First Century of the United States Steel Corporation, 1901–2001* (Univ. of Pittsburgh Press, 2001), 52.

24. Warren, *Big Steel*, 303.

25. Mike Mahoney, "2-Prong Attack Is Mounted," *Youngstown Vindicator*, July 20, 1979.

26. Christina Rouvalis, "Crumbs, 1,200 Protesters Jam East Liberty Rally to Save Nabisco Plant," *Pittsburgh Post-Gazette*, Dec. 17, 1982.

27. Staughton Lynd, "Remembering Local 1330," *Unbound: Harvard Journal of the Legal Left* 7, no. 45 (2011): 49.

28. Irwin M. Marcus, "An Experiment in Reindustrialization: The Tri-State Conference on Steel and the Creation of the Steel Valley Authority," *Pennsylvania History: A Journal of MidAtlantic Studies* 54, no. 3 (1987): 194.

29. Staughton Lynd, *Living Inside Our Hope: A Steadfast Radical's Thoughts on Rebuilding the Movement* (ILR Press, 1997), 243n101.

30. Peter Perl, "'Dorothy Six' Is Hope of Pennsylvania Steelworkers Coalition," *Washington Post*, Apr. 26, 1985.

31. David Roderick to Allegheny County Commissioners, Apr. 15, 1985, Archive of Industrial Society, Tri-State Conference Archives, Archives & Special Collections, University of Pittsburgh Library System.

32. Statement of Eugene Keilin, General Partner—Lazard Freres & Co., circa 1986, box 16, Tri-State Conference on Manufacturing Records 1982–93, Archives & Special Collections, Univ. of Pittsburgh Library System.

33. "Unions and US Steel Agree: Furnace Not Worth Saving," *New York Times*, Jan. 9, 1986.

34. David Morse, "Surrender Dorothy," *In These Times*, Feb. 19, 1986, 8–9.

35. Jim McKay, "Factory Fixers," *Pittsburgh Post-Gazette*, Apr. 12, 1988.

36. Peter K. Eisinger, *The Rise of the Entrepreneurial State: State and Local Economic Development Policy in the United States* (Univ. of Wisconsin Press, 1988), 328.

37. Philip Shapira, "Industrial Restructuring and Economic Development Strategies in a Japanese Steel Town: The Case of Kitakyushu," *Town Planning*

Review 61, no. 4 (1990): 405; Mi-Gyeung Yeum, "Corporate Governance Regimes, Industrial Restructuring, and Community Responses: A Comparison Between Kitakyushu and Pittsburgh," *Asian Perspective* 28, no. 2 (2004): 157.

38. Thomas Jäger, "Die verhinderten Free Riders von Rheinhausen," *Kölner Zeitschrift Für Soziologie und Sozialpsychologie* 42, no. 1 (1990): 81.

39. Thomas Rommelspacher, "Krupp-Rheinhausen: A Conflict over the Consequences of Decline in the West German Steel Industry," *International Journal of Urban and Regional Research* 12, no. 4 (1988): 627–35.

40. Judith Stilgenbauer, "Landschaftspark Duisburg Nord [EDRA/Places Awards]," *Places Journal* 17, no. 3 (2005): 6–9.

41. *Remaking the Monongahela Valley* (Regional Urban Design Assistance Team, a service of the American Institute of Architects, 1988), 80.

42. Diana Nelson Jones, "Blasting Out of the Past," *Pittsburgh Post-Gazette,* Oct. 12, 1995.

43. Dan Hopey, "Grant Offers Mon Valley Revitalized Future," *Pittsburgh Post-Gazette,* Mar. 13, 1999.

44. Staughton Lynd, "The Genesis of the Idea of a Community Right to Industrial Property in Youngstown and Pittsburgh, 1977–1987," *Journal of American History* 74, no. 3 (1987): 939; Local 1330, United Steel Workers of America et al., Plaintiffs-appellants. v. United States Steel Corporation, Defendant-appellee, 631 F.2d 1264 (6th Cir. 1980), argued June 18, 1980, decided July 25, 1980.

45. Linda S. Wilson, "Union Hall Converted to Care Home," *Pittsburgh Post-Gazette,* Feb. 5, 1987.

46. Bill Steigerwald, "Steel's Decline Cripped Valley," *Pittsburgh Post-Gazette,* Dec. 28, 1989.

47. Mark Belko, "Old Mills a Bonanza in Scrap, Equipment," *Pittsburgh Post-Gazette,* Aug. 19, 1988.

9. Diaspora

1. Mary Ann Lickteig, "Chance at Police Jobs in Texas Attracts Jobless Steelworkers," *Pittsburgh Press,* June 27, 1985.

2. Christopher Briem, "How Many People Left Pittsburgh During the 1980s?," *Pittsburgh Economic Quarterly,* June 2014, 4.

3. Bob Gradeck, *The Root of Pittsburgh's Population Drain* (Carnegie Mellon Univ., Center for Economic Development, Nov. 2003), 3.

4. "Stable Population Forecast for Area," *Pittsburgh Post-Gazette,* Oct. 2, 1976.

5. Committee for Progress in Allegheny Committee (ComPAC), Background Materials—Exhibit D, 1980, 2, box 91, folder 28, H. John Heinz Archives, Carnegie Mellon Univ., https://digitalcollections.library.cmu.edu/node/128473.

6. Norman Robertson, "Forecast of the Southwestern Pennsylvania Regional Economy for the Next Ten Years," circa 1978, Heinz Archives.

7. "Staying Put," *Pittsburgh Post-Gazette,* May 30, 1983, 3.

8. Douglas Root, "Down and Up, Population Here Continues to Decline, but Crime Rate Is Safest for Big Cities," *Pittsburgh Press,* July 31, 1985.

9. Ramit Plushnick-Masti, "After 250 Years, Pittsburgh Remains an Anomaly," *USA Today,* Nov. 26, 2008.

10. Sally Kalson, "City No Champion for Single Women," *Pittsburgh Post-Gazette,* Nov. 28, 1984.

11. Christopher Briem, "Outmigration Steady in Region," *Pittsburgh Economic Quarterly,* June 2000, 2.

12. Robert W. Bednarzik and Joseph Szalanski, *An Examination of the Work History of Pittsburgh Steelworkers, Who Were Displaced and Received Publicly-Funded Retraining in the Early 1980s,* Institute for the Study of Labor (IZA), 2012, 11, http://repec.iza.org/dp6429.pdf.

13. Arnold Katz and Frederick Tannery, "Adjusting to Structural Change: A Profile of the Work Experiences and Earnings of Dislocated Workers in the Pittsburgh Region: 1979–1986" (Univ. of Pittsburgh, Economics Department and Univ. Center for Social and Urban Research, 1988), 24, author's collection.

14. Linda Babcock, Mary Ellen Benedict, and John Engberg, "Pittsburgh Labor Market Adjustments in the 1980s: Who Gained and Who Lost?," *Journal of Urban Affairs* 20, no. 1 (2016): 66.

15. Frederick Tannery and Patricia Beeson, "The Impact of Industrial Restructuring on Earnings Inequality: The Decline of Steel and Earnings in Pittsburgh," *Growth and Change* 35, no. 1 (2004): 21–41.

16. Briem, "How Many People Left Pittsburgh During the 1980s?," 5.

17. Lena Andrews, *Destination Pittsburgh* (Center for Economic Development, Carnegie Mellon Univ., 2003), 1.

18. Frederick Tannery, "Labor Market Adjustments to Structural Change: Comparisons between Allegheny County and the Rest of Pennsylvania: 1979–1987," Working Paper (Economic Policy Institute, Univ. of Pittsburgh, 1991).

19. Peter A. Morrison, *A Demographic Overview of Metropolitan Pittsburgh* (RAND Corporation, 2004), 3.

20. Douglas A. Fisher, *Steel Serves the Nation 1901–1950: The Fifty Year Story of United States Steel* (U.S. Steel Corporation, 1951), 89.

21. Ronald Reagan, "Remarks at the National Conference on the Dislocated Worker in Pittsburgh, Pennsylvania," Apr. 6, 1983, available at Gerhard Peters and John T. Woolley, *American Presidency Project,* Univ. of California, Santa Barbara, https://www.presidency.ucsb.edu/documents/remarks-the-national-conference-the-dislocated-worker-pittsburgh-pennsylvania.

22. Steven R. Weisman, "Reagan Jeered By 4,000 Protesters on Visit to Pittsburgh Job Forum," *New York Times,* Apr. 7, 1983.

23. Reagan, "Remarks at the National Conference on the Dislocated Worker in Pittsburgh, Pennsylvania."

24. Weisman, "Reagan Jeered by 4,000 Protesters on Visit to Pittsburgh Job Forum."

25. Associated Press, "People in the News," *Pittsburgh Press,* Apr. 18, 1983.

26. "Around the Nation; Man Who Gave Resume to Reagan Gives Up Job," *New York Times,* July 4, 1983.

27. Associated Press, "Kennedy, Holland Talk Automation; Pittsburgher Gives First Data on Effects of Automation," *Pittsburgh Post-Gazette,* Dec. 16, 1960.

28. Gladys Roth Kremen, "MDTA: The Origins of the Manpower Development and Training Act of 1962," US Department of Labor, 1974, available at http://www.dol.gov/general/aboutdol/history/mono-mdtatext.

29. David E. Nye, *America's Assembly Line* (MIT Press, 2015), 166.

30. Robert Guttman, "Job Training Partnership Act; New Help for the Unemployed," *Monthly Labor Review*, Mar. 1983, 3.

31. *Job Training Partnership Act—Inadequate Oversight Leaves Program Vulnerable to Waste, Abuse and Mismanagement* (US General Accounting Office, 1991).

32. "Uncertainty Tempers Workers' Confidence in Retraining Efforts," *Pittsburgh Press*, Apr. 4, 1984.

33. Paul Maryniak, "'Real Help' Elusive in Job Training Partnership," *Pittsburgh Press*, Apr. 13, 1986.

34. Maryniak, "'Real Help' Elusive in Job Training Partnership"; also James Bovard, *Cato Institute Policy Analysis No. 77: The Failure of Federal Job Training* (Cato Institute, 1986).

35. Maryniak, "'Real Help' Elusive in Job Training Partnership," 1.

36. "Uncertainty Tempers Workers' Confidence in Retraining Efforts," 4.

37. Ronald Reagan, "Statement on the Worker Adjustment and Retraining Notification Act," Aug. 2, 1988, Peters and Woolley, *American Presidency Project*, https://www.presidency.ucsb.edu/documents/statement-the-worker-adjustment-and-retraining-notification-act

38. Thomas K. Glennan et al., *Education, Employment, and the Economy: An Examination of Work-Related Education in the Pittsburgh Metropolitan Area* (RAND Corporation, 1989), vi.

39. "Education, Training, and Retraining Issues," in *Computerized Manufacturing Automation: Employment, Education, and the Workplace* (US Congress, Office of Technology Assessment, 1984), 253.

40. Bednarzik and Szalanski, *Examination of the Work History of Pittsburgh Steelworkers.*

41. Morton Inger, *Community-Based Strategies for Work-Related Education*, NCEE Brief, no. 10 (National Center for Education and Employment, US Department of Education, 1990).

42. Barnaby J. Feder, "Struggle to Survive in Town That Steel Forgot," *New York Times*, Apr. 27, 1993.

43. Pittsburgh Regional Planning Association, *Region with a Future*, vol. 3 of *Economic Study of the Pittsburgh Region* (Univ. of Pittsburgh Press, 1963), 284.

44. Elizabeth Dole to John Heinz, Mar. 30, 1989, box 112, folder 12, Heinz Archives; US Department of Labor, *Coordination of Housing and Job Training Services: A Review of Best Practices in 12 Cities*, Research and Evaluation Report Series 92-D (US Department of Labor, 1992), 11–18.

45. Econometric Institute, "Long Range Outlook for the Pittsburgh Industrial Area," Feb. 12, 1947, box 3, folder 9, Allegheny Conference Archives, Archive of Industrial Society, Univ. of Pittsburgh Archives.

46. Melvin K. Bers, "Labor Force Participation in the Pittsburgh Standard Metropolitan Area," Economic Study of the Pittsburgh Region, Working Paper No. 2 (Pittsburgh Regional Planning Association, 1960), 9.

47. Bers, "Labor Force Participation in the Pittsburgh Standard Metropolitan Area," 33.

48. John H. Hinshaw, *Steel and Steelworkers: Race and Class Struggle in Twentieth-Century Pittsburgh* (State Univ. of New York Press, 2002), 89; Maurine Weiner Greenwald, "Women and Class in Pittsburgh, 1850–1920," in *City at the Point: Essays on the Social History of Pittsburgh*, ed. Samuel P. Hays (Univ. of Pittsburgh Press, 1991), 28.

49. Pittsburgh Regional Planning Association, *Region with a Future*, 33.

50. Pittsburgh Press Co. v. Pittsburgh Commission on Human Relations, 413 U.S. 376 (1973).

51. "Day Care Toddles Here, Despite Need," *Pittsburgh Post-Gazette*, Jan. 17, 1982.

52. Sabina Deitrick and Christopher Briem, "Gender Wage Disparity in the Pittsburgh Region," *American Behavioral Scientist* 53, no. 2 (2009): 239–60.

53. Data on employment by gender available from the Department of the Census, Longitudinal Household-Employer Dynamics program, Quarterly Workforce Indicators, online at https://lehd.ces.census.gov/data/.

54. Dan Fitzpatrick, "Region Is Portrayed as a 'Cool' Place to Live," *Pittsburgh Post-Gazette*, Dec. 19, 2000.

55. Richard L. Florida, "Competing in the Age of Talent: Environment, Amenities, and the New Economy," Jan. 2000, author's collection.

56. Florida, "Competing in the Age of Talent," 50.

57. Pittsburgh Regional Planning Association, *Region with a Future*, 288.

58. Pittsburgh Regional Planning Association, *Region with a Future*, 286.

59. Regional Economic Revitalization Initiative, Robert Mehrabian, and Allegheny Conference on Community Development, eds., *The Greater Pittsburgh Region: Working Together to Compete Globally* (Initiative, 1994).

10. Beyond Smokestack Chasing

1. William H. Wylie, "Industry to Spread 'The Pittsburgh Story,'" *Pittsburgh Press*, May 22, 1981; Penn's Southwest Association, *Dynamic Pittsburgh: It's a Vital, Vibrant, Historic, Sporting, Bright, Breakthrough, Resourceful Place to Live and Work* (Penn's Southwest Association, 1981), available in Historic Pittsburgh Book Collection, Univ. of Pittsburgh, https://digital.library.pitt.edu/islandora/object/pitt:31735051651598.

2. Committee for Progress in Allegheny Committee (ComPAC) and Pennsylvania Economy League, "Promoting Economic Development in Allegheny County," July 28, 1977, 27, H. John Heinz Archives, Carnegie Mellon Univ., https://digitalcollections.library.cmu.edu/node/201650?search_api_fulltext=compac%20and%201977.

3. Charlie Kelly, "Panel to Map Region's Economy," *Pittsburgh Post-Gazette*, July 23, 1981.

4. Michael Schroeder and Barbara White Stack, "Game Plan: Allegheny Conference Strategy Eschews 'High-Tech Fix,'" *Pittsburgh Post-Gazette*, Nov. 16, 1982.

5. "Fortune 500: A Database of 50 Years of FORTUNE's List of America's Largest Corporations—1980 Full List," available at *CNNMoney,* accessed May 8, 2025, https://money.cnn.com/magazines/fortune/fortune500_archive/full/1980/.

6. Associated Press, "Loss of Gulf Would Be Costly in Pittsburgh," *Beaver County Times* (Beaver, PA), Mar. 8, 1984.

7. Schroeder and Stack, "Game Plan," 19.

8. Schroeder and Stack, "Game Plan," 35.

9. Douglas Root, "Business Leaders Here Map Economic Rescue," *Pittsburgh Press,* Nov. 16, 1982.

10. For one concise criticism of regional leadership at the time see Roger S. Ahlbrandt, "A Cry for Leadership," prepared for a presentation at the Joint Ventures in Housing and Economic Development Conference, cosponsored by US Department of Housing and Urban Development and ACTION-Housing, Inc., Pittsburgh, Oct. 23, 1984.

11. Univ. of Pittsburgh, *Recommendations for Southwestern Pennsylvania's Regional Development Strategy for the 1980s and 1990s: From a Conference June 1–3, 1983* (Univ. of Pittsburgh, 1983).

12. Allegheny Conference on Community Development, ed., *A Strategy for Growth: An Economic Development Program for the Pittsburgh Region: A Report* (Allegheny Conference on Community Development, 1984).

13. Ellen M. Perlmutter and Cynthia Piechowiak, "Power in Pittsburgh—Growth Strategy Collides with Changed Times," *Pittsburgh Press,* Nov. 15, 1987.

14. City of Pittsburgh et al., *Strategy 21: Pittsburgh/Allegheny Economic Development Strategy to Begin the 21st Century: A Proposal to the Commonwealth of Pennsylvania* (City of Pittsburgh, 1985).

15. City of Pittsburgh et al., *Strategy 21.*

16. Clyde Mitchell-Weaver, "Public–Private Partnerships, Innovation Networks and Regional Development in Southwestern Pennsylvania," *Canadian Journal of Regional Science* 15, no. 2 (1992): 275.

17. Alberta M. Sbragia, "Pittsburgh's 'Third Way': The Nonprofit Sector as a Key to Urban Regeneration," in *Leadership and Urban Regeneration: Cities in North American and Europe,* ed. Dennis R. Judd and Michael Parkinson (Sage, 1990), 51–68.

18. Jonathan Williams, "Estimated Costs: $200 Million—Commissioners Hail Airport Growth Plan," *Pittsburgh Post-Gazette,* Apr. 9, 1969.

19. William Pade, "Cautious Nod Given Airport Facelifting," *Pittsburgh Press,* Aug. 10, 1967.

20. Associated Press, "Greater Pitt Expansion Announced," *Observer-Reporter* (Washington, PA) Nov. 10, 1978.

21. Al Donalson, "Greater Pitt Project Cut $119 Million," *Pittsburgh Press,* Apr. 27, 1982; Jim Wilhelm, "Airport Price Tag Too High," *Beaver County Times* (Beaver, PA), Mar. 12, 1982.

22. Chet Wade, "USAir: No New Terminal Needed," *Pittsburgh Post-Gazette,* May 25, 1984.

23. Wade, "USAir," 4.

24. Ed Blazina, "USAir Insisting on More Funds, Foerster Says," *Pittsburgh Press,* Feb. 6, 1986.

25. P. J. Boyle, "Terminal Dilemma—To Land a Slice of 21st-Century Pie, County May Have To Wing It," *Pittsburgh Press,* July 1, 1984.

26. Ed Blazina, "State's Airport Funding Plan Lauded," *Pittsburgh Press,* July 2, 1986.

27. Bernie Kohn, "Alternate Funding Sought for Airport," *Pittsburgh Press,* Mar. 6, 1987.

28. Mark Belko, "Biggest Tenant Makes Commitment to New Terminal," *Pittsburgh Post-Gazette,* June 10, 1988.

29. "Finance/New Issues; Allegheny County Offering of Airport Revenue Bonds," *New York Times,* July 21, 1988.

30. Michel Marriott, "Pittsburgh Builds Airport of Future Now," *New York Times,* Nov. 12, 1991.

31. "Press Release: 1986–87 Budget Proposal Will Include a Renaissance Communities Program," Jan. 29, 1986, box 169, folder 1, Dick Thornburgh Papers, ser. 11, Governor of Pennsylvania, 1979–89, Univ. of Pittsburgh Library System, also online at http://digital.library.pitt.edu/islandora/object/pitt%3Aais9830.11.02.1801; Allen Dieterich-Ward, "Mines, Mills and Malls: Regional Development in the Steel Valley" (PhD diss., Univ. of Michigan, 2006), 336n114.

32. UPI, "Thornburg Signs Economic Package," *Pittsburgh Press,* July 9, 1986.

33. Linda S. Wilson, "Some Officials Question Study Team's Suggestions," *Pittsburgh Post-Gazette,* Mar. 3, 1988.

34. Jim McKay, "Decline of Industry Here Sets Stage for Rebirth, Fed Study Says," *Pittsburgh Post-Gazette,* Apr. 1, 1987; *Annual Report 1986* (Federal Reserve Bank of Cleveland, 1987), 18.

35. "Editorial: Dreams in the Mon Valley," *Pittsburgh Press,* Mar. 3, 1988.

36. Regional Economic Revitalization Initiative (Pittsburgh, PA), Mehrabian, and Allegheny Conference on Community Development (PA), *The Greater Pittsburgh Region* (Regional Economic Revitalization Initiative, 1994), 8,

37. Committee to Prepare Allegheny County for the 21st Century, *Preparing Allegheny County for the 21st Century: A Report to the Allegheny County Board of Commissioners* (Pennsylvania Economy League, 1996), 4.

38. Steve Massey, "Reviving Region's Economy," *Pittsburgh Post-Gazette,* Nov. 7, 1993.

39. "Developing a Unified Approach," *Pittsburgh Post-Gazette,* Nov. 8, 1995.

40. Southwestern Pennsylvania Strategic Investment Partnership, *Investing in the Future: Strategies for Strengthening Southwestern Pennsylvania's Regional Core and Restoring Its Manufacturing Base,* 1995, copy in Main Library—Pennsylvania Department, Carnegie Library of Pittsburgh.

41. Steve Rushen, "Competitiveness of the Steel Industry in the Pittsburgh Region," Univ. Center for Social and Urban Research, Univ. of Pittsburgh, July 1996, 22.

42. Raymond R. Christman, "Pittsburgh Can Make It," *Pittsburgh Post-Gazette,* Aug. 27, 1995.

43. Karen Kovatch, "SPIRC Spars with Agencies over Funding—Ben Franklin, Pitt Centers Get Less for Manufacturing Aid Program," *Pittsburgh Business Times,* Feb. 3, 1997.

44. Al Haas, "End of the Line for PA's WV Plant," *Philadelphia Inquirer,* July 14, 1988.

45. Pamela Gaynor, "Incentives Race Among States Is Cooling Off," *Pittsburgh Post-Gazette,* Mar. 4, 1991.

46. Christopher Briem, "Recent Trends in Manufacturing Employment," *Pittsburgh Economic Quarterly,* June 2009, 4.

47. Reuters, "LTV Plans to Close Coke Plant in Pittsburgh," *New York Times,* July 15, 1997.

48. Tom Barnes, "Close Look at a Coke Plant—Officials Urge Sun Coke to Build Its $350 Million Facility in Hazelwood," *Pittsburgh Post-Gazette,* July 31, 1998.

49. Tom Barnes, "Sun Coke Plant Sets a Shining Example," *Pittsburgh Post-Gazette,* Aug. 2, 1998.

50. Cliff I. Davidson et al., "Soiling Patterns on a Tall Limestone Building: Changes over 60 Years," *Environmental Science & Technology* 34, no. 4 (2000): 560.

51. Joel A. Tarr and Denise Di Pasquale, "The Mill Town in the Industrial City: Pittsburgh's Hazelwood," *Urbanism Past & Present* 7, no. 1 (1982): 10.

52. Stephen Piper et al., *Odor Study and Engineering Evaluation of the LTV Steel Company Coke Plant in the Hazelwood Area of Pittsburgh, a Report for the Allegheny County Health Department, Bureau of Air Pollution Control* (Alliance Technologies Corporation, Apr. 1989), table 2–5, available in Pennsylvania Department, Carnegie Library of Pittsburgh.

53. Walter Goldburg, "The Proposed Non-Recovery Coke Plant in Hazelwood," Group Against Smog and Pollution website, accessed Jan. 10, 2012, available via Internet Archive, https://web.archive.org/web/20141002205718/http://gasp-pgh.org/projects/past-projects-2/ltv-hazelwood-news/the-proposed-nonrecovery-coke-plant-in-hazelwood/.

54. U.S. V. LTV Steel Company, Inc. (W.D.PA. 2001).

55. Cindi Lash, "Neighbors, City Clash at Forum on Coke Plant," *Pittsburgh Post-Gazette,* Aug. 6, 1998.

11. How Now Brown Town?

1. "Monessen Steel Works," *Historic American Engineering Record* (National Park Service, Department of the Interior, n.d.).

2. "Monessen Steel Works"; "Wheeling-Pittsburgh to Spend $140 on Two New Casters," *Pittsburgh Press,* June 26, 1981.

3. "Wheeling to Close Rail Mill," *New York Times,* Dec. 25, 1986.

4. Peter B. King, "Hollywood Turns to Monessen," *Pittsburgh Press,* Oct. 29, 1986.

5. D'Appolonia, "Environmental Remediation of Former Steel Manufactur-

ing Site," n.d., *ContenTree,* https://www.contentree.com/caseStudy/environ mental-remediation-of-former-steel-manufacturing-site_62957.

6. "ArcelorMittal Holdings Idles Monessen Coke Plant, lays off 93," *Pittsburgh Tribune-Review,* May 6, 2009.

7. Ramit Plushnick-Masti, "Monessen Now Famous for Vacancy, not Industry," *Pittsburgh Tribune-Review,* May 5, 2009.

8. "About ArcelorMittal Monessen," ArcelorMittal, June 2018, available via Internet Archive, https://web.archive.org/web/20160418214842if_/http://usa .arcelormittal.com:80/globalassets/arcelormittal-usa/our-operations/2015 -updated-fact-sheets/5184-monessen.pdf.

9. Binyamin Appelbaum, "Struggles in a Steel Town Highlighted by Donald Trump," *New York Times,* July 4, 2016.

10. Agis Salpukas, "LTV's Steel Operations Prospering After Merger," *New York Times,* Nov. 23, 1979.

11. Andrew Blum, "J&L Department Closing Inevitable, but No Disaster, Parent Firms," *UPI Archives,* Nov. 19, 1980, https://www.upi.com/Archives /1980/11/19/JL-department-closing-inevitable-but-no-disaster-parent-firms /4700343458000/.

12. "Council Urges City to Purchase J&L's Property in Hazelwood," *Pittsburgh Press,* May 19, 1981.

13. Lorna Doubet, "J&L Sells Closed Mill to Private Developer," *Pittsburgh Post-Gazette,* June 16, 1981.

14. Jane-Ellen Rosenberger, "URA May Buy J&L Site for High-Tech Park," *Pittsburgh Press,* Mar. 18, 1983.

15. *Pittsburgh Technology Center—Final Land Development Plan* (Urban Redevelopment Authority of Pittsburgh and Regional Industrial Development Corporation of Southwestern Pennsylvania, 1989), 3.

16. City of Pittsburgh et al., *Strategy 21: Pittsburgh/Allegheny Economic Development Strategy to Begin the 21st Century: A Proposal to the Commonwealth of Pennsylvania* (City of Pittsburgh, 1985), 3B.

17. Joel A. Tarr, "Pittsburgh and the Manufactured Gas Industry," *Pittsburgh Engineer* (Winter 2006): 14.

18. Steve Massey, "Union Switch Move Sends a Signal," *Pittsburgh Post-Gazette,* May 4, 1993.

19. "Tax-Increment Financing Successful, City Data Indicate," *Pittsburgh Tribune Review,* May 18, 2008.

20. "Park Corp. History," *Funding Universe,* accessed May 9, 2025, http:// www.fundinguniverse.com/company-histories/park-corp-history/.

21. Allegheny County Department of Economic Development, *Allegheny County Tax Increment Financing Program Project Evaluation 2015,* Allegheny County Economic Decelopment, 2015, https://www.alleghenycounty.us/files /assets/county/v/1/government/economic-development/documents/lerta -amp-tifs/tif-program-evaluation-2015.pdf.

22. Hatch Associates and Arthur D. Little, Inc., *Steel Retention Study* (County of Allegheny [PA] Department of Planning, 1988), author's collection.

23. Tom Barnes, "City Seeking Riverfront 'Land Bank,'" *Pittsburgh Post-Gazette,* Apr. 16, 1994.

24. Klaus R. Kunzmann, "Creative Brownfield Redevelopment: The Experience of the IBA Emscher Park Initiative in the Ruhr in Germany," in *Recycling the City: The Use and Reuse of Urban Land,* ed. Rosalind Greenstein and Yesim Sungu-Eryilmaz (Lincoln Institute of Land Policy, 2004), 4–5.

25. Kunzmann, "Creative Brownfield Redevelopment," 5.

26. Henry S. Prellwitz, "A Mineralogical and Geochemical Study of the Nine Mile Run Slag Area, Squirrel Hill, Pittsburgh, Pennsylvania" (PhD diss., Univ. of Pittsburgh, 1998), 4.

27. Chriss Swaney, "Houses Are to Replace a Pittsburgh Slag Heap," *New York Times,* Jan. 28, 2001.

28. Nicki Puit, "Guide to the Nine Mile Run Greenway Project Records, 1945–2005 AIS.2006.19A," Digital Collections, Univ. of Pittsburgh Library System, accessed May 9, 2025, https://digital.library.pitt.edu/islandora/object/pitt%3AUS-PPiU-ais200619a/from_search/4b4fb7a17096a1a509c15e7734 0df864-3.-3.

29. Bernard D. Goldstein et al., *Ensuring Environmental Health in Postindustrial Cities: Workshop Summary* (National Academies Press, 2003), 39.

30. Charles Bartsch, *Analysis of Pennsylvania's Brownfields Program* (Northeast Midwest Institute, 2003), 9

31. Bartsch, "Analysis of Pennsylvania's Brownfields Program," 10.

32. James T. Hathaway, "Geographical Dynamics of Environmental Service Firms at Metropolitan and National Scales in the United States: The Case of Pittsburgh, Pennsylvania," *Urbani Izziv* 23 (2012): S107–16.

33. Edward K. Muller, "River City," in *Devastation and Renewal: An Environmental History of Pittsburgh and Its Region,* ed. Joel A. Tarr (Univ. of Pittsburgh Press, 2003), 41–63.

34. *A Master Plan for the Development of Riverfronts and Hillsides in the City of Pittsburgh: An Analysis of Their Best Possible Uses, For the Enhancement of the City, and the Enjoyment of Its Citizens* (City of Pittsburgh Dept. of Parks and Recreation, 1959), dedication, 506.

35. H. R. Preston, *Monongahela River Basin Aquatic Biology: Part 1. Fish Population Studies of the Monongahela River* (US Environmental Protection Agency, Wheeling Field Office, 1974), 3.

36. Pittsburgh Regional Planning Association, *Region in Transition,* vol. 1 of *Economic Study of the Pittsburgh Region* (Univ. of Pittsburgh Press, 1963), 439n9.

37. Mark Shelton, "The Prince Comes to Pittsburgh," *Pittsburgh Magazine,* Mar. 1988.

38. *Remaking Cities: Proceedings of the 1988 International Conference in Pittsburgh* (American Institute of Architects, 1988), 52.

39. Sherie Mershon and Tim Palucka, *National Energy Technology Laboratory: A Century of Innovation* (U.S. Department of Energy, 2010), 52.

40. Goldstein et al. *Ensuring Environmental Health in Postindustrial Cities,* 21–22.

41. "How Now Brown Town?," *Economist*, Sept. 14, 2006, http://www.economist.com/node/7914950.

12. Energy Burgh

1. Remarkably, only 3 percent of the estimated undiscovered unconventional gas was in the Marcellus Shale. Robert C. Milici et. al, *National Assessment of Oil and Gas Fact Sheet: Assessment of Undiscovered Oil and Gas Resources of the Appalachian Basin Province* (US Geological Survey, 2002).

2. Michael Quenton Morton, "Unlocking the Earth—A Short History of Hydraulic Fracturing," *GEO ExPro*, Dec. 9, 2013, https://archives.datapages.com/data/geo-expro-magazine/010/010006/pdfs/86.htm.

3. Michael Shellenberger and Ted Nordhaus, "A Boom in Shale Gas? Credit the Feds.," *Washington Post*, Dec. 16, 2011.

4. Jeff Ventura, Ray Walker Jr., and Greg Davis, "The Discovery of the Marcellus Shale Play," *Pittsburgh Engineer* (Winter 2013), 18.

5. Seamus McGraw, *The End of Country: Dispatches from the Frack Zone* (Random House, 2013), 54.

6. Kristin M. Carter et al., "Unconventional Natural Gas Resources in Pennsylvania: The Backstory of the Modern Marcellus Shale Play," *Environmental Geosciences* 18, no. 4 (2011): 229.

7. Pittsburgh Regional Planning Association, *Region in Transition*, vol. 1 of *Economic Study of the Pittsburgh Region* (Univ. of Pittsburgh Press, 1963), 251.

8. David A. Waples, *The Natural Gas Industry in Appalachia: A History from the First Discovery to the Tapping of the Marcellus Shale*, 2nd ed. (McFarland, 2012), 47.

9. America's Industrial Heritage Project et al., *Coal and Coke Resource Analysis: Western Pennsylvania, Northern West Virginia* (US Dept. of the Interior, National Park Service, Denver Service Center, 1992), 36.

10. Pittsburgh Regional Planning Association, *Region in Transition*, 228.

11. Walter H. Voskuil, "Coke: A Key Industrial Material," *Journal of Land and Public Utility Economics* 22, no. 4 (1946): 343.

12. Pittsburgh Regional Planning Association, *Region in Transition*, 229–36.

13. "Report of the Conference Sub-Committee Assigned to Review Section III, Chapter XI Wages and Cost of Living of the Econometric Institute Report," Allegheny Conference on Community Development, Oct. 31, 1946, box Z, Pittsburgh Regional Planning Association Archives, Oliver Room, Carnegie Library of Pittsburgh.

14. "Biggest Story in the History of Coal," *Pittsburgh Press*, Mar. 25, 1947.

15. W. L. Russell, "Gigantic New Concern in Prospect, Bringing New Era for District," *Pittsburgh Press*, Mar. 25, 1947.

16. John J. Kane and George Rankin Jr., *Your Future in Allegheny County* (North River Press, 1947), 42.

17. "Sub-Zero Wave May Continue Until Tuesday," *Pittsburgh Post-Gazette*, Feb. 9, 1948.

18. Don Ball, *The Pennsylvania Railroad, 1940s–1950s* (W. W. Norton, 1986), 30.

19. Russell, "Gigantic New Concern in Prospect," 1.

20. "Leaders of City Given View of New Coal Plan," *Pittsburgh Post-Gazette,* Mar. 26, 1947.

21. "Leaders of City Given View of New Coal Plan," 7.

22. "100 Years with Coal Age," *Coal Age News,* Sept. 14, 2012, 4, https://www.coalage.com/features/100-years-with-coal-age/4/.

23. Joel A. Tarr, "The Changing Face of Pittsburgh: A Historical Perspective," in *Ensuring Environmental Health in Postindustrial Cities,* ed. Bernard D. Goldstein et al. (National Academies Press, 2003), 19. Maury Klein, *A Call to Arms: Mobilizing America for World War II* (Bloomsbury Publishing USA, 2013), 499; Waples, *Natural Gas Industry in Appalachia,* 173.

24. Dudley Dillard, "Big Inch Pipe Lines and the Monopoly Competition in the Petroleum Industry," *Journal of Land and Public Utility Economics* 20, no. 2 (1944): 118.

25. "War Emergency Pipeline," *Historic American Engineering Record* (National Park Service, Department of the Interior), 23, accessed Jan. 10, 2018, page discontinued as of May 13, 2025, http://lcweb2.10c.gov/master/pnp/habshaer/tx/tx0900/tx0944/data/tx0944data.pdf.

26. Dillard, "Big Inch Pipe Lines," 120n.

27. Joel A. Tarr and Karen Clay, "Pittsburgh as an Energy Capital," in *Energy Capitals: Local Impact, Global Influence,* ed. Joseph A. Pratt, Martin V. Melosi, and Kathleen A. Brosnan (Univ. of Pittsburgh Press, 2014), 24.

28. E. E. Kintner, "Admiral Rickover's Gamble," *Atlantic,* Jan. 1959, 31–35.

29. Jack M. Holl, Richard G. Hewlett, and Ruth R. Harris, *Argonne National Laboratory, 1946–96* (Univ. of Illinois Press, 1997), 70.

30. William R. Beaver, "Duquesne Light and Shippingport: Nuclear Power Is Born in Western Pennsylvania," *Western Pennsylvania History* 70, no. 4 (1987): 346.

31. Beaver, "Duquesne Light and Shippingport," 344–45, 348.

32. Thomas L. Neff and Henry D. Jacoby, "Supply Assurance in the Nuclear Fuel Cycle," Working Paper No. MITEL:79-007WP (MIT Energy Laboratory, Feb. 1979), 27.

33. Raymond Pikna, "The Uranium Cartel Saga—Yellowcake and Act of State: What Will Be Their Eventual Fate," *Case Western Reserve Journal of International Law* 12, no. 3 (1980): 592.

34. Steve Massey, "Who Killed Westinghouse? Chapter 2: Sue Me, Sue You Blues," *Pittsburgh Post-Gazette,* Mar. 3, 1998.

35. Pikna, "Uranium Cartel Saga," 593.

36. Douglas Martin, "Suit Ended on Supplies of Uranium," *New York Times,* Jan. 30, 1981.

37. Beaver, "Duquesne Light and Shippingport," 344.

38. See chapter 7 for more on the minimill Worldclass Inc. proposed.

39. U.S. Steel Corporation, "Comments of United States Steel Corporation," Pennsylvania Public Utility Commission website, June 15, 2006, https://www.puc.pa.gov/PcDocs/616283.pdf.

40. Carter et al., "Unconventional Natural Gas Resources in Pennsylvania," 238.

41. Jennifer Cruz, Peter W. Smith, and Sara Stanley, "The Marcellus Shale Gas Boom in Pennsylvania: Employment and Wage Trends," *Monthly Labor Review,* US Bureau of Labor Statistics, Feb. 2014, https://doi.org/10.21916/mlr.2014.7.

42. Timothy J. Considine, Robert Watson, and Seth Blumsack, *The Economic Impacts of the Pennsylvania Marcellus Shale Natural Gas Play: An Update* (Penn State Univ., College of Earth and Mineral Sciences, Department of Energy and Mineral Engineering, 2010), iv.

43. "Drilling Is Just the Beginning—American Manufacturing," posted Oct. 30, 2012, by Range Resources Corporation, YouTube, https://www.youtube.com/watch?v=-p-ozr4FiEU.

13. Knowledge Town

1. UP, "U.S. Steel to Use 'Electronic Brain,'" *Monessen Daily Independent,* Aug. 26, 1954.

2. Herb Mitchell, "Chapter 10: We Move to New York (1953–1956)," *My Biography,* 3rd ed., 2007, https://herbmitchell.info/Chap10a.htm.

3. Paul E. Ceruzzi, *A History of Modern Computing* (MIT Press, 1999), 54.

4. "Mellon Bank Installs 'Electronic Brain,'" *Pittsburgh Post-Gazette,* Nov. 11, 1955.

5. Tom Lassman, Interview of Dr. John W. Coltman, June 30, 2004, Niels Bohr Library & Archive, College Park, MD, available via Internet Archive, https://web.archive.org/web/20150523000703/http://www.aip.org/history/ohilist/30547.html; "Milestones: Westinghouse 'Atom Smasher,' 1937," last edited Dec. 13, 2019, *Engineering and Technology History Wiki,* http://www.ethw.org/wiki/index.php/Milestones:Westinghouse_Atom_Smasher,_1937.

6. Charles C. Bates, Thomas Frohock Gaskell, and Robert B. Rice, *Geophysics in the Affairs of Man: A Personalized History of Exploration Geophysics and Its Allied Sciences of Seismology and Oceanography,* 1st ed. (Pergamon Press, 1982), 21.

7. Keith Lindblom, *Mellon Institute of Industrial Research, Carnegie Mellon University,* National Historic Chemical Landmarks (American Chemical Society, Mar. 28, 2013), 2.

8. Allen V. Astin, *Paul Darwin Foote: Biographical Memoir* (National Academy of Sciences, 1979), 181.

9. Bates, Gaskell, and Rice, *Geophysics in the Affairs of Man,* 22.

10. Patrick S. Vitale, *Nuclear Suburbs—Cold War Technoscience and the Pittsburgh Renaissance* (Univ. of Minnesota Press, 2021).

11. Pittsburgh Regional Planning Association, *At the Forks,* vol. 4 of *Economic Study of the Pittsburgh Region* (University of Pittsburgh, Department of Economics, 1964), iii–39.

12. Pittsburgh Regional Planning Association, *Region with a Future,* vol. 3 of *Economic Study of the Pittsburgh Region* (Univ. of Pittsburgh Press, 1964), 176.

13. Vitale, *Nuclear Suburbs,* 35; Ira Lowry and Pittsburgh Regional Planning Association, *Portrait of a Region,* vol. 2 of *Economic Study of the Pittsburgh Region* (Univ. of Pittsburgh Press, 1963), 98.

14. Benjamin Chinitz, "Contrasts in Agglomeration: New York and Pittsburgh," *American Economic Review* 51, no. 2 (1961): 284.

15. Steven N. Czeti, "High-Tech in Steel City: The Way We Were," *Pennsylvania Business and Technology* 4, no. 2 (1993): 14.

16. Pittsburgh Regional Planning Association, *Region in Transition,* vol. 1 of *Economic Study of the Pittsburgh Region* (Univ. of Pittsburgh Press, 1963), 417.

17. "The Organization and Operation of a University Medical System with Particular Reference to the University of Pittsburgh," circa 1952, box 48, file 328, Fitzgerald Papers, Univ. of Pittsburgh Archives.

18. "Preliminary Analysis of Facilities Required for the School of Industrial Administration," June 1, 1949, Pittsburgh Regional Planning Association Archives, Oliver Room Archives, Carnegie Library of Pittsburgh.

19. D. S. Greenberg, "Pittsburgh: The Rocky Road to Academic Excellence (I)," *Science* 151, no. 3710 (1966): 552.

20. Albert W. Bloom, "Post-Gazette for Two Years Eyed Development of Silent Struggle Between Scientist and Chancellor," *Pittsburgh Post-Gazette,* Mar. 12, 1960.

21. "Hopes Brighten for Center for Scholars, Scientists," *Pittsburgh Press,* Jan. 21, 1964.

22. Edward Litchfield, "Research: The Key to Pittsburgh's Economic Growth," speech before the Pennsylvania Economy League, Pittsburgh, May 4, 1962, Chancellor of the Univ. of Pittsburgh, Edward H. Litchfield, Administrative Files, folder 1308, 1956–65, UA.2.10.1956–1965, Univ. Archives, Archives & Special Collections, Univ. of Pittsburgh Library System.

23. "New Research Park," *Science News-Letter* 83, no. 25 (1963): 391; "Research Center to Rise in Ravine," *New York Times,* June 30, 1963; Oakland Corporation, "This Is an Urban Area: Panther Hollow Project Plans," box 97, Litchfield, Administrative Files.

24. Herbert Stein, "Research Center Due by 1970," *Pittsburgh Post-Gazette,* June 6, 1963.

25. *Time for Decision—Valley of Tomorrow* (Oakland Corporation and WTAE Channel 4, 1963), film.

26. "The City: Renaissance, Phase 2," *Time,* June 21, 1963.

27. "Hopes Brighten for Center for Scholars, Scientists," 38.

28. D. S. Greenberg, "Pittsburgh: The Rocky Road to Academic Excellence (III)," *Science* 151, no. 3712 (1966): 800.

29. US Department of Labor, "Pittsburgh: A Study of a Static Economic-Area Situation," 6, Report Prepared for Congressman Elmer J. Holland, Feb. 2, 1968, box 290, Papers of Elmer J. Holland, Archives of Industrial Society, Univ. of Pittsburgh.

30. "Pittsburgh Area a Research Center," *New York Times,* Oct. 27, 1968.

31. Regional Industrial Development Corporation of Southwestern Penn-

sylvania, *Imaginative Research; Pittsburgh's Gateway to the Future* (Regional Industrial Development Corporation of Southwestern Pennsylvania, Pittsburgh, 1968).

32. Michael N. Geselowitz, "From Alcoa to Anacom—Pittsburgh," *IEEE Annals of the History of Computing* 1, no. 2 (June 26, 2008): 72.

33. Mike Moyle, "RIDC Urges Area Stress on Scientific Innovation," *Pittsburgh Post-Gazette,* Oct. 17, 1978.

34. Walter H. Plosila, "State Science- and Technology-Based Economic Development Policy: History, Trends and Developments, and Future Directions," *Economic Development Quarterly* 18, no. 2 (May 1, 2004): 114.

35. David Osborne, *Laboratories of Democracy* (Harvard Business School Press, 1988), 48.

36. Governor's Office of Policy and Planning (Pennsylvania), "An Advanced Technology Promotion Program for Pennsylvania," Dec. 17, 1981, 1, box 233. folder 5, Dick Thornburgh Papers, Univ. of Pittsburgh Library System Archives & Special Collections.

37. Lorna Strauss, "The Future of High-Technology: Is Pittsburgh Missing Its Chance?," *Pittsburgh Post-Gazette,* Jan. 26, 1981.

38. Christopher Briem and Vijai Singh, "The Role of Universities in the Evolution of Technology-Based Economic Development Policies in the United States," in *The Role of Universities in the Evolution of Technology-Based Economic Development Policies in the United States,* ed. Ulrich Hilpert (Routledge, 2015).

39. Associated Press, "High Technology Business Started," *Observer-Reporter* (Washington, PA), May 16, 1985.

40. Letter from Charles A. Garber, PhD, President Structure Probe West Chester, PA, Nov. 12, 1982, box 233, folder 6, Thornburgh Papers.

41. Michael Schroeder, "As Smoke Clears, High-Tech Allure Grows," *Pittsburgh Post-Gazette,* July 24, 1983; Frederick Cusick, "State Job Program Criticized Report: What Has It Done?," *Inquirer* (Philadelphia), Mar. 6, 1988.

42. Lee Hotz, "State, Industry Grants Could Create 8,000 Jobs," *Pittsburgh Press,* Aug. 13, 1983.

43. Czeti, "High-Tech in Steel City."

44. Roy Lubove, *Twentieth-Century Pittsburgh: The Post-Steel Era* (Univ. of Pittsburgh Press, 1995), 33.

45. Allen Dieterich-Ward, *Beyond Rust: Metropolitan Pittsburgh and the Fate of Industrial America* (Univ. of Pennsylvania Press, 2015), 240.

46. Arthur S. Levine et al., "The Relationship Between the University of Pittsburgh School of Medicine and the University of Pittsburgh Medical Center—a Profile in Synergy," *Academic Medicine: Journal of the Association of American Medical Colleges* 83, no. 9 (2008): 819.

47. Mary Brignano, *Beyond the Bounds: A History of UPMC* (Dorrance, 2009).

48. Levine et al., "Relationship Between the University of Pittsburgh School of Medicine and the University of Pittsburgh Medical Center," 819.

49. R. D. Gordon et al., "Liver Transplantation at the University of Pittsburgh, 1984 to 1990," *Clinical Transplants* (1991): 105.

50. R. W. Evans, D. L. Manninen, and F. B. Dong, "An Economic Analysis of Liver Transplantation. Costs, Insurance Coverage, and Reimbursement," *Gastroenterology Clinics of North America* 22, no. 2 (1993): 451–73.

51. Enterprise Corporation of Pittsburgh, "A Survey of Venture Capital in Pittsburgh in 1989," June 1989, 1, author's collection.

52. "State Slashes Funding for Ben Franklin," *Morning Call* (Allentown, PA), July 19, 1989.

53. "Speed Rail Needs Subsidy, Experts Tell Commission," *Pittsburgh Post-Gazette*, July 10, 1985.

54. Lubove, *Twentieth-Century Pittsburgh*, 41–42.

55. "Innovation Works a New Approach to Technology Business Development | University of Pittsburgh News," Univ. of Pittsburgh, Nov. 17, 1998, http://www.news.pitt.edu/news/innovation-works-new-approach-technology-business-development.

56. Corilyn Shropshire, "Unfinished Business," *Pittsburgh Post-Gazette*, Apr. 15, 2004.

57. Maria Guzzo, "Frangos Development Lands Tenants to Take Space in Rubicon Building—Company Has Filed Suit vs. Sony over Electronic Giant's Exit," *Pittsburgh Business Times*, Oct. 28, 2002.

58. "Foundry, Greenhouse Merge," *Pittsburgh Business Times*, Dec. 15, 2004.

59. Colin Edwards, "Useful Stats: Higher Education R&D Performance by Metro, 2009–2018," State Science and Technology Institute (blog), Dec. 12, 2019, https://ssti.org/blog/useful-stats-higher-education-rd-performance-metro-2009-2018.

60. Joyce Gannon, "Talking with . . . William Thomasmeyer," *Pittsburgh Post-Gazette*, July 21, 2007.

61. Christina Dyrness, "Tech Transformation," *TECHcapital—Washington Post*, Nov.–Dec. 1998.

62. Jessica Livingston, *Founders at Work: Stories of Startups' Early Days* (Springer-Verlag 2007), 420.

63. Hiawatha Bray, "20 Years Later, Lycos Searches for Rebirth," *Boston Globe*, Sept. 11, 2015.

64. Livingston, *Founders at Work*, 421.

65. Stephen Lawson and Cheri Paquet, "GEC Bids $4.5 Billion in Fore Systems Buyout," *InfoWorld*, May 3, 1999, 16.

66. "Fore Systems Remnants Fading Away," *Pittsburgh Business Times*, Oct. 31, 2005.

67. Stephen Kiehl, "City Is Last Maglev Contender if MD Quits Race," *Pittsburgh Post-Gazette*, Dec. 16, 2002.

68. "Specter, Casey, Doyle, Shuster Announce Pennsylvania's Maglev to Receive $28 Million in Federal Funding," Sept. 10, 2009, Bob Casey website, available via Internet Archive, https://web.archive.org/web/20201009013541/https://www.casey.senate.gov/newsroom/releases/specter-casey-doyle-shuster-announce-pennsylvanias-maglev-to-receive-28-million-in-federal-funding.

69. Patrick Cloonan, "Maglev's Funding 'Dried Up,'" *McKeesport Daily News,* July 29, 2011.

70. John Carreyrou, "Doing a Volume Business in Liver Transplants," *Wall Street Journal,* Nov. 21, 2008.

71. Oral History of Mark Kryder, interviewed by Chris Bajorek, Computer History Museum, Apr. 14, 2017, 20, https://archive.computerhistory.org/resources/access/text/2017/12/102738245-05-01-acc.pdf.

72. Patricia Lowry, "Places: Nabisco Plant Deserves Historic Status," *Pittsburgh Post-Gazette,* Sept. 8, 2004.

73. Paul S. Goodman, 2002, *Plant Closings,* video, *Plant Openings,* video, and *Object: 65,* mixed materials, The Changing Nature of Work, 1996–2003, Paul S. Goodman Collection (2012–0001), Carnegie Mellon Univ. Archives, https://findingaids.library.cmu.edu/repositories/2/archival_objects/37029.

74. "Nabisco Plant Attracts Interest from Philly," *Pittsburgh Business Times,* Feb. 7, 2005.

14. Cooperation and Fragmentation

1. Franklin Toker, *Fallingwater Rising: Frank Lloyd Wright, E. J. Kaufmann, and America's Most Extraordinary House* (Knopf Doubleday, 2007), 36.

2. "Mr. Mellon's Patch," *Time,* Oct. 3, 1949, 14.

3. Patrick S. Vitale, "Anti-Communism, The Growth Machine and the Remaking of Cold-War-Era Pittsburgh," *International Journal of Urban and Regional Research* 39, no. 4 (2015): 774; Patrick S. Vitale, *Nuclear Suburbs—Cold War Technoscience and the Pittsburgh Renaissance* (Univ. of Minnesota Press, 2021), 29; John David Weidlein, "The Allegheny Conference for Community Development for Pittsburgh, Pennsylvania" (BA thesis, Princeton Univ., 1950), 81.

4. "The History of the Allegheny Conference on Community Development," Allegheny Conference on Community Development website, Aug. 2016, https://www.alleghenyconference.org/wp-content/uploads/2016/08/AlleghenyConferenceHistory.pdf.

5. Pittsburgh Railways Co., Appellant, v. Port of Allegheny County Authority. July 30, 1964.

6. J. Steele Gow, "Goals and Government of the Metropolis," 10–11, paper presented at the Community Goals Forum, Feb. 24, 1972, Univ. of Pittsburgh, University–Urban Interface.

7. Thomas G. Greig, "The Metropolitan Plan of Pittsburgh—Allegheny County" (BA thesis, Princeton Univ., 1937).

8. Southwestern Pennsylvania Regional Planning Commission, ed., *Issues in a Region of Contrasts* (Southwestern Pennsylvania Regional Planning Commission, 1968), 3.

9. Mark Solof, *History of Metropolitan Planning Organizations* (North Jersey Transportation Planning Authority, Inc., Jan. 1998), 15.

10. Roger S. Ahlbrandt and Morton M. Coleman, *The Role of the Corporation in Community Economic Development as Viewed by 21 Corporate Executives* (Univ. Center for Social and Urban Research, Univ. of Pittsburgh, 1987).

11. Cynthia Piechowiak and Ellen M. Perlmutter, "Region's Fast Change Challenges Old Boy Network," *Pittsburgh Press*, Nov. 15, 1987.

12. John G. Craig Jr., "Waxing and Waning of the Allegheny Conference," *Pittsburgh Post-Gazette*, Sept. 5, 1987.

13. Roger S. Ahlbrandt, "Mill Town Renewal: Patience and Partnerships," Working Paper (Univ. of Pittsburgh, Joseph M. Katz School of Business, circa 1989), 10–11; Ahlbrandt and Coleman, "Role of the Corporation in Community Economic Development," 21–36.

14. Piechowiak and Perlmutter, "Region's Fast Change Challenges Old-Boy Network."

15. Quote in James P. DeAngelis, "Some Elements of a Regional Economic Development Strategy for Southwestern Pennsylvania," presentation to the Southwestern Pennsylvania Regional Planning Commission (Univ. of Pittsburgh, Oct. 29, 1984), 1; original in Roy Kahn, "The Dream Merchants," *Pittsburgh Magazine*, Oct. 1984.

16. "Getting SPRPC Off Shelf," *Pittsburgh Post-Gazette*, Apr. 10, 1975.

17. Roger S. Ahlbrandt, "The Revival of Pittsburgh—A Partnership Between Business and Government," *Long Range Planning* 23, no. 5 (1990): 33.

18. One conflict was described as a "titanic power struggle" with the Pennsylvania Department of Transportation. See Clarke M. Thomas, "ISTEA: A Different Kind of Highway Act" (Institute of Politics, Univ. of Pittsburgh, circa 1992), 4.

19. Dan Fitzpatrick, "All Together Now?," *Pittsburgh Business Times*, Dec. 1, 1997.

20. Neal Peirce, "Steel City Synthesis: Knitting Pittsburgh Together," *Nation's Cities Weekly*, June 4, 2001, 2.

21. Pennsylvania Economy League, Western Division, Pittsburgh: A *Regional City with a Local Tax Base* (Pennsylvania Economy League, Western Division, Oct. 1982).

22. Clyde Mitchell-Weaver, "Public-Private Partnerships, Innovation Networks and Regional Development in Southwestern Pennsylvania," *Canadian Journal of Regional Science* 15 (Summer 1992): 277.

23. Henry Cisneros, *Regionalism: The New Geography of Opportunity* (Diane Publishing, 1995), 25.

24. Committee to Prepare Allegheny County for the 21st Century. *Preparing Allegheny County for the 21st Century: A Report to the Allegheny County Board of Commissioners* (Pennsylvania Economy League, 1996). 4, 16.

25. The margin in support of the legislation was 126–73 in the Pennsylvania House and 36–12 in the Senate. See Peter J. Shelly, "Ridge Expected to Sign Tax Referendum Bill," *Pittsburgh Post-Gazette*, June 12, 1997.

26. "Commonwealth of Pennsylvania Legislative Journal—House" 41 (June 11, 1997): 1334; Paul R. Flora, "Clarion's Call to Vote on Sales Tax Unintended," *Pittsburgh Post-Gazette*, June 20, 1997.

27. Robert Trumpbour, "Media Coverage of Sports and Politics: An Examination of the Press' Role in Campaigns for Professional Sports Stadium Construction," *Proceedings of the Eighty-Second Annual Meeting of the Association for Education in Journalism and Mass Communication* (Association for Education in Journalism and Mass Communication, 1999), 24.

28. Trumpbour, "Media Coverage of Sports and Politics," 21–22.

29. Paul Furiga, "Redefining an Epithet," *Pittsburgh Business Times,* June 8, 1998. For older references to "Creeping Metropolitanism," see Christine Altenburger, Kevin Kearns, and B. Guy Peters, "Strengthening Pennsylvania Local Governments: Implications for the Mon Valley," prepared for the Univ. of Pittsburgh President's Conference on the Mill Towns, Pittsburgh, May 5, 1988, 20; American Council on Intergovernmental Relations, *Metropolitan Organization: The Allegheny County Case* (Advisory Commission on Intergovernmental Relations, 1992), 16; "City-Type Rule Stirs Boros' Ire," *Pittsburgh Post-Gazette,* June 19, 1958.

30. Allegheny County Division of Computer Services, "Official Election Results (Computer Printout)—Nov. 4. 1997, General County of Allegheny Regional Renaissance Initiative Economic Development Tax?," Nov. 24, 1997, Allegheny County (PA) Elections Division.

31. Dan Fitzpatrick, "How Goes Regionalism? After Sales Tax Defeat, Concept May Evolve," *Pittsburgh Business Times,* Dec. 29, 1997.

32. Karen Kovatch, "PRA Members Can't Agree on Consolidation," *Pittsburgh Business Times,* Apr. 6, 1998.

33. *Allegheny Conference on Community Development 2001 Report* (Allegheny Conference on Community Development, 2001).

34. George Anderson, "Triangle Tattler: Waiter Sings Way into Opera," *Pittsburgh Post-Gazette,* Mar. 25, 1980.

35. "A Brief History, 1985–2015," Grantmakers of Western Pennsylvania website, accessed June 10, 2018, https://gwpa.org/sites/default/files/files/pages/GWP%201985%20-%202015%20history%20FINAL.pdf.

36. Victoria B. Bjorklund and David S. Chernoff, "Draft Examples of Program-Related Investments ('PRIs') (For Addition to Treas. Reg. Sec. 53.4944–3[B]) and Analysis of Each," MacArthur Foundation, n.d., https:///pubpolicy/2002/020515pri.authcheckdam.pdf.

37. Justin B. Hollander, *Polluted and Dangerous: America's Worst Abandoned Properties and What Can Be Done About Them* (Univ. Press of New England, 2009), 132.

38. Jeffrey Cohan, "Waterfront Deal a Bit Taxing for Homestead," *Pittsburgh Post-Gazette,* Apr. 18, 2004.

39. Loysen and Kreuthmeier Architects, *Hazelwood—Second Avenue Design Strategy,* June 2005, 9, available at the City of Pittsburgh website, https://apps.pittsburghpa.gov/ura-files/HAZELWOOD-050124Lloysen&Kreuthmeier.pdf.

40. "Carnegie Mellon Robot Will Run Time Trials to Enter $2 Million Desert Race," *Space Daily,* May 2, 2005, http://www.spacedaily.com/reports/Carnegie_Mellon_Robot_Will_Run_Time_Trials_To_Enter_$2_Million_Desert_Race.html.

15. Left Behind

1. Mary Niederberger, "Duquesne School Closing Facing Legislative Hurdles," *Pittsburgh Post-Gazette,* May 30, 2007.

2. Bobby Kerlik, "Duquesne Student's Transfer Upheld," *Pittsburgh Tribune Review,* Sept. 5, 2008.

3. Michael Gruendl, "Duquesne Ponders Fate with Steel Cuts," *McKeesport Daily News,* June 2, 1984.

4. "Taking Stock in Brownsville a Generation After Liggetts Bought Much of Town," *Observer-Reporter* (Washington, PA), Feb. 7, 2020.

5. Cindi Lash, "Brownsville Lays off All but One Employee," *Pittsburgh Post-Gazette,* Dec. 17, 2006.

6. Linda S. Wilson, "Steel Valley Officials Dispute Authority of Pitt Conference on Area," *Pittsburgh Post-Gazette,* May 12, 1988.

7. Frank Lucchino, *Reclaiming Hope—Municipal Disincorporation in Allegheny County* (Allegheny County Controller, Jan. 23, 1994), author's collection.

8. Melanie McGinness, "The Long-Awaited Eight Miles: Economic Development in Mon Valley 'Rides' on Expressway Link," *Gazette* (State College, PA), Dec. 31, 2022.

9. "Commissioners Seek Mon Valley Highway," *Washington Reporter,* Apr. 3, 1965.

10. "Mon Road Called Lifeline by Shapp," *Pittsburgh Press,* Feb. 23, 1973.

11. Rich Gigler, "State Toll Road Plans Getting Support," *Pittsburgh Press,* Sept. 23, 1983.

12. City of Pittsburgh, Allegheny County, University of Pittsburgh, and Carnegie-Mellon Univ., "Strategy 21: Pittsburgh/Allegheny Economic Development Strategy to Begin the 21st Century: A Proposal to the Commonwealth of Pennsylvania," Pittsburgh, 1985, 4B, author's collection.

13. "Housing Prices Have Stood Still at Six Towns in Mon Valley," *Pittsburgh Post-Gazette,* Jan. 16, 2011.

14. Tripp Umbach and Associates and Perkins Eastman, "Mon Valley Economic Development Strategy," A Comprehensive Redevelopment Initiative of the County of Allegheny Department of Economic Development and the Redevelopment Authority of Allegheny County, Feb. 2005, iii–viii, author's collection.

15. Peter A. Morrison, *A Demographic Overview of Metropolitan Pittsburgh* (RAND Corporation, 2004), 3.

16. Henry Hamman, "Diamond in the Rust," *Financial Times,* Apr. 24, 2009.

17. Mindy Thompson Fullilove, *Root Shock: How Tearing Up City Neighborhoods Hurts America, and What We Can Do About It,* 1st ed. (One World / Ballantine, 2004), 171.

18. Sarah H. Sharp, "Artist's Billboard Declaring 'There Are Black People in the Future' Taken Down by Landlord," *Hyperallergic,* Apr. 9, 2018, https://hyperallergic.com/436763/alisha-wormsley-the-last-billboard-pittsburgh-there-are-black-people-in-the-future/.

19. Ralph Bangs, *Black and White Economic Conditions in the City of Pittsburgh* (Univ. Center for Social and Urban Research, Univ. of Pittsburgh, 1994), author's collection..

20. Barry T. Hirsch and William E. Even, "Union Membership and Coverage Database from the CPS," Union Coverage and Membership Database from the CPS, 2025, https://unionstats.com/.

21. Gabriel Winant, *The Next Shift: The Fall of Industry and the Rise of Health Care in Rust Belt America* (Harvard Univ. Press, 2021).

22. Alan Mallach, *The Divided City: Poverty and Prosperity in Urban America* (Island Press, 2018), 48, 85, 203–4.

23. Emily Ashton, "The Faded Town Where Britain's Brexit Vision Lives or Dies," *Bloomberg*, May 14, 2022, https://www.bloomberg.com/graphics/uk-levelling-up/darlington-north-east.html.

24. Andrés Rodríguez-Pose, Javier Terrero-Dávila, and Neil Lee, "Left Behind versus Unequal Places: Interpersonal Inequality, Economic Decline and the Rise of Populism in the USA and Europe," *Journal of Economic Geography* 23, no. 5 (2023): 970

25. Edward L. Glaeser and Charles Redlick, "Social Capital and Urban Growth," *International Regional Science Review* 32, no. 3 (2009), 4.

26. Andrés Rodríguez-Pose, "Revamping Local and Regional Development through Place-Based Strategies," Working Paper (Penn IUR/Federal Reserve Bank of Philadelphia, Sept. 2016), https://www.penniur.upenn.edu/uploads/media/Rodriguez-Pose_-_Wilkie_PennIUR-Philly_Fed_working_paper_091616.pdf?utm_source=chatgpt.com.

27. "Levi's Gives Struggling Town Cinderella Treatment," *NPR*, Oct. 3, 2010, https://www.npr.org/2010/10/03/130306219/levis-gives-struggling-town-cinderella-treatment; "Levi's Go Forth to Work—Braddock, PA," posted Nov. 4, 2010, by TheBestCommertials, YouTube, https://www.youtube.com/watch?v=B-LUqzvtS14.

28. Joshua Bernstein, "Captain of Industry," *ReadyMade*, Sept. 2007, 68–73.

29. John Fetterman, "Here's Why I Wear Braddock on My Sleeve," *Medium*, Mar. 16, 2021, https://john-fetterman.medium.com/the-truth-about-my-tattoos-cc4b2940ceb6.

16. Termination Shock

1. *Russian Economic Report* (World Bank, June 2010), 23.

2. *Russian Economic Report*, 26.

3. David Streitfeld, "For Pittsburgh, There's Life After Steel," *New York Times*, Jan. 8, 2009.

4. Pittsburgh Regional Planning Association, *Region in Transition*, vol. 1 of *Economic Study of the Pittsburgh Region* (Univ. of Pittsburgh Press, 1963), 149–50. For more on the history of the *ESPR*, see chapter 5.

5. Michael J. Madison, "Contrasts in Innovation: Pittsburgh Then and

Now," in *Entrepreneurship and Innovation in Evolving Economies: The Role of Law,* ed. Megan M. Carpenter (Edward Elgar, 2013), 136.

6. Sean Safford, *Why the Garden Club Couldn't Save Youngstown: The Transformation of the Rust Belt* (Harvard Univ. Press, 2009).

7. Michael E Porter, Council on Competitiveness, and ontheFRONTIER, *Pittsburgh: Clusters of Innovation: Regional Foundations of U.S. Competitiveness* (Council on Competitiveness, Oct. 2001), 51.

8. Economists will recognize Douglas for his role in the formulation of the ubiquitous Cobb-Douglas production function. See Gregory S. Wilson, *Communities Left Behind: The Area Redevelopment Administration, 1945–1965* (Univ. of Tennessee Press, 2009).

9. Benjamin Chinitz, "The Regional Problem in the U.S.A.," in *Backward Areas in Advanced Countries,* ed. Edward A. G. Robinson (Springer, 1969), 57.

10. A. Bruce Johnson, "Federal Aid and Area Redevelopment," *Journal of Law and Economics* 14, no. 1 (1971): 275–84.

11. J. David Woodard, *Ronald Reagan: A Biography* (ABCCLIO, 2012), 51.

12. Ronald Reagan, inaugural address, Jan. 20, 1981, available at Reagan Library website, https://www.reaganlibrary.gov/archives/speech/inaugural-address-1981.

13. Ronald Reagan, "Address Before a Joint Session of the Congress on the Program for Economic Recovery," Feb. 18, 1981, online by Gerhard Peters and John T. Woolley, *American Presidency Project,* Univ. of California, Santa Barbara, http://www.presidency.ucsb.edu/ws/index.php?pid=43425.

14. Marcia Coyle, "Northeast Faces Loss in Budget Study Forecasts Damage to Industries and Cities," *Morning Call* (Allentown, PA), Feb. 7, 1986.

15. Francine S. Kiefer, "In the Ruhr, Duisburg Scrambles to Replace Industrial Base," *Christian Science Monitor,* Mar. 22, 1993.

16. Madison, "Contrasts in Innovation," 136.

17. Paul Krugman, "The Narrow Moving Band, the Dutch Disease, and the Competitive Consequences of Mrs. Thatcher: Notes on Trade in the Presence of Dynamic Scale Economies," *Journal of Development Economics* 27, no. 1–2 (1987): 41–55.

18. Stein Østbye et al., "The Creative Class: Do Jobs Follow People or Do People Follow Jobs?," *Regional Studies* 52, no. 6 (2018): 745–55.

19. John Lowensohn, "Uber Gutted Carnegie Mellon's Top Robotics Lab to Build Self-Driving Cars," *Verge,* May 19, 2015, https://www.theverge.com/transportation/2015/5/19/8622831/uber-self-driving-cars-carnegie-mellon-poached.

20. AnnaLee Saxenian, "Institutions and the Growth of Silicon Valley," *Berkeley Planning Journal* 6, no. 1 (1991): 37.

21. E. C. Stone et al., "Voyager 1 Explores the Termination Shock Region and the Heliosheath Beyond," *Science* 309, no. 5743 (2005): 2017–20.

22. "'Invest Here' Theme Echoed," *Pittsburgh Press,* Jan. 16, 1964.

23. Edgar Malone Hoover and Frank Giarratani, *An Introduction to Regional Economics,* 3rd ed. (Knopf, 1984), 359.

24. Pittsburgh Regional Planning Association, *Region with a Future,* vol. 3 of *the Economic Study of the Pittsburgh Region* (Univ, of Pittsburgh Press, 1963), 286.

Epilogue

1. Reid Frazier, "Pittsburgh Mayor's Comments Set off Controversy over Petrochemical Industry's Impact to Western Pa.," *StateImpact Pennsylvania,* Nov. 25, 2019, https://stateimpact.npr.org/pennsylvania/2019/11/25/pittsburgh-mayors-comments-set-off-controversy-over-petrochemical-industrys-impact-to-western-pa/.acknowledgem.

2. Daveen Rae Kurutz, "'Pittsburgh Isn't in Beaver County': County Officials Disheartened by Pittsburgh Mayor's Dismissal of Petrochemical Development," *Beaver County Times* (Beaver, PA), Oct. 30, 2019.

3. Ryan Deto, "Allegheny County Executive Rich Fitzgerald Denounces Peduto's Anti-Cracker Plant Stance," *Pittsburgh City Paper,* Nov. 1, 2019.

4. "Major Energy Company Withdrawing from Allegheny Conference, Citing 'Marginalization' of Energy," *KDKA News,* Nov. 12, 2019, https://pittsburgh.cbslocal.com/2019/11/12/company-withdraws-from-allegheny-conference/.

5. National Geographic, "'Paris to Pittsburgh'—Trailer," posted Sept. 12, 2018, by National Geographic, YouTube, https://www.youtube.com/watch?v=sFznn8FNRbU.

6. Brian O'Neill, *The Paris of Appalachia: Pittsburgh in the Twenty-First Century* (Carnegie Mellon Univ. Press, 2009).

7. ConocoPhillips, "ConocoPhillips Completes Acquisition of Marathon Oil Corporation," *Business Wire,* Nov. 22, 2024, https://www.businesswire.com/news/home/20241121025978/en/ConocoPhillips-completes-acquisition-of-Marathon-Oil-Corporation.

Index

Page numbers in *italics* refer to illustrative material.

www.ingramcontent.com/pod-product-compliance
Lightning Source LLC
LaVergne TN
LVHW050951080826
845145LV00005B/1473
9781606355022